THE PROTESTANT
DISSENTING DEPUTIES

The D.r also reported that an Address had been sent to him as y.e Chairman from the Pastors of New England That he had intended to have desired the Committee or a Competent Number of them to have gone w.th him to have presented the same to his Majesty But the Duke of Newcastle had told him he had better present it alone or at most not being more than Three or 10.r him And therefore he only desired that M.r Eliakim Palmer to accompany him & present the same ——

D.r Avery also acquainted the Deputys that he had Opened a Subscription to defray raise a sufficient Sum of money to defray the yearly Charges of the Deputation. ——

Ordered that the Chairman write to the Ministers of the three Denominations within Ten Miles of London Some time in this Month of October to desire them to return their Deputys for their respective Congregations for the Ensuing Year to him by the last Day of Nov.r next. ——

Ordered that the first Meeting of the New Deputys be in this place on the second day of Dec.r next And that on that Day a new Committee be chosen by Ballott beginning at 9 in the Morning ending at One & that notice hereof be accordingly given to the s.d Deputys

Ordered that Seven of the Committee be a Quorum ——

No Committee y.e last Wednesday in Oct.r

Margin) Gen.l Meeting 8.th Oct.r
Report from the Comm.ee to the Deputies. viz.t
Relating to the printed Acc.t of y.e Services of y.e Deputation
Sundries relating to the Carnarvonsh.r Riot
Relative to a Freeholder's being Imprefs'd
The Secry of War to be waited on once more
Also y.e Bishop of Bangor & M.r Bodvil, Memb.r for Carnarvon
A Meeting House settled at Anglesea.
An Address to the King from the Pastors of New England,
A Subscription opened to Defray the yearly Charges of y.e Deputation

MINUTES OF 8 OCTOBER 1746

THE PROTESTANT
DISSENTING DEPUTIES

BY

BERNARD LORD MANNING

EDITED BY

ORMEROD GREENWOOD

CAMBRIDGE
AT THE UNIVERSITY PRESS
1952

PUBLISHED BY
THE SYNDICS OF THE CAMBRIDGE UNIVERSITY PRESS
London Office: Bentley House, N.W.I
American Branch: New York
Agents for Canada, India, and Pakistan: Macmillan.

Printed in Great Britain by The Carlyle Press, Birmingham, 6

CONTENTS

Frontispiece. Minutes of the Protestant Dissenting Deputies, Vol. I, p. 291. 8 October 1746.

The page has a threefold interest. It records the first visit of the Deputies to court as representatives of New England; it minutes the opening of their permanent funds; and it refers to typical cases of riot and alleged illegal impressment.

CONTENTS

EDITOR'S NOTE

THIS WORK was left uncompleted by its author on his death in 1942. The editor owes it therefore to his readers to describe his own connection with the book, the condition in which its author left it, and the extent of his revision.

In November 1931 the Protestant Dissenting Deputies appointed a sub-committee to discuss with Bernard Manning the preparation of some account of their history for their forthcoming bi-centenary in 1932. It was at first intended that the history should be a short popular account for the Deputies, their constituents, and Nonconformists in general, to be based on the series of Minute Books, which had been preserved since the inception of the Deputies in 1732.

When, however, he had reviewed the material contained in the 7,500 pages of the Minute Books, and the number of important issues which they affected, Manning became convinced that a summary treatment was inadequate; he felt that 'a fully documented history, giving the dates of the Minutes concerned at all important points, ought to be written . . . it is more laborious, but I think that the political importance of the Deputies . . . justifies it . . . the Minutes seem to me too valuable a historical document to warrant a less minute treatment.'[1]

A more detailed estimate of the importance of the material is given in a letter which Manning wrote to the Cambridge University Press in 1938:

As far as I am aware no one has ever read these Minutes except for severely practical purposes. They appear to be unknown to 19th-century historians. Even a writer like Halevy has the most sketchy notions about the Deputies. Yet they are the most important of all the keys to an understanding of the political importance of Dissent in the 18th and 19th centuries, because they record the day-to-day activities of

---

[1] From a letter addressed to the Deputies' Treasurer, 1 May 1938.

the most active of all the Dissenters. Much has been made of the political activities of the Methodists, of the importance of the Quakers and Unitarians; but the three historic bodies of Dissenters have never taken their natural place in the story. They acted until far into the 19th century mainly through the Dissenting Deputies. The Deputies, as their Minutes shew, were behind nearly all the legislation which is vaguely attributed to the Dissenting Interest and left at that.

After indicating the range of the book, he continues:

I should like to make it clear that the Minutes are of wider interest than denominational or ecclesiastical. There is no feature of 19th-century history in particular which they do not illustrate. They provide a definite example of the way in which public opinion organized and mobilized itself and made itself effective in the Parliamentary government of that age. They shew one form of ecclesiastical opinion modifying general tendencies of legislation. They bring out the peculiar position of the Dissenting Bodies under the Toleration Act with their privileged status on one side and their lack of ordinary rights on the other. In short they illustrate in detail and at close range some unique features of English political thought and practice.

The circumstances of this letter may provoke a suspicion of partiality; it is for the reader to judge whether the claim is too great.

The traditional patience of the Deputies has been exercised over their history. Soon after he had undertaken the work, Manning was unexpectedly called to the Senior Tutorship of his College, a position which left little opportunity for detailed historical research. He discussed the book with me, and I was able to assist him by making an abstract of the Minute Books (which had been deposited in the Guildhall Library of the City of London in 1933), and by making drafts of some sections of the proposed book, in which we hoped at one time to collaborate. Although this did not prove possible, I felt when he died that I was perhaps better placed than others to put the work in order and prepare it for publication.

Manning had spent the greater part of several Long Vacations on the work, and before the end of his life had arranged for the Minute Books to be withdrawn from the Guildhall for closer study. He had completed about two-thirds of the book in revised form in typescript; and there were manuscript drafts of varying degrees of completeness for the remaining third. From an outline of the contents which he had left, it was clear that there were no important sections missing; on the other hand it was clear that the manuscript sections, particularly, were not in final form. I have had to take the responsibility of revising, of excising, and some-times of adding, as I thought necessary. The shape of the book, too, has undergone some alteration.

In its original form, it was proposed to reprint the *Sketch of the History of the Deputies*, published in 1813, as part of the present work. In spite of its charm and interest, this has proved imprac-ticable; among other difficulties, it involved a harassing amount of cross-reference. The long 'Introductory Essay' which Manning wrote for the *Sketch* has therefore been broken up, and the sections assimilated to the later history to make one continuous story.

I have felt free to condense where I could, and to prune rough-nesses of style in the unrevised sections; but not to delete expres-sions of opinion, even where these may sometimes seem too forceful for an academic work. It may well be that the author himself would have modified these; but because to those of us who knew him it is precisely at those moments that Bernard Manning speaks most clearly and with his own accent, I have left them untouched, especially where my own attitude is different. For it is not the only value of this book that it treats of a neglected side of 18th- and 19th-century history: it also reveals a man.

O. G.

PART I

THE CONSTITUTION

CHAPTER 1

WHO THEY WERE

THE PROTESTANT Dissenting Deputies have left two memorials. One is the series of changes in our laws and habits of thinking to which they contributed, and which it is the purpose of this book to record; the other is in the 'memorials and the things of fame, that do renown this city'—the face of London itself.

Those who have passed at any time through Ludgate Circus will have noticed the obelisks there; and the curious may have made their way through the traffic to read the inscriptions on them. The one on the right, facing St Paul's, is inscribed from his fellow-citizens to Robert Waithman; the other, across the road, to John Wilkes. The two obelisks represent the two Londons, one raffish, the other 'respectable'. John Wilkes, 'Liberty' Wilkes, the hero of the *North Briton* and the Middlesex elections, has his place in every history book; but the fame of Robert Waithman has gone, like his linen-draper's shop which once stood where the obelisk now stands. To have been M.P., and Sheriff, and Lord Mayor of London—even that does not ensure immortality, it seems.

In Trafalgar Square stands a column, with Nelson at the top, and lions by Landseer at the base; but Sir Morton Peto, Bart., M.P., who erected it—and built also the Hungerford Market, the Lyceum and St James's Theatres, the Reform and Constitutional Clubs—Sir Morton Peto is a name in books of reference.

The City of London has a famous Library and Museum, which grew from the vision of one man, Sir Charles Reed, M.P. A well-known educational institution on the south bank of the river Thames, Morley College for Working Men and Women, derives an endowment from the Victorian philanthropist, Samuel Morley; whose fortune contributed also to the foundation of the 'Old Vic'. Men like these made London what it is, a grimy, ugly, fascinating, eccentric, human, and sometimes lovely city. 'Si monumentum requiris, circumspice.'

Yet these men, because they were *Dissenters*, lived under a stigma. Through the accidents and the prejudice of history, their country reserved certain duties, powers, rights, honours and responsibilities for members of the National Church alone. The issues fought out at Marston Moor and Naseby, symbolized on the scaffold outside the Banqueting Hall of Whitehall, and recorded in the Petition of Right and the Clarendon Code left a legacy of hatred expunged only with the passing of centuries.

The Protestant Dissenting Deputies consisted (and consist) of two members chosen annually from each congregation of the 'three denominations, Presbyterian, Independent and Baptist,' (to use their time-honoured phrases) 'in and within twelve miles of London' (originally ten miles), 'appointed to protect their civil rights'. From these Deputies is elected the Committee of 21; and by the Committee are chosen the officers: the Chairman (frequently a distinguished Nonconformist active in public life, but not necessarily a member of the body), the Vice-Chairman and Treasurer, and the Secretary, who for two hundred years has always been a solicitor. Sir Morton Peto and Sir Charles Reed held the office of Chairman; Robert Waithman and Samuel Morley sat on the Committee. Men like these have been the Protestant Dissenting Deputies.

But why of three denominations only, and why chosen from within ten (or twelve) miles of London? The answer to these questions lies in the historical circumstances of the Deputies' inception.

The story begins with the penal code imposed by the victorious Royalists returning to power with Charles II in 1660. In spite of the Declaration of Breda, which had promised 'liberty for tender consciences', and in spite of the King's avowed desire for toleration, the Cavaliers rejected a scheme for widening the Church of England to include at least the Presbyterians, and still more emphatically the notion of giving civic recognition to different faiths. They sought a National Church on the old Elizabethan model, and imposed the Act of Uniformity (1662).

But half a century of civil strife lay between them and the

Elizabethan Church, though it took them twenty years to recognize this. The first result of the Act of Uniformity was the expulsion of 2,000 clergy from their cures on 'Black Bartholomew's Day', 1662—the division of English life into Church and Dissent was set. Once again, in 1689, an attempt was made to secure 'comprehension'—that is, to reconstitute a National Church by dispensing with the Thirty-Nine Articles of the Church of England, recognizing Presbyterian ordination as valid, making forms of ritual optional, and revising the liturgy, canons, and constitution of the ecclesiastical courts. But by 1689 no one wanted this solution; instead of *comprehension* we got *toleration*.

Before the end of 1661 the Cavaliers had passed the Corporation Act, preventing anyone for the future from holding municipal office unless he received the sacrament according to the Church of England. In 1664 the Conventicle Act interfered directly with liberty of worship by preventing more than four persons from assembling with a household for religious worship outside the forms of the Church. The Five Mile Act of 1665 excluded Dissenting ministers and schoolmasters from the towns, their chief strongholds. Like other persecuting Acts, from the time of Elizabeth onwards, these laws were only spasmodically enforced; but after the failure of Charles's effort to remit them by the Declaration of Indulgence, the Test Act (1673) extended the ban of the Corporation Act to all offices of trust under the Crown. From 1673 until the Deputies achieved the repeal of the Test and Corporation Acts in 1828, it was impossible in form of law for anyone but a member of the Church of England to be a minister of the Crown, a member of a Corporation, an officer in the armed forces, or a responsible Civil Servant. Although from the beginning of George I's reign indemnity Acts were passed which gave some relief, the Indemnity was not merely partial and unsatisfactory, but left the stigma of the 'penal laws' (as the Dissenters called them), a stigma which bred fresh grievances.

In 1689 the Toleration Act brought hope to the Dissenting bodies. Macaulay, in a famous passage of his *History*, makes a vigorous defence of this measure.[1] He admits that it 'abounds with

---

[1] *History of England*, vol. III, pp. 87-8.

contradictions', and that the provisions are 'cumbrous, puerile, inconsistent with each other, inconsistent with the true theory of religious liberty', and even that 'it recognised persecution as the rule, and granted liberty of conscience only as the exception'. But Macaulay condemns these objections as doctrinaire, and defends its practical value: 'it put an end, at once and for ever . . . with scarcely one audible murmur . . . to a persecution which had raged during four generations'.

Such praise may be considered excessive when it is realized that the Act applied only to Protestants who accepted the Trinity; that Catholics and unorthodox Dissenters were barred (except for the Quakers, who had specific provision made for them); and that the Act did not repeal the Clarendon Code, it merely stated that the statutes should not be construed to extend to any person 'who should testify his loyalty by taking the oaths of Allegiance and Supremacy, and his Protestantism by subscribing the Declaration against Transubstantiation'.[1] According to Macaulay, 'the rule remained in force only against a few hundreds of Protestant Dissenters, and the benefit of the exception extended to hundreds of thousands'. But if this were true in 1689 (which is not proved), what was to prevent it from becoming less true with the passage of time, the shift of opinion, and the growth of new religious movements? During the 18th century a large part of the Presbyterian body became Unitarian—and this excluded them from the benefit of the Act. The same period saw the growth of Methodism and attempts were made, and successfully made, to put the Conventicle Act into force against the Methodist congregations. In 1689, Baptists were excused from affirming the validity of infant baptism, and Quakers had merely to express their recognition of the Trinity and the validity of the Scriptures; but all others had to profess their belief in the Articles of the Church of England, four only excepted. The Independents and Presbyterians of 1689 might have no difficulty about doing this, but their grandchildren might feel differently. Historians have too confidently followed Macaulay in supposing that the Toleration Act put an end to Dissenting grievances; so far from being ended, they were in

---

[1] Macaulay, *op. cit.*, p. 82.

certain ways augmented during the 18th and 19th centuries.
Until 1753, Dissenters might be married in their own meeting-
houses, for the *public contract* between the parties constituted a
legal marriage, though the *ceremony* was not recognized. But Lord
Hardwicke's Act, passed in 1753 'against clandestine marriages',
made all weddings illegal except those celebrated by the clergy
of the Established Church; this state of affairs continued (in law)
until 1836, but even after that date marriages were celebrated
outside the Church under a series of disabilities.

During the 18th century also, the Dissenting bodies had a hard
struggle to maintain recognition of the validity of their forms of
baptism, although during the Middle Ages and up to the end of
the 17th century it was clearly understood by Canon Law that
baptism even by a heretic, a layman, or a woman was valid, if it
had been performed in the name of the Father, the Son, and the
Holy Ghost.

This question was of particular importance, because it involved
the right to burial in parish churchyards, which might be denied,
by the rubric of the Book of Common Prayer, to 'any that die
unbaptised, or excommunicate, or have laid violent hands on
themselves'. No other dispute gave such prolonged trouble to the
Dissenters (and to the Committee of Deputies) as the right of
burial; for in country places the churchyard was often the only
burial place, and where the clergy were ignorant, prejudiced, or
at loggerheads with Dissenters in the parish, the legal ruling which
the Deputies secured was not enough to secure the end of the
trouble. Cases were frequent down to the end of the 19th century,
and have even been known during the twentieth.

As the 19th century wore on, and the 'penal laws' passed into
history, a new crop of controversies came to exacerbate the relations between Church and Dissent, and at last to raise the demand
for Disestablishment and Disendowment of the Established Church.
The bitterest of these vexed questions were Education and Church
Rates, but the developing mechanism of the modern State brought
other problems as well. The old theory that every Englishman was
born a member of the National Church, with his place in the
parish as well as the city or county, was not abandoned when the

Test and Corporation Acts were repealed; it was so deeply rooted in our history and tradition that in some form it still remains. With the complexities of modern society it became important, for instance, to have a proper register of births, marriages and deaths; but until 1836 the only official registers were those kept in the parish churches; these were neither complete nor always adequately preserved, and, among other disadvantages, they recorded baptisms, not births, though the baptism, which took place at no fixed date after the child's birth, had less value as a record. The Dissenters might keep their own registers (as the Deputies did at Dr Williams's Library), but these were not official, and the courts would not always recognize them.[1] Yet to get a civil registration, applying in the same form to all citizens, proved a difficult matter.

Then came the Education question, which still holds (and perhaps from its nature must ever hold) matter for disagreement. The Church had been responsible for teaching since the Middle Ages, and religion and education seemed inextricably entangled. At Oxford and Cambridge, still semi-clerical in their organization, no one but a member of the Church of England could take a degree (until 1870) without violating his conscience; and those familiar with Victorian biographies will remember how frequent and how intense were the struggles in the minds of young men called on to avow dogmas against which their hearts rebelled.[2] One solution was to establish new Universities without religious tests; the Deputies, for instance, had their share in the foundation of University College, London.

The movement for primary education began with a struggle between rival voluntary societies with the backing of opposed religious bodies. When the provision of State schools was mooted,

---

[1] 'This register is only considered as a private entry, and not as a public record. An entry in a father's family Bible—an inscription on a tomb-stone—a pedigree hung up in the family mansion—are all good evidence.' Note, p. 167, in *Sketch of the History of the Protestant Dissenting Deputies*, 1813.

[2] 'Yes, I have lied, and so must walk my way,
Bearing the liar's curse upon my head'
A. H. Clough, *Early Poems*, p. 10.
Clough, after resigning his fellowship at Oriel, was appointed head of University Hall, London.

there were divisions among the parties themselves. Not all Dissenters, for instance, accepted the notion that the State should control or provide schools; and if there were State schools, ought they to be free from religious instruction altogether, or if religion was to form part of a State system, who should control it? The Birmingham League represented a powerful party of Nonconformists who wanted education to be secular as well as free and compulsory; and two of its leaders, Henry Richard and Edward Miall, were Deputies; but, in the Deputies and outside, there was also a body of Nonconformist opinion which rejected the theory of secular education. The Church of England still asserted its old claim to represent the nation, and the compromises with which this claim has been met are perhaps neither satisfactory nor final.

The question of Church Rates, let us hope, is settled for ever, for nothing aroused more barren strife among the fellow-Christians of Victorian England. Nonconformists were touched in their pockets by the necessity of contributing to the upkeep of a Church to which they did not belong; they were touched also in their principles; and pocket and principle foster righteous indignation, a luxury which communities and individuals can often ill afford.

From matters of this kind it is only a step to the cry for Disestablishment and Disendowment, and there were those among the Dissenters very ready to raise the cry, but the Deputies lent only half-hearted assistance. It was their deepest instinct to distrust the doctrinaire proposal; they had always proceeded against specific practical grievances, and general campaigns were outside their field.

CHAPTER 2

THE MINUTE BOOKS AND
THE *SKETCH*

THE MATERIAL from which this history is principally drawn is contained in sixteen volumes folio, the Minutes of the Protestant Dissenting Deputies, deposited in the Library of the City of London at Guildhall (Guildhall MSS. 3083, 1/16). The seventeenth volume of Minutes was destroyed by fire at the Secretary's office on the night of 10/11 May 1941, in the last and worst raid of the first 'blitz' on the City of London. An eighteenth volume was opened in 1946.

In addition, there exists one Letter Book, containing the correspondence of the Deputies from 10 April 1826, to 12 March 1834—that is, during the climax of the campaign for the repeal of the Test and Corporation Acts—and three volumes of proceedings of a Joint Committee called into being by the Deputies and sympathetic bodies at the same period:

1. 'Minutes of the United Committee appointed to conduct the application to Parliament for the Repeal of the Corporation and Test Acts.'

   20 April 1827 to 15 December 1828.

2. 'Minutes of the United Committee appointed to consider the grievances under which Dissenters now labour with a view to their distress.'

   19 March 1833 to 18 December 1835 [i.e. after Repeal].

3. *Ibid.*, 18 Jan. 1836 to 9 July 1838.

These, with six volumes of draft Minutes, for the period 1786-1828, mainly of the Deputies' Committees, are also deposited at Guildhall (the word 'Rough' is written and scratched out on a flysheet of the second volume of this last series). Some use has also been made of the *Minutes of the General Body of Ministers of the Three Denomina-*

8

tions, deposited at the Memorial Hall, Faringdon Street. But of these there can only be traced at present (1950) Volume IV, 10 April 1827—12 April 1836, and Volume VI, 18 January 1864—12 July 1897.

As all the references in this History are given by date to the Deputies' Minutes, it is advisable to give here the dates covered by the sixteen volumes of the main series:

Volume I.	9 Nov. 1732 to 25 Feb. 1767
II.	4 Mar. 1767 to 20 May 1791
III.	6 July 1791 to 27 Dec. 1805
IV.	31 Jan. 1806 to 17 Dec. 1813
V.	14 Jan. 1814 to 25 Jan. 1822
VI.	22 Feb. 1822 to 14 Mar. 1828
VII.	16 May 1828 to 31 Dec. 1830
VIII.	5 Jan. 1831 to 24 Feb. 1837
IX.	29 Mar. 1837 to 23 June 1840
X.	26 June 1840 to 6 May 1844
XI.	9 May 1844 to 11 Dec. 1848
XII.	15 Jan. 1849 to 17 Mar. 1854
XIII.	24 Mar. 1854 to 10 June 1870
XIV.	14 June 1870 to 15 Feb. 1881
XV.	23 Feb. 1881 to 24 April 1890
XVI.	6 May 1890 to 20 April 1909
XVII.	18 June 1909 to May 1941
	(destroyed by enemy action)
XVIII.	Current volume, commencing 1946

The conscientious enthusiasm of the Deputies for their work has a memorial in the excellence of their Minute Books. Not quite the same level is maintained through two hundred years; but despite natural ups and downs the general level is very high. The early volumes almost deserve to be called works of art. Not only is the script delightful; the same pains were lavished on the phrasing, and the routine proceedings are recorded in an almost liturgical set of formulae:

That the thanks of this Meeting be given to the Chairman for his able and impartial conduct in the chair this day. . . .

For the Election of the Committee: that a Ballot be taken, to begin now and close in half-an-hour, and that Messrs. A. and B. be the Scrutineers to examine the Ballot and decide on which 21 Gentlemen the election has fallen. . . .

and at the close of General and Committee Meetings in the mid-eighteenth century:

The Toleration Act was read.

Anyone who has read the Act will find it hard to believe that it was not sometimes taken as read; but the formula testifies that the orthodox Dissenters regarded the Act as the cornerstone of their liberties, and accepted it with an enthusiasm almost equal to Macaulay's.

The early Minute Books were not merely Minute Books, they took the place too of letter files. All important and many trivial documents were copied into them, and the early volumes present for this reason a fuller picture of the Deputies' doings than can be drawn from the later. Modern minutes usually record results reached without the full documentation which formerly accompanied the decision, though even the fullest Minute Books have, as sources, their inevitable limitations.

The excellence of the early volumes is due no doubt to their having been transcribed by one who was probably a professional scrivener, Benjamin Johnson. He appears to have written up a great deal at one time, for in 1767 he received £30 for transcription, making marginal notes, references, and an index. Ten guineas more were to be paid when he completed the work.[1] Fourteen years later his death is recorded; he had then been employed at £5 5s. per annum for many years to 'enter the minutes fair in the "folio book"'. The Secretary was to do this work in the future, and to receive the same sum for doing it.[2] His work, though good, did not approach Johnson's. The full marginal notes and splendid index were continued in Volume III. These were so full and so well done that it is clear that a great deal of time was spent on them.[3]

[1] 24 June 1767.   [2] 19 Jan. 1781.

[3] Ordered 28 Feb. 1806; finished 29 Sept. 1809. In 1824 the Secretary, John Webster, asked forty guineas for making the index to the 4th volume of Minutes, and after arbitration was allowed the full amount. 5 Mar. and 17 Dec. 1824.

Only occasionally is there a blank in the Minutes, as where a name is not filled in.[1] It is of interest to note that January 1752 is the first date when the older notation, 1751/2, ceased. About the beginning of the 19th century 'chapel' appears beside 'meeting-house'.[2] As an example of the punctiliousness of the records it may be mentioned that in a reference to 'the Committee of Mr Wesley's Societies' in 1812, the entry has been perfected later by the addition of 'the late Reverend' before 'Mr Wesley'.[3] In the early 19th century, too, 'congregations' give place to 'Churches' (1827) and 'Ministers' are referred to for the first time as 'Clergy' (1829); while by the sixties the older term 'Dissenters' has given way to 'Nonconformists'.

In accordance with modern editorial practice, it has been thought wise to preserve the spelling and use of capital letters in the Deputies' records; the time has surely gone by when we think of the usage of our forefathers as 'incorrect'. A point of interest which may be given as an example is the spelling of such words as 'honor, favor' in the Latin instead of the French form.

Besides the manuscript material, we have also made considerable use of the previous history of the Dissenting Deputies, printed in 1813. At one time it was proposed to reproduce the text of the *Sketch*,[4] as we propose to call it, as an integral part of this volume —a course to which its limpid, Augustan prose, its occasional gentle irony, its precision, moderation, and candour seemed to entitle it. As the work of a partisan body engaged in continuous conflict, and anxious to win support, the *Sketch* must be unique: it illustrates the Deputies' belief in one of their favourite maxims—truth needs no adventitious support or recommendation, it is its own best advocate.

But though the *Sketch* needs no correction, some addition to it is inevitable, and to avoid an intolerable amount of cross-reference it seems best to tell the whole of the Deputies' story as a continuous narrative. Fortunately, each period of their history had its

---

[1] As 27 Sept. 1752. [2] First noted 5 Oct. 1806. [3] 29 May 1812.
[4] '*A Sketch of the History and Proceedings of the Deputies appointed to protect the Civil Rights of the Protestant Dissenters*, to which is annexed a Summary of the Laws affecting Protestant Dissenters. With an appendix of statutes and precedents of legal instruments.' 8vo. London, 1813.

dominant problem, and an arrangement by subject rather than purely by chronology has seemed preferable. The severe taste of the Deputies excluded from the *Sketch* almost all picturesque detail, and if the Deputies cannot be accused of overstatement they are at times guilty of understatement. The restraint of the Editors, admirable as it is, has deprived their readers of some legitimate entertainment and some precious glimpses into the life of the 18th century. A few illustrations will suggest the wealth of the Minute Books, which bring us very close to ordinary life, even when they present a plain tale. The formal language of the attorney-at-law who is the Deputies' Secretary does not prevent our overhearing the emphatic and picturesque expressions of his clients. There is a bogus Dissenter in Southwark who is trying to use his bogus Dissent as a means of escaping constable duty. A friendly informant of the Deputies tells the story because 'he would not for the world be the means of leading the Committee into a scrape', and that if the Chairman would consent, 'he and Mr Ward would go to Mr Grace and make the best end of it they could'.[1] An injured party elsewhere protests that 'he never had a farthing of the money'.[2] Attempts to get justice after a riot at Midhurst prove difficult: 'The fellow they were going to proceed against' is run away.[3] A minister has been dismissed from a Woolwich meeting-house. Is the dismissal valid? It may depend on the validity of the votes cast. Fourteen communicants seem to wish the minister to remain, and ten wish to see him go. The qualifications of some of the voters are in question. Of one we are told that she 'is generally in her right senses but is sometimes disordered'. Of another, 'Mr Pattison don't attend, neither the daughters but when the old gentlewoman her mother does which is about once a year.' The Deputies' informant 'don't remember whether those persons Mr Stokes objected to did communicate for some time or not'.[4]

· With such detail in our minds we must clothe the skeleton accounts in the *Sketch*.

What is reported coldly as an assault on a minister at Beaumaris must be expanded until we see the minister in the act of administering the sacrament of baptism to several adults and Humphrey

[1] 24 Nov. 1767. [2] 10 Feb. 1768. [3] 26 May 1775. [4] 12 Mar. 1755.

Tyer approaching. Tyer assaulted the minister 'and behaved very rudely and with both his hands threw water in the minister's face'. We can almost hear the scandalized Welsh narrator catch his breath.[1] The *Sketch* does indeed mention the masks of seven men who committed a violent outrage at Llanfellyn (called Llanryllyn in *Sketch*), but hardly suggests the romantic scene portrayed in the Minutes. In the depth of winter the minister, Mr Lewis, was visiting Mr and Mrs Hughes, when all three were attacked by seven masked men who formed part of a body of eighteen. In the scuffle one man's mask fell off and he only could be identified with certainty.[2]

On one subject the Minutes tell us little. The planning and furniture of the meeting-houses come less than might be expected into a story that concerns the temporalities of Dissent. We have a glance at a sixteen-branch chandelier from the meeting-house in Hare Court, Aldersgate Street: it was distrained on account of rates for the repair of St Botolph's Without, Aldersgate. The Deputies advise the church that if they cannot get the sale postponed they should appoint someone to buy back the chandelier. They should appeal in good time against the next rate, as they are probably not liable to pay it.

The *Sketch* had several forerunners. As early as 2 April 1746 the printing of an account of the services of the Deputies drawn up by Dr Avery, the Chairman, was ordered. Caution prevented the Deputies from broadcasting the account. After considerable thought a copy was supplied to each Deputy. He might shew it to whom he thought fit, but it was not to go out of his custody.[3] In 1749, in 1759, and in 1762 supplements were ordered.[4] The victory over the City in the House of Lords naturally called for a new edition to be issued when the Committee should think fit.[5]

Twenty-five years later a new abstract of the proceedings was drawn up for printing.[6] Much care and nearly four years were devoted to the compiling and revising of the cases. A sub-committee, William Smith, Stephen Lowdell, and James Smith,

---

[1] 27 Feb. 1784 and *Sketch*, p. 128.   [2] 14 Dec. 1787.

[3] 8 Oct. 1746.   [4] 25 Oct. 1749; 31 Oct. 1759; 24 Nov. 1762.

[5] 11 Mar. 1767.   [6] 7 Nov. 1792.

was charged with the task of printing.[1] By April 1795 the sub-committee produced the following: The Preface; History of Proceedings relative to the Test and Corporation Acts; Abstract of the business transacted relative to the colonies in America; History of the Sheriffs' Cause; present state of the laws respecting Nonconformists; and the index.[2] The *Sketch*, as we have it, appears to have been faithfully built on these foundations, and if the length of time that William Smith detained the Minute Books be any measure of his services in the compilation, we may regard him perhaps as the principal author of the *Proceedings* of 1796.[3] It is then tempting to see in the *Sketch* itself a work at least inspired by him. Certainly all that we know of his ability, his moderation. and his dignity is consonant with the character of the *Sketch*.[4] A thousand copies were printed and 916 promptly distributed in different counties.[5]

A brief account of the Origin, Design, and Principles of the Deputation was produced in 1803 and entered on the Minutes. It is very slight, but adds to our knowledge the interesting informa-tion that the foundation of the Deputies' funds was laid when the Committee subscribed to fight the City in 1742. This historical memorandum does not appear to have been intended for publica-tion, but in 1804 a sub-committee of eight was appointed to bring out a new edition of the *Proceedings*.[6]

In 1811 the Committee asked the Rev. Mr Joyce to compile for them a 'New Abstract of the Proceedings of the Deputies' for publication. During the eighty years which he chronicled since the foundation of the Deputies, they had successfully defended Dissenters all over the country against petty abuses, disturbances of worship, assaults, unjust demands, refusals of magistrates to discharge their duty because of prejudice. They had defeated attacks such as that of Lord Sidmouth,[7] and had gained one or two victories, such as the judgment in 'The Sheriffs' Cause',[8]

[1] 7 Nov. 1793.

[2] 24 April 1795. A copy of this Abstract, dated 1796, is in Dr Williams's Library (Tracts 2:14:2).

[3] 25 April 1794 and 24 April 1795. [4] Lady Stephen's Memoir.
[5] 22 Dec. 1796 [6] 27 April 1804.
[7] *Sketch*, pp. 83 ff. See below. [8] *Sketch*, pp. 25 ff. See below.

which were more significant because of the opinions incidentally expressed than because they gave a wide measure of relief. It had to be admitted that the principal grievances remained unremedied, and, above all, that the Test and Corporation Acts, in spite of the partial indemnity, still remained upon the Statute Book.

The calmness and lucidity of the *Sketch* must not blind us, therefore, to the fact that it is really no academic document, but a strictly practical one. The Dissenters needed to be reminded of the extent of the disadvantages under which they laboured, and of the value which had been proved to attend united action for redress. The practical value of the *Sketch* is shown by the fact that within a few months a second edition of 1200 copies[1] was called for.

In continuing the history of the Deputies a century and a quarter after the publication of the *Sketch*, our attitude can be more detached, for the practical grievances have almost entirely vanished, and the jealousies of religious bodies have greatly diminished. Nevertheless, we should be sorry to pretend that it is quite detached. There is still a price on the head of liberty, and a more than academic interest in this unfinished story. We need to know under what conditions such a group as the Deputies may profitably operate, and even more under what conditions it may legitimately operate.

In this story Charles James Fox, Lord Holland, the Duke of Sussex, Lord John Russell, Mr Gladstone, and Mr Lloyd George have their part—but they are not the heroes; they must rub shoulders with Dr Benjamin Avery, Josiah Conder, and John Remington Mills; and yield place to William Smith, M.P. for Norwich; to John Wilks, son of a Whitefields minister, popular orator, and father of an international criminal; and to Henry Richard, interpreter of Wales and apostle of European peace. Yet even these must give place to the institution itself. It is a natural part of our constitutional machinery that we are continually binding ourselves into fresh groups, begun quite casually in tavern or coffee-house, growing, becoming recognized, developing a tradition and a code, being invoked by outsiders or by the State

---

[1] Nov. 1813.

itself for advice or assistance, and finally perhaps, our original object fulfilled, finding a way of changing so that we go on, as the City Companies have gone on, with a new kind of life and activity.

For a large part of their history, the conduct of the national campaign for the relief of Dissenters remained in the hands of this committee of London lawyers and merchants; indeed, in the 18th century they might almost have been called ambassadors of international Nonconformity at the Court of St James. Before the railway age, national (and, still more, international) associations were impracticable—the Deputies themselves discovered this very early on. In the 19th century national organizations with similar objects arose in numbers: the 'Protestant Society for the Protection of Religious Liberty'; the 'Church Rate Abolition Society'; the 'Religious Freedom Society'; the 'Liberation Society'—but the Committee of Deputies remained the 'Deputies in and within twelve miles of London', the extension of their constituency from ten miles to twelve was their only concession to the times.

Because they represented a small area, and drew their personnel from a limited class of society, they were always on the spot, ready to be called together at a few hours' notice, able to meet daily in emergency, well acquainted with each other, and so able to trust each other's discretion, closely in touch with events and the men behind them, and represented in the House of Commons by their Chairman, who after 1800 was by custom almost always an M.P.

With friends in the House of Commons and the House of Lords, they knew exactly whom to approach for assistance with the particular point at issue; and if he were an Anglican hunting squire so much the better—he would appear less prejudiced, and their regular spokesmen would be spared for other occasions. The Deputies would keep their member primed with all he needed for their case: information, a suitable amendment for a clause, or the draft of a Bill. Even to their enemies they never blustered; and so far from being intransigent, they reconciled differences, proposed compromises, and inspired United Committees of bodies with some common ground. When occasion arose, they could collect petitions with over two million signatures (they did so in 1843, with the aid of the new penny post and the new railways),[1] but even at such a moment the warmth of their tone was free from abuse.

There is even an interest to be drawn from the newspapers in which they advertised their appeals or their legal victories, or whose representatives they admitted to their gatherings. In the period of greatest activity, between 1820 and 1850, the list was often *The Times, The Morning Chronicle,* and *The Morning Advertiser,* with *The Globe, The Patriot, The Monthly Repository,* and *The London Gazette.* Others are sometimes in the list, but when *The Daily News* came into being it sometimes refused to print evidence friendly to the Deputies' cause. About the 1860s *The Morning Advertiser* falls out of the conventional list of papers used; and in the later part of the century it was perhaps the last newspaper to which men would have turned for a vindication of Calvinistic orthodoxy, or an elucidation of the Nonconformist conscience. Yet it had not always been so. Readers of Dr Peel's history of the Congregational Union, *These Hundred Years,* will remember the *Rivulet* controversy concerning the theology of the Rev. T. T. Lynch, a 'Controversy that nearly killed the Union.' A publisher's advertisement of 1856 quoted opinions from *The Gospel Herald* and *The Morning Advertiser* side by side: the two papers were equally likely to appeal to Dissenters interested in the orthodoxy or heterodoxy of the Congregational Union.[2] *The Morning Advertiser* complained that Mr Lynch's hymns 'might have been written by a Deist', and added, with picturesque imagination, 'a very large proportion might be sung by a congregation of Freethinkers'; there was in them 'not one particle of vital religion or evangelical piety; no mention of our Saviour's divinity, atoning sacrifice, and mediatorial office'. It would be easy for the modern reader to sneer at this alcoholic Saul among the Dissenting prophets; but the sneer would be worse than ungenerous, it would be anachronistic. It would overlook what was still, in the middle of the century, the traditional and natural relation of brewing and Dissent, both of them well established

---

[1] See Chapter 2 of Part III, on Marriage Laws.   [2] *These Hundred Years,* p. 224.

activities of the substantial middle class. In old-fashioned rural churches the connexion may still be traced. The maltster until yesterday in many small towns was a deacon, but so far has the trade now parted from Dissent that an effort of imagination is needed to reconstruct that earlier state of things.

An equal effort is needed to remind ourselves of the standing once enjoyed among Dissenters the world over by the London Committee of Deputies. Governors of the New England colonies corresponded with it on equal terms; if the Baptists of Jamaica were forbidden to preach to the slaves, it was to the London Committee that they appealed for intervention with the home Government; and to the Deputies also that the Dissenters of Melbourne came when they wished to prevent the endowment of the Episcopalian Church in Victoria. At the other end of the social scale, a Welsh villager thrown into gaol for refusing to attend his parish church found the London Committee ready to intercede with Lord Melbourne on his behalf.[1] This local body kept its authority while more pretentious organizations had their day and disappeared again; and its exceptional standing was recognized by a right of approach to the Throne.

[1] 7 Dec. 1838. See p. 181 below.

CHAPTER 3

THE FIRST YEARS OF THE DEPUTIES

IT IS ALWAYS possible, often easy, and usually silly to be iconoclastic about origins. To be iconoclastic about the origins of the
Deputies is possible, and easy, and silly. There is abundant opportunity (and no need) to disturb the tradition which represents a
general meeting of Protestant Dissenters held in 1732 as the
beginning of the Deputies: doubtless Dissenters had met before to
consider matters of common interest—therefore an earlier date can
be called for. Doubtless the decision to have an annual election of
Deputies from London congregations was not made until more
than three years later, on 14 January 1735/6: therefore a later date
can be called for. Those who themselves made the history saw
direct continuity from the meeting of 1732; and posterity may be
content to err with them rather than with other people.

On the 9th of November, 1732, a general meeting of Protestant
Dissenters was held, at the meeting-house in Silver-street, London, to
consider of an application to the legislature for the repeal of the Corporation and Test Acts. At this meeting a Committee of twenty-one persons
was appointed, to consider, and report to a subsequent meeting, when,
and in what manner, it would be proper to make the application.
Another general meeting being held on the 29th of the same month,
the Committee reported that they had consulted many persons of
consequence in the state; that they found every reason to believe such
an application would not then be successful; and therefore could not
think it advisable to make the attempt. This report was not very
cordially received. The Committee was enlarged by the addition of
four other gentlemen, and instructed to reconsider the subject. It was
at the same time resolved, that every congregation of the three denominations of Protestant Dissenters, Presbyterians, Independents, and Baptists, in and within ten miles of London, should be recommended to

appoint two Deputies; and to a general assembly of these Deputies, the Committee were instructed to make their report. . . .

It soon became evident that whatever might be the fate of their attempts to procure a repeal of the Corporation and Test Acts, the Dissenters would derive considerable advantage, in other respects, from establishing a permanent body to superintend their civil concerns. It was accordingly resolved, at a general meeting of the Deputies, held at Salter's Hall meeting-house, on the 14th of January, 1735-6, 'That there should be an annual choice of Deputies to take care of the Civil Affairs of the Dissenters'. In order to carry this resolution into effect, it was further resolved, 'That the chairman do write to the ministers of the several congregations, some convenient time before the second Wednesday in January next, to return the names of their Deputies to him fourteen days before'.

The first meeting of the Deputies, elected in pursuance of these resolutions, was held at Salter's Hall meeting-house, January 12, 1736-7, when Dr Benjamin Avery was called to the chair. The meeting, after some preliminary business, adjourned for a fortnight, to give each member time to determine upon the most proper persons to form a Committee of twenty-one, on whom the principal business of the year was to be devolved. Accordingly, on the 26th of the month, the Deputies met, and elected their Committee by ballot. These several elections—of the Deputies by the congregations, and of the Committee by the Deputies—have been continued annually from that time to the present.[1]

Behind the tact of this account we may discern signs of the birth-pangs of the new body. These signs may be described more fully.

The 'Three Denominations' still constituted the bulk of the Dissenting body. The Quakers stood apart, both in their own estimation, in that of their fellows, and in the eyes of the State; their stubborn resistance in the days of the Restoration had brought them special legal recognition; their doctrine and organization were unorthodox; and in the 18th century their special dress and usages made them a semi-monastic order in lay society. They hardly co-operated with the Deputies on any single occasion. On the other hand, in 1732, the 'Methodists' were a score of

---

[1] *Sketch*, pp. 1-3.

Oxford High Churchmen; there were still six years to go before 24 May 1738, when John Wesley went 'very unwillingly' to the meeting in Aldersgate Street, and heard Luther's preface to Romans being read; and it was nearly the end of the century before 'The Rev. John Wesley's Societies' were avowing themselves Nonconformist, and entering into correspondence with the Deputies on matters of common concern.

After the passing of the Toleration Act, the Dissenters had been satisfied for a time with their gains; and if they had wished to improve their condition they would hardly have found the Tory Governments of Queen Anne sympathetic. They greeted the Hanoverian accession with enthusiasm, but they dared do nothing to shake the new Government, faced with the threat of Jacobite revolt. But by the thirties they were becoming bolder. Walpole had based his policy on the development of trade, and the Dissenters were the backbone of the trading interest. At last 'the Minister's' complacency seemed to be shaken by the Excise Bill and the opposition led by Bolingbroke, and a General Election was anticipated.

Ever since the return of Charles II the affairs of the Dissenters had been in the hands of their ministers; but the first sign of formal union between them for political purposes had been at the accession of Queen Anne, when four Presbyterian, three Baptist, and three Independent divines united under the leadership of Dr Daniel Williams to present the new Queen with an address (1702); it will be noted that at this date the Presbyterians retained the leadership of the Dissenting body which they had claimed all through the 17th century. In 1727 the ministers of the Three Denominations formally constituted a 'General Body' which was henceforth to deal on behalf of them all with the Court and the Government of the day.

But the new body soon found itself under heavy and constant pressure from Dissenters 'in the country'. Meetings were held in the big provincial cities, especially Liverpool[1] and Bristol; pamphlets were published and protests showered on the London Committee of Ministers, who were freely accused of

[1] *Historical Memoirs of Religious Dissention*, p. 46, n.

being publicly and strongly suspected to have abused the interest they have with Men in Power by obtaining pensions or charities.[1]

Whether right or wrong, the tone of Walpole's Administration made this accusation particularly difficult to counter. What gave it point was the establishment by the Government of a Fund for poor ministers' widows. According to Edmund Calamy[2] this Fund had come about in the following way. Daniel Burgess, secretary to the Princess of Wales, had been bred a Dissenter; and it was he who proposed to Townshend an annual allowance for necessitous Dissenting ministers. Townshend discussed it with Walpole, and they put it to George I, who

was very free to it, and soon ordered £500 to be paid out of the Treasury for the use and behoof of the poor widows of dissenting ministers.

The sum was later augmented to £1000 a year and regularized in half-yearly instalments, which were paid over to Burgess personally, and by him given over to trustees, Calamy himself being one of the original body. No conditions were imposed by the Crown, or stipulations entered into by the trustees or the recipients—it was a pure act of charity without political motive.

But there were many Dissenters who resented 'a pure act of charity' and others who thought there must be secret strings to an annual payment made 'without stipulations.' It was therefore not an accident that the man who found a way to relieve the Ministerial Body of their embarrassment was Dr William Harris. At the meeting of the Ministers' Committee on 29 August 1732, Dr Harris, seconded by Mr George Smith, reported that

a considerable number of their brethren had proposed that gentlemen of weight in the three denominations should meet and consult what steps are fit to be taken in relation to the repeal of the Corporation and Test Acts, the next ensuing session of Parliament.[3]

---

[1] 'Report to the Deputies by the Committee of Enquiry and Proposals' (Edmund Calamy's copy in Dr Williams's Library, in a volume of tracts mostly relating to the Deputies' early history [5: 17: 47]).

[2] Quoted in 'A Brief Statement of the Regium Donum and Parliamentary Grant to Poor Dissenting Ministers' by the Trustees, N.D. c. 1835. (Dr Williams's Library 12: 66: 18).

[3] *An impartial account of the late transactions of the Dissenters, in reference to their committee and deputations.* 1734. Copy in Dr. Williams's Library, 5: 17: 47. Unfortunately the original Minutes of the Ministerial Body for this date are missing (see p. 9 above).

The operative word here is *gentlemen*; the proposal was that the laity should be made responsible, and at the next Annual Meeting of Ministers in October this was done.

Now Dr William Harris was one of the Trustees of the Royal Fund,[1] and if his motives in the matter were honourable, they did not remain without suspicion. The original form of motion put to the Ministers' General Meeting on 3 October 1732 was

that the Civil Affairs relating to the General Interest should be referred to Gentlemen,

but an amendment was carried, whittling this down to more precise terms of reference:

that a considerable number of gentlemen might meet to consider what steps were fit to be taken with relation to the repeal of the Corporation and Test Acts the ensuing session of Parliament.[2]

No machinery was provided for carrying this Resolution into effect; but later about 19 gentlemen were got together in a quite haphazard way by request of one or two ministers, and agreed to call a conference on the subject in Silver Street. This was the inaugural meeting described in the passage quoted from the *Sketch*,[3] held on 9 November 1732, which led to the appointment of the original Committee of Deputies.

To the account in the *Sketch* we may add the accusations contained in an anonymous pamphlet of the time,[4] not necessarily because they are wholly accurate but because they show the mood of the moment very vividly. According to this pamphlet, an attempt was made by a caucus meeting in advance to wreck this conference. All Dissenters opposed to any attempt at Repeal were canvassed to attend, 'pressed to be early, and to fill the body of the place' in this 'promiscuous and voluntary meeting.' Mr Samuel Holden, who had always refused to attend Dissenters' meetings before, appeared and took the chair, without any vote. He then took names for the Committee in his own order, put them to the vote affirmatively and not negatively, declared eighteen elected,

---

[1] 'A Brief Statement of the Regium Donum' (see above).
[2] 'A Narrative of the Proceedings of the Protestant Dissenters of the Three Denominations, relating to the Repeal of the Corporation and Test Acts, &c.' Dr Williams's Library (5: 17: 47).   [3] See above, p. 19.   [4] 'A Narrative' as above.

and then put up several more candidates for the last three places.

Nobody knew what method was being taken except a few close to the Chair, among whom things passed in a kind of whisper. Nor was the counting exact, as it was a numerous assembly, held by candle-light.

Before giving up the attempt at Repeal that year, the General Body held two more meetings. At the first, on 29 November, it refused to accept the Committee's report that 'an application was not likely to be attended with success'; and reminded the Committee that its terms of reference were 'when and in what manner to appeal'. But at a meeting on 28 December the Committee again reported that 'application was not likely to be attended with success' and adjourned for a year. This last meeting was the first to which two deputies from each congregation were summoned; and an account in the *Courant* (1 Dec. 1732) declares that this measure was adopted 'to avoid the inconveniences and disorders which attend such general meetings'.

The Committee sent to Bristol, Liverpool, and Exeter letters reporting their views on postponement as 'the almost concurrent sentiments of the representatives of the Three Denominations in and about London'. These letters were signed by Samuel Holden, the Chairman, as 'Your affectionate friend'.[1] No doubt there was some anxiety that the hot-heads should not get control, but the letter of Isaac Watts, quoted below, and the subsequent history of the Deputies suggest that the worst accusations were unfounded.

In October 1733, at the Annual Meeting of Ministers, it was decided 'after a violent discussion' to have a new choice of Deputies for the ensuing year; but the Deputies did not actually meet until 6 February 1733/4, and this meeting was provoked by the action of a group of dissidents who had called a rival meeting at Pinners' Hall on 28 January. The letter which had been sent out to the country was heard and approved; it was resolved that 'the said Committee doth subsist and be desired to continue'. It ordered a third General Meeting for the following January. There are signs of care about procedure, to prevent recurrent accusations of irregularity. The ministers of the several congregations are to

[1] 3 Jan. 1732/3.

be warned in good time about the choice of Deputies for the date prescribed. Their names are to go to the Chairman fourteen days before the meeting. Meanwhile the Chairman is to summon the Committee 'if any special matter arises', or if eleven members sign a requisition.[1]

The malcontents provoked a new General Meeting within a month; they wanted more energetic action, a fresh committee, and a national organization. It claimed to be the true body of Deputies of the Three Denominations, and had summoned a General Meeting of Dissenters from England and Wales and Berwick-on-Tweed for the first Wednesday in April. Much light is thrown on the situation by the following letter of Isaac Watts to the Rev. Samuel Say:

LONDON

March 26, 1734

Dear Sir

I have delayd an Answer to your Letter till I can give a better account of everything.

The Deputies of the Dissenting Congregations in and neer London are wretchedly divided into two parties, one acknowledging the subsistence of the Committee of Gentlemen which were chosen 16 months ago upon the talk of repealing the Test, who mett at Salters hall, and have almost all the Independents with them. The other part denounced the Committee, disclaiming their power to act or to call the Deputies together & some Presbyterians & some Baptists join with them.

As far as I can find, the body which owns the Committee are almost two thirds of the whole, if not quite, some say more: yet the others have chosen one Capt. Winter their chairman, & thus they act in Separate Bodies, mutually ruinous. The business of chusing Deputies all over England, recommended by this lesser body in London, will, I suppose, have very small effect. Their cry ag^t the Committee is that they are too much influenced by the Court: but I think we are by no means in a Case to sett up against the Court, even if the Majority shou'd incline to it, which is far from the Truth. Your remarks in your own Letter are perfectly Just. My Salutations to Mr Baxter & tell him so...[2]

The discontented, though summoned, had not come to the

---

[1] 6 Feb. 1733/4.
[2] From the original letter in the Congregational Library, Memorial Hall, London. Attention was drawn to this letter by Dr Albert Peel.

third General Meeting. This meeting deplored the schism as weakening the influence of Dissenters, but made no concession to the malcontents. No action was taken beyond recommending Dissenters to vote at the forthcoming Election for candidates well affected to His Majesty's person and government, and friendly to civil and religious liberty.[1] These resolutions the Committee sent to country Dissenters, explaining very temperately that the far greater part of the Deputies disapproved of the plan for a meeting in London on a national scale.[2] The main body of them, it is clear from the Chairman's speech, were afraid that too vigorous an agitation in the Dissenting interest would alienate and alarm public opinion, and by reviving the cry of 'The Church in Danger' might even endanger the stability of the friendly House of Hanover. To ensure the stability of Whig government, 'putting their own and the nation's concerns into those hands who are known friends to the civil and religious liberty of both' appeared to them to be at that moment the best way of serving the interest of Dissenters. It may be argued that they took an unduly gloomy view, but they had been in serious danger in Anne's time. There can be no doubt of the genuineness of their fear lest a national assembly of Dissenters 'may draw after it consequences more fatal to us and more detrimental to the public in the present situation of affairs'.

The tactics of the Deputies appear to have succeeded and even not to have alienated their opponents, for in 1735 the name of Capt. Jas. Winter appears as a Committee man, though it was over the signature of Jas. Winter that the Pinners' Hall section had issued their notices.

At its next meeting the Committee had before it two items of business which were prophetic of all its future activities. The first item concerned an individual case of one Mr Humphreys at Cirencester of which unhappily no detail is given. The Minutes reveal only, in words almost identical with those which the Secretaries were to write hundreds of times henceforth, 'That Mr Bowles be desired to write to Mr Humphreys to send him a full statement of his case'. The Chairman and three more of the

[1] 6 Mar. 1733/4.   [2] 7 Mar. 1733/4.

Committee were authorized to act and asked to report; but as there appears to be no report recorded it is impossible to say how they acted.

The second item concerned 'the affair of the Test'. The Committee authorized a general letter on the subject, explaining to the Dissenters at large that the Deputies had the matter at heart and were considering the most prudent steps to secure success.[1] The letter sent out was jubilant over the result of the 1734 Election, and expressed confidence that the Government were sensible of the services of the Dissenters. But again the note of caution was struck: 'prudence and privacy' were necessary in any endeavour to remove the Dissenters' grievances.

We therefore desire you would as far as your influence reaches use your interest to prevent any rash or precipitate steps from being taken in this affair which may awaken our adversaries, revive the cry of the danger of the Church, inflame the nation, and give its and our enemies great advantages over us.[2]

Following the Election, the Committee sent the Chairman and another Deputy to interview Sir Robert Walpole on the Test.

He returned for answer, 'That on account of the situation of public affairs, both foreign and domestic, His Majesty's servants were not of opinion that the time was then proper; but as the Dissenters had more than once deferred their application, in deference to the wishes of ministers, and in the late elections had behaved so exceedingly well, they would leave it to them to make the attempt, if they saw fitting, the next session.[3]

The Committee in 1735 corresponded with country Dissenters urging them 'to engage as many members as you can to be in our interest'. The need to proceed 'quietly and silently' was pointed out, lest opposition should be roused and hostile petitions presented.[4] Encouraged by replies from the country, the sixth General Meeting instructed the Committee to prepare for next session.[5] The Committee accordingly prepared a Bill,[6] and sought the help of the Administration.[7]

[1] 14 Aug. 1734.   [2] 15 Nov. 1734.   [3] *Sketch*, p. 4.
[4] 15 May 1735.   [5] 26 Nov. 1735.   [6] 10 Dec. 1735.
[7] 31 Dec. 1735.

Again the Deputies had an experience prophetic of much of their future; a party which had secured their support at the Election went back on its undertakings:

> From the administration, so far as we know their minds, we have not the least encouragement; but on the contrary must expect opposition from them. Those members of parliament, now out of power, tell us the attempt will be vain unless the administration concur, and decline giving us the promise of their assistance. Others, though the numbers be small, declare their readiness to assist us in all events.[1]

The Committee in the circumstances made no recommendation; but the General Meeting decided to go on with the attempt: it re-elected the old Committee but added six new members. The decision was probably wise in view of the resentment aroused on earlier occasions amongst those Dissenters who had thought the Committee apathetic. It was at this crisis in their affairs that (possibly without having in mind the full significance of the resolution) the General Meeting put the Deputation on a permanent basis by ordering an *annual* choice of Deputies 'to take care of the civil affairs of the Dissenters'.[2]

The Committee of thirty felt obliged to report next month that, the Administration being unsympathetic, most of their advisers in all parties dissuaded them from continuing the attempt. They saw that much could be said both for and against action, and urged the General Meeting to see to it at least that 'a good harmony and understanding amongst our selves' was maintained.[3]

The General Meeting confirmed its earlier decision to continue, and in the event accepted defeat without despairing of future success. The *Sketch* thus reports the outcome:

> On the 12th of March, 1735/6, Mr Plumer, the distinguished member for the county of Herts, moved for leave to bring in a Bill for repealing the Test and Corporation Acts. After a debate of considerable length, in which he was supported by a number of gentlemen, who were known friends to the established church, the question was lost by a majority of 251 to 123.[4]

The tactics pursued by the Committee are of interest. Besides approaching Members of Parliament privately, they circulated

---

[1] *Sketch*, p. 4   [2] 14 Jan. 1735/6.   [3] 25 Feb. 1735/6.   [4] *Sketch*, p. 4.

pamphlets among them, and thanked those who voted favourably.[1] To their letter giving the country Dissenters an account of the application to Parliament they added this characteristic postscript:

> It is not our design to send about lists of the names of those gentlemen who appeared in our favour, but we think it would be ungrateful and unjust should we not hint to you that ———— acted a very friendly part on that occasion.[2]

The blank was, it seems, to be filled by the local member's name. An interesting letter to an Irish correspondent reveals the mood of the Deputies in defeat: they had felt it wise to make the attempt, and could only hope that in time Civil Polity and Religion would be thought of as different things, and no longer blended together as they had been for a long course of years to the destruction of both.[3] It was following this failure that the first Chairman, Samuel Holden, resigned, and was succeeded by Dr Benjamin Avery, who was to remain the Deputies' Chairman until 1762.

Dr Avery, who is an interesting figure, had been one of the critics in the disputes of 1732. He had been a Presbyterian minister, but quitted the ministry in 1720 as a result of the Salters' Hall controversy,[4] one of the landmarks in the spread of Arianism among the Presbyterian body. He then became a physician, and was appointed Treasurer of Guy's Hospital, which had a Baptist founder. As well as being Chairman and Treasurer of the Deputies, he was a trustee of Dr Williams's Library, where his portrait still hangs; and he found time, too, for a good deal of polemical journalism.

But to return to the Deputies' campaign. Hope was not quite abandoned; a further attempt at Repeal was made in 1739. To the joint Deputation which waited on him, Walpole made his stock reply: 'The time has not yet arrived.' 'You have so repeatedly given this answer', said Dr Chandler, the head of the Deputation, 'that I trust you will give me leave to ask when the time will

---

[1] 18 Mar. 1735/6.
[2] 13 April 1736. Duncan Coomer, in *English Dissent under the Early Hanoverians* (Epworth Press, 1946) gives evidence of the voting strength of the Dissenting interest.
[3] 24 Mar. 1735/6.
[4] See Coomer, *op. cit.*, for a good account.

come'. 'If you require a specific answer', said Walpole, 'I will give it to you in a word—never'.[1]

Nevertheless, the Dissenters decided to press on, with or without the Minister's support. With this in view, a Treasurer was for the first time appointed 'to receive the voluntary contributions of the several congregations';[2] and the indefatigable Dr Avery offered to fill this office as well as the Chairmanship. The new Committee appointed on 10 January 1738/9, drew up for Members of Parliament a printed statement of its objections to the Test, whose main heads were as follows:

The Protestant Dissenters can and do readily take the oaths of allegiance and supremacy required by these Acts; but some of them scruple receiving the sacrament after the manner of the church of England; and many of them refuse to take the sacrament, after the manner of any church, as a qualification for an office.

It is humbly hoped, therefore, that so much of these acts as relates to the taking the sacrament as a qualification for offices, may be repealed, for the following reasons:

1. Every man has an undoubted right to judge for himself in matters of religion. No one therefore ought to be punished, by being deprived of any of the common rights of subjects, and branded with a mark of infamy, merely for exercising this right in things that no way affect the public welfare and prosperity of the kingdom.

2. The sacrament of the Lord's supper was appointed only for religious purposes; and the using it as a qualification for civil offices, seems, in a great measure, to have occasioned that disregard and contempt of this institution in particular, and of religion in general, of which all good men have so long and justly complained.

3. As the Dissenters are universally acknowledged to be well affected to His Majesty and the established government, they think it hard, that by the Corporation Act they are rendered incapable of holding offices in the corporations where they live, though in many places their property is at least equal to that of their neighbours; especially since many of them have been fined for not taking upon them such offices; and in particular, as a very large fine is now insisted on, by the city of London, from a known Dissenter, for not serving the office of sheriff, and a prosecution for the same is actually commenced.

[1] Coomer, *op. cit.* p. 100, quoting H. S. Skeats and C. S. Miall, *History of the Free Churches of England (1688–1891)*, 1891, p. 275.　　　　　　[2] *Sketch*, p. 8.

4. Many persons of substance and capacity being excluded by this act, the government of several corporations has fallen into the hands of the meaner sort of people, to the great prejudice of such corporations, the discouragement of industry, and the decay of trade.

The statement concluded by asserting that the Test Act, which had been designed against Popish recusants, had been applied against Protestant Dissenters, and that

nothing seems more likely to heal our divisions, put an end to party names and distinctions, and unite the friends of liberty, than removing those incapacities from a body of men, whose dissent is founded on the right of private judgement, and who are confessedly a great support and security to the religion and liberties of this kingdom.[1]

Members of Parliament, however, proved deaf to the eloquence of this statement; and when the application had been rejected by a majority of 188 to 89—'rather more unfavourable' than before, as the *Sketch* says—it was half a century before the Deputies found circumstances favourable enough to renew the application.[2]

The frustration of this second attempt led the Deputies to entertain for a moment the plan of the Pinners' Hall party for a national organization. Their 'Committee of Correspondence'— the first sub-committee set up after their institution—kept lists of the principal Dissenters in each county and large town.[3] Some of the provincial towns imitated the constitution of the Deputies by convening their own Deputies from time to time.[4]

Now, in 1739,[5] the London Deputies attempted to 'obtain a Representation from the country to meet them Yearly, in order to join with them and give them assistance with relation to the Civil Affairs of the Dissenters'. A circular letter was drafted inviting each county to send properly authorized representatives to a General Meeting in April every year. A General Meeting was indeed held on 2 April 1740, when the Deputies from the country were thanked for attending; but there is no indication of the number present, little business appears to have been transacted, and with the waning hopes of a fresh appeal to Parliament, the

[1] *Sketch*, pp. 7-10.   [2] See pp. 217 ff. below.   [3] 23 Feb. 1736/7.
[4] E.g. Leicester, 1790. R. W. Greaves, *The Corporation of Leicester, 1689-1836*, records 'the Dissenters holding a meeting of their Deputies under the very noses of the Aldermen and Councillors'.   [5] 31 Oct. 1739.

scheme quietly dropped. Not merely the notion of a national representation, but even the Committee of Correspondence was allowed to languish; for in 1756[1] a new sub-committee was appointed to 'revive the Correspondence of the Deputation with the Country'. In 1758 fresh lists of correspondents were produced; but again ten years later it was reported that 'there were none of the old Committee remaining but the Chairman and Mr Crisp who is gone to the West of England and settled there'. So a new Committee of ten were appointed; this time to deal specifically with colonial as well as country matters. In January 1772 we hear of new names being added, but there is little further mention of the committee under its former title, although it is clear that the Deputies' links with Dissenters throughout the country continued firm at all times of national agitation or local emergency:

Nothing but the circumstance of proximity to the seat of power, can ever induce those Dissenters who constitute what is here called the General Body, to act upon any occasion independently of their brethren in other parts of the kingdom, and that only upon sudden emergencies, on which the sentiments of the Dissenters at large cannot be collected. But as a common interest must dictate similar feelings, we are confident that in general we express your sentiments whenever we declare our own.[2]

This declaration in a letter of 1788, though dictated by policy, can be taken as substantially correct. If, in the 1730s, the campaign for repeal proved abortive, the Deputies had discovered other profitable grounds for unity, and these concerned the country at large. By the time the *Sketch* was published in 1813, the Deputies had intervened in 240 cases affecting Dissenters, of which only 20 were in the bounds of their own constituency—and of these 20, thirteen came into the category of parochial disputes.[3]

Already in 1738 the Deputies were writing to their country correspondents:

You well know that the Corporation and Test Acts were the important business that gave rise to our thus meeting. But though this be

---

[1] 28 Jan. 1756. [2] *Sketch*, pp. 48-9.
[3] Supplement to *Sketch*, pp. 123-144. Discussed below.

the chief, it is not the only thing we have in view. We would willingly attend to every thing that may remedy or prevent any inconveniency to the cause of civil and religious liberty; and we have the satisfaction to inform you, that we have already seen some desirable fruits of this our watchfulness and care.[1]

The reference is to the success of the Deputies in preventing Dissenters in two London parishes (St Olave's, Southwark; and St Leonard's, Shoreditch) from being subjected to new and unreasonable rates on burials:

In the first draughts of these bills there were several clauses which would have subjected many of the inhabitants of the parishes above named, and particularly such of them as dissented from the established church, to new and unreasonable exactions: and these seemed to us, designed as precedents and rules for the drawing and modelling all future acts of parliament of a like nature. These therefore we thought it nearly concerned us to oppose, and have been so happy as to get those clauses struck out of each of the bills before they passed into laws. In our attendance upon these affairs, we found that the want of a proper attention and of a timely notice had manifestly occasioned many of the inconveniences we have laboured under. We judged it, therefore, a matter of great consequence to engage a solicitor, who should make it a part of his stated business to acquaint us with any thing that may fall under his notice, which he apprehends can in any way affect the cause of civil and religious liberty, which the Protestant Dissenters have always professed to have at heart: and we have accordingly retained a person in this character, who is thought to be well qualified for this purpose; and though we have had but a short trial of it, yet we are already convinced, by our experience, of the usefulness of this measure.[2]

In this characteristically empirical way the constitution of the Protestant Dissenting Deputies took shape. Let us now examine the constitution in more detail.

---

[1] *Sketch*, p. 5.　　　　　　　　　　[2] *Ibid.* p. 6.

CHAPTER 4

THE CONSTITUTION OF
THE DEPUTIES

THE FORMAL constitution of the Deputies has undergone little change since the early days which have just been described. Deputies were welcomed from any recognized Presbyterian, Independent (now called Congregational) or Baptist congregation. The methods by which congregations satisfied the Deputies that they deserved representation varied from time to time, and it is much to be regretted that the records, perfect as they are in most respects, do not contain for any period a list of the congregations represented.

The Secretaries have worked, it seems, from lists brought up to date from year to year, and replaced by new lists when emendations became numerous. The foundation of the Congregational and Baptist Unions, and the re-organization of the true Presbyterian Churches as the Presbyterian Church of England, provided in the 19th century official year-books; from them without enquiry the Secretary could learn the names of the congregations in and about the cities of London and Westminister which could properly be asked to send Deputies. In the 18th and earlier part of the 19th century his task was not so simple. If he wanted to secure new recruits he collected as well as he could the names of congregations which might properly be approached. The Congregational and the Baptist Fund Boards, for instance, were appealed to.[1]

More often, in the early days before denominational organization, congregations asked for permission to send Deputies; at first it appears to have been left to the Secretary to decide which congregations were qualified. In 1802 it was ordered that any

[1] 13 Feb. 1854.

future applications should be laid before the Committee;[1] and in 1805 a form of certificate was sent to the ministers whose congregations returned Deputies. This stated that the Deputies in question were elected at a meeting of the subscribers of the congregation of Protestant Dissenters of . . . . Denomination meeting for public worship at . . . .[2] The great growth of Dissent after the Evangelical revival and the ambiguous character of some Methodist congregations made it less clear than in the early years whether a congregation had or had not the required status. Admission was not given carelessly; the application was received at one meeting and a decision made at the next. Applications were sometimes refused: a casual congregation not under the regular pastoral care of a minister was not recognized. When a Barnet congregation nominated the Rev. Alexander Stewart as its Deputy in 1839, it was ordered that 'Mr Stewart be respectfully informed that this Deputation has always been composed of laymen',[3] and a fresh return made. Until 1931 the Deputation consisted exclusively of men; in that year women representatives from congregations were first admitted.

Towards the end of the year notices were usually sent out to the ministers asking for an election of Deputies for the following year. In November 1768 for the first time the list of Deputies returned for the ensuing year is set out in full. It contains some 140 names carefully graded: two are baronets; between thirty and forty are esquires; there is one captain; the rest are plain misters. It is gratifying to see that one baronet was put on the Committee. Unfortunately the value of this list and of many similar lists which follow is reduced because there is no indication of the congregations which the Deputies represent. 'N.B.', says a persistent footnote, 'the place of abode and by whom returned are in the book kept for that purpose by the secretary'. Nothing is to be more regretted than the disappearance of that series of books.

It is not always possible to determine the profession or rank of the Deputies and the Committee, but a few things are obvious. The legal profession—barristers, solicitors, and even judges[4]—has

---

[1] 26 Nov. 1802.   [2] 13 Dec. 1805.   [3] 8 Feb. 1839.
[4] E.g. Lord Justice Lush, Vice-Chairman in 1856. He sat as one of the three judges in

always had a good representation; and lawyers who were also Members of Parliament had particular value. In the 18th century the medical profession was prominent, and supplied three Chairmen—Benjamin Avery, Thomas Lucas (of Guy's) and Edward Jeffries (of St Thomas's). After the 18th century the connection of the Deputies with the City was prominent, and in 1859 the list of Committee-men was headed by 'The Right Honourable the Lord Mayor', while Charles Reed, M.P., Chairman of the Deputies from 1867-74, was later to become Sir Charles Reed and to take an even more prominent part in London government. More often than might be expected a military title occurs; but the majority, we can but assume, was made up of business and professional men.

The number of Deputies tended to grow slightly until the repeal of the Test and Corporation Acts, but it is difficult to estimate what proportion of congregations sent Deputies. Only incidental references give a hint. In a petition of 1843 the Deputies claimed to represent nearly one hundred congregations;[1] but in the same year eighty circulars sent out to unrepresented congregations secured only five additions. In 1857, 128 congregations were circularized.[2]

The General Meeting of the whole body of Deputies met seldom. In the early part of the 19th century there were often two meetings a year at more or less fixed dates. In the latter part of the century the regular meeting was annual. At all periods exceptional meetings have been summoned for special business.

The work of the Deputation has fallen usually on the Committee of twenty-one. The Deputies have altered from time to time the plan according to which they elected the Committee; and its quorum varied from about eleven to five. It was elected with considerable formality by ballot. It tended to consist of a core of more or less permanent members, and a floating population often changed. At times the desire to retain experienced

the Tichborne Case. On 24 Jan. 1882 a resolution on his death recalled his career at the bar, as a Judge of First Instance, and as Lord Justice of Appeal. He had sat for fourteen years on the Deputies Committee, 'and though from his high position he must have had many inducements to join the Established Church, yet the Lord Justice throughout his life remained conscientiously a Nonconformist'.   [1] 11 Jan. 1843.   [2] 2 Dec. 1857.

members led to so little change that a reaction set in, and it was ordered that after a certain length of service no member should be re-elected unless by the Committee's special request.[1] At another period, it was ordered that the seven senior Committee-men should go out each year, and for a year be ineligible.[2] This was amended two years later, so as to prohibit any Deputy from being elected for more than three successive years.[3] But these attempts at rigidity rarely gave satisfaction and did not endure long. The tables shew that members served from one to forty years.

The Committee has exercised powers of almost every sort except the election of officers. At most periods it would be difficult to shew that there were any classes of business beyond its competence. As a matter of course it consulted the General Meeting on the most important problems, but the differentiation was one of feeling rather than of legislation. This peculiarly English neglect of formal definition led to no clashes; only occasional differences of opinion between the General Meeting and the Committee are revealed by the Minutes, and it is a fact that the Committee's decision has hardly ever been revised. It was sometimes the practice to read all Committee Minutes to the General Meeting, but this did not continue; an Annual Report was prepared instead. The absolute confidence of the Deputies in their officers and Committee was one of the conditions of their success: it meant that the Committee could act quickly, could collect evidence without publicity, and take decisions without having to defend itself to a public meeting at every stage.

During the greater part of the 19th century regular meetings of the Committee took place on fixed days once a month (usually in the morning), but frequent special meetings were summoned. The Committee in early days was summoned at 9 for 10, the General Meeting at 10 for 11, business to begin when a quorum arrived. Later the hour was named 'precisely'. Only on rare occasions could no meeting be held for lack of a quorum. Throughout the two centuries the Deputies have been inclined to take good summer vacations; their meetings were often most needed when

---

[1] 10 Jan. 1823; 2 May 1833; 26 June 1840.   [2] 29 Jan. 1802.   [3] 14 Dec. 1804.

Parliament was sitting, and from June to October in normal years meetings were much less frequent, or not held at all.

The first two General Meetings were at the meeting-house in Silver Street. From the beginning the Committee met usually at Salters' Hall, and the General Meetings after 1732 were also held there. In 1745 a less expensive place was sought, and Pinners' Hall replaced it.[1] Some twenty years later the Committee thought the vestry at Pinners' Hall cold and inconvenient and not to be altered cheaply. They moved to Silver Street vestry,[2] and held the General Meetings there as well. Towards the end of the century the King's Head Tavern in the Poultry became the favourite place for the Committee and the General Meeting, and for long it remained the favourite place.

Throughout the 18th century the Committee and sub-committees met at other places for special purposes, at the Crown Tavern behind the Exchange, for instance, to sign a letter;[3] at Pontack's in Abchurch Lane;[4] at the Amsterdam Coffee House;[5] and at Dr Williams's Library,[6] though it is interesting to find that later, in 1828, a request to allow the Committee to meet regularly at the Library was refused.[7]

The regular habit of meeting at the King's Head Tavern was broken early in the eighteen-fifties. For some years the Committee met at a number of places: at the Guildhall Coffee House, at the Milton Club in Ludgate Hill, at the Guildhall Hotel; at the London Coffee House; at the Sunday School Union Office in Old Bailey; and latterly at the Secretary's office, where sub-committees had met from early days. The larger General Meetings were still held usually in hotels. In the seventies the Memorial Hall became the regular meeting-place and had no rival, until the new Baptist Church House in Southampton Row claimed about equal attention.

The Deputies, as has been made plain, have never had a headquarters of their own apart from their Secretary's office. There

[1] 27 Feb. 1744/5; 27 Mar. and 24 April 1745. [2] 13 May 1767.
[3] 7 Mar. 1734 and often later. [4] 26 Oct. 1737.
[5] 22 Feb. 1737/8. [6] 16 July 1755.
[7] 11 Jan. 1828. (The Ministerial Body, however, continued to meet there for some time longer.)

their records and property have been kept—or not kept. On one occasion a reasoned argument was put to the Deputies in favour of their acquiring premises of their own. In 1838[1] the Secretary reported that his offices were to be demolished, and he suggested that it would be to the advantage of the Deputies as well as himself to acquire a house: 'No change takes place in the Secretaryship without a certainty of accidental loss, damage, and detention'. The Deputies' property, he reported, would fill an ordinary room. There were at that time five boxes full of legal and other papers; 226 copies of the *Test Act Reporter*; 150 copies of the *Sketch*; 300 medals (struck at the time of Repeal); two large closets full of papers; a score of Minute Books, and the like. Not all the Deputies' papers were there: the Dudley papers relating to a suit that cost £2,000 were in Spital Square.

The Deputies postponed discussion; the secession of the Unitarians and the low state of the funds made increased expense inopportune. A year later the Secretary resigned[2] and the plan lapsed. But the proposal had some effect. It was ordered that loose papers should be bound and indexed.[3] Old Minute Books were to be repaired and bound. New boxes were to be procured for the papers.[4] Repercussion continued for some years. A 'Committee of Waste Papers' was appointed.[5] It was followed by a Record Committee of two with the powers of the 'late Waste Paper Committee',[6] and in later years the Minutes record resolutions about arranging the papers.[7] Little of significance, however, remained when the Secretary's office was burnt in an air raid in 1941; the Minute Books (except the current one) had been removed, and escaped damage.

The 'Record Committee' and the 'Committee of Correspondence' were only two of the Deputies' sub-committees. Besides *ad hoc* committees, there was, under one name or another, almost always a legal committee; and latterly there was always a Parliamentary Committee to watch and promote legislation; these two often combined. A finance committee was regularly held. The

---

[1] 2 Mar. 1838.   [2] 3 May 1839.   [3] 21 Nov. 1838.
[4] 14 Dec. 1838.   [5] 14 Sept. 1839.   [6] 30 Mar. 1842.
[7] 27 Nov. 1844, 7 April 1876.

Deputies' sub-committees co-operated with other bodies in such campaigns as the agitation for Repeal, or the education crisis of 1843. The Parliamentary Committees of the Deputies and the Liberation Society very frequently sat together in the late nineteenth century. The Deputies' Minute Books usually contain a full record of these joint meetings. Even Victorian Dissenters had human frailties; occasionally therefore a meeting failed for lack of a quorum; but in the records of hundreds and hundreds of meetings summoned, the rarity of this entry is an impressive testimony to the enthusiasm and devotion of the Deputies.

The officers of the Deputation have been few. From the beginning there was a Chairman. At first he seems to have been elected for each meeting, but on 10 December 1740 Dr Avery was elected for the ensuing year, and the appointment may be considered annual thereafter. Since the days of William Smith M.P. (Chairman 1805-32), the Chairmen have with two exceptions been Members of Parliament (the exceptions are Henry Waymouth, who succeeded William Smith, and the present Chairman, C. T. Quesne, Q.C.). When age, illness, or Parliamentary duties prevented the Chairman from attending ordinary meetings, a Vice-Chairman was appointed, and became an important figure.

As we have noted, Dr Avery was also the first Treasurer of the Deputation, appointed in January 1738/9; but ten years later the offices were separated, and have remained so.[1]

The appointment of the first Secretary is not recorded, but William Hodgkin was already regarded as Secretary as early as 6 December 1732, and held the office till his death in 1743. There appears to be no record in the Minutes of payment to him, but his successor, Nathaniel Sheffield, was appointed with a salary of £20 a year.[2] The same salary was paid to his successor, Thomas Cotton (1767-88), of whom we learn that he was an attorney-at-law chosen out of two applicants.[3] From this time forward, the Secretary was always a lawyer; a fixed fee has covered as a rule his attendance at ordinary meetings and his transaction of routine business. For exceptional work there has been additional payment.

[1] 12 Oct. 1748.   [2] 12 Oct. 1743.   [3] 25 Feb. 1767.

In another way, the appointment of Thomas Cotton established a precedent, for he was succeeded by Bayes Cotton (1788-95), presumably a relative, and probably a son. In 1863 Charles Shepheard was appointed, and succeeded in 1878 (after a year of joint service) by Alfred J. Shepheard, who was in turn succeeded by Harold B. Shepheard, the present holder of the office. The Deputies were almost always fortunate in their officers. Ability, enthusiasm, diligence, long tenure of office: these are their characteristics. During the two centuries of its existence, the Deputation has had but twenty-one Chairmen, and, more remarkable still, only twelve Secretaries. Only on one or two occasions (not without their humorous side) has there been friction. It is clear that the resolutions which mark the death or resignation of officers are no mere conventional tributes; behind the vivid and affectionate phrasing we can still plainly discern the forms of the competent and trusted leaders. We may remind ourselves, too, of the close ties of blood and friendship which must at all periods have existed between the leading figures. The preservation in the Congregational Library of a series of letters from Joshua Wilson, a leading Committee-man of the 1830s and '40s, gives a vivid insight into these relationships. He was the son of a Congregational minister, Thomas Wilson; a cousin of John Remington Mills, M.P., the Deputies' Chairman (1836-44); related also to another member of the Committee, David Williams Wire, Alderman and afterwards Lord Mayor of the City of London; a brother-in-law of the Rev. J. A. Coombs, and connected with Dr Raffles, a prominent Liverpool minister. It was through such links as these that the preliminary work and private conference of the Deputies was done in all their campaigns—the all-essential ferment of activity which has left no trace in the formal resolutions of the Minute Books.

In the early period, as we have noted, a solicitor was employed as well as the Secretary; the first was Mr Cann, appointed at ten guineas a year 'to keep a watchful eye on everything that shall be moved in Parliament that can any way concern our interest'.[1] On Mr Cann's death ten years later, a successor was appointed at the

[1] 25 Aug. and 2 Nov. 1737.

same salary,[1] but after Mr Yates, appointed in December 1749, the Secretary, being himself an attorney, took over the duties.

On 21 December 1821 a request was made for a written report from the Committee to the general body, setting out the work done in the year; this was ordered to be done, but 'at the discretion of the Committee' was added. The work of 1822 seemed to the Committee not worthy of a report, but the General Meeting expressed disappointment at this interpretation of the order of 25 Jan. 1822, and the series of Annual Reports began. The first was voted 'satisfactory', printed, and sent to each Deputy. It has not been possible to recover the whole series. For many years the Secretaries maintained the admirable practice of copying the report verbatim into the Minute Book, but the last to be so treated was that of 1853.

It is perhaps a tribute to the shrewdness of the Deputies that we cannot record any comprehensive account of their finance. Without a fairly considerable income they could never have done their work. Legal expenses were continuous: in the earlier part of their history, in legal action against those who defied the laws protecting Dissent, or those who failed to carry out their duties as trustees; in the latter part of their history, expenses connected with Parliamentary proceedings, the drafting of Bills and the like.

At all times the Deputies fortified themselves with the best legal opinion that they could get. They took no decision of importance without consulting counsel; and the excellence of the advice they obtained is shewn by the small number of cases they lost. They never went to law rashly; but once assured of the goodness of their case, they never abandoned it for financial reasons. The thought of an appeal to a higher court never deterred them. Doubtless they benefited by the legal learning of members of the Committee, but it is clear that they preferred very often to pay for professional advice in the ordinary way—we find members resigning from the Committee because they are regularly consulted professionally, and do not wish to mix their functions. Their numerous petitions, their organized agitation, the public meetings and luncheons and breakfasts which directly or indirectly

[1] 7 Oct. 1747; 22 Mar. 1748/9.

they supported, their use of the press and the pamphlet cost no small amount. They were rigid in declining to give financial help to rectify an abuse or to prosecute an offender unless they were consulted in advance and their advice scrupulously followed; but if their conditions were observed, they were liberal. They expected corporations or churches or individuals who could afford to pay not to leave them with the whole burden. Often they made financial terms first; but where the aggrieved party was poor they undertook the whole charge without hesitation or quibbling. They accepted a merely nominal contribution when a gesture of gratitude was all that their clients could afford.

How were these expenses met? The first appeal for contributions was made by Dr Avery when appointed Treasurer in 1739; but the substantial basis of a permanent fund was laid when the Committee subscribed to fight the City in 1742. In defending the wealthy Dissenters nominated by the City as Sheriffs,[1] the Deputies required before undertaking their defence that they should be responsible for expenses to the extent of the fine to which they were liable (usually £413 6s. 8d.); and they declined to fight several cases when their financial terms were not accepted. The unfortunate nominees found the demand heavy: several times the phrase occurs: 'He desired time to advise with his friends before he could come to a final resolution.'[2] The Deputies may have appeared severe, but they won their case against the City, and they set by a valuable nest egg of capital, which their successors never dissipated, although when income shrank or a special call was made on the funds, part of the stock was ordered to be sold.[3] A note of the amount of stock held appears at random intervals in the Minutes; but though in the late 19th century a fairly full account of the current expenses appears annually, it is not possible to reconstruct a balance-sheet of value for any period.

Of course the Deputies looked for regular support from their own constituency, the London congregations. For every reason

---

[1] See below, p. 122.   [2] E.g. 19 and 21 May 1748.
[3] E.g. 28 May 1834: £1500 sold to defray expenses of the United Committee. 27 Oct. 1882: £100 sold to meet expenses of lawsuits and drafting Parliamentary Bills.

the Deputies wished to see all congregations represented, but not unnaturally the efforts to get in touch with unrepresented congregations often coincided with periods of financial stringency. The numbers attending the annual meetings might vary, sinking, for example, as low as 22 in 1863, when the Secretary reported that out of 110 congregations, only 25 ministers had made a return. The annual subscriptions might also vary, sinking, for example, as low as £47 in 1859. At such times appeals more or less urgent might be made. Efforts were made in various ways, and had varying success at different times. Ministers were written to; appeals were made in the press; from 1837 to 1882 a collector was employed to gather subscriptions and to increase the number of subscribers—he was paid 5 per cent on what he collected,[1] and sometimes a larger percentage on new subscriptions stimulated his efforts. But after 1882 no collector was appointed, and it was found that subscriptions still came in satisfactorily.[2]

Although congregations returning Deputies were expected to give financial support, there appears to have been no rigid rule making a subscription a necessary qualification for membership; we hear of congregations sending representatives but no subscriptions.[3] The secession of the Unitarian Deputies in the thirties brought financial difficulties, for, as they rather boastfully claimed, they had provided a good deal of the financial stability hitherto. An examination of the amounts contributed by the congregations[4] led the General Meeting to resolve to ask for a minimum subscription of two guineas a year from each.[5] It was at this time that a collector was first appointed. But it is to be remarked that the Committee were rarely very liberal in affording detailed information about their funds to the General Meeting; for instance, in 1803 a proposal that the Treasurer should report to the next General Meeting on the funds of the Deputies and their sources was negatived by the previous question. In 1804, however, the enquirers persisted and won their point. The auditors reported a balance of £33 7s. 8d., while the Trustees held £6,500 of 3 per cent Consolidated Bank Annuities and £2,000 reduced Bank

[1] 31 Jan. 1838. [2] 17 June 1884.
[3] 13 Feb. 1854. They are to be asked why they send none.
[4] 12 June 1837. [5] 27 Dec. 1837.

Annuities. When we next learn the state of the funds, in 1828, the campaign for Repeal had taken its toll. The 3 per cent Consols had shrunk to £3,500; the reduced stock stood slightly higher at £2,500; but the Treasurer also had in hand £1,417 2s. 4d.

As the Deputies did not confine their activities to the interests of the London Dissenters, they looked for help farther afield. From time to time reminding the provincial Dissenters of their labours in national or in peculiarly provincial affairs, they sought subscriptions or collections. Some sent casual, some annual, subscriptions; a Baptist congregation at Medbourn in Derbyshire, for instance, sent five guineas for a number of years. In 1844 the Deputies devised a neat plan for disseminating sound opinions and collecting money at the same time. Ministers in the metropolis and throughout the Empire were to be asked on or near St Bartholomew's Day to preach sermons commemorative of the principles of Dissent, and to secure public or private collections for the Deputies' work. As St Bartholomew's Day approached this was urged by letters and in the press.[1] Memories of the Great Ejection on the 'Black Bartholomew' of 1662 produced £171 13s. 6d. There followed an attempt 'in accord with the cherished spirit of voluntaryism' to replace the annual subscription of two guineas by a collection. This doctrinaire proposal failed.[2]

Donations and legacies came from the Deputies themselves and other sympathizers: legacies like that of £720 from Dr Newman in 1845; occasional votes from such funds as those of the Coward Trustees—£100 in 1817 and £50 the following year.

The Deputies never came within sight of serious trouble from any quarter, but there were occasional internal disputes. In 1863, the annual subscriptions having been for a number of years insufficient to discharge current expenses, the Secretary had got into the habit of receiving lump sums on account. He was now owed £177, besides £70 for the current year. One of the auditors, Mr Potter, refused to confirm the accounts, and there was considerable feeling between him and the Secretary, Hull Terrell. A special committee had to be set up to examine the accounts. This brought in a unanimous report, and reintroduced the procedure

[1] 9 July 1845.   [2] 17 June 1846.

of the forties, which had arranged a regular scale of payments, and passed the Secretary's charges annually.

We have now completed our study of the Deputies' constitution and financial resources, but two questions need special treatment. One of these is the relation of the three constituent bodies—the Presbyterians, Independents, and Baptists. The other is the relation of the Deputies and other Societies working in the same field. As this is simpler, we will deal with it first.

After the failure of the Pinners' Hall dissidents at the very outset of the Deputies' history[1] to form a national organization of Dissenters, the Deputies remained for a long time in undisputed possession of the field, maintaining contacts with Dissenters in the provinces and abroad through their Committee of Correspondence. But the agitation over Lord Sidmouth's Bill[2] in 1811 provoked those who had been feeling for some time that the Deputies made slow progress and that a more militant policy was desirable. The militants found their natural spokesman in John Wilks, one of the most fascinating of Dissenting figures in his time. His father was a famous Moorfields minister. Wilks himself was a man of wide culture, possessed of a fine library and a notable collection of works of art. Like the Deputies' Chairman, William Smith, he was interested in politics, and sat for a time in Parliament as Radical M.P. for Boston in Lincolnshire. But his personal qualities were as different from those of Smith as could be imagined; he was possessed of extraordinary eloquence in an age when eloquence was prized; one would call him a demagogue if the word were not so derogatory in its connotations.

In 1811 he invited all Dissenting and Methodist congregations to unite in founding the 'Protestant Society for the Protection of Religious Liberty';[3] he and Thomas Pellatt persuaded 217 congregations to join and to subscribe, and became joint secretaries. The organization was novel in two ways—first, it was national; second, it united the Methodists for the first time with the older Dissenting bodies. The years immediately following the Society's

---

[1] See pp. 24 ff. [2] See p. 130.
[3] See *Cong. Hist. Soc. Transactions*, vol. VI, no. 6 (Oct. 1915), pp. 364-76; anonymous article on the Protestant Society.

foundation were very favourable to its growth. On the one hand, Dissenters in the provinces were feeling the constant prick of petty persecution; both the Deputies and the Protestant Society heard constant complaints of local riot and disturbance; of the right of burial unjustly refused; of tolls and rates unjustly levied. On the other hand, the Dissenters made progress in having the law altered. Lord Sidmouth's Bill was rejected; in 1812 the Conventicle and Five Mile Acts were formally repealed; and J.P.s who had been refusing to administer the oath required under the Toleration Act were compelled to do so. In 1814 the Chancellor of the Exchequer promised to exempt chapels from local rates. At its fourth Annual Meeting in 1815 the Protestant Society was able to claim that it had got more for the friends of religious liberty than their effort had secured since 1688.

It may be imagined that the first reaction of the Deputies to the formation of this new body, so different in tone and structure from their own, was one of disdain mingled with something approaching dismay. Annual Meetings organized with all the arts of publicity, with distinguished national figures in the Chair,[1] and speeches that breathed Gallic fire, were as opposed as they could be to the Deputies' quiet unobtrusive persistence and conciliatory manners. Yet by a curious paradox, when it came to the main issue of Repeal, it was at first the Protestant Society that held back and the Deputies who wished to go forward. Perhaps the foundation of the new Society put the Deputies on their mettle; at least it is notable that in the year following the Protestant Society's inception we find the Deputies speaking for the first time of 'breaking every bond and abolishing any shackle'.[2]

After the first few years, however, the Deputies and the Protestant Society began to work together on the United Committee for the Repeal of the Test and Corporation Acts;[3] and from then on it says much for both bodies that their relationship was singularly harmonious, and in financial matters generous.

[1] Among those who presided over the Protestant Society's Annual Meetings were the Duke of Sussex (1818 and 1839), Lord John Russell (1822), Lord Holland (1820, 1824, 1828), Lord Ebrington (1829 and 1836), Lord Nugent (1830 and 1837), Sir Jas. Macintosh (1819), Samuel Whitbread M.P. (1821), Lord Dacre (1823) and Lord Brougham (1835).
[2] See below, p. 143.   [3] In 1827. See Part III, Chapter 1, below.

But, Repeal once achieved, the momentum of the Protestant Society began to fall away. It was essentially the creation of one man; and it had all the initial advantages and long-term disadvantages of that kind of origin. After 1839 it held no more public meetings, though its Committee continued in being and continued to pass resolutions and advertise them in the press for at least four more years. After 1843 it disappeared from public view.

It still had, however, substantial funds; and the Deputies did not forget. Ten years later, when John Wilks appeared to be nearing the end of his life, they began to make tactful enquiries. Mr Drake, the former sub-secretary of the Society and Mr Wilks's confidential clerk, shewed himself at first 'indisposed to give any information' on the subject. But it was learnt that two members only of the Committee were alive and well; and that Drake's salary, which had once been £100 a year, had been reduced to £20, and had subsequently shrunk to an occasional gratuity. Mr Wilks died, and it was clear that there was no time to be lost, but it was three years before the negotiations, which had been begun in 1854, were ended by a memorandum which transferred the Protestant Society's funds, amounting to £800, to the Deputies' Treasurer. The memorandum[1] set out the former co-operation of the Societies and the Deputies' intention to pursue the aims of the Protestant Society by procuring an amendment of the law relating to Church Rates, the trust deeds of chapels, and the right of Dissenters to burial in parochial churchyards by their own ministers. The two remaining representatives of the Protestant Society, acknowledging that the Deputies 'can more efficiently obtain the proposed alteration', declared themselves dissolved.

As late as 1906 the Deputies considered the possibility of making a similar claim. The Charity Commissioners were seeking for an order to divide the proceeds of the sale of a chapel between the Baptist and Congregational Unions. The trust deed had provided that such proceeds should go to the Protestant Society, and of that Society the Deputies had established their claim to be the most legitimate representative. The Deputies, though they had no reason to shew tenderness to the wishes of the Charity Commis-

[1] Recited in full in the Minutes, 20 Nov. 1857.

48

sioners, decided not to oppose an order which, on this occasion at least, did no substantial injustice to the Dissenting founders' wishes.[1]

But, to return to the moment when the Protestant Society, though still in being, was losing its impetus and fading from sight. At that moment, the Deputies found themselves confronted with a new rival and a new enemy organization. In 1837 a letter sent by the Deputies[2] to 148 unrepresented congregations points out that 'their old and powerful adversaries' have adopted new means, and that Dissenters' rights are not more secure than in the days before 1829 when their social status was worse. 'Measures of prudent and cautious policy' says the Committee 'replace open acts of cruelty and oppression'; and it instances the recent institution of a 'Lay Union for the Defence of the Established Church' with 15 Members of Parliament among its officers and committee, and representatives all over the country to resist more concessions. The Lay Union claimed that the Established Church needed a system of defence 'as well organized and sustained as the system of attack adopted by its adversaries'.

Although this sounds like a direct hit at the Deputies and the Protestant Society, it is probable that the Lay Union had also other enemies in mind. Readers of Mr G. M. Young's *Portrait of an Age* will remember the picture he draws of the weakness of the Established Church in the years following the Reform Bill and before the growth of the Oxford Movement. The Benthamites were at this moment the protagonists of Disestablishment, and there were many who thought that they would succeed in having the parish churches taken over and put to secular use.

But the Dissenters were also active. In 1839 (the year of the Protestant Society's last public meeting) was founded a new 'Religious Freedom Society', whose objects and methods were practically identical with those of the Protestant Society, but whose basis was broader; it was composed of local associations in various parts of the United Kingdom 'for promoting the Civil Equality of all Religious Denominations'. For several years it held annual meetings; its practical efforts were mainly directed

---

[1] 20 Sept. 1906.   [2] 27 June 1837.

against Church Rates and sectarian bias in administrative abuses, but it resisted also attempts to establish schools at public cost under Church control. Soon it was definitely committed to the Disestablishment principle, and stimulated, if it did not actually originate, the conference which in 1844 gave birth to the Anti-State Church Association. The birth of this new body was accompanied by a dispute as to whether it should admit to membership men of any religion and no religion—or in other words, whether Utilitarians and Dissenters should lay joint siege to the citadel of Establishment. In the end it emerged as a predominantly Dissenting body.

The evolution of the 'Religious Freedom Society' into the 'Anti-State Church Association', which in 1853 turned itself into the 'Society for the Liberation of the Church from State Patronage and Control' (or Liberation Society for short) owed a great deal to one man. Edward Miall played in the development of the Liberation Society almost the same role as John Wilks in the Protestant Society. Born in 1809, he had been an usher in a school and then an Independent minister before he came to London in 1841 to found a periodical called *The Nonconformist*. He had strong political interests and was much influenced by Chartism; he was involved in the founding of the National Complete Suffrage Union in 1842, and sat as M.P. for Rochdale (1852-7) and for Bradford (1869-74). With these political and journalistic gifts and his background of north-country Congregationalism, Miall was well equipped to lead the campaign against Establishment, and the position he achieved was shown after the Liberation Society's triennial conference of 1862, when he received a testimonial of £5,000 and a service of plate. Nor was that the end, for in 1873 a wider body of admirers subscribed 10,000 guineas for him.

But the Liberation Society was never Miall's single enterprise in the same sense as the Protestant Society was Wilks's. It is not surprising that his strongest backing came from Welshmen, for they felt particularly strongly about the Establishment. Thus at the time the Anti-State Church Conference was held in 1844 we find a Mr J. C. Evans moving a series of resolutions on the evils

of Establishment at the Deputies Annual Meeting.[1] Another
Welshman, J. Carvell Williams, became secretary of the Anti-
State Church Association in 1847, remained the secretary of the
body when it became the Liberation Society, and did not relinquish
the office until 1877. Yet another, Henry Richard, who was M.P.
for Merthyr for twenty years, lent strong support.

Miall himself was a Deputy for a time, but never took much
part in the Deputies' activities; but on the other hand both Richard
and Williams were prominently associated with the Deputies, and
Carvell Williams sat on their Committee for a long period. The
story of the Deputies' attitude to Disestablishment is told below,
and need not be repeated here; but the course of their relationship
with the Liberation Society is of interest. In 1844 the Deputies
rejoiced on hearing that an Anti-State Church Conference was
being convened, and in 1854 they declared that they welcomed
co-operation, though they rejected a proposal that the two bodies
should unite for Parliamentary action. Three years later the more
spectacular methods of the new Society caused the Deputies
disquiet; the question was raised whether the Liberation Society
was not getting all the credit for Dissenting agitation, and it was
recommended that a statement should be issued by the Deputies
to show how they differed from the Liberation Society.[2] But
again, as with the Protestant Society, a *modus vivendi* was found.
One of the Liberation Society's methods of publicity was an
annual Parliamentary Breakfast given at the opening of each
Parliamentary session to sympathetic M.P.s. In the course of the
next decade an invitation to the Deputies to be represented had
grown (by 1867)[3] into a recognized joint affair, which persisted
into the 20th century, and re-appeared, in the form of a Joint
Luncheon, as late as 1912. The Deputies also made a practice after
1877 of sending representatives to the Triennial Conferences of
the Liberation Society,[4] and it became customary to hold joint
conferences on matters of immediate importance, such as Burial
Bills, Education, the attitude of the Charity Commissioners and,

---

[1] 14 Feb. 1844. See Chapter on Disestablishment in Part III below.
[2] 5 May 1857.   [3] 10 April 1867.
[4] In 1871 the Committee of Deputies had thought it 'desirable that members should
attend in their individual capacity'.

of course, Disestablishment. Yet from time to time the old caution of the Deputies characteristically re-appeared;[1] it was their instinct to distrust publicity and to prefer to work quietly behind the scenes; and about Disestablishment, as will be seen, they always made reservations.

The Liberation Society continued to be very active up to the First World War, but in the twenties it began to be caught in the changing current of opinion about Disestablishment. As the word 'Reunion' began to acquire currency, and the feeling spread among Christians that they were once more a threatened minority in a pagan world, the force of the campaign against a State Church lost most of its vigour; while the spectacle of bishops unable to maintain their palaces, and vicars on bicycles supplementing their stipends by doing odd jobs or living in apostolic poverty, made 'Disendowment' seem a shabby instead of a powerful war-cry. In 1931 the Liberation Society approached the Deputies with a proposal for amalgamation; but this was declined.

One other body needs to be mentioned, though it needs little more than mention—the National Free Church Council. The Deputies welcomed the foundation of the new body and have maintained amicable relations with it, without ever facing, up to the present, the problem created by this new body, which with its national and federal basis must now inevitably fulfil some of the purposes originally discharged by the Deputies. The Deputies, however, continue to feel, though without defining spheres, that there remains a special field for their own activities, and that a constitution whose flexibility has stood the test of two hundred years is not to be lightly abandoned.

[1] E.g. in 1877 over a pamphlet called *Practical Suggestions* issued by the Liberation Society.

WHO WERE THE PRESBYTERIANS AMONG THE DEPUTIES?

IN A NOTE to his *Apologia*, John Henry Newman observes: 'Had I been born an English Presbyterian, perhaps I should never have known our Lord's divinity'. This observation may serve to remind us of the change in English Presbyterianism in the course of the 18th century. From the ebullient orthodoxy of the Westminster Confession, English Presbyterians had sunk through Arianism and Socinianism to Unitarianism. At one time or another almost every shade of theological opinion had had its representatives in the Presbyterian congregations. The gradualness of the change had given no particular moment at which it had seemed necessary to consider the propriety of still using the old name 'Presbyterian'. The legal situation had made any such consideration distinctly unattractive. Until 1813 Unitarians were particularly excluded from any enjoyment of the Toleration Act, and were particularly included among the persons affected by King William's Act to suppress Blasphemy and Profaneness.

After 1779 it was indeed no longer necessary to subscribe the selected Articles of Religion in order to obtain the benefits of the Toleration Act; it was sufficient to declare

I, A. B., do solemnly declare, in the presence of Almighty God, that I am a Christian and a Protestant, and as such, that I believe the Scriptures of the Old and New Testament, as commonly received among Protestant churches, do contain the revealed Will of God; and that I do receive the same as the rule of my doctrine and practice.

This ambiguous declaration might be so glossed as to cover Unitarian consciences; and certain new congregations of Unitarians had founded new meeting-houses in the later part of the 18th century without using the cover of the word Presbyterian.

Where the word did cover an existing congregation, however, it was generally retained. If no questions were asked, the meeting-houses, manses, and endowments were secure, though they were used to teach precisely that one doctrine which the founders had feared and hated and denounced as worse than Popish idolatry itself.

By the beginning of the 19th century most English congregations retaining the name Presbyterian were Unitarian; so were some General Baptist congregations which retained their old name for the same reasons. The Independents, though they had felt the Arian and Socinian influences in the early part of the century, were almost all orthodox at the end of it. Their numbers had indeed been increased by the addition of certain originally Presbyterian congregations which passed over to Independency in order to retain their orthodoxy. All generalization is difficult and inaccurate, for each congregation had its own history. It is beyond doubt, however, that in 1813, under the ancient and honourable description Presbyterians, Independents, and Baptists, no small number of Unitarians appeared among the Deputies as the representatives of congregations which (whatever they might once have been) were now Unitarian.

When the *Sketch* was published in 1813 this circumstance appears to have received no comment and to have aroused, at least among the Deputies themselves, no bitter or doubtful feeling. The last document in the *Sketch* is indeed the brief Act—Mr Wm. Smith's Act—which relieved 'Persons who impugn the Doctrine of the Holy Trinity from certain Penalties'; and the Preface refers complacently to it as extending toleration 'to a respectable class of Protestant Dissenters, who were before tolerated by the liberality of their countrymen but not by law'.

An incident in 1814 well illustrates the attitude of the Deputies at this time. A Unitarian congregation in Parliament Court, Artillery Street, Bishopsgate, asked to be allowed to send deputies. The Deputies replied that they consisted of Presbyterian, Independent, and Baptist Deputies, adding that 'under either of those denominations the Committee would with pleasure admit the gentlemen you have named'. 'By this', they continued significantly, 'you will perceive that this Institution has carefully guarded against any Theological distinctions'. The minister, the Rev. Wm. Vidler, played up at once. By return of post he replied 'I am sorry that I omitted the Denomination of the Congregation of Parliament Court Chapel. We are of the Baptist Profession'. In this reply, which secured the admission of the congregation's representatives, there was perhaps more agility than honesty, for Mr Vidler had not omitted to describe the congregation in his original letter. That letter opened with the words 'The Unitarian Church in. . .'. There was of course no intent to deceive and no one was deceived. A Baptist congregation had lapsed into Unitarianism, but it wished to retain the advantages of its original faith and status, and the Deputies were anxious that it should succeed in so doing. The viciousness of a persecuting law, a sentimental attachment to tradition and an eye for the main chance had combined to put many a Unitarian congregation in an essentially false position. They were living under a false name and the fact that it often assured them of considerable pecuniary advantages did not make the position pleasanter. To charge such congregations with living under a false name is not too strong, for neither of the names 'Baptist' and 'Presbyterian' had become a mere meaningless antiquarian curiosity to be used as well by one sort of person as another. Each was used by contemporary congregations which still professed the doctrines properly indicated by the name.

The reply of the Deputies merits close attention. It rests on the doctrine for which Unitarians were to fight far into the century. The Deputies take credit for ignoring, or, as they put it, 'guarding against', any theological distinctions among Protestant Dissenters. There is one body of Protestant Dissenters, that is to say; historically it has been known indifferently by the names Presbyterian, Independent and Baptist, but it is essentially one class. That is what matters. This was to be the assumption and the contention of the Unitarians; there was and is some one thing known as Protestant Dissent and it existed and exists without reference to theology. Only on this assumption could Unitarian Protestant Dissenters make good a claim to be the legitimate descendants of Trinitarian Protestant Dissenters. Protestant Dissent appeared to be a common factor. It must be shewn to be the only important factor.

This point of view—far removed as it is from history—commended itself to most of the Deputies at the beginning of the 19th century. In itself it indicates how strong the influence of the Unitarians was among them. It is to be distinguished from the still more mischievous doctrine of the 'Open Trust'; of which more later.

Several causes contributed to its strength. Presbyterianism in England had had two main centres: London was one of these two; Lancashire the other. No small proportion of the whole number of the English Presbyterian congregations was therefore within the area represented by the Deputies; and the influence of the Unitarians was for this reason probably greater among the Deputies than among the Dissenters of England as a whole.

Another cause was personal. William Smith was a Unitarian, and for many years he had no rival among the Deputies; his personal qualities and his national position gave him a unique influence. Yet he did not stand alone. Among the United Committee during the campaign for the Repeal of the Test and Corporation Acts the Unitarians were remarkably prominent. The Repeal Bill was drafted and seen through Parliament by the Unitarian, Christopher Richmond. That the Rev. Mr Aspland was chosen to edit the *Test Act Reporter*[1] shews that among the ministers as well as the laymen the Unitarians had a conspicuous influence. Mr Edgar Taylor, a Unitarian Deputy, was not only prominent in the Repeal campaign, but outstanding in the appeal for civil registration of Births, Marriages and Deaths.[2] At this period, too, the Unitarians supplied two of the four Trustees of the Deputation—William Smith and Edward Busk.[3] But perhaps it is more important than stressing that the Unitarians included a high proportion of the ablest Dissenters, to indicate the other causes which helped to maintain the Unitarians in their position in the early part of the century, and to discuss what occurred to challenge this influence and in the event to oust the Unitarians from the Deputies and indeed from the common life of Protestant Dissent.

[1] See p. 231.   [2] See p. 264.   [3] 27 Oct. 1837.

To answer this question we have to remember that the development of Dissent in the later part of the 18th century was two-fold. On the one side there was the drift through Arianism and Socinianism to definite Unitarianism. This was gradual and it is easy to ante-date it. There were still people living in the twenties of the 19th century who could remember this and that chapel passing from orthodox or semi-orthodox ministers to Unitarians. The change was not of long standing. It might well appear not beyond hope of redress.

On the other side there was in late 18th-century Dissent an increasing current of Evangelical doctrine and experience. The decline of the Dissenting interest had ended. Old congregations were reviving; new congregations were gathering; and in most places the fresh life was orthodox. Under the influence of these two movements, Dissent was certain to experience a schism. The old formula to which the Unitarians were to cling—'Protestant Dissent'—was coming to cover things too unlike to be held in unity. In some of the things that mattered there was more communion between Evangelicals inside and outside the Established Church than between orthodox and Unitarian Dissenters.

Not seldom this schism appeared in the same congregation. The legal holders of the property were the trustees, and especially in Presbyterian churches they suffered little control from the members. Neglect in maintaining a church-roll meant that only an ill-defined body of subscribers faced the trustees. Trustees who had Unitarian leanings could put a Unitarian minister in possession and maintain him, though a majority of his congregation was orthodox and desired orthodox teaching. Trustees and congregations were sometimes divided into two factions. The old drift to Unitarianism was being more than equalled by the new Evangelical movement; and, though partisans on each side exaggerated, there seems little reason to doubt that in a number of places the orthodox majority in the congregation had to leave a building and endowments originally orthodox in Unitarian hands and then to build new and unendowed chapels for their own worship. Such incidents rankled and the effect was cumulative. It is important to remember that the nature of the situation at the end of the 18th century meant that more of the grievances were on the orthodox side. For, in the first place, there was no great accession of numbers to Unitarian congregations. The appeal of unorthodox doctrine remained a somewhat hard intellectual appeal to the few, and in congregations untouched by the Evangelical revival the Dissenting interest continued to decay. The Unitarians therefore did not suffer from an inadequate supply of buildings as the orthodox did; and, in the second place, when the orthodox did win the contest, at least they could not be charged with malversation of trust property. For no trust was unorthodox though not all were explicitly orthodox. The orthodox victory simply mean that things remained as they had originally been.

A special form of this situation existed in the Wolverhampton case. In 1813 a minister with views acceptable to the congregation, which was chiefly Unitarian, was appointed for three years. At the end of the period he was preaching Trinitarian doctrine, and the trustees wished him to retire, but with the aid of an orthodox party he retained the chapel. The Unitarian majority kept the funds and built a new chapel, until after some years the orthodox at the old chapel instituted a suit for recovery. Lord Eldon cut the Gordian knot by giving the chapel and endowments to the Anglicans, on the ground that 'A Trust for the worship of God pure and simple is a Trust for maintaining and propagating the Established Religion of the country'. Neither party, of course, would accept this award, and the case dragged on to a re-hearing in 1836, giving to the Unitarians 'a growing sense of insecurity and to the orthodox a deepened sense of injustice'.[1]

Into these disputes the Deputies were sure at times to be drawn, for in no duty were they more punctilious and successful than in holding trustees to their duty. Often no doctrinal issue appeared. The trustees were merely idle or corrupt or ill-tempered. They yielded to argument or to threat, and did their duty. But there were cases of another sort. There were disputes between trustees and congregations where both sides were active and enthusiastic. The Deputies avoided entering into doctrinal quarrels; their business was civil right, not dogma; but sometimes we can feel

---

[1] H. Gow, *The Unitarians*, 1928, p. 100.

sure, and more often we can suspect, that the clash of claims is a clash of theologies. Where the Deputies decline to act on the ground that the dispute is of a sort not within their purview, where they counsel that the contending parties should try to come to terms, we may suspect the same thing.

At times we have direct evidence. A problem of this type came before the Deputies in 1810 from the church in Broad Street, Plymouth. This was a Presbyterian church, and 'many years since' the trustees had received a little South Sea Stock for the minister, provided that he held, and declared on applying for the money, his belief in the doctrine of the Holy Trinity. If he held contrary doctrines, the interest was to be paid to the next Presbyterian minister in Plymouth who made the declaration specified in the will. For several years the Rev. Christopher Mends, the only Presbyterian minister in Plymouth, had received the interest. On his death it was for some years paid to his son, the Rev. H. Mends, who was his immediate successor in the same church. The trustees now informed Mr Mends that he had no right to it, alleging that

although their minister could not claim it, preaching doctrines perfectly opposite to the doctrine of the Trinity, yet it remained with them to give it to whom they pleased, whether Independent or Baptist.

The Deputies as usual tried to avoid discussing the doctrinal issue. They advised Mr Mends that they had doubts about his right, as they were not sure whether the present government of his church was Presbyterian or Independent: if the former, his title may be good; if the latter, it may be uncertain.[1] Mr Mends replied that the government was Presbyterian, as it had always been; and the Deputies asked the trustees why they had discontinued the payment, since it appeared that Mr Mends was entitled to it.[2] After three months all that the Deputies could learn was that Mr Welsford, 'the acting manager of the concerns of the Unitarian Meeting' and of the Fund, refused to furnish a copy of the will or any information about the trustees. Whether Mr Welsford was himself a trustee was uncertain, but he received and dealt with the money in question, about £3 per annum. The

[1] 26 Oct. 1810.   [2] 30 Nov. 1810.

Committee told Mr Mends that they needed more information; and there, it appears, they left the matter.[1]

The incident is peculiar in revealing the manager of a Unitarian meeting zealous for Trinitarian tests. Was Mr Welsford simply anxious to irritate a minister whom he disliked? Was he doing his best for the Unitarian cause by trying to prevent awkward enquiries about the Unitarians' rights to a Presbyterian meeting-house? Did he feel that if he openly flouted a will which had specifically called for a Trinitarian declaration he was asking for trouble in a generation when the orthodox were beginning to question the process by which Unitarians had come into possesion of much property once in orthodox hands? This particular bequest was an awkward point at which to meet enquiries, if enquiries should be made; and trouble once begun might not stop at the sum of £3 a year? Whatever Mr Welsford's motives may have been, the Deputies' attitude is clear and somewhat remarkable. In 1810 they were inspired and led mainly by Unitarians, and they took the usual Unitarian point of view. It was proper to ignore completely the doctrinal issue, clearly as it might be expressed. If the church was 'Presbyterian' in government, the minister and congregation had the right to 'Presbyterian' property, whether Trinitarian or not. The incident also reveals what might be described by a 'Presbyterian' minister as 'Presbyterian' government at the beginning of the 19th century. It was a system which might be alternatively described as the supremacy of 'the acting manager of the concerns of the Unitarian Meeting'.

Not all English Presbyterian churches presented the same aspect. Not quite all had moved towards Socinianism or Unitarianism. In the north of England the influence of the Church of Scotland had counted for something in maintaining orthodoxy. A faint indication of such conditions is to be seen at Morpeth. There was indeed trouble at Morpeth in 1806. The minister, Mr Trotter, was also the sole surviving trustee, and he declined to have others appointed. He had appointed an assistant minister, contrary (it was reported) to the wishes of the congregation.[2] To Mr Trotter's contention that the trust deeds required a Presbyterian minister

---

[1] 22 Feb. 1811.   [2] 25 April 1806.

and moreover a regular licentiate of the Church of Scotland, the Deputies replied that an abstract of the deed shewed that the minister need not be a licentiate of the Church of Scotland: he must be a Presbyterian Dissenting Minister holding the doctrine of the Articles of the Church of England. Moreover he ought not to be a trustee.[1] Mr Trotter was not to be moved,[2] and the last that the Deputies could learn was that he had probably appointed new trustees, but that he treated enquirers with contempt.[3] The requirement about the Articles of the Church of England is a valuable commentary on the doctrine that all Presbyterian churches in England had a so-called 'open trust'.

The Presbyterian church at Stafford, as is well known, had a very distinctive history. It resisted the general drift of English Presbyterianism to Unitarianism, and continued an orthodox ministry by maintaining connexions with Scotland and Northern Ireland.[4] To maintain these connexions was at times an arduous business. The church had its bad days and its isolation nearly ended in extinction. The Deputies' Minutes give us a fleeting glimpse of the church in a dangerous situation. In 1813 the Deputies learnt that since the last minister died the two surviving trustees had taken possession of the property. They talked of turning the meeting-house into tenements. The endowment was said to be more than £100 a year; from this the trustees allowed the widow of the late minister £40 a year.[5] More enquiries brought worse news. The endowment was now said to be only £35 a year, and the meeting-house was shut up, as there was no congregation. The revival of the church was thought hopeless at least by one correspondent. The Deputies' correspondents were in Nottingham and Stockport. From Stafford they could learn nothing. We leave them seeking more information.[6] Happily the later history of the church falsified the forebodings of 1813.[7]

In one set of disputes, however, the Deputies' influence tended to help the Unitarians. When the majority of the congregation wanted orthodox teaching they often had to call a Congregational

[1] 30 May 1806.
[2] 5 Sept. 1806.
[3] 3 Oct. 1806.
[4] See K. M. Black, *Scots Churches in England*, 1906.
[5] 25 June 1813.
[6] 30 July, 27 Aug., 24 Sept. 1813.
[7] See K. M. Black, *op. cit.*

(or occasionally a Methodist) minister as so many Presbyterians were Unitarian. When this happened, and a trustee declined to allow the use of the building or the endowments on the ground that the meeting-house was Presbyterian not Congregational, the Deputies tended to support the nominally Presbyterian party without enquiring if the alleged Presbyterian was not, in doctrine, less of a Presbyterian than his Congregational rival was.[1] The Unitarians were already securing the advantage of the name Presbyterian without recognizing the implications of the name. Cases of dispute between trustees and congregation on doctrinal grounds increased at the end of the 18th century, and there were more and more frequently cases in which the Deputies declined to intervene. These internal troubles, they said, not only brought Dissent in general into contempt; they 'strengthen the hands of those who watch opportunities to dissolve the Deputation' itself.[2]

A case at Bristol has another point of general interest. In 1820 the congregation of the Old Meeting House of Marshfield expressed fears lest the Independents in the district were about to claim the meeting-house, on the grounds that the persons who assemble there are Unitarians, and not, as according to the old trust deed they should be, Independents or Presbyterians.[3] The Deputies asked to see the deed. Although it appeared that the Independents would be right in claiming the meeting-house, the Deputies learnt that in fact no hostile step had been taken.[4] They found such appeals particularly distressing at a time when their Chairman was a Unitarian and they were greatly under Unitarian influence, because in the country at large the Unitarians did not hold the same proportion of the Dissenting interest as in the Deputies' constituency, as well as because of their genuine desire for peace among Dissenters at a time when the campaign for Repeal was gathering momentum.

But the special significance of the Bristol case is this: the threat to the Unitarians who enjoy what was once orthodox property comes from the Independents. This was typical of the situation in

---

[1] E.g. Shaftesbury, 3 Nov. 1780; Lincoln, 13 April 1804 and 26 Oct, 1804; Leek, 16 Jan. 1784 and 30 April 1784.
[2] 8 April 1767.   [3] 25 Feb. 1820.   [4] 26 May 1820.

most parts of England. The Presbyterians who had remained orthodox were too few to be dangerous. The Baptists would have found it difficult to claim for themselves: their original divergence from both Presbyterians and Independents was too well known and too easily identified. But, failing orthodox Presbyterians, the Independents had a very colourable claim to Presbyterian property and endowments. English Presbyterianism had never developed on lines very different from the Independent polity; and in doctrine the Independents stood for precisely that orthodox Calvinistic ground which the Presbyterians had once defended, and which it might well be argued they had been endowed to defend. The battle would therefore be joined, if and when it should be joined, between the Independents and the Unitarian Presbyterians.

The passing of Mr William Smith's Act in 1813 made it possible for Unitarians openly to claim the benefits of the Toleration Act. No longer needing the legal cover of one of the three denominations, they were sure to find their relations with the orthodox altered. A change in the temper of at least some of the Unitarians was discerned as the years passed. Some of them began to organize themselves definitely as a denomination. These years saw the founding of the specifically Unitarian societies. In 1819 was founded the Association to protect the Civil Rights of Unitarians, and in 1825 the British and Foreign Unitarian Society incorporated this and two earlier bodies, the Unitarian Book Society (of 1791) and the Unitarian Fund Society (of 1806).

The name Unitarian began to be in common use among them and partly to replace the old and less accurate 'Presbyterian' or 'Baptist' description of some of their meeting-houses. 'Presbyterian' had almost died out in ordinary use in the early 19th century; it was revived with the qualification 'English Presbyterian' about 1825 and became prominent in the Wolverhampton and Hewley cases.[1] Not all Unitarians welcomed the change. Some (like Dr Martineau) objected to a distinctive sectarian name, hoping to permeate all churches as formerly English Presbyterianism had been permeated and so to produce not a new sect but a so-called liberal Christianity. For the moment, however, an

---

[1] W. Lloyd, *Protestant Dissent and English Unitarianism*, 1899, p. 83.

aggressive, self-conscious sectarian spirit took advantage of the new legal security. This shewed itself in the teaching of such a man as Belsham, the minister of the most important Unitarian congregation (in Essex Street, for which in 1813 he applied to send Deputies).[1] He did not hesitate to denounce the worship of the Saviour as 'idolatrous', and called for an end of the cautious compromising Arianism which had used old formulae in a new sense and had avoided an open clash with the orthodox. It was not enough to claim the right to interpret the Scriptures according to the individual conscience and to make that, and that alone, the basis of Protestant Dissent. Belsham and his party saw as plainly as the orthodox saw that such a formula was a mere sham. It did not touch the vital questions which divided him and his opponents and which he and his opponents agreed in thinking more important than any matters on which they were united. The theory of a common basis for Protestant Dissent might have been useful before 1813. It had served its purpose. The time for plain speaking had come. The doctrines of the Holy Trinity, the Incarnation, the Redemption, the Mediatorial work of the Son of God were revealed truths or they were false superstitions. As Dr Mellor said in 1878, and candid Unitarians agreed, 'They did not worship the same Being and preach the same Gospel'.[2]

The clash between the new unveiled Unitarianism and the new Evangelical Independency, it might be prophesied, would occur either in London or in Lancashire. In London and Lancashire the English Presbyterians had had their strongholds. In those two districts, therefore, the Unitarians appeared with peculiar prominence as their legitimate or illegitimate heirs. In London the co-operation of the denominations in the Deputation and the personal influence of William Smith helped to preserve the peace; but in Lancashire battle was joined. It is not by accident, therefore, that the decisive collection of documents was issued as *The Manchester Socinian Controversy*. Failing London, the Socinian Controversy was sure to be a Manchester controversy.

---

[1] 28 May 1813, see below, p. 65.
[2] W. Lloyd, *op. cit.* pp. 153-4. Prayers and hymns, says Lloyd, prove the accuracy of Dr Mellor.

This is—unhappily—not the place in which to set out the contents of that entertaining book, the most delightful piece of theological controversy ever published. It is important to us only as indicating the tension in the twenties between the Independents and the Unitarians. The Lancashire Unitarians, flown with eloquence and (it seems) with wine, had trailed their coats not in vain before Geo. Hadfield the Independent, who played in the north of England exactly the opposite part to Wm. Smith in the south. In August 1824 they held a dinner at the Spread Eagle to present the Rev. John Grundy, on leaving Cross Street Chapel for Liverpool, with a silver tea service as a tribute to his zeal for 'Unitarian Christianity'. The Rev. George Harris delivered a violent attack on orthodoxy, which caused the correspondence included in *The Manchester Socinian Controversy*.

It appears, by the Report of their Meeting, that they devoted seven hours (from 4 to 11 at night) to the task of eating and drinking, talking, clapping, and shouting, sometimes laughing at the wit of one of their clergy, and sometimes weeping at the pathos of another.[1]

Convinced that the Unitarians possessed an immense amount of property to which they had neither moral nor legal right, the *Malleus Unitariorum*, 'The Coryphaeus of persecuting Independency',[2] accepted the challenge and blew through the pages of *The Manchester Socinian Controversy* a shrill call to war. He gave details of 223 Unitarian chapels, shewing 178 to have been orthodox in foundation;[3] many were well endowed; a few had large congregations but most were very small. The Unitarians were boasting of their separation from and superiority to the miserable orthodox Dissenters, still fast bound in Calvinistic dogma. Be it so, retorted Hadfield, be separate, but as you shake off the dust from your feet leave to the orthodox the orthodox property. The hosts moved to war; the campaigns lasted from the Wolverhampton case (1816-36), through the Lady Hewley case (settled in 1842 at a cost of £30,000), to the Dissenters' Chapels

[1] Hadfield, *Manchester Socinian Controversy*, 1825, p. 33.

[2] The phrase is Mr R. D. Darbishire's, quoted in Lloyd's *Protestant Dissent and English Unitarianism*, p. 85.

[3] The same figures are given in another amusing tract of this pamphlet war, *Hackney Gravel Pit* by G. C. Smith (1830), of which there is a copy in Dr Williams's Library.

Act of 1843—and in the process the Unitarians ceased to be
counted among the Deputies. The Three Denominations from
which they accepted representatives became again what they had
originally been, three bodies of orthodox Presbyterians, Independents, and Baptists. We have now to trace the process.

The passing of Mr William Smith's Act in 1813 was followed
immediately by what was probably the high-water mark of
Unitarian influence in the Deputies' history. In the autumn of
that same year the Essex Street congregation applied for leave to
send deputies. This application was a test case indeed. The congregation had never been even in name Presbyterian, Independent,
or Baptist. It had gathered around Theophilus Lindsey, the
Socinian Anglican who resigned from the incumbency of Catterick.
The meeting-house trust declared in general terms that the congregation were Protestant Dissenters, to bring them within the
provisions of the Toleration Act; but their Unitarianism had never
been in doubt.[1] In 1813, as we have seen, the minister was Jas.
Belsham. With the frankness which marked their minister's own
proceedings the congregation admitted that 'being neither Presbyterians, Independents, or Baptists' they could send deputies only as
Nonconformists, if the Deputies would receive them as such.[2] The
unusual character of the application might well cause delay. On
14 January 1814 the Deputies' Secretary wrote to Belsham:

However much they may regret the loss of such Deputies as your
Congregation would send, they are of opinion that they cannot with
propriety depart from the letter of their constitution . . . if you could
unite with them under the name of *Protestant Dissenters* or *Nonconformists* without declaring you are *not* of either of the three Denominations the Committee think the difficulty would be removed.

It was removed.[3] The Essex Street congregation crowned their
achievement by naming as one of their representatives the most
distinguished person among the Deputies, Mr William Smith.
This of course was not Smith's first appearance. He had been a
member of the Committee since December 1791 and Chairman
since 1805 and had been most active and useful both in and out

[1] 'The Deeds of Essex Street Chapel', *Unit. Hist. Soc.* vol. I, no. 3.
[2] 17 Dec. 1813. [3] 28 Jan. 1814.

of Parliament in pressing the claims of Dissenters for more liberty and in enforcing such rights as they had.[1] It is not surprising that the first avowed Unitarian congregation should pay this compliment to the man who had just secured toleration for Unitarians. The Deputies in accepting him as the representative of a congregation which had no just claim to be represented among them at all paid Smith a well-deserved compliment and signalized their gratification at the toleration of Unitarians. But they did more. They accepted at least on this occasion the Unitarian view that to use the names Presbyterians, Independents, and Baptists was only a verbose way of saying Nonconformists and Protestant Dissenters; and that in consequence anyone who came under the latter description might claim to come under the former too.

If this incident be compared with the application from the Parliament Court congregation[2] its significance is the plainer. The Parliament Court congregation's application came between the first and second applications from Essex Street. It could be dealt with by winking at a conventional misuse of the word Baptist; but the triumph of Unitarianism was unveiled and blatant in Essex Street; and the name of Wm. Smith was used of set purpose to grace it.

The old fiction did not die, however; when one of the conventional names could be used, it was used still. In 1823 a self-confessed Unitarian congregation asked in a somewhat unusual way to be allowed to send deputies.[3] When the application was renewed as from the Presbyterian congregation at White Horse Court it was received favourably[4] and granted.[5]

Through the twenties, despite the rumblings in the provinces, the Unitarians under whatever title held their places among the Deputies. The influence of William Smith, now at its height, and the need for unity in the struggle for the repeal of the Corporation and Test Acts help to explain this. The Deputies indeed worked in close touch with the Unitarians. They wished to see the marriage

---

[1] E.g., attacks on the Woodstock meeting-house and minister, 1 Feb. and 30 May 1793; 12 Dec. 1794; 27 Feb. 1795; riots at Needham and Stowmarket, 6 Nov. and 18 Dec. 1795; 29 Jan. 1796.
[2] See p. 54.   [3] 10 Jan. 1823.
[4] 31 Jan. 1823.   [5] 14 Feb. 1823.

laws amended—only Quakers and Jews had the privilege of celebrating their own rites—but they left the matter to the Unitarians, as the Unitarian objection to the Prayer Book service was more radical than that of the orthodox Dissenters. This was the generation when avowed or crypto-Unitarians had great influence in politics, especially in legal circles.[1]

The Unitarian Association for protecting the civil rights of Unitarians in 1822 sought the co-operation of the Deputies in agitation for Repeal;[2] and two and a half years later the Association's Committee reported that 'in the event of pecuniary aid being at any future time needed by the Committee of Deputies the Unitarian Association will be ready to contribute such aid according to the state of its funds'. No clearer evidence of goodwill and co-operation could be desired. In the celebrations which followed the Repeal, as well as in the agitation which preceded it, the Unitarians had a prominent part.

But a change was at hand. The forces making for peace were weakened. One great common task ended with Repeal in 1828, and early in 1832 Smith resigned because of age. Meanwhile the contests in the provinces grew more acrid. The Wolverhampton case, the Lady Hewley case were but indications of the gigantic legal struggle which might be in the offing. The letter which William Smith wrote to the Deputies on retiring is as full of fear for the future as of gratitude for the past.[3] Scarcely were the Dissenters relieved from the heavy hand of legal oppression than their unity departed. 'Some of our brethren seemed to think differences of opinion on controverted points of theology sufficient grounds of separation even as to the common intercourse of life in civil affairs'. What, he asks, is the foundation of Dissent but the right of private judgement limited only by the inquirer's conscience and a decent respect for other inquirers? This is the basis of the revised declaration for ministers and schoolmasters under the Toleration Act.[4] It is the basis of Protestantism. 'If Christians attempt to stigmatize each other on account of their differences as unworthy of Christian fellowship, is not this as far as lies in their

---

[1] See *Manchester Socinian Controversy.*   [2] 28 June 1822.
[3] 27 Jan. 1832.   [4] See p. 53 above.

power inflicting punishment for opinion?' How can such people blame the *autos da fe* of Madrid? The letter ended with an appeal to the Deputies to discountenance such inconsistent and non-charitable presumption.

Smith's melodramatic reference to the *autos da fe* of Madrid, however worthless as an argument, indicates the bitterness aroused. His contention that Protestantism is simply the right of private judgment and that the declaration of 1779 ought to satisfy Dissenters only showed how far the Unitarians were from the orthodox Dissenters. Calvinistic theology and the Evangelical experience counted for more than the Unitarians could understand. There was in fact no religious communion between the two parties, and the time had come to recognize it. Orthodox Dissent was in its origins and its life primarily a religious movement. The political grievances which it shared with Unitarianism were, especially after 1828, insufficient to render ineffective fundamental religious differences.

William Smith lived on till the middle of 1835;[3] and it would be pleasant to think that consideration for his feelings delayed the storm. The first inkling of trouble is a note in the Deputies' Annual Report for 1834 that the Rev. Dr Rees and Rev. Thos Russell had 'withdrawn from the United Committee on Grievances'.

Trouble had begun, apparently, when the Ministerial Body were making their arrangements for presenting an Address on the accession of William IV and Queen Adelaide. A meeting summoned by requisition 'regularly and numerously signed by ministers of each of the three denominations' was called for 16 July 1830, and objection was raised to the presentation of the Address by a Presbyterian. The nature of the objection implied by the Minutes of the Ministerial Body is that each denomination ought to present in turn. Precedents were raised and the following resolution passed:

Whereas it appears by the minutes of the General Body of the dates of Nov. 11th and Dec. 14th 1760, that it is the acknowledged privilege of the Presbyterian Body to present the Address on an accession to the Throne, the Presbyterian Body would claim to exercise that privilege

[1] 9 June 1835.

on the present occasion, but that hereafter they would relinquish it, and on all occasions take their rotation in the presentation of Addresses.

A motion thanking the Presbyterians 'for this act of Liberality and Courtesy' was then passed 'with a few dissentient voices' (the Presbyterians, of course, abstaining), after an attempt to move the previous question had been made and defeated.[1]

There can be no doubt that the Presbyterians derived from their 17th-century predominance the privilege of presenting the Address; but it is also clear that deeper motives than precedence were involved. The nature of these may be gathered from a gibe in *The Record*, an Evangelical organ of the Church of England; in its number of 2 August 1830 it commented on the 'Address of the Protestant Dissenting Ministers being presented to the throne by the Blasphemers of our Lord Jesus Christ'.[2] Other correspondence and virulent attacks on the Presbyterians followed, and during the next few years feelings were more and more exacerbated. In January 1832 *The Monthly Repository* declared:

It was by the Unitarians that the Petitions to Parliament in favour of Catholic Emancipation from the General Body of Ministers were saved from being smothered by the previous question

and the Ministers at their meeting in April deplored this statement as likely to produce an incorrect impression, and in its tendency injurious to the reputation of those to whom it refers, and likely to impair the union and harmony of the three Denominations.[3]

But the press campaign and the unfriendly feeling fanned by recent litigation had done its work. When in 1835 the re-election of the Presbyterian secretary of the Ministerial Body, Dr Rees, was proposed, another candidate, Mr George Clayton, was put up. The meeting adjourned for a fortnight, and at the end of that time, 'after a considerable debate', Clayton was elected.[4] At the same meeting a split among the Baptists showed itself, some General Baptists being Unitarian, while the Particular Baptists were orthodox:

The General Baptists are as essentially a part of that denomination as

---

[1] Ministers' Minutes, vol. IV, pp. 146-9.
[2] Quoted in *Hackney Gravel Pit* by G. C. Smith, 1830.
[3] Ministers' Minutes, 10 April 1832 (vol. IV, p. 224).   [4] *Ibid.* p. 386, 27 April 1835.

their Particular Brethren, and it is utterly incompetent to one division to pass any resolutions affecting the right of the other, and especially to set up a standard of religious belief by which the members of that other division shall be approved or rejected.[1]

During the next twelve months the split became final, and on 9 March 1836, the Ministers met by requisition to hear a letter read from Dr Rees, as secretary of the Presbyterian Body, declaring the Union dissolved. Five Presbyterian ministers, however, headed by Dr Broadfoot,[2] challenged the dissolution, and claimed to maintain the Presbyterian connexion. The protest read by Dr Broadfoot condemned the secession as 'reckless and improper', recited the influence the General Body had exercised, declared their own orthodoxy and

that they, properly speaking, are the only Presbyterians of the Body, those withdrawing being only so in name, besides their being by the late decisions in the case of Lady Hewley's Charity, legally adjudged to be no Presbyterians; all that was Presbyterian of the Body remains, with its identity unaffected by the circumstance of a majority of its members being in favour of the vote.[3]

In spite of a written protest made by the Rev. Benjamin Mardon, one of the General Baptist Ministers who shared the Unitarian position and withdrew, the General Body of Ministers resolved:

That this Body, having heard the Documents read by Mr. Broadfoot, do *approve* the proceedings of their protesting Brethren, and do hereby declare that *they* together with any other member or members of the Presbyterian Denomination who have not withdrawn from this Body, do continue to possess all the privileges they have been understood to enjoy, in that general union.

The Unitarian Seceders became a separate body, which still exists, under the name of 'The Body of Protestant Dissenting Ministers of the Presbyterian Denomination in and about the Cities of London and Westminster'. It came to include ministers of churches which had no imaginable connexion with Presby-

[1] This protest, dated 7 April 1835, was signed by George Smallfield, Benjamin Mardon, J. C. Means, and J. O. Squier.
[2] The others were Jno. Young, Jas. Gates, Tho. Cooper, and Robt. Redpath, three of the five representing Scots Presbyterian congregations.　　　　[3] 9 Mar. 1836.

terianism of any sort.[1] In 1727 the Presbyterians had numbered 73. In 1836 the Unitarian Presbyterians numbered only 12, and the orthodox Scottish Presbyterians three.[2]

We must now leave the story so far as it concerns the Ministerial Body, noting merely that steps were taken to inform Lord John Russell of the position, and that a deputation saw him at the Home Office on Thursday, 17 March 1836; while the Baptists closed their ranks against the seceders, and the orthodox Presbyterians were able, at the General Meeting of 5 April, to announce the accession of Rev. Thos. Archer of Oxenden Chapel and Rev. Robert Simson of Colebrook House.

Meanwhile, a similar struggle was taking place in the lay body, the Unitarian Deputies being recommended by their ministers to withdraw. The laymen, like the ministers, considered friendly co-operation with the orthodox no longer possible. On 25 March 1836 the Deputies considered a letter dated 9 March from Edgar Taylor of Hampstead, whose prominence in the Deputation we have already noticed. This letter enclosed resolutions passed

at an Aggregate Meeting of Ministers and Deputies of the Presbyterian Denomination in and about London and Westminster, and of the Committee and other Members of 'The Association of English Presbyterians and others holding the right of the free and unlimited exercise of private judgment in matters of religion and of full Christian Communion on the great principle of the Divine Mission of our Lord without any other doctrinal test whatever'.

Included in Taylor's letter were certain other resolutions described in the Deputies' Minutes as 'purporting to be passed at a Meeting of the Deputies of Congregations of the Presbyterian Denomination.' The Deputies' Minutes contain no detail of the resolutions of the larger meeting, but present in full those from the smaller meeting composed of the Deputies only. These resolutions were as follows:

At a Separate Meeting of the Deputies of Congregations of the Presbyterian Denomination (who were appointed in January last to join the general body of Deputies of the Protestant Dissenters of the three Denominations in and about London) Held the 5th day of March 1836.

---

[1] W. Lloyd, *Protestant Dissent and English Unitarianism*, p. 96 f.   [2] Lloyd, *loc. cit.*

JAMES GIBSON, ESQ. IN THE CHAIR

Resolved

That the existing bodies of London Ministers and Deputies of the three denominations were formed more than a hundred years ago, and have till lately been uniformly considered to be based and conducted upon the footing of the perfect independence and equality of each denomination, to have for their object the promotion of the broad and acknowledged principles of nonconformity and to have no reference whatever to doctrinal opinions, distinctions, or qualifications.

That before and at the time of the formation of these unions of the general bodies, the denomination of English Presbyterian Dissenters had publicly asserted and have ever since maintained the principles of perfect freedom of investigation in matters of religion, and of resistance to every species of restraint upon, or interference with a complete liberty of action upon the results of such investigation.

That in the earliest period of these Associations of the three denominations and down to the present time, the result of this principle of action among the Presbyterians has been that many of their Ministers and Laymen have from time to time adopted doctrinal opinions differing more or less widely from the Calvinistic standard.

That notwithstanding such known diversity of opinion, and the departure of the English Presbyterians in many particulars from those forms of Church discipline in which their name originated, the identity and succession of their Ministers and Congregations have been on all occasions formally and officially recognized by the other constituent parts of the bodies with which they have been connected.

That this Meeting lament that within a short period (and particularly since the establishment of the Civil and Social rights of Protestant Dissenters by the Repeal of the Corporation and Test Acts) they have witnessed an obvious and continued disposition on the part of many members of the other denominations to act upon Exclusive distinctions, subversive of the equality and independence of such portions of the aggregate Dissenting Societies, as do not coincide with the doctrinal creed of the majority, hostile to the principles on which they have combined their efforts and contributions and constantly tending to the comparative depression and degradation of the Presbyterian Denomination in particular.

That open challenge has of late been repeatedly and publicly made of the title and identity of the Ministers and Congregations hitherto invariably recognized as composing the Presbyterian denomination and that legal proceedings have been successfully instituted by Dissenters, founded on the denial of such title and identity and seeking to inflict the forfeiture and transfer of the endowments now held by the Presbyterians as the penalty for the exercise of their conscientious privileges as Christians and Protestant Dissenters.

That the adoption of proceedings (operating as restraints upon the Christian liberty of Congregations of another denomination) is in the opinion of this Meeting at variance with the principles which occasioned and justified the separation of Non-Conformists from an Established Church. That such proceedings are mainly founded on inferences drawn from penal laws long since repealed, and which it is the duty of every consistent Dissenter to condemn and disregard. That the consequences of their successful prosecution are personally vexatious and oppressive in the highest degree to those who have for a long course of years peaceably occupied the foundations of their Ancestors, and that the injury is deeply aggravated by the attempt thus made to fix upon those Ancestors exclusive intents, repugnant to their known principles of action and opposed to the honest and consistent tenor of their lives and characters.

That the establishment of the legal principles thus involved against Dissenters by their Brethren strikes at the root of that Protestant liberty for the attainment of which their Forefathers made their noblest sacrifices to conscience and tends to convert every Chapel though founded for free and independent worship into a petty establishment, more objectionable than that connected with the State both in *principle* because it is the work of men who profess to be free, and in *practice* because the State possesses the power and means of improvement in its Institutions; while on the other hand the tenets of Dissenters would be doomed to continue perpetual and invariable.

That the community of principle and feeling which have been assumed to characterize the Associations of Protestant Dissenters being thus disturbed, the freedom which the Presbyterians have sought to protect in such Associations being attacked by those with whom they associated for mutual defence, and it being plainly necessary to direct their energies and resources towards their own protection not provided for elsewhere, this Meeting cannot but consider it useless and undesirable that the body to which they belong should continue outwardly to maintain a connection which has no common or consistent object, and which tends rather to strengthen an influence that experience shows may not improbably be directed against themselves.

That the Deputies here present therefore, while they respect the characters and principles of many of those with whom they have so long co-operated, and while they greatly lament the necessity for the present measure, feel themselves imperatively called upon in conformity with the example of their respected Ministers and with the prevalent feeling of their Country Brethren to withdraw from the union of their denomination with the Deputies of the other two denominations and in so doing to co-operate in the formation of a new union founded on enlarged and consistent views, and directed to the maintenance of the great essential principles of Protestantism.

That this determination be forthwith communicated to the Chairman of the present body of Deputies.

The intention of the Unitarian Deputies was plain: they intended to disintegrate the Deputation. 'You will no doubt,' wrote Taylor, 'take proper steps to make that alteration in the style of your body (if the other two denominations continue united) which this withdrawal of ours renders necessary.'[1]

Why did the Deputies stubbornly and even insolently decline to comply with this apparently reasonable request? Because it touched the fundamental question at issue in the whole controversy between the Unitarians and the orthodox Dissenters. Were the Unitarians the genuine English Presbyterians or were they quite a different sort of people who had continued to use a name which no longer belonged to them? On the answer to that question depended at that moment, for instance, the issue of the Lady Hewley case. The attitude of the Deputies was that, as long as the question was not raised in their Body, they were prepared for the purposes of their own Body to accept as Presbyterians and Baptists any Unitarians who thought it proper to present themselves under those names; but that the Unitarians had the exclusive right to the name Presbyterian in England the Deputies would not allow.

At this time most of the so-called Presbyterian Deputies came from what were either openly or in effect Unitarian congregations, but it is important to note that, as there was a leaven of orthodox Presbyterians in England at large, so there was also in

---

[1] 25 Mar. 1836.

the Deputies. In 1818, for instance, Deputies were admitted from the Scots Presbyterian congregation in Oxenden Street, Piccadilly.[1]

For the moment, however, the Deputies laid down no general principles. They asked for the names of the Deputies who had adopted the resolutions on 5 March. It appeared from Taylor's reply that only representatives of the English Presbyterian congregations had been summoned. All of these, ten in number, had been represented by one, if not both, of its Deputies.[2] The only dissentients had been the deputies from South Place, Finsbury; these had had no instructions from their congregation. Since the meeting Taylor had learnt that 'a Scotch church' sent deputies, but the proceedings on 5 March concerned English Presbyterian Deputies only. The General Baptists, he added, must speak for themselves. The seceders had not yet organized themselves; Taylor did not hold, and did not propose to hold, any official position among them; but he indicated on a printed list supplied by the Deputies which congregations among their constituency had been represented on 5 March. The Deputies then consulted the ten congregations separately.[3]

The ten congregations were (i) Brentford Butts, (ii) Carter Lane, (iii) Essex Street, Strand, (iv) South Place, Finsbury, (v) Hackney Gravel Pit, (vi) Hampstead, (vii) Jewin Street (Old Jewry), (viii) Newington Green, (ix) Old Ford, Bow, (x) Stanford Street. No reply seems to have come from Old Ford, and South Place, Finsbury, persisted in its dissent from the proceedings on March 5; but by 25 May the other eight congregations, it seems, had expressed their wish to secede.

The reply from South Place, Finsbury, contained much of interest. It took the form of an extract from the Minute Book of the Committee of that congregation under date 28 February 1836. On that date the two gentlemen who represented the congregation on the Deputation reported that they had had 'from Dr Thomas Rees and others of the Presbyterian and General

---

[1] 27 Nov. 1818. In 1811 the historic church in Crown Court, Covent Garden, sent £30 for the use of the Deputies. This was the largest, or among the largest, of the donations received at that time. The Rev. Geo. Grieg was then minister. 28 May 1811.

[2] An eleventh congregation in Portland Place, Taylor said, appeared not to have representatives among the Deputies. [3] 6 April 1836.

Baptist portion of that Society'[1] a recommendation that they should separate themselves from it. There was no time to consult the congregation, but the Committee of the congregation did not 'deem it expedient to accede to the recommendation of the Presbyterian and General Baptist portion of the United Assembly of Protestant Dissenters', and requested its two Deputies to protest against the proposal for separation. The South Place Deputies attended the meeting on 5 March at Dr Williams's Library. A resolution in favour of separation from the other denominations had been passed at a previous meeting of the Presbyterian Association, the Body of Presbyterian and General Baptist Ministers and the Presbyterian and General Baptist Deputies. When this was considered by the meeting of Deputies the South Place representatives took the initiative and moved three resolutions opposing separation. Edgar Taylor's amendment, the resolutions finally adopted by the meeting, was carried, and the South Place representatives found that they 'constituted the entire minority'. They therefore left a written protest and withdrew. Their main contention was that the Deputies were concerned with civil rights only; that each party had shewn itself 'equally earnest, unwearied, and consistent'; that disagreements about endowments and other matters need not prevent united action on civil rights. Finally, by a clever turn, the seceders' own argument was used against them. 'The flagrant violation by the Independent Dissenters of the right of private judgment' was alleged as the main reason for secession. But the course proposed appeared 'liable to the same censure'. To refuse to act with the Independents as Deputies (in which character their interests and prospects were identical) 'because our particular interests and opinions may differ from theirs upon subjects totally unconnected with the objects *for which alone we were deputed* is of the essence of intolerance and breathes the spirit of persecution'.[2]

A General Meeting of the Deputies accepted the resignation of the eight dissatisfied congregations, but declined, like the Ministerial Body, to accept their assumption that this amounted to a withdrawal of one of the Three Denominations.[3] In view of

---

[1] Presumably the Body of Ministers of the Three Denominations.
[2] 6 May 1836.   [3] 25 May 1836.

resolutions which had been passed by 'certain Presbyterian deputies' on 5 March 1836 the meeting set forth its views in a reasoned historical statement. For many years after the foundation of the Deputies the Presbyterians constituted a very large proportion of the whole number and had a preponderating influence on the Committee. 'Of late years their number has undergone great diminution while that of the other Denominations has increased, which has produced a corresponding alteration in the Committee.' There were before the secession fourteen Presbyterian congregations, fifty-three Independent and thirty-six Baptist. If the complaints about attempts to depress and degrade Presbyterians were aimed at the Deputies, they were unjustified. The Presbyterians have had representation on the Deputies' Committee fully adequate to the number of their congregations. The statement from South Place, Finsbury, was quoted as evidence of the fairness of the Deputation. With 'recent successful legal Proceedings', to which the seceders allude, the Deputies have nothing to do: all complaints on that subject are wholly inapplicable to the Deputies.

There was only one dissentient from these resolutions. It was then unanimously resolved that the Deputies would carry on their work for civil liberty; after an unsuccessful amendment (no figures given) declaring the Deputation 'virtually dissolved' since the withdrawal of the major part of the Presbyterian deputies had destroyed its essential character as representing the several London congregations of the Three Denominations, there came the decisive resolution. In this it was stated that no claim was made to represent the seceding congregations, but since several Presbyterian congregations continued their connexion the meeting saw no occasion for making any alteration in the title under which it had hitherto been known.

A resolution regretting the occurrences, recording appreciation of the services of many Deputies of the Presbyterian denomination to civil and religious liberty and expressing confidence that they would not cease in their separate proceedings to aim at the same object was proposed and seconded, but withdrawn. There may have been a discussion; a considerable space was left as if for such, but another hand than the Clerk's has recorded the withdrawal and drawn a pen through the vacant space. Without accepting responsibility for what went on outside and without entering into theological disputation, the Deputies had cleverly weakened the general claim of the Unitarians to be the legitimate successors of the Presbyterians; and in view of all the legal controversy of the thirties this was of the highest importance. The decision of the Deputies was advertised in the usual newspapers.

The seceders meanwhile organized themselves with chairman (Edward Busk) and secretary (Chas. Bischoff); and on 7 June 1836 held a meeting and sent more resolutions. The Deputies 'having deliberately considered' these resolutions adhered to their earlier decision of 25 May and so reported.[1] These later resolutions of the seceders were not included in the Deputies' Minutes. The Deputies' Report for 1836 states simply that the Deputies decided not to alter their name at the request of Presbyterian seceders.

The seceders did not at once accept defeat and found means of revenge. More was at stake than a name. The Deputies possessed funds, and two of the four trustees were Unitarians, William Smith and Edward Busk. A year after the secession a new set of resolutions from the Presbyterian Deputies arrived.[2] The propriety of entering them on the Minutes was questioned; one of the Deputies was instructed to investigate the question of the title of the Deputies and in a long report vindicated the Deputies' claim to be the same body as before the secession. In the end the Deputies retained the funds, as they remained in their own and in general opinion identical before and after the secession of the Unitarians. The Unitarian trustees could, and did, cause some difficulty when it was desired, for example, to sell the shares in the University of London held by the Deputies.[3]

The secession of the Unitarians was more serious in finance than in numerical strength, for among the Unitarians were reckoned some of the wealthier of the Deputies' supporters. The need for improving the financial position was much in the Deputies' mind in 1837. When, on 31 May 1837, £300 of stock was ordered to be sold there was a hitch. One of the trustees, Busk, was a Unitarian

---

[1] 6 July 1836.   [2] 28 April 1837.
[3] E.g. 10 Mar. and 29 Oct. 1841, 24 April and 11 Dec. 1846.

seceder and chairman of the 'Presbyterian' Deputies. He declined to concur in the sale till he had consulted the seceding Presbyterian Deputies. The seceders argued that two denominations could not dispose of what had been invested for three without the consent of the third. They had seceded, however, on other considerations than those of mere property, and did not propose to be 'unnecessarily tenacious upon such points'. They would not withhold concurrence if the circumstances were laid before them and the purpose was unobjectionable.

To this pronouncement the Deputies replied by a resolution which must have been intended to irritate. It was desirable, they affirmed, to appoint new trustees in place of Busk, who has retired, Smith, who has died, and the two survivors.[1]

Busk now declined to budge unless the title of the Deputies was altered and the funds divided by arbitrators. The suggestions for the new name are significant: The Deputation from the Independent and Baptist Denominations and of the United Associate Presbytery' or 'Deputies of Congregations of Protestant Dissenters'. At all costs the Unitarians must assert their title to the name Presbyterian, for on their alleged identity with the old English Presbyterians their title to hold the property of Presbyterians depended. The Deputies adopted stone-walling tactics. They left the main issue and appointed their Chairman and Mr Hale to receive any dividends now or hereafter due, to invest them in Consols, and to hold stock as trustees.[2] This proved to be no empty threat. On 30 May 1838 the Chairman reported that he had bought £100 3 per cent. Consols from dividends received.

The seceders now re-stated their demands. The presence of some Scottish Presbyterians might indeed be held to justify the Deputies' retention of the old title, but these were newcomers[3] and the public would still imagine from the unchanged title that the old Presbyterians were included. If the Deputies would drop the name Presbyterian, or simply use the name Dissenters, the seceders would perhaps waive their right to a share of the funds, though they believed that 'Presbyterians' chiefly had provided

[1] 21 July 1837.   [2] 1 Dec. 1837.
[3] Deputies had been admitted from Oxenden Street, Piccadilly, in 1818.

them. They would pay bills to prevent inconvenience to individuals. They asserted that no congregation in touch with the Presbyterian Board was now represented. (This was perhaps an over-statement, for South Place, Finsbury, was still represented.)[1]

At the General Meeting the Committee was empowered to negotiate with the seceders about the stock held and the shares in London University.[2] Six months later the deadlock remained. The seceders replied to requests to transfer stock and London University shares by enquiries about what the Deputies proposed in the main matter.[3] The problem was deferred, but financial needs and the desire to sell the University shares led the Committee to be again empowered[4] to deal with the seceders. How long the war of attrition would have continued it is impossible to forecast. The decisive stroke came from outside. Mr Busk died and with him the main legal obstacle to the Deputies' wishes disappeared. The Bank authorized the two surviving trustees (the Chairman, Waymouth, and Hale) to sell out the stock originally held by them and Smith and Busk. It was agreed to sell out the whole and to appoint new trustees;[5] and no time was lost in doing this.[6] The disposal of the London University shares proved more difficult and dragged on for years. These were held by individuals, not by trustees in blocks.

In concluding our account of the secession itself, we may note that the seceding ministers made a permanent organization whose title, 'The Presbyterian Divines of London and Westminster', still echoes the controversy which we have examined. By a most characteristic piece of English compromise the ministers and the Deputies of the Three Denominations retained unaltered their privileges in approaching the Throne, but to the new body, the Presbyterian Divines, similar privileges were also allowed.

An epilogue to the Ministerial Secession came before the Deputies in 1839. The Rev. Dr Rees still retained the Minute Book of the joint Ministerial Body of which he had been secretary. What did the Deputies advise? The Committee pointed out that the legal difficulties about title were not inconsiderable, and the results

---

[1] 22 Dec. 1837. [2] 22 Dec. 1837. [3] 27 June 1838.
[4] 1 Aug. 1838. [5] 12 Oct. 1838. [6] 31 Oct. 1838.

of a prosecution uncertain; only the expense would be certain. The Committee could therefore do no better than advise that an amicable settlement should be reached.[1]

At first it appeared as if Unitarian influence in high political circles might destroy the Deputies' status as the recognized representatives of the great body of English Dissenters. A trivial incident indicated how the wind was blowing. Lord Holland had often shewn himself a friend of the Deputies. As late as 29 June 1836 he had agreed to present a petition on Church Rates to Parliament on their behalf, and he was of course as good as his word.[2] But a month later his attitude had changed. The Deputies had approved on 6 July a petition in favour of the Registration and Marriage Bills, and hoped that Lord Holland would again present it, but he declined 'on the ground of its purporting to be a Petition from the Presbyterians as well as from the Independent and Baptist denominations'.[3] Now the 6th of July was the date on which the Deputies finally declined to alter their style and Lord Holland's language is reminiscent of the second Unitarian Resolutions passed at a meeting of the Deputies of the congregations of the Presbyterian denomination 'withdrawn from the *late* Body of the Deputies of the Several Congregations' etc. It is hard to believe that Lord Holland had not been got at by some of the Unitarians like Edgar Taylor who had hitherto carried on the negotiations between the Whig politicians and the Deputies.

Though feeling ran high, co-operation in matters of common interest did not cease completely. In the late summer the secretary of the Presbyterians sent a copy of their resolution on a General Registry Bill;[4] and in the winter Edgar Taylor and another of the seceders helped the sub-committee of the Deputies to prepare the Dr Williams's Library Register for the Commissioners.[5]

Throughout these years the faithful Finsbury congregation continued to send Deputies. It sent its £2 2s. subscription, when that plan was recommended,[6] but in doing so it expressed dissatisfaction because no Presbyterians were now on the Committee.

---

[1] 17 May 1839. [2] See Annual Report for 1836.
[3] 27 July 1836. [4] 31 Aug. 1836.
[5] 16 Nov. 1836 and 26 Dec. 1836. See p. 264. [6] 27 Dec. 1837.

All denominations ought to be represented.[1] Next year the protest was renewed. It was pointed out that the protest had been reported to the General Meeting, and that though the Committee found it difficult to influence elections, in fact there was now a Presbyterian Committee-man.

One other reference to this congregation has a somewhat pathetic interest. On 24 December 1844 it was pointed out that South Place, Finsbury, was not recognized by the Presbyterian body. The Secretary was accordingly ordered not to invite it again to send Deputies. By 'the Presbyterian body' the Deputies almost certainly meant the orthodox Presbyterians. The Dissenters' Chapels Bill had just become law; the Unitarians had contrived a revenge for the doubts cast on their claim to be Presbyterians; and in the bitterness of this tragic defeat, it seems, the Deputies wanted to end the last shred of connexion with the Unitarians. It was logical and it was right, at a moment when Parliament sanctioned a gross misuse of title, that the Deputies should clear themselves of any complicity; but it was a sad parting from loyal and tried friends.

We have next to examine the Deputies' part in the controversy that ended in the passing of the Dissenters' Chapels Bill. This was the climax of the events of almost a quarter of a century. It is unnecessary to tell again the whole story but a summary is needed. The legal toleration of Unitarians as such since 1813 had had two results: the Unitarians, assured of safety, were more loud and aggressive in their denunciation of orthodoxy, and in the eyes of the other Dissenters and of most serious Anglicans they had lost the only excuse for not organizing themselves under their true colours as an anti-Trinitarian sect. On their side the Unitarians wanted to make the best of both worlds: to retain the status (as among the Ministers and Deputies of the Three Denominations) and the property which they had acquired under the titles of Presbyterians and Baptists, and at the same time to use that status and property exclusively for the advantage of anti-Trinitarian doctrine.

Their moral right, and then their legal right, to do this was challenged by the orthodox. The Independents, led by Wm.

[1] 27 June 1838.

Hadfield, mainly organized the attack. Desultory controversy in the twenties made it clear that the Unitarians would give up nothing to argument.

Unitarian trustees, it was freely alleged, appointed Unitarian ministers sometimes against the wishes of orthodox congregations in chapels known to have been built and endowed by orthodox founders. Even where the congregation agreed with the trustees the views of the founders were flouted. Trusts established for the benefit of orthodox ministers were used only for Unitarians or their nominees. Hadfield carried the controversy from the columns of local newspapers to the law courts; and after years of controversy won a sufficient number of cases to shew that, as he had contended in *The Manchester Socinian Controversy*, the Unitarians had no legal claim to most of the property that they enjoyed. In many places their congregations were small and diminishing. It was certain that without the property they could not carry on their work. This might be used as an *ad misericordiam* appeal. It might be used as an argument to emphasize the moral wrong of bolstering up a dying error by money left for the express purpose of combating it.

The decision in the Lady Hewley Charity brought the controversy to a head. Lady Hewley, of the Presbyterian congregation in York, had died in 1710 leaving a large fortune in trust for the benefit of 'poor and godly preachers of Christ's Holy Gospel'. In 1830, after the Manchester Socinian controversy, Evangelical Congregationalists asked for the removal of the trustees on the grounds that grants had been made to Unitarian ministers who were not proper objects of the benefaction. The 1829 account shewed that of 237 ministers who had benefited, 38 were known Unitarians, in addition to the minister of St Saviour's Chapel, York, who had a special position under the deeds. The trustees pleaded that benefactions were intended for Presbyterians regardless of religious opinions. After 12 years of legal actions and the expenditure of nearly £30,000[1] the control of the Charity was

---

[1] Lloyd, *Protestant Dissent and English Unitarianism*, p. 91. Hadfield, however, put the costs at £10,000. See 'Manchester Socinian Controversy', G. H. McLachlan, in *Unit. Hist. Soc.* vol. II, no. 2.

restored to the orthodox, the Lords ruling that 'no Trust might be held for any purpose which was illegal at the time when the Trust was established', though the Unitarians were allowed to retain St Saviour's Chapel, York, to which they had no better claim, strictly interpreted, than to the rest of the bequest. Every old foundation had a slightly different history, but there was enough similarity to make the orthodox hope and the Unitarians fear that a great proportion of the property in Unitarian hands would be taken from them. 'I know', said the Lord Chancellor, 'that two or three hundred suits are already talked of as likely to be initiated for the purpose of ousting the present possessors.' To prevent this the Dissenters' Chapels Act was passed by Peel's Government in 1844.

The Unitarians constructed an ingenious title which (although it was completely exploded in advance by Hadfield in *The Manchester Socinian Controversy*) served its purpose for the moment and imposed on the mass of Englishmen for almost a century. It was first cautiously modified and then quietly abandoned by scholarly Unitarians at the end of the century when it had served its practical purpose; and it has lately been held up to the deserved ridicule of scholars by a Unitarian scholar in the *Transactions of the Unitarian Historical Society*. The title by which the Unitarians claimed in many places to defend their possession was the so-called doctrine of the Open Trust.

According to this doctrine a distinction could be drawn between two main sorts of trusts for meeting-houses founded after the Toleration Act of 1689. In some the trustees were bound to use the property for the benefit of strictly orthodox Calvinistic doctrine often defined by reference to the Westminster Confession. In others they were not so bound. The only condition expressed was that the building should be used for the worship of God, possibly qualified by some reference to Protestant Dissenting use. It was argued that the difference implied a different state of mind in the two sorts of founders. The one sort—and it was further alleged that these were mainly Independent—wished to tie their successors to a definite body of doctrine for all time. The other sort—and it was alleged that these were mainly Presbyterians—

wished to leave their successors freedom to think for themselves with a minimum of restriction. They had foreseen, it was even claimed by some, that theology would move far from the standards of the Westminster Confession and they definitely desired to encourage such a movement. Even where such intention was not definitely attributed to them, it was argued that no malversation occurred if the freedom left were used. The Unitarians were worshipping Almighty God as required, and the Open Trust was satisfied.

Against this somewhat attractive theory two main arguments could be advanced, one general and one particular. In general it overlooked the very relevant fact that, far more often than not, everything that was known concerning the wishes of the founders and their temperaments made it certain that Unitarianism was the last thing (Popery, Mohammedanism, and Paganism possibly excepted) that they would have desired in any conceivable circumstances to encourage. Only a very ingenious or a slightly disingenuous person could brew up for the dogmatic Presbyterians of the late 17th and 18th centuries the state of mind in which the Open Trust was alleged to have been thought out. In particular the theory of the Open Trust overlooked the very relevant fact that Unitarianism was expressly forbidden by law at the time when the meeting-houses were founded. There was no need to prescribe orthodox doctrine for the meeting-house. The law of the land had already done that. The trust was only valid on that assumption, and the pious Presbyterian founders knew and rejoiced in the definite proscription of the Unitarian heresy.

Both these points were made by Hadfield in 1825. Both have been confirmed and admitted by later scholarship; but there was an interval in which the doctrine of the Open Trust misled enough people to make it dangerous. And in that interval the Dissenters' Chapels Bill was passed.

The matter appears first in the Deputies' Minutes in connexion with a deputation from Ireland. In the 18th century Presbyterianism had suffered in Ireland as in England from Socinian tendencies, though to a less degree. Scottish influence was stronger in Ireland than in England and more congregations remained orthodox. The

Unitarians and the orthodox were organized separately. The legal position was much the same in the early 19th century, and the Unitarian title to Presbyterian property was as effectively shaken as in England by decisions in the courts. Cases were pending or threatened which were certain to restore very considerable properties in Dublin and elsewhere to the orthodox. The Unitarians saw that special legislation only could save them and busied themselves to procure it. On 2 August 1843 the Moderator of the General Assembly of Ireland and a member of the Privilege Committee attended a Committee of the Deputies and produced a draft Bill which the Unitarian minority of the Irish Presbyterians contemplated introducing into Parliament.

The Committee at once took up the position from which it never receded. It began by asserting its attachment to the rights of conscience and disclaimed any wish to interfere with the rights of Unitarians to preach and teach and hold any property 'to which they are legally entitled'. The Unitarians' Bill appeared to be 'an anomalous attempt' to divest other persons of their rights to their property 'for the purpose of investing Unitarians with such property'. It interfered with the sacredness of trusts and was a dangerous precedent for other interference. The Committee resolved to petition against it in every clause.

The alarm was well founded. On 13 March 1844 a Committee was summoned to consider some resolutions about Church and State which had aroused the keenest interest, but the Chairman set such business aside to deal with the Dissenters' Chapels Bill introduced into Parliament for Peel's Government by the Lord Chancellor. The Deputies opposed the Bill as unjust and unnecessary for five reasons:

(1) The wish of the original donors of property deduced either from express declaration or from fair presumption should be the sole guide for courts of equity. Only when it was impossible to discover the donors' wishes should the usage of the congregation be admitted as evidence.

(2) In practice this rule has been satisfactory: 'it being evidently calculated to secure as far as possible the just application of property according to the intentions of the donors, a right' (as the

87

Committee acidly observes) 'hitherto enjoyed by Dissenters as well as other members of the community.'

(3) For this rule the Bill substitutes a new rule: unless doctrines are expressly defined in the deeds a usage of some agreed term of years will be taken as conclusive evidence of the doctrines for the preaching of which a chapel was founded.

(4) This will prevent restoration of property according to the beliefs of the founder and will tempt Unitarians to acquire still more property unlawfully.

(5) Amendments will apply the Bill to Ireland, where, even more than in England, property has been diverted from its rightful use.

All friends of Evangelical religion were asked to help in opposition; and a petition to the Lords was to be made. The Deputies had the co-operation of the Ministers of the Three Denominations, the Irish Deputation, and the Congregational Board.

A deputation met members of the Government, but only to find that the matter was pre-judged. Peel said that the Bill was a Government Bill and had two Chancellors behind it, so it could not be dropped. He denied that the Government could have any disposition to favour Unitarians as against Trinitarian Dissenters, but this of course was precisely the point at issue. Lord Denman's remarks threw a flood of light on the actual situation. He said he was personally unacquainted with the Bill, but he was desirous of preventing litigation about chapels.[1] The claim that the Bill would prevent more cases like Lady Hewley's was undoubtedly its strongest attraction to people who had no inclination to acquaint themselves with the questions at issue.

The sub-committee shewed all the activity characteristic of the Deputies at an important crisis. First, they took steps to enlighten the Peers, in whose House the Bill first appeared. They were of course in touch with Mr Hadfield. They discussed with him the best dates for petitioning and arranged that Lord Lyndhurst's judgment in the Hewley case should be used in the circulars for the press. The Lord Chamberlain was interviewed—no doubt in vain, for no result is recorded.[2] The Committee secured the

[1] 27 Mar. 1844.   [2] 3 April and 11 April 1844.

co-operation of the Wesleyans, whose chapels were threatened by the sweeping clauses of the Bill.[1] To all the Peers were sent reasons against the Bill and copies of a letter to the Lord Chancellor.

After the Peers, the public. A meeting at the Freemasons' Hall was organized for 1500 ticket-holders under the auspices of the Deputies, the Irish Presbyterians, the Congregationalists and the Wesleyans. There was difficulty in getting a Peer to preside, though several expressed their intention of opposing the Bill. In the end Mills (the Deputies' Chairman) presided and four resolutions were passed. These deplored dangerous interference with trusts and emphasized that though the Bill was represented as a benefit for Dissenters it was in fact disapproved of by the three Dissenting Bodies in England and Wales, by Methodists, by the orthodox Presbyterians and Dissenters in Ireland, by the Free Church and Secession Kirk in Scotland. It had been contrived by a small party, not one-hundreth part of the Dissenters in the Three Kingdoms, 'to prevent just and legal consequences similar to the triumph achieved by the law in the celebrated case of Lady Hewley's Charity'. Its success would encourage the perversion of trust estates by 'any parties happening to have interest with any administration or with a majority in Parliament'. The meeting asserted its devotion to freedom of conscience and—with a pretty cut at the Unitarian use of the name Presbyterian—declared that it would not directly 'or indirectly persecute any persons who assume, however unjustly, the name of Unitarians' nor deprive them of meeting-houses actually conferred on them. They discountenanced vexatious litigation but would be traitors to the Christian faith if they did not oppose a Bill to enable the promoters of error to acquire property by infringing all established legal rules and by violating indisputable rights. At least there should be an enquiry before any legislation took place.[2]

All through the spring and early summer the fight raged. The Deputies were the central part of an enlarged united committee representing all Dissenting interests. At a time when on other grounds feeling between the Established Church and Dissenters was bitter, the Deputies had the unusual experience of co-operating

[1] 8 April 1844.
[2] 25 April 1844.

with bishops. The Bishop of London presented the petition against the Bill; his speech was used as propaganda by the Deputies; the Archbishops spoke and voted against the Bill.[1] At a public meeting on 7 May in Oxenden Chapel, Haymarket—one of the orthodox Scottish Presbyterian chapels—Lord Mountcashel took the chair, and the case against the Bill was restated with great ability in masterly resolutions.

If it be thought desirable by the Legislature to establish and endow the Unitarian form of faith this meeting is of opinion that such a proposition should be made openly; that as this meeting would find itself bound to oppose any such proposition it feels itself doubly bound to enter its solemn protest against the proposition now made to transfer the property of Trinitarians to Unitarians and thus to apply the property of the pious dead to the subversion of the faith which they cherished and supported while alive and for the maintenance of which after their deaths they have founded these charitable trusts.

Petitions from the provinces were organized and statements circulated to the press, to Anglican clergy, to Dissenting ministers, and to members of the Lower House. The Government was at first unmoved. The Lord Chancellor declined even to postpone the discussion and the Bill passed the Lords. The Deputies seem to have turned in vain to their old ally, Lord John Russell.[2] Lord Aberdeen made an appointment, but cut it.[3] Peel at last had to yield to pressure and agreed to delay until after Whitsuntide in order to allow opinion in the country to be expressed.[4] On 25 May an Exeter Hall meeting, representing all denominations, constituted an enlarged committee which managed the subsequent opposition.[5]

This unusual alignment of forces was not to everyone's taste. The Anti-State Church Association was just coming into existence as a result of an Anti-State Church Conference held in this year, 1844. To those whose main concern was the redress of Dissenters' political grievances and the Disestablishment of the Church of England, it appeared deplorable to divide Dissent over the Bill

[1] E.g., 26 April; 29 April; 1 May; 2 May; 13 May; 15 May; 17 May; 20 May.
[2] 17 May 1844.   [3] 3 May 1844.
[4] 13 May and 20 May 1844.   [5] 20 May and Report of 1844.

and to alienate perhaps for all time the Unitarians. Though they might be represented as numerically feeble, legally insecure and morally questionable, they had vast political influence. The Dissenters' Chapels Bill was itself convincing evidence of that. Accordingly we find that in the heat of the fight a Special Meeting of the whole body of Deputies was summoned on the request of eight Deputies, of whom it is significant that Edward Miall, the leader of the Anti-State Church movement, was one. The tension may be guessed at from the Chairman's acid remark in opening that the address of the requisition was incorrect. The requisitioners proposed that it was undesirable to oppose the Bill further, 'particularly because the influence of the Dissenting body would be materially injured by the divisions inevitably consequent on such opposition'. Others called for strenuous opposition at all stages and the advertisement in all papers of the Deputies' determination.[1] Voting was postponed until a further meeting after a week's adjournment. By forty-eight votes to ten continued resistance to the Bill was approved. It is tempting to fancy that we can discern the influence of the South Place, Finsbury, congregation here; and that the discontinuance of a summons to them was not wholly unconnected with this incident. But that is mere speculation.

Macaulay, Monckton Milnes, Lord John Russell, Gladstone and Peel supported the Bill. Gladstone's argument, conveyed with typical Gladstone fuzziness, was as follows:

When I look at these Chapel Deeds I find . . . that the most general words are used, and if the parties themselves who were willing to subscribe, when they came to found meeting houses, which of course were intended to be used by posterity as well as themselves, no longer referred to doctrinal tests, but framed their deeds in the largest and most general language, does not that raise a strong presumption that, though they were themselves believers in particular doctrines, yet they objected on principle to binding their posterity to the maintenance of them for ever?

The favourable reception given to the Bill in the House of Commons made the Committee shift its tactics to amendments limiting the operation of the Bill: only existing meeting-houses,

[1] 2 May 1844.

which must be registered by 1 Jan. 1845, should be affected.[1] The Government refused the amendments, but modifications were made to secure the Wesleyans in possession of their threatened chapels. The Wesleyans, for all that, being opposed in principle to the Bill, won the gratitude of the Deputies by 'nobly' continuing their co-operation.

The Act as passed was less violent than as at first drafted. As drafted, by legal experts ignorant of the fundamental question, it had at first declared

that when no particular religious doctrines were enforced by the Trust Deeds the usage of — years (the number left to be fixed by Parliament) should be taken as conclusive evidence of the doctrines for the promotion of which the meeting houses were founded.

Martineau and others protested; the difficulty was raised in Committee by Mr J. Stuart-Wortley and Mr Cardwell and removed on the report stage by amendments introduced by the Solicitor-General to secure

the more ample recognition of the power of such Dissenting Congregations as had no tests or creeds to change their opinions as they saw fit in the lapse of time.

A majority of 161 approved the final division on the Bill, on 15 July 1844.

Its effect may be summarized in the words of the Deputies' Report of 1844. The object intended by the projectors of the Act, who were Unitarians, has been obtained. Unitarians in England and Ireland have had a title given them to chapels from which they were in fear of being ejected by the Law of Charitable Trusts, which required that the objects and principles intended by the founders if ascertainable by legal evidence should be ever regarded as sacred and unchangeable. This Act applied to all Dissenting chapels. Since the passing of the Act the judgment of the Lord Chancellor in the case of the Eustace Street Chapel, Dublin, had been given whereby the possession of large property originally devoted to Trinitarian purposes had been continued in the power of Unitarians, although previous to the Act Lord Chancellor

[1] 10 June 1844.

Lugden had given his opinion that Trinitarians were the rightful parties to enjoy the same.

To guard against the application of Meeting Houses to purposes not intended by the founders it will be necessary in future to state with distinctness in Trust Deeds the doctrines intended to be taught and the usages to be followed.

The Deputies in the bitterest hour of their humiliation did not lose their traditional sagacity. They took steps instantly to advise the Congregational and Baptist Boards about the need for very explicit trusts in order to safeguard their property in future. They promptly found occasion—even if an irrelevant occasion—to have a cut at the organizers of the Unitarian victory, Sir Jas. Graham and the Attorney-General. A week after the passage of the Bill they noted that the Poor Law Amendment Bill described Dissenting ministers incorrectly. Graham and the Attorney-General were informed that the proper title is not 'licensed' but 'certified' and 'a satisfactory reply' about the correction was drawn from Graham.

The expenses of the United Committee, apart from the earlier expenses, it seems, of the Deputies, were £566. A year after the passing of the Act, the unpaid balance, £313 7s. 8d., was met from equal grants from the four parties: Church of England, Wesleyans, Irish and Scottish Presbyterians, the Deputies.

The Act roused fears for the integrity and sanctity of trusts, as was shewn in a petition to the Commons on Charitable Trusts. Commissioners, it was urged, ought to be bound in the doctrine of *cy près*[1] and to the execution of founders' intentions as nearly as possible. The Deputies henceforth regarded any State supervision of religious trusts with the gravest suspicion, and, as we shall observe, were at no pains to conceal their distrust of the Charity Commissioners. Their distrust of all State interference with religious trusts was well founded in their memory of the infamous legislation of Peel's Government; and for many years the Charity Commissioners did nothing to induce Dissenters to modify their opinions.

[1] See Chapter 4 of Part II below, on the Temporalities of Dissent.

PART II

ON THE DEFENSIVE

CHAPTER 1

THE DEPUTIES GO TO LAW

As we have seen, the Protestant Dissenting Deputies came into being for a specific purpose—the Repeal of the Corporation and Test Acts. To procure Repeal would be to improve their legal status; but it was almost a century before they succeeded in this. Meanwhile they were not, of course, without rights. They possessed common rights as citizens by Common and Canon Law; and they possessed privileges as a special class under the Toleration Act. There was an urgent need, which became apparent in the first years of the Deputies' existence, to see that these rights were respected. As early as 1734 the Deputies were consulted about a case at Cirencester; in 1737 they made their first intervention in Parliament on a question of rates; and

very soon after the appointment of the Deputies, they received complaints from various quarters, of clergymen refusing the rites of burial to those who had not been baptized according to the forms of the established church. In 1740 they took the opinion of the Attorney General upon this subject, and received instructions how to proceed for the future in cases of the same kind.[1]

From this time on, the Deputies were regularly asked to help country Dissenters in legal and internal disputes in which they were involved. So far from diminishing as time went on, the number of these cases grew at the end of the century, partly because the Dissenters were more conscious of their rights and better able to defend them; partly because of the antagonisms of the stormy French Revolutionary period. After Repeal the number of cases rapidly diminished, except in two categories—those involving burial rites, and those involving trust property. These are treated in separate chapters.

[1] *Sketch*, p. 13. Their relations with the Attorney-General were such that he returned the fee as a friendly gesture (15 Oct. 1740).

In a special supplement, the *Sketch* reports 241 cases in which the Deputies intervened between 1740 and 1812. They are arranged in the following categories:

Unjust demands and prosecutions:	45	(8 in Wales)
Riots, assaults and disturbances:	38	(4 in Wales)
Refusal of Magistrates to execute their office:	27	(8 in Wales)
Refusal of Clergy to perform their duty:	42	(3 in Wales)
Parochial disputes:	24	(most in London; none in Wales)
Private disputes:	65	(7 in Wales)

The rapid increase in the number of cases at the end of the century is shown by the following analysis of the number of cases in each decade:

1740-49	17 cases
1750-59	6 cases
1760-69	15 cases
1770-79	33 cases
1780-89	27 cases
1790-99	45 cases
1800-09	79 cases
1810-12	19 cases

That is, there were 23 cases before 1760, 120 between 1760 and 1800, and almost as many—98—in the 12 years between 1800 and 1812. Of these, only 23 occurred in the Deputies' own constituency (within ten miles of London) and 13 of the 23 were in the comparatively unimportant category of appeals against parish rates. On the other hand, 30 cases of a much more serious character, many involving personal violence, bigotry and rancour, are recorded from Wales.

It is clear that Wales in the 18th century produced more than its fair share of outrages of all kinds. They seem to have increased as the Evangelical revival disposed the people everywhere to practise their religion outside the Established Church. It is difficult to resist the impression that magistrates were more truculent in Wales than elsewhere in refusing to register meeting-houses and ministers under the Toleration Act, that the Deputies had to force their hands more often by *mandamus*, that riots, insults, disturbance of divine service, and 'barbarous usage' of Dissenters were reported more frequently from Wales than from the rest of the kingdom.

In 1745, for example, Dissenters, it was claimed, were illegally impressed. The Deputies took up the matter in September 1745. In April 1746 the Secretary for War promised to release one who was a freeholder on an affidavit of fact. In November the Deputies learnt that at last the man was at liberty.[1] What happened when the Deputies did not interfere? An enquiry from a Welsh minister in 1754 lights up an immense background of envy, hatred, malice, and all uncharitableness. Was it safe for him, he asked the Deputies, to speak over the grave of a person buried in the parish churchyard, even if the vicar had consented, or would such an action provide material for a case in the spiritual courts?[2] As late as 1838 we find two Welshmen imprisoned for not attending church; a technical error prevented the Deputies from attempting to liberate them; but another technical point secured their freedom.[3] Even in 1870 the Deputies contributed £21 to a fund for the relief of Welsh Nonconformists evicted because they voted against their landlords' political views. When the long unbroken tale is pondered, the bitterness of the Welsh against the Anglican Church in the 19th century may be more easily understood.

Nothing is more striking than the contrast between the quiet competence and recognized status of the Deputies in London and the utter defencelessness of many of those whom they assisted in the provinces. In the provinces when a riot had occurred, when magistrates refused to register meeting-houses, or when some property was flagrantly misappropriated, it was often hard to get a solicitor in the neighbourhood to undertake a case for the injured church. Local bigotry and the social and financial power of the Establishment made it too dangerous for a professional man. The Deputies would sometimes send down one of their number to investigate, or would employ a London lawyer; they could put the best legal advice at the service of a tiny congregation.

[1] 25 Sept. 1745; 2 April and 26 Nov. 1746. [2] 9 Oct. 1754.
[3] See Chapter 5 on Church Rates and Church Courts.

Nevertheless, all was not easy, even for London Dissenters in touch with friendly Whigs in high places. We recall the remark made by the Chairman of the Deputies when Mr Evans (the hero of the 'Sheriffs' Cause') died: 'He exposed himself so to the displeasure of the Great as to suffer considerably in his secular affairs'. The Chairman continued: 'I verily believe that the bitterest enemy the Dissenters now have would gladly excite animosities amongst us and destroy the Deputation'.[1] In the 19th century the same fears were sometimes expressed. In 1837 the Deputies sent a letter to 148 unrepresented London congregations of Dissenters, warning them that their 'old and powerful adversaries' have adopted new means, and that Dissenters' rights were not more secure than when their social status was worse (before Repeal). 'Measures of prudent and cautious policy' replace 'open acts of cruelty and oppression' —that is all. 'The Lay Union for the Defence of the Established Church' (with 15 Members of Parliament among its officers and committee, and representatives all over the country) had been established to resist more concessions, declaring that the Church needed a system of defence 'as well organized and sustained as the system of attack adopted by its adversaries'.[2]

But if in the 19th century the Church of England sometimes paid the Deputies the flattering compliment of imitation, in the 18th century any association of Dissenters was in itself a dangerous matter, likely to arouse suspicion and to give ground to those who wished to raise prejudice. Some Dissenters thought that such a body as the Deputies by its very existence was likely to harm the Dissenting interest. In these circumstances the Deputies had reason to behave with the greatest prudence; this is clearly the reason why they so often held back over Repeal. The earliest petition which they organized concerned a Bill for rebuilding St Olave's, Southwark, 'which tended to subject the Dissenters in that parish' (and there were similar cases at St Leonard's, Shoreditch, and St Mary's, Rotherhithe) 'to certain new and unreasonable rates on burials'.[3] The Deputies agreed to bear the expenses since the matter was of public interest; but it is typical of their methods that neither the Deputies themselves, nor even the Dissenters as such, are

[1] 11 Mar. 1767.   [2] 27 June 1837.   [3] April 1737; see *Sketch*, p. 5.

mentioned in it. A short petition from 'several inhabitants' of the parish asks that they may be heard by counsel against the Bill.

Not only were the Deputies abnormally cautious about the accuracy of any legal instrument prepared for them;[1] they had qualms about their own legal status. Whenever possible, legal action was taken in the name of some trustee or person directly interested in a case; but this could not always be done. Not infrequently some obstinate chairman of Quarter Sessions, some High Church incumbent, or some recalcitrant trustee knew well that no local Dissenter had money or independence enough to face him. Such folk the Deputies brought to heel best by themselves taking or threatening to take legal action. In 1802 they decided to take counsel's opinion on the matter. Was the Committee guilty of barratry, champerty, or maintenance in cases where they acted but had no personal interest? The reply was reassuring. No question of barratry (vexatious litigation) or champerty (the hope of receiving a share of the proceeds of the case)—no question of these arose. Only in some civil causes did the Committee run the risk of maintenance; but it appeared to be agreed that it was legitimate to advance money to help a poor man to carry on his suit, and this probably covered most of the Committee's actions.[2]

Nothing but the exact perusal of the sixteen volumes of Minutes will suffice to shew the vast extent, the meanness, the venom, the relentlessness of the persecution which went on, sometimes within the law, sometimes outside it. No matter was too paltry, no grief too poignant, no place too sacred, no rite too solemn, no violence too scandalous, no unchivalry too despicable. It is a squalid but a necessary enquiry. So much has been heard of the dissidence of Dissent and the unreasonable readiness of Dissenters to take offence that it is important to examine the soil which produced the unlucky side of Nonconformity. The Anglicans were often the wealthier, the better educated, the better bred; but too often—more often than in these milder times we remember—the ancient motto *noblesse oblige* was the last thought in their mind and the last rule of their conduct.

On public occasions—in petition and resolution—the Deputies

[1] E.g. 14 Nov. 1764.   [2] 1 Jan. and 28 May 1802.

knew how to use vigorous language and the devices of rhetoric. But where matters of law are concerned there is the quiet coolness of a solicitor's office. The facts are recorded without comment. Enquiry is made to ascertain that the facts are as recorded, and that evidence will be forthcoming. Before action, legal opinion is sought. Great care is taken to secure accuracy—for example, in 1764, when getting a *mandamus* against the Anglesey Justices of Peace, the Committee returned an affidavit made by the local people as not in proper form.[1]

If the outrage was not plainly against the law as well as against justice, the Deputies would not touch it. If there was a plain case, the offender was approached in an unprofessional way, and an amicable solution found. If he shewed any disposition to be reasonable the Deputies would meet him: for an apology they would waive claim to damages. 'Use all gentle methods first' is a characteristic piece of advice.[2] 'In point of prudence'[3] it might not always be best to insist on full legal rights. Sometimes the issue was not worth the expense; sometimes a legal victory would have cost the local church more in reputation than it would have won in other ways.

The Deputies' funds were not available for actions which had been begun without their being consulted, or which were not carried on under their direction.[4] They expected clients to help themselves; for instance, they said in 1810 that the Committee

takes it for granted that such pecuniary aid as may be necessary will be rendered by the opulent and benevolent Dissenters and friends of religious liberty in the surrounding neighbourhood

though ultimately they would help, they admitted, as far as the limited funds and the demands on them allow, if need be.[5] Often the local congregations were poor, and the whole cost fell upon the Deputies.

On many occasions their strict adherence to the rules they had set themselves stood the Deputies in good stead; and local people who proceeded in defiance of their advice generally regretted it. At Stansted in Essex, for instance, the Dissenters seem to have been

[1] 14 Nov. 1764.   [2] 13 Oct. 1769.   [3] 10 Mar. 1769.
[4] 29 Nov. 1816.   [5] 30 Nov. 1810.

defrauded of a coachway to the meeting-house. The uncertainty of the trust deed gave poor vantage for a fight, and when after much litigation the Dissenters could have secured a coachway by the payment of a small rent the Deputies advised them to close with the offer, inequitable though it might be. But Stansted's blood was up; the case was continued; and in the event the Dissenters emerged with no credit and, one hopes, a respect for the Deputies' judgment.[1]

When there was no legal redress, the Deputies advised patience. One of the Overseers of the Poor at Edenbridge, Kent, asked if he was bound by a resolution of the vestry forbidding the Overseers to purchase anything whatever from any person who was a member of the Dissenting congregation lately established there. He received the advice to comply with the resolution. 'The orderly peaceful conduct of Protestant Dissenters' said the Committee, 'is the most likely means to lessen prejudice and silence those who clamour against us'.[2]

The Deputies were determined not to prejudice their general usefulness by injudicious vigour on particular occasions. An incident in 1808 illustrates this, and at the same time reveals a little drama in village life. The curate of Milborne Port refused to bury a young woman except on a Sunday, though her mother asked that the funeral might be on Saturday evening. As the young woman was a Dissenter, the Deputies informed the Bishop of Bath and Wells. The Bishop reported that the curate had had an excellent reputation for twenty-three years and had a reason for his action.

The last time he interred a Dissenter upon a weekday the friends of the deceased in an improper manner procured the keys of the singing gallery, and introduced their own singers contrary to the forms of the Established Church.

Having sufficient reason to expect a repetition of such conduct, the curate fixed on Sunday to prevent it. The Deputies agreed that they could not interfere in the affair, as the Dissenters had acted irregularly in the past; but they add, perhaps somewhat illogically, that in future they will compel the curate to do his duty.[3]

[1] 17 Jan. 1777.   [2] 29 Oct. 1802.   [3] 24 June 1808.

The Deputies shewed a steady determination to discountenance ill-mannered truculence even among Dissenters suffering flagrant injustice. Their attention was drawn to the wrongs of a man who was smarting under an inequitable demand for burial fees, though the burial took place in another parish. He was also under distraint of goods for tithe. The Committee responded:

As by his letters it appears his conduct has been very intemperate and that he has used insolent language the Committee lament they cannot, consistent with the duty which they owe the Dissenters at large, interfere in a case where a person has so conducted himself.[1]

A second appeal did not make them change their attitude.[2]

Nothing could be more admirable than their courteous diligence in pursuing enquiries even when the immediate effect might be to discredit a cause in which they had already succeeded.[3] Admirable, too, was their refusal to budge from a decision carefully taken, even when it was represented later that by merely writing 'a sharp letter' they could secure what was asked.[4] In a similar spirit they declined to support the Rev. Mr Anthony, of Bedford, in his refusal to pay for an organ in the parish church and for alterations which he considered unnecessary. The charge, the Deputies said, falls on him as a parishioner, not as a Dissenter. They can distinguish law and justice: this claim is a matter of law.[5]

Sometimes when the Deputies had been unable to perceive any legal redress of injustice they had the pleasure of hearing that in the end the grievance ceased. Here is a not uncommon case of petty persecution. A Mr Sawbridge of East Haddon, near Daventry, forbade his tenants to deal with Dissenters. As a direct consequence one Dissenting tradesman would not only have to leave the place, he would also have to sell his premises without any business now attached to them.[6] The Deputies could see no ground for action;[7] and were the more delighted to hear later that 'a pleasing change' had taken place in 'the conduct of Sawbridge towards the Dissenters.' The restrictions were removed. Peace and order reigned again in the village.[8]

[1] 26 June 1807.   [2] 26 July 1807.
[3] 3 Oct. 1806: was a request for burial improperly made?
[4] 30 May 1806: interest on a legacy of £20 long withheld.
[5] 28 Aug. 1807.   [6] 25 Oct. 1811.   [7] 29 Nov. 1811.   [8] 17 Jan. 1812.

Unfortunately, this was not always so; sometimes the Deputies found themselves involved in a running feud. The *Sketch* tells how, in 1808,

Several persons guilty of disturbing the public worship of the Dissenters (at Aylsham, Norfolk) and personally ill-treating the minister, were indicted by order of the Committee. At the trial, the defendants offered to make a public apology and pay the costs. The proposition being acceded to, they were reprimanded by the judge, who observed, that if the affair had not been compromised, and the defendants had been found guilty, the sentence would have been very severe.[1]

But in 1813 the Deputies were again receiving complaints. A large stack of corn had been built so near the windows of the meeting-house 'that the shutters will but just open'. The annoyance was undoubted, but the meeting-house was private property; and the Deputies did not allow their sympathies to lead them to positions where they might have no legal foothold—this time, they declined to intervene.[2] On the other hand, though there was no legal redress, publicity sometimes helped. In a similar case near Swindon seven years later, stacks were not only built near the windows of a chapel, but the property was damaged by rain-water being allowed or directed to run into the foundations. The meanness of this conduct wilted when dragged into the daylight; the farmer promised to build no more stacks there, and to make a drain.[3]

A case which occurred very early in the Deputies' history, in 1747, at Fairford in Gloucestershire, illustrates their tact admirably. A congregation of Independents there 'scrupled marriage' according to the rites of the Established Church. They 'marry amongst themselves in their own congregation'. Before the passing of Lord Hardwicke's Act in 1753[4] such marriages were irregular, but not invalid. Nevertheless one Greenwood who had been so married was put into a spiritual court for living in fornication with his wife.[5] When the Chairman of the Deputies induced the incumbent, Dr Attwell, to withdraw the prosecution, the Committee advised the Fairford Independents 'to behave themselves civilly to

---

[1] *Sketch*, p. 130. [2] 26 Nov. 1813. [3] 28 Jan. 1820.
[4] See p. 271. [5] 28 Jan. 1746/7.

Dr Attwell and not to triumph as if they had gained a victory over the Doctor'.[1]

The same shrewdness appears in the reply sent to a minister on his liability to take a parish child. Since the Toleration Act does not exempt him,[2] he can only 'make interest' with the parish or the justices.[3]

Many of the struggles with trustees, magistrates, incumbents, rioters dragged on year after year. Legal fees mounted. Dexterous opponents, often unjustly in possession, used every artifice of delay to wear down the patience, enthusiasm, and income of the Deputies. In the procedure of unreformed Chancery such persons had an advantageous arena for a struggle. News of an outrage often reached the Deputies considerably after it had occurred. Often, especially in citations before spiritual courts, it was found that the case had gone by default; no one had appeared in court, and though the charge might be preposterous and though decisive precedents might be on the Dissenters' side, the village clergyman scored his mean triumph. The payment of a fine which might at an earlier stage have been contested successfully was now the only way to avoid excommunication or imprisonment. The Deputies could only pay—it might be £20, it might be £50, it might be more[4]—and urge their poor and ignorant clients not to let the case go by default next time; they must put in an appearance in court, secure precise information of the charge, and send the information promptly to the Deputies.[5] No doubt by these means the Deputies prevented a repetition of the vexatious proceedings in the same parish. Either the incumbent did not risk a second venture, or the Dissenters knew how to counter him; but in some other parish the same squalid drama was played out: ignorant Dissenters, information supplied too late, a substantial fine needlessly paid, and a careful locking of the stable door when the horse was stolen and the thieves busy elsewhere.

Anyone who will study the Appendices to the *Sketch* will understand that to secure exemption from earlier statutes given by the

---

[1] 1 April 1747.　　　　[2] Cf. 24 April 1778.　　　　[3] 14 Mar. 1783.
[4] 6 Oct. 1786: £43. 14. 5 paid to save poor people at Swansea from excommunication.
[5] E.g. 22 May 1789: Deputies send a proctor to attend with a man in court for not attending church.

Toleration Act a man might need a considerable knowledge of legal process. Ignorant Dissenters neglected to make the declarations required by the Toleration Act. In practice this did not usually matter; not only laymen but ministers at times omitted the formality, but such persons were liable to be prosecuted, and (unless competently advised) involved themselves in no small expense before they understood what was happening. It was only too easy to make vexatious threats to fine people for not attending parish churches, for keeping schools, for preaching without making the necessary declarations[1] or in buildings not properly registered at the time. Sometimes the threats could be carried out; sometimes they could not. At almost every meeting of the Committee during the period covered by the *Sketch* there was one or more of such cases to be disentangled. Threats against schoolmasters were extremely common, but perhaps because on such occasions their clients were better able to understand the legal situation, it was almost always enough for the Deputies to advise the schoolmaster how to proceed, and no action followed. On the other hand, fees not legally enforcible, such as fees for churching women, were collected from Dissenters.[2]

Burial fees were often collected under threat of legal proceedings, or after proceedings had been begun, though the burial had been in a Dissenting graveyard with the rites of Dissenters, and no fee was due.[3] The Deputies found it very difficult, because information reached them too late, to defeat this peculiarly mean manoeuvre to increase the incumbent's income; the costs of fighting even a good case made it often better to pay.

The improper assessment of church property for rates constantly received the attention of the Deputies, and nowhere was their judicious caution more admirably illustrated. The ignorance of the victims and the expense of proceedings often combined to put Dissenters at the mercy of those who had the wish to injure them. It cost £71 5d., for instance, to clear a meeting-house of an unwarranted claim for rates for repairs to the parish church and

---

[1] I.e. taking the Oaths of Allegiance and Supremacy, and subscribing the Declaration against Popery, at the General Sessions of the peace. *Sketch*, p. 157.

[2] E.g. 9 May 1764.

[3] For further details, see Chapter 2 of Part III on the Burial Laws.

the building of a workhouse. The Deputies paid half the expense.[1] But wherever property was not used exclusively for sacred purposes; where preaching occurred in a room put at times to secular purposes; or where pews let at advertised rates brought the premises legally though inequitably under assessment, they advised prompt submission to the law, and (where possible) such an adroit change in custom as would put the premises on the right side of a statute or legal decision.[2]

Tolls were another tricky matter. They could not legally be demanded from church- and chapel-goers, and the Deputies, by warning enquiries, caused efforts to persecute Dissenters by exacting them to cease. But Dissenters at Buckland (near Dover) had to be told in 1819 that a recent decision of the Court of King's Bench held that the exemption only applied within a parish boundary; and worshippers who crossed into another parish (as in this case) had no redress.

In 1832 this point was still giving trouble. Richard Fox of Barlestone, Leicestershire, was encouraged to resist a claim for toll on his way to his usual place of worship at Barton. In the Deputies' view at this date, it did not make any difference that there was a place of worship at Barlestone—it was not his 'usual' place. However, the Gatekeeper, the Clerk of the Turnpike Trust, and the Commissioners of the Road treated the Deputies' letters on the point with 'perfect indifference, if not with contempt'.[3] The Deputies therefore decided to consult the Attorney-General, who held that there was no liability to pay. The Committee thereupon asked the Commissioners if they would test the case at law by seizing Fox's goods (as the Attorney-General suggested). The Commissioners at first agreed, and the Deputies prepared to fight; but later they heard that the Commissioners had discontinued taking toll; their attorneys would not pursue the case; and the Deputies suspended proceedings 'for the present'.[4]

There were also many complications caused by local Acts; the position might not be clear without a test case; and often the

[1] 30 Jan. 1795: Hornton Street Chapel, Kensington.
[2] For further details, see Chapter 4 on Temporalities.   [3] 24 Feb. 1832.
[4] 26 June 1833.

collectors persisted up to the point of going to court before they gave way. Thus at Huntingdon, near Kington (Hereford), in 1815, the demands were abandoned at the last minute, but the Deputies were involved in fees amounting to £15 12s. Much later, in 1849, we find the Deputies making enquiries about the local Acts when Sunday tolls were demanded on a bridge at Wallingford.

The Deputies charged themselves not only with the defence of the rights of Dissenters against the attacks of outsiders, but also with disputes inside the congregations. Most of these were concerned with property, for many of the meeting-houses were endowed, but the provision of proper trustees, the correction of negligent and the punishment of corrupt trustees were constant difficulties, which are treated more at large in the next chapter.

But other disputes were doctrinal or personal. On such occasions the Deputies gave good counsel, but declined to adjudicate; the number of such cases was very considerable, as may be seen from the analysis of those mentioned in the *Sketch*.[1] Some were trivial, some little more than begging appeals. In 1797 the Deputies declined an appeal from a Cockermouth congregation who could not raise a decent sum for the maintenance of their minister.[2] In 1822 a Lowick minister complained that a 'person in affluent circumstances had attended the Meeting house from Nov. 1802 to Nov. 1819 without contributing to the Pastor'. He was told that

A person (however affluent) cannot be compelled to contribute towards the support of the Ministry from attending Divine Worship at a Meeting House unless he agrees to pay for a seat or sitting.

In 1813 the Rev. Wm. Turner of Newcastle-on-Tyne complained for the Elders of Castle Garth Chapel that a former minister—the Rev. Jas. Chambers—withheld the 'sacramental plate and other things belonging to the Chapel'. When approached, Chambers wrote on behalf of 'the Managers and Elders of his present congregation' promising to return 'the principal articles except the Register Book of Births'; and the Deputies advised the Castle Garth congregation to adjust the remaining matters in the best way they could. In such cases, doctrinal divisions are plainly

---

[1] See above, p. 98. [2] 15 Dec. 1797.

evident, and (as we have shown in the chapter on the Presbyterians) the Deputies neither could nor would intervene in such
disputes. But there were enough internal disputes of other kinds
to cause the Deputies serious disquiet, and in 1770 they thought it
wise to draw up a scheme, for general circulation in the country,
to prevent disputes, especially those arising from the choice of a
minister. A characteristic instance may first be mentioned. Mr
Patrick, the minister at Southill, was shut out of the meeting-
house by some trustees and others on account of a doctrinal
difference. The Deputies succeeded in getting a scheme accepted
by which there was to be a delay of six weeks, and then a vote on
the continuance or discontinuance of Mr Patrick's ministry. With
some insight the Deputies recommended that

in order to preserve the decorum and propriety which become persons
calling themselves Christians they should request the attendance of two
respectable persons in the neighbouring churches to preside on the
occasion.[1]

The Deputies noted later that the ministry was to end amid mutual
complaints. They regretted that their plan had not succeeded, but
saw no need for interfering further.[2]

The *Sketch* describes another case, with the Committee's
resolution:

The Committee were appealed to, about the year 1770, respecting
some differences among a congregation of Dissenters at Shrewsbury, as
to the choice of an assistant minister. The adherents of one candidate
applied for the assistance of the Committee in regard to the temporalities
belonging to the congregations alledging that the other had been
elected by a minority. On this the Committee directed their secretary
to write for a statement from the other party, with properly authenticated documents. Before any progress could be made in the investigation, the elected candidate died; and the chairman of the Committee
wrote to one of the principal people connected with the congregation,
urging him by all means to endeavour to unite both parties. The
Committee highly approving of his conduct, came to the following
unanimous resolution, which is strongly recommended to the attention
of those who may in future be interested in similar cases:

[1] 18 Jan. 1811.
[2] 31 May 1811. Other typical cases in 1824 (Saffron Walden and Maryport), 1828
(Bath), 1832 (Maidenhead), 1858 (Southwark).

'That it is the opinion of this Committee, that differences like those above mentioned, weaken the Dissenting Interest, and tend to bring Dissenters into contempt; and strengthen the hands of those who watch opportunities to dissolve the Deputation:—a Deputation that reflects great honour on the Dissenters; and has been of the utmost utility and advantage to the Dissenting Interest, and without which several of their congregations must have fallen a prey to their adversaries. For Providence has, in several instances, favoured the attempts of the Deputation and Committee, to defend the legal civil rights of the Dissenters against oppression. This is their proper business, and not to settle disputes and controversies in particular churches, which should always be adjusted with a spirit of meekness and humility by the congregations themselves, or their friends and neighbours.

'That as it is the undoubted right of every congregation of Protestant Dissenters in England to choose their minister, they have also the sole right to fix the qualifications of an elector. And therefore it is the opinion and resolution of this Committee, that it be recommended to the congregation at Shrewsbury, and to all other congregations, that before they come to the choice of a minister, it should be plainly settled by them what kind of persons have a vote.'[1]

Internal disputes did not always concern trusts or the choice of a minister. In 1811 the introduction of an organ at the New Tabernacle, Plymouth, caused dissention. The majority of the congregation, the Deputies' Committee were told, wished to remove it; but some of those who like it threatened prosecution if it were removed. The Committee declined to intervene.[2] This case will serve as a reminder to readers of Thomas Hardy's novels and Francis Kilvert's Diary that internal disputes of this kind were not confined in the 19th century to congregations of Dissenters; they were part of the tissue of all Church life, though many 'mute, inglorious' Mrs Proudies found no Anthony Trollope to chronicle them.

Trollope himself would have enjoyed the Deputies' contest with his old school and its redoubtable headmaster. On 9 July 1816 the Rev. Richard Thatcher was ordained to the ministry of Harrow

---

[1] *Sketch*, pp. 40-1. The Minutes add: 'In order to preserve the spirit of peace and love which is so much the stability and glory of religious societies.' (9 Dec. 1767.)
[2] 11 Jan. 1811.

Baptist Church, and the boys of Harrow School in pursuit, it appears, of a standing feud turned out to enjoy the occasion. Five ministers and others who attended complained that between fifty and a hundred of the boys had endangered more than fifty people, much hurt some, used very opprobrious and insulting language, and threatened to demolish the meeting-house. They had begun by taking out the linch-pins of the carriages; and when one of the coachmen answered this mischief with blows, the boys answered the blows with stones.

Complaint was made to the Deputies, but they did not meet in the summer, and so did not consider the matter until 25 October. On 15 November they wrote to the Headmaster, the Rev. Dr Butler, reporting this 'most outrageous transaction', stating the legal advice they had received, and asking for co-operation.

The young gentlemen of Harrow School must learn, that they cannot with impunity insult and injure persons who never attempt to molest them.

In his reply on 28 Nov. Dr Butler handled the situation with great skill. The Deputies had referred to former 'aggressions' by Harrow boys; he refers to his former efforts to satisfy injured parties. He complains of the five months delay in reporting the matter as making his task now needlessly difficult; in particular had he been informed when the linch-pins were removed from the carriages during service, he could have checked everything. Instead one or more offending boys were violently struck, their school-fellows were exasperated, and in that way the only serious part of the affair began. The threat to demolish the meeting-house was unworthy of inclusion in a case drawn up for the serious consideration of counsel: it is 'the idle effusion of some thoughtless boy'; does not a master live close by the House? He asks for the names of the offenders, and neatly contrasts in passing the unhelpful, dilatory Deputies with 'the enlightened and liberally minded counsellors whose opinion has been ultimately taken upon the case'.

Six names were sent and more promised, though after enquiry no more could be reported. On 3 Dec. Dr Butler promised to punish 'duly' any boys of whose guilt he was convinced. What other 'atonement', he asked, had the Deputies in mind; and what 'distinct pledge' that such insults would never again occur? He could but promise to be ready to interfere to prevent disorder. On 30 Jan. 1817, Dr Butler was informed that no indictment would be preferred if the boys sent a written apology and thanks for being left to the discipline of the school and not prosecuted. (The apology would not be published.) Minute enquiry had shewn that one of the coachmen caught one of the young gentlemen at the linch pins and took him by the collar, or by the arm, and shook him; no other reprisal was made.

I have transmitted the statements of the Persons who were of the Party, from which you will perceive the nature of the Outrage, the deliberation with which it was planned, the violence with which it was executed, and the great number of scholars engaged in it.[1]

The names of the Deputies' informants Dr Butler was asked to keep to himself lest they should incur the ill-will of the school.

On 17 February, Dr Butler sent a letter of apology signed by five boys, in which they 'thankfully acknowledge the delicacy and liberality' of the treatment, sending £10 for the compensation of anyone injured. Dr Butler added his own assurance, tantalizingly mysterious, that 'the measures which I have adopted for punishment have been adequately severe'.

What of the sixth offender? He was Lord Ashley, son of the great Earl of Shaftesbury; and of him Dr Butler could only report that he had left Harrow, that he was free of Dr Butler's authority, and that Lord Shaftesbury's objection to his signing any paper whatever appeared insuperable. As he could no longer cause offence, probably proceedings against him were not worth taking. Moreover, Lord Shaftesbury was anxious that compensation should be made for any violence, and authorized Dr Butler to tender £10 in consideration of any share which Lord Ashley might be supposed to have taken in the affair.

The Deputies, as their custom was, took care that the honours of war were theirs. They accepted the apology and returned the boys' £10,

assuring them and you, Sir, that pecuniary satisfaction formed no part

[1] 30 Jan. 1817.

of that object to obtain which the Committee thought it their duty to interfere.

Out of feeling for Dr Butler and for the five boys who have apologized they will not make the matter the subject of public discussion by prosecuting Lord Ashley. But they will not take Lord Shaftesbury's £10, for the reason already stated, and they end in a mood of truculently complacent reflectiveness:

It is not thought that the accidental circumstance of withdrawing from the school ought to exempt the party from making a proper apology to insulted and injured individuals; nor can the Committee persuade themselves that the true dignity of a Legislator is to consist in evading the submission due to violated order and offended justice.

There were many other cases besides that at Harrow in which meetings were disturbed; and they did not all arise from boyish high spirits and the love of practical joking. The first reported and dealt with was at Stratton in Wiltshire in 1741, where a mob broke the windows of a meeting-house and insulted and 'barbarously used' the congregation. The Justices of the Peace refused to grant warrants against the rioters, and the Deputies took the case to King's Bench; but here, as so often, they failed to get satisfaction because those concerned could not be satisfactorily identified. A case with particularly serious implications of this kind occurred at Guilsborough in Northamptonshire, where a meeting-house was burnt down on Christmas Day, 1792, with strong suspicion of arson.

The Committee being applied to, obtained an authenticated statement of facts, which they laid before his Majesty's ministers, who readily offered a reward of £200, by public advertisement, to any person or persons, for bringing the offenders to justice. No discovery was made; but the vigilance of the Committee, and the prompt attention of His Majesty's government to their representations, were probably the means of preventing farther outrages in other parts of the kingdom.[1]

No action was possible in cases of disturbance or damage unless the meeting-house had been properly registered. Even when it was, often all the satisfaction that could be obtained was a public

---

[1] *Sketch*, p. 57.

apology, for both the Dissenters and their assailants were frequently poor and illiterate. The *Sketch* quotes the judge's summing-up in a typical case of this kind, at Reigate in 1797:

This is an indictment founded on a statute which passed in the reign of King William and Queen Mary, and known by the name of the Toleration Act. The object of that statute was, what every man in his heart must commend, to leave every man to worship God in his own way, to follow the dictates of his own conscience, and to observe them in such a manner as he thinks right, he not doing any mischief to any other member of the community. It is undoubtedly to be wished that that indulgence should be granted to all ranks of men.

The ground of this prosecution is, that when this Dissenting Congregation were met for the purposes of worship, the defendant Yeoman thought fit to go into this congregation, disturb them in that worship, and according to the evidence, to insult and disturb the minister to a great degree.

Having proved what I may call the introductory parts of this case, namely, that this place was registered, and that the minister had a certificate granted to him, which is also required, for the purpose of the government of the country knowing who are intitled to the exemptions given by the statute, and who not; they proceed to state what passed on the 4th of December, when the congregations were assembled.

[Mr Justice Buller stated the evidence, and then proceeded.]

This is the evidence on the part of the prosecution, and this evidence is not contradicted.

To be sure, there cannot be more insolent or more abusive conduct than that proved on the defendant. It is said by his counsel, that he did not mean to disturb the congregation. Disturbing the minister, who was then performing his duty as the minister of that congregation, was the greatest insult that could be offered to that congregation. The others who were silent were not the object of abuse: the most likely object of abuse was the minister in the act of preaching.

It is proved that there were no words used on the part of the minister that should give him any provocation.

It should be remembered, that where people are assembled together in a place of worship for the purpose of paying their respect to the Divine Being, a man who does not agree in opinion with them is not at liberty to go into that assembly and quarrel with the minister because he does not happen to utter the doctrine which is agreeable to his mind.

The object and purpose of their being allowed to have such a meeting-house, is because they do not agree with the established church. They have ideas particular to themselves, and they have as much right to be pleased with their mode of worship as we have with ours, and they are protected by the law in worshipping God in their own way, if they comply with the requisites of the law, as much as we are.

Then these people were doing no more than by law they had a right to do when this man chose to go into this chapel, insult the minister, and disturb the congregation in the manner you have heard. I am bound to tell you the evidence brings this man's offence clearly within the Act of Parliament, and if you believe the evidence, it is your duty to find the defendant guilty.

It is conspicuous that the majority of these cases were from small and isolated villages. Such cases occurred in 1813 at Chadwell, Essex; in 1817 at Hartington, Middlesex; in 1819, near Coventry; in 1825 at Stretton-under-Fosse; in 1827 at Cove, near Blackwater, Hants. In the last case four men were gaoled for disturbance, but the church was too poor to prosecute, the defendants too poor to pay costs, and in view of their poverty and the imprisonment they had suffered, the Deputies paid the costs of the action. The atmosphere characteristic of these cases is vividly called up by that which occurred in 1828 at Kingston near Ringwood, Hants, where a Wednesday evening meeting in a licensed room was disturbed, not for the first time, by 'horns, kettles, bells, and shouts proceeding from some forty or fifty human throats'. Stones were thrown through the door and windows, and those who expostulated were thrown to the ground.

Sometimes the Dissenters were as disreputable as their opponents. In 1821 the Deputies undertook a case at Tolton (Southampton) as 'a most obstinate defence' was threatened and, as so often, the church was poor. It then appeared that the minister, the Rev. Mr Davies, had been guilty of immoral conduct and brought disgrace on religion; but still, the disturbance was most flagrant. The minister died during the progress of the action, but care had to be taken about the 'general character and situation in life' of other witnesses. The case dragged on until 1829, and though one defendant appeared personally and made apologies 'which his own heart told him they were entitled to', the Deputies found themselves eventually due to pay £51 19s. 2d. costs.

Not all such riots were organized. In 1830 one of the Deputies reported a disturbance in his own congregation at Great Suffolk Street, Southwark. A young married man, Field, who ill-treated his wife and (it was alleged) had been responsible for the death of his two-year-old baby, sent up a note by the pew-opener to tell his wife that he would 'fetch her out and rend her veil' if she should stand up to sing 'as is the custom among our singers to do'. The preacher was giving out the second hymn when Field went up the stairs—but her father resisted and the police carried her off.

Doubtless the 'New Police' had much to do with the diminution of such riots after this date. The last to be mentioned in the Minutes came from Horsham in 1878, when the Congregational minister, the Rev. A. E. Lord, was disturbed by 'noisy playing on the Green opposite his Chapel'. He was advised to try the effect of a strong letter to the authorities; if it failed to apply to the magistrates.

So often were the Deputies concerned to get redress for congregations disturbed by rioters that it was natural for them in the early period to hear of assaults on Methodist preachers. The cautious and unfriendly attitude with which the Dissenters and the early Methodists eyed one another has often been described. Perhaps it has been exaggerated. In America they intervened to plead with the New England authorities for toleration.[1] And at home the records, at the very few points where they concern Methodists, shew more co-operation and sympathy than might be expected. But several cases on which they were consulted were, for technical reasons, unsuitable for legal action. The first was when the Grand Jury refused to find a true bill against the Silvertown rioters. As the place of preaching was unlicensed, no redress was obtainable.[2] Twenty years later the Committee had made no general decision whether or not to interpose on behalf of Methodists. Without establishing a precedent, they agreed to try and force a recalcitrant J.P. to do justice after riots and ill-usage at Lingfield. The case would not have formed a happy precedent; it was long, expensive,

---

[1] See Chapter on America, below, p. 407.   [2] 31 Jan. 1753.

and unsatisfactory. It cost the Committee a good deal, and the local people refused arbitration against the Committee's advice.[1]

On another occasion the evangelicals were the offenders. A new chapel of Lady Huntingdon's in Mulberry Gardens in Nightingale Lane disturbed the Rev. Dr Mayo's meeting-house, 'the singing being so loud that he could not be heard when preaching'.[2] The Committee urged Dr Mayo to try, not for the first time, to accommodate matters with the Countess; but, like many another man, he made no impression on the elect lady. The Committee heard counsel's opinion, but no detail and no action appear to be recorded.[3]

By the end of the century the Committee had definitely decided not to touch cases which did not affect the Three Denominations,[4] though they continued to invite, and sometimes to obtain, the co-operation of the Methodists in applications to Parliament for specific reforms.[5]

---

[1] 6 and 13 Aug. 1776; 9 Oct. 1778.   [2] 29 May 1778.   [3] 9 Oct. 1778.
[4] E.g. 25 Jan. 1799: Stoke Abbas riot.
    24 April 1801: Hull minister's right to remove baptismal registers.
[5] E.g. Places of Worship Enfranchisement Bill, 1920 (see below).

CHAPTER 2

'THE SHERIFFS' CAUSE'

NOTHING WOULD have astonished the Protestant Dissenting Deputies of the 18th century more than to know that a hundred years later their Committee would be headed by the Right Honourable the Lord Mayor of London, and that they would find themselves acting from time to time as a sort of unofficial sub-committee of the Common Council of the City on causes which they had in common. For in the 18th century the bitterest battle between Church and Dissent was fought *à l'outrance* between the Deputies and the City of London.

In the two other great defensive actions which the Deputies fought at this period—the battle for the right of burial, symbolized in the case of Kemp *v*. Wickes;[1] and the attempt of Lord Sidmouth to impose new conditions for the registration of Dissenting ministers[2]—it was easy to see the right on the side of the Church. There were Anglican clergymen who conscientiously scrupled to bury those whom they regarded as 'unbaptized'; and Lord Sidmouth could justly claim that under altered conditions the Toleration Act of 1689 needed revision. But in 'The Sheriffs' Cause' the attitude of the City Corporation was vexatious and intransigent, and the struggle was the more bitter because of the great and growing weight of Dissent in the City.

The first rumbling of distant thunder was heard in a 'Paper of Reasons for Repealing the Test and Corporation Acts' drawn up by the Deputies in January 1739. The third reason states:

As the Dissenters are universally acknowledged to be well affected to His Majesty and the established government, they think it hard, that by the Corporation Act they are rendered incapable of holding offices

---

[1] See Chapter 2 of Part III below on the Burial Laws.
[2] See Chapter 3 below on Lord Sidmouth's Bill.

in the corporations where they live, though in many places their property is at least equal to that of their neighbours; especially since many of them have been fined for not taking upon them such offices; and in particular, as a very large fine is now insisted on, by the city of London, from a known Dissenter, for not serving the office of sheriff, and a prosecution for the same is actually commenced.[1]

But the information which had reached the Deputies was premature. In March the Committee learned that no action had yet been entered against the Dissenter in question, a Mr Wightman, and the reference in the paper was ordered to be deleted; but the information was not inaccurate in substance: we learn from a note four years later that, in the event, Mr Wightman *was* prosecuted.[2]

It seems clear from the form of the paragraph quoted, and from references to a similar case at Hull (in which the Deputies agreed to assist the Dissenters in their case, though without accepting any financial responsibility)[3], that this attack began outside London, and that it was a fairly common weapon against Dissent. It is impossible to tell in whose brain the fertile notion originated of appointing Dissenters to offices which they could not conscientiously discharge, and then fining them for their refusal. But London became the great test case—a case which was not to be settled until 1767, and then in dramatic fashion, with a race against time as the defendant lay dying.

It was three years after the first mention of the matter that issue was joined. In October 1742

Mr Mauduit reported that the City of London intend to move for an Information against Mr Robert Grosvenor for not taking on him the Office of Sheriff. *Resolved* that this Committee will endeavour to defend Mr Grosvenor in such manner as they shall be advised by Counsel learned in the Law, and Mr Tomkins be desired to appear for him in case he be prosecuted.[4]

Exactly a year later the Chairman reported to the General Meeting:

An affair of great Importance to the Dissenting Interest. The City of London (not contented with prosecuting Mr Wightman a Protestant Dissenter for his fine which they Claimed for his refusing or neglecting to take on him the Office of Sheriff) had moved the Court of King's Bench for an Information against Robert Grosvenor Esqr for his

---

[1] *Sketch*, p. 9, quoted more largely above, p. 30.   [2] 12 Oct. 1743.   [3] *Ibid.*   [4] 27 Oct. 1742.

refusing to give Bond to serve that Office when he had been Chosen by the Common Hall.

Mr Grosvenor on his being chosen had applyed to the Committee for Advice, and as he thought himself incapable of being chosen[1] into & Consequently not obliged to hold or execute that Office he had intimated that he would refuse to serve it if the Committee would stand by him and assist him in his Defense. This the Committee promised him to do, thinking his Refusal and Contesting this matter with the City was an Affair of Common Concern to the Dissenters and might answer very valuable purposes.[2]

Mr Tomkins, the Deputies' solicitor, was asked whether he would enter into the same rule of court as in the Wightman case, to the effect that the only question to be argued was whether the defendant was

eligible or not to the Office of Sheriff of London and Middlesex or his Nomination or Election thereto being void or not void according to the Acts of Parliament commonly called the Corporation or Toleration Acts.[3]

But the Deputies refused to enter into this agreement in the Grosvenor case; and the Court of King's Bench in a two days' hearing unanimously refused to grant the information. The City then threatened a prosecution for a fine of £620 in the Sheriffs' Court, 'and we hear have given orders accordingly' noted the Deputies' Committee, instructing Tomkins to have the case removed by *habeas corpus* from the City Courts to the King's Bench. In April 1745 the case was still dragging on; the Deputies had succeeded in getting it removed to the Court of Common Pleas, and were opposing an attempt to get it referred back to the City Courts. At last the City abandoned the prosecution.

Here the affair ended for a time; and when fresh attempts were made, they appear to have been rendered unavailing by the vigilance and activity of the Committee.[4]

In 1748 the Common Hall made a new bye-law with the object of bringing the Dissenters within their jurisdiction.

[1] 'apprehending that the Corporation Act . . . was an effectual bar to his election, and that the Toleration Act would protect him in refusing to qualify' he being 'a Protestant Dissenter who had never taken the sacrament according to the usage of the Church of England, and who scrupled to do it as a qualification for an office'—*Sketch*, p. 25.

[2] 12 Oct. 1743. [3] 20 Nov. 1744. [4] *Sketch*, p. 26.

It was notorious that this bye-law was contrived for the double purpose of oppressing the Dissenters, and raising money. The fines were expressly appropriated towards defraying the expense of building the Mansion-house. Many Dissenters were nominated and elected to the office, not because their services were wanted—for some were wholly incompetent, through age or infirmity, but because it was known they would rather submit to the fine, than serve an office, for which, they supposed, they were disqualified by law, except upon a condition with which they could not conscientiously comply. Numbers of them, accordingly, paid their fines; and above fifteen thousand pounds were thus obtained by the corporation of London.[1]

It is clear that not all the Dissenters had the same fighting spirit as Mr Robert Grosvenor, and it was six years before the Deputies found a suitable test case. Among the first to be nominated was Mr Reynolds of Spitalfields; he came with an offer to the Deputies —he would pay one quarter of the cost of the suit if they would defend him, and the whole fine himself if he was cast. But the Deputies did not think it a proper case; for he had not taken the oaths and subscribed the declaration required by the Toleration Act, and he 'can't now within time', and also 'the said Mr Reynolds has withdrawn himself from the Religious Society of the Dissenters for a Considerable time last past'.[2] Within a few days Mr Reynolds had been followed by a Mr Robinson.[3] Mr Robinson had a better case than Mr Reynolds, but he haggled over the Committee's terms for his defence. His final offer was to pay £200 down, and a further £300 if he lost the case; but the Committee wanted him to promise the £300 if the expenses of the suit exceeded £700. 'He refusing to consent thereto, nothing was done in the affair'. Mr Robinson was the first of many opulent Dissenters who found the Deputies' terms hard; in 1752 we hear of Mr Whitbread desiring 'time to advise with his friends before he could come to a final resolution', although the Deputies agreed that 'as he had already subscribed to this fund £26 5s., that the same shall be taken as part of the said sum he is to pay';[4] in 1753 Mr Harrington and in 1754 Mr Trueman similarly 'desired time to consider of the said proposal'.[5] But the Deputies were firm;

---

[1] *Sketch*, pp. 26-7.   [2] 9 May 1748.   [3] 19 May and 21 May 1748.
[4] 22 June 1752.   [5] 14 June 1753; 19 June 1754.

they knew what they were up against, and they would not move if their terms were not agreed to. They did not leave everything to individuals; they raised a national guarantee fund of nearly £4,000, and before they had done they had to call up 40 per cent of this in three stages.[1] Special appeals were made to certain districts—for instance, in 1758 to Bristol and Norfolk—as Dissenting strongholds, or perhaps because similar prosecutions were threatened there.

In the early 1750s a number of prominent Dissenters, who saw the eyes of the City Fathers fixed on them, agreed to pay to the Deputies 'the fine they must have paid to the City to be excused from serving the Office of Sheriff' if the Deputies would indemnify them; the money was to be vested in the Deputies' trustees, and after the defendants were indemnified was to be 'to the use of the Deputation'. Among those who paid their fines in this way to the Deputies instead of to the City were the three men whose cases came for trial—Messrs Sheafe, Streatfield, and Evans; Mr Sheafe paid his £400 and twenty marks down 'then and there' on agreement.[2]

The Deputies had not mistaken their opponents; the City were determined to make the suit as awkward and expensive as possible. They refused to shorten the procedure by consent, or to take one case and let it decide the others. When the three separate actions were begun, that against Streatfield could not be maintained, as he was found to be out of the jurisdiction, but the City refused his offer of trying the merits of the cause in the courts above. The defendants were compelled to apply to the Court of Chancery before they could get authority to inspect the books of the Corporation; and they had to have more than fourteen hundred sheets of transcript made in each case, which was both expensive and unnecessary.[3]

In the first court, the Sheriffs' Court ('the judges of which are persons appointed by the Common Council', says the *Sketch*) the verdict went in favour of the City (September 1757),[4] and this

[1] 20 per cent in April 1759 (£720 received); 15 per cent in 1761; 5 per cent in 1767.
[2] 26 April 1751. On 29 May the Treasurer reported having bought £800 3½% Bank Annuities with part of the money received from Messrs. Sheafe and Streatfield.
[3] 22 Feb. 1758.   [4] *Sketch*, p. 28.

verdict was confirmed by the Court of Hustings, of which the Recorder of London was sole judge. The cases were then brought by *certiorari* before the Court of St Martin's,[1] a special commission to examine and correct errors, composed of Lord Chief Justice Willes, Lord Chief Baron Parker, and Justices Foster, Bathurst and Wilmot. The Lord Chief Justice died before judgment was given; the other judges unanimously reversed the decision of the City Courts, in a verdict given at Guildhall on 5 July 1762. Here are some observations from Mr Justice Foster's argument:

It hath been said, that the construction now contended for is over-partial to the Dissenters; it excuseth them from offices of burden. But doth it not at the same time exclude them from all offices attended with honour and profit? And it would sound extremely harsh to say, that the same law which, for the reasons given in the preamble, excludes them from the one, as persons unworthy of public trust, hath still left them liable to the other, be the trust that attends the office what it may. The shrievalty is indeed an office of burthen, but we all know that it is likewise an office of great importance and signal trust. The present defendant hath solemnly pleaded it (the Toleration Act) and shewn himself intitled to the benefit of it. And he doth not plead it in order to excuse one fault by another, but in order to shew that the Rubric which requires all persons to communicate with the established church three times at least in the year, is not now obligatory on him. The Toleration Act, he saith, hath taken away the force and effect of the Rubric with regard to him. Whether it hath or hath not done this remains to be considered. And I am clearly of opinion with my brothers who have spoken before me, that it hath. This opinion I ground, not barely on some particular branches of the act, but likewise on the spirit and general frame and tenor of it. It is not to be considered merely as an act of connivance and exemption from the penalties of former laws; it doth, in my opinion, declare the public worship among Protestant Dissenters to be warranted by law, and intitled to the public protection. It no less than four times, upon different occasions, speaks of the religious worship practised among them as a mode of worship permitted and allowed by that act. What is this but saying, that it is warranted by law? The magistrate may sometimes connive, where he cannot punish or reform; but what the legislature permits, allows, and takes under its protection, ceaseth from that moment to be

---

[1] From having been formerly held in the Church of St Martins le Grand.

an offence. I conclude therefore . . . that the Act having dispensed with the defendant's conformity to the Rubric, the judgement against him must be reversed.[1]

In spite of this decision, the City took the case to the House of Lords by writ of error. By this time Sheafe was dead, and Evans was dying; his case only could go forward, and had he died too the expense and trouble of fourteen years had perhaps been lost.

Mr Evans's life was at that time so precarious, and an object of such importance to the Dissenters, that numerous inquiries were continually made at his house respecting the state of his health.[2]

But Providence lengthened out 'the dying life of the defendant' just far enough to sustain the cause till it was judicially determined.

On 21 and 22 January 1767, Mr Yorke and Sir Fletcher Norton appeared at the bar of the House of Lords for the plaintiff, and the Attorney-General and the Solicitor-General for the defendant, before Lord Mansfield and all the judges except those who had sat as commissioners. Though neither the *Sketch* nor the *Minutes* ever say so, we may gather from the persons of the defending counsel that the Government now considered the defence of the Dissenters a matter of public policy. Lord Mansfield proposed that to draw a line 'between the *bona fide* Dissenter and the occasional Conformist, the Infidel and the Profligate' a question should be put to the judges 'so as to prevent all future applications to Parliament, either from corporations or *bona fide* Dissenters'. The question was as follows:

Whether, upon the facts admitted by the pleadings in this cause, the defendant is at liberty, or should be allowed, to object to the validity of his election, on account of his not having taken the sacrament according to the rites of the church of England within a year before, in bar of this action.

All the judges, except Mr Baron Perrott, were full and clear in stating it as their opinion,

that the defendant is at liberty, and should be allowed to object to the validity of his election on account of his not having taken the sacrament according to the rites of the church of England within a year before, in bar of the action.

[1] *Sketch*, pp. 29-30. [2] *Sketch*, p. 39.

Lord Mansfield then rose in his place, as a Peer, and said:

In moving for the opinion of the judges, I had two views. The first was, that the House might have the benefit of their assistance, in forming a right judgement in this cause before us. The next was, that the question being fully discussed, the grounds of our judgement, together with their exceptions, limitations, and restrictions, might be clearly and certainly known, as a rule, to be followed hereafter, in all future cases of the like nature.

He did not think that the action could be supported on any view. The express provision of the Corporation Act was that no person could be elected who had not taken the sacrament within a year; its general design to exclude Dissenters from office; and on both grounds the prosecution must fail. But if the plaintiffs grounded the action on their own bye-law, 'professedly made to procure fit and proper persons to serve the office', they must fail too, since the defendant is not fit and able, being expressly disabled by statute law. Nor is the defendant guilty of criminal neglect in not having taken the sacrament, since the Toleration Act freed Dissenters from the obligation.

Lord Mansfield continued:

It is now no crime for a man to say he is a Dissenter; nor is it any crime for him not to take the sacrament according to the rites of the church of England; nay, the crime is if he does it contrary to the dictates of his conscience. . . . It hath been said, that 'this being a matter between God and a man's own conscience, it cannot come under the cognizance of a jury'. But certainly it may: and though God alone is the absolute judge of a man's religious profession, and of his conscience, yet there are some marks even of sincerity; among which there is none more certain than consistency. Surely a man's sincerity may be judged of by overt acts. It is a just and excellent maxim, which will hold good in this as in all other cases, 'By their fruits ye shall know them.' Do they—I do not say go to meeting now and then,—but do they frequent the meeting-house? Do they join generally and statedly in divine worship with Dissenting congregations? Whether they do or not, may be ascertained by their neighbours, and by those who frequent the same places of worship. In case a man hath occasionally conformed for the sake of places of trust and profit, in that case, I imagine, a jury would not hesitate in their verdict. . . . The defendant in the present cause pleads, that he is a Dissenter within the description of the Toleration Act; that he hath not taken the sacrament of the church of England within one year preceding the time of his supposed election, nor ever in his whole life; and that he cannot in conscience do it.

Conscience is not controllable by human laws, nor amenable to human tribunals. Persecution, or attempts to force conscience, will never produce conviction; and are only calculated to make hypocrites, or martyrs. My lords, there never was a single instance from the Saxon times down to our own, in which a man was ever punished for erroneous opinions concerning rites or modes of worship, but upon some positive law. The common law of England, which is only common reason or usage, knows of no prosecution for mere opinions. For atheism, blasphemy, and reviling the Christian religion, there have been instances of persons prosecuted and punished upon the common law: but bare non-conformity is no sin by the common law: and all positive laws inflicting any pains or penalties for non-conformity to the established rites and modes, are repealed by the Act of Toleration; and Dissenters are thereby exempted from all ecclesiastical censures. What bloodshed and confusion have been occasioned from the reign of Henry the Fourth, when the first penal statutes were enacted, down to the Revolution in this kingdom, by laws made to force conscience! There is certainly nothing more unreasonable, more inconsistent with the rights of human nature, more contrary to the spirit and precepts of the Christian religion, more iniquitous and unjust, more impolitic, than persecution. It is against natural religion, revealed religion, and sound policy.

Sad experience, and a large mind, taught that great man, the President DE THOU, this doctrine. Let any man read the many admirable things which, though a Papist, he hath dared to advance upon the subject, in the dedication of his History to Harry the Fourth, of France (which I never read without rapture), and he will be fully convinced, not only how cruel, but how impolitic, it is, to persecute for religious opinions. I am sorry that of late his countrymen have begun to open their eyes, see their error, and adopt his sentiments. I should not have broke my heart (I hope I may say so without breach of Christian charity), if France had continued to cherish the Jesuits, and to persecute the Huguenots. There was no occasion to revoke the Edict of Nantz; the Jesuits needed only to have advised a plan similar to what is contended for in the present case:— make a law to render them incapable of office:— make another to punish them for not serving. . . . If they accept, punish them; if they refuse, punish them; if they say yes, punish them; if they say no, punish them. My lords, this is a most exquisite dilemma, from which there is no escaping; it is a trap a man cannot get out of; it is as bad a persecution as that of Procrustes:— if they are too short, stretch them; if they are too long, lop them. Small would have been their consolation to have been gravely told, the Edict of Nantz is kept inviolable; you have the full benefit of that Act of Toleration; you may take the sacrament in your own way with impunity; you are not compelled to go to mass. Was this case but told in the City of London as of a proceeding in France, how would they exclaim against the Jesuitical distinction! And yet in truth it comes from themselves: the Jesuits never thought of it; when they meant to persecute, their Act of Toleration, the Edict of Nantz, was repealed.

This bye-law, by which the Dissenters are to be reduced to this wretched dilemma, is a bye-law of the City, a local corporation, contrary to an Act of Parliament, which is the law of the land; a modern bye-law, of very modern date, made long since the Corporation Act, long since the Toleration Act, in the face of them: for they knew these laws were in being. It was made in some year of the reign of the late king: I forget which; but it was made *about the time of building the Mansion-House*.[1] Now if it could be supposed the City have a power of making such a bye-law, it would entirely subvert the Toleration Act, the design of which was to exempt the Dissenters from all penalties; for by such a bye-law they have it in their power to make every Dissenter pay a fine of six hundred pounds, or any sum they please; it amounts to that.

The professed design of making this bye-law, was to get fit and able persons to serve the office: and the plaintiff sets forth in his declaration, that if the Dissenters are excluded, they shall want fit and proper persons to serve the office. But were I to deliver my own suspicion, it would be, that they did not so much wish for their services, as for their fines. Dissenters have been appointed to this office, one who was blind, another who was bed-ridden; not, I suppose, on account of their being fit and able to serve the office. No, they were disabled both by nature and by law. We had a case lately in the courts below, of a person chosen mayor of a corporation, while he was beyond the seas, with His Majesty's troops in America; and they knew him to be so. Did they want him to serve the office? No; it was impossible. But they had a mind to continue the former mayor a year longer, and to have a

---

[1] Italics in original.

pretense for setting aside him who was now chosen, on all future occasions, as having been elected before.

In the cause before your lordships, the defendant was by law incapable at the time of his pretended election: and it is my firm persuasion that he was chosen because he was incapable. If he had been capable, he had not been chosen: for they did not want him to serve the office. They chose him, because without a breach of the law, and an usurpation on the crown, he could not serve the office. They chose him, that he might fall under the penalty of their bye-law, made to serve a particular purpose: in opposition to which, and to avoid the fine thereby imposed, he hath pleaded a legal disability, grounded on two acts of parliament. As I am of opinion that his plea is good, I conclude with moving your lordships, that the judgement be affirmed.'[1]

'The judgement' says the *Sketch*, 'was immediately affirmed *nemine contradicente*, 4th of February 1767. . . . By this decision the important question, in which the property, not to say the liberties, and even the lives of Protestant Dissenters were so much involved, was finally set at rest'. And the *Sketch* then describes how the news was brought to Mr Evans, the defendant:

He was sufficiently sensible, when the cause was determined, to receive the information, and to express, with a faint smile and faultering accents, the satisfaction it afforded him in the immediate prospect of death. He was a man of considerable opulence, and great respectability; and had been for several years a member of the Committee.

But the Minutes are more explicit:

The good man was spared to hear of the success, and sufficiently sensible to smile and say 'Aha! Aha!' By his attachment to the Deputation 'he exposed himself so to the displeasure of the Great as to suffer considerably in his secular affairs.' Nor was he alone in this. 'I verily believe' said the Chairman, reporting to the Deputies 'that the bitterest enemy the Dissenters now have would gladly excite animosities amongst us and destroy the Deputation.'

On this ominous note, in spite of the ringing victory they had won, ended 'The Sheriffs' Cause'.

---

[1] *Sketch*, pp. 32-7. A footnote says: 'It is stated by Mr Dodson, that this speech was brought away *memoriter* by Dr Furneaux' (note, p. 31).

CHAPTER 3

LORD SIDMOUTH'S BILL OF 1811

ON 18 JUNE 1810 Lord Sidmouth made a speech in the House of Lords,

respecting the abuses of the Toleration Acts; he asserted that these abuses were disapproved of by many of the Dissenters themselves; and concluded with giving notice of his intention to bring in a bill to prevent any person taking out a certificate as a preacher or teacher, unless he had attained the age of twenty-one, was appointed to a congregation, and could produce testimonials of his fitness for his office from some persons of the same religious persuasion.[1]

A year previously, on 2 June 1809, his Lordship had stated in the House

that he had reason to believe many persons took out licenses as Dissenting ministers, under the Toleration Act, for no other purpose than that of obtaining an exemption from parish offices and the militia.[2]

He had begun, therefore, by asking for an account of licences granted in each year since 1780; a proposal which the House accepted, amending the initial date of the statistics to 1760. The *Sketch*, having paused to denounce the 'invidious and unwarrantable' word *licences*, makes an interesting analysis of the returns:

Number of persons who have taken the oaths and subscribed the declarations prescribed by 1st W. and M. c. 18, and 19th G. 3. c. 44, at the Quarter Sessions, in periods of seven years, and in each year of the last period.

From 1760 to 1766	80	From 1788 to 1794	610
From 1767 to 1773	38	From 1795 to 1801	1318
From 1774 to 1780	179	From 1802 to 1808	1068
From 1781 to 1787	379		
			3672

---

[1] *Sketch*, p. 91.   [2] *Sketch*, p. 83.

In 1802	105	In 1806	171
In 1803	188	In 1807	162
In 1804	113	In 1808	215
In 1805	114		
			1068

Number of places of worship registered, or recorded, conformably to the Act of 1st W. and M. c. 18, at the Bishop's Registries, or the Quarter Sessions, in periods of seven years.—N.B. Many of these places have long ago ceased to be used for public worship.

	Bp's Reg.	Qr. Sess.	Total
From 1760 to 1766	387	284	671
From 1767 to 1773	391	193	584
From 1774 to 1780	652	246	898
From 1781 to 1787	665	213	878
From 1788 to 1794	1486	386	1872
From 1795 to 1801	3185	393	3578
From 1802 to 1808	3388	292	3680
	10154	2007	12161[1]

It may be proper to illustrate the situation revealed by these statistics. The religious and ecclesiastical conditions were very different from those that had prevailed when the Toleration Act of 1689 settled the status of Dissenting ministers. In 1689 the number of congregations was comparatively small. Most of these had a settled minister whose clerical status was, for all practical purposes, as clear as that of the incumbent of the parish; his time was devoted to ministerial and scholastic work. By the end of the 18th century the Evangelical revival had multiplied the number of congregations among the old orthodox Dissenters and had called into being the new Methodist congregations. The multiplication of congregations had multiplied the ministers too, and ministering to these new congregations there were in many places ministers of a new type: less well educated than the older sort of Dissenting minister, engaged during much of the week in secular work, carrying out their spiritual duties in their spare time, yet exercising

---

[1] *Sketch*, p. 85 n.

a regular ministry, sometimes itinerant, sometimes settled in one place. To give such men the status of ministers was to use the Act in a manner not perhaps contemplated by its makers; laws designed for one situation were in fact giving a more extended form of toleration than anyone had conceived in 1689. Whether this was in accord with the spirit of the Acts of 1689 and 1779 might be a matter of opinion, but it was not altogether unreasonable for Lord Sidmouth to argue that the new situation called for new regulations.

Lord Sidmouth claimed that 'these abuses were disapproved by many of the Dissenters themselves'. The Deputies, on the other hand, claimed that their resistance to his proposals was based on a national decision. During the winter recess of Parliament in 1809-10 they held a conference with the ministers, and agreed to lay the matter before Dissenters throughout the country.

Various reports were made to the Committee in the course of the winter, which concurred in reprobating any design to explain or alter the law so as to abridge the freedom in religious matters then enjoyed by the Dissenters, but *differing as to the description of persons who, it was thought, might reasonably expect from the legislature the advantages of Dissenting ministers.* The general opinion appeared to be, that no alteration in the law was desirable, except to render the operation of the Act of His present Majesty co-extensive with that of 1st William and Mary, *and to establish the right of students in divinity to the same advantages as regular ministers.*[1]

There seem to have been elements in Dissent itself which were not entirely averse from some check on the new activities. Some of the older, more sober, more scholarly ministers (and perhaps some of the less orthodox) had no wish to be confused with the itinerant hot-gospellers of the Evangelical revival. This aspect of the questions is referred to in *The Manchester Socinian Controversy*[2] and we may see it reflected also, from the field-preacher's point of view, in a tract called *Hackney Gravel Pit*[3] directed against the London Presbyterians, and in particular against the Rev. Mr Aspland, who, as acting chairman of the Protestant Ministers of the Three Denominations, read an Address presented to William IV

---

[1] *Sketch*, p. 85. Italics not in original. [2] Above, p. 64.
[3] *Hackney Gravel Pit*, by G. C. Smith (1830), quoted from a copy in Dr Williams's Library (Tracts 12:66:18).

on his accession, by the General Body.[1] The author of the tract disclaims personal knowledge of Mr Aspland:

I merely knew that there was such a man, and that he was a leading man among the Socinians, and that he had once been at Bristol Baptist Academy. . . . Had he been connected with the New Police, I should certainly have known him, or had he preached in a street at Wapping, or on the deck of a collier . . . but situated as he is at the top of all that is learned, elegant, and wealthy in Hackney; and placed as I am among all that is filthy vulgar miserable and poor in Wapping, it was not likely that we should have much acquaintance.

He goes on to quote the remark of *The Record* (an Evangelical newspaper) on an Address to the Throne being presented 'by the Blasphemers of Our Lord Jesus Christ'.

It is in the light of such utterances that we must read Lord Sidmouth's speeches.

Far be it from him [he said] to object to the low situation in life of the persons applying for licences. Upon that ground he never had the slightest intention of urging any objection; his object being that there should be a security, as far as it could be applied, for their moral fitness for the exercise of the important duties of religious instruction. He had had communications upon the subject from several magistrates, complaining of the situation in which they were placed with respect to the construction of the law; and he had understood, from the communications he had had with several respectable Dissenters, that they were desirous that some such measure as this should be adopted, or at least that they approved of it.[2]

Nevertheless it would be merely malicious to suggest that the Socinian Dissenters separated themselves from the rest at this crisis in order to curry favour and to win toleration for themselves. The part taken by the Deputies at a time when Socinian and Unitarian influence was most prominent among them is proof enough to the contrary; but if some unorthodox ministers lacked enthusiasm in securing their own privileges for preachers whose illiteracy they despised and whose doctrine they detested there is no need for surprise.

In 1807 the Bury Quarter Sessions refused to allow a minister to take the oath unless the leading men of his congregation certified

---

[1] See pp. 70 and 460.   [2] *Sketch*, p. 107.

that he was their minister.[1] The Deputies were advised that the Bury magistrates could be compelled by *mandamus*, but thought it worth while to put the opinion before the Attorney-General. In the next year the Norwich Quarter Sessions refused to allow an applicant to qualify because he was not settled with a congregation. The uncertainty of the whole problem led the Deputies to express the opinion that it would not be discreet to agitate the question in a court of justice at the present time.[2] Eighteen months later they gave the same advice to enquirers at Axminster and Cardiff.[3] The Axminster enquiry raised the point of the registration of divinity students before their ordination to a settled congregation.

The question of exemption from militia duty and parish offices was clearly prominent. Persons inadequately qualified might seek to evade public duties, and persons adequately qualified might be unjustly accused of so doing. As early as 1799 the Bristol justices had tried to refuse to allow students of the Bristol Academy to qualify as Dissenting teachers.[4] The Committee found that the ambiguity of the relevant Acts gave some ground for the justices' refusal. The young men would therefore be liable to serve in the militia or to find substitutes.[5] The Lord Chancellor had been in correspondence with a clergyman who was chairman of the Quarter Sessions; and he was thought to be about to introduce a Bill to prevent future difficulties. Mr William Smith was asked to watch the matter for the Deputies.[6]

A month later the Committee had their eye on a Bill respecting the qualification of Dissenting teachers, to be introduced by Mr Michael Angelo Taylor.[7] They assured a correspondent who wished Dissenters and Methodists to take common action that they were not inattentive to the matter, but were postponing a decision until the nature of the Bill was known.[8]

When in 1802 Quarter Sessions refused to allow Mr William Burn of Kirk Ella, Yorkshire, to qualify on the ground that he was a farmer, the Deputies held that this was not a disqualification. They were prepared to get a *mandamus* to force the justices, but

---

[1] 26 June and 28 Aug. 1807.   [2] 29 July 1808.   [3] 26 Jan. 1810.
[4] 29 Nov. 1799.   [5] 27 Dec. 1799.   [6] 31 Jan. 1800.
[7] 28 Feb. 1800.   [8] 25 April 1800.

they shewed some interest in the question 'whether he means to qualify with any view to the being exempted from serving parish or other offices' and did not propose to act unless the answer to that question were satisfactory.[1]

The difficulty was not a new one. An amusing case in which the Deputies burnt their fingers badly occurred in 1778, and no doubt accounts in part for the cautious attitude which we have observed them to take. It was not uncommon to annoy Dissenting ministers by trying to deny their ministerial status and make them Overseers of the Poor. The Deputies had just successfully defended a minister against this claim when a similar appeal reached them for a Mr Hatch of Crediton. For once the Deputies appear to have been hasty; and only after an appeal had been filed did they learn that Mr Hatch was an illiterate layman, who had no registered meeting-house and no regular congregation. Though it came late, they received as usual full information. One correspondent

cannot find that any beside his own family attend his preaching on Lord's day mornings or afternoons, but that in the evenings a great rabble assemble for ridicule and riot.

Mr Hatch is said to have preached at a country place some seventeen miles distant, but the Deputies' correspondent 'does not apprehend he is paid anything for preaching'. Only a Mrs Tanner and his family approve of Mr Hatch's conduct;

All serious persons who have any concern for the Dissenting interest lament the Society's undertaking to defend him in his refusal to do parochial offices.

The Committee interviewed the writer of this letter, and decided to compromise. They had to pay the costs of the prosecution amounting to £39 17s. 11d.[2]

The fullness with which the Deputies record this example of their discomfiture provides the best possible assurance that their Minutes do not suppress incidents unfavourable to Dissenting interests. Mr Hatch's case is remarkable because it has few if any parallels. The rareness of attempts to abuse the position of a Dissenting minister and the Deputies' attitude to such attempts justify

---

[1] 2 April and 28 May 1802.   [2] 27 Mar. and 24 April 1778.

their claim that Lord Sidmouth's Bill was unnecessary, that it was designed to provide against evils which did not exist.

At an interview with Lord Sidmouth, in May 1810, a sub-committee of the Deputies put their point of view as follows:

The Sub-committee represented to his lordship, that any new restrictions upon persons who wished to qualify as Dissenting teachers would be very objectionable to the Dissenters at large, and therefore ought not to be imposed without adequate cause; that no evidence had been, or, as they conceived, could be produced, to shew a necessity for new restrictions: that though unworthy individuals might be found among those who had qualified, their moral character was, in most cases, an ornament to their profession, and would not suffer from a comparison with any description of ministers whatsoever: that a minister whose conduct was found to be immoral was almost invariably dismissed from his situation, and seldom could get appointed to any other, or even obtain permission to preach; so that no interposition of the legislature was necessary even in the rare case of immorality: that, as to other qualifications, most ministers of congregations had received a competent education, and that some were men of the most eminent talents and attainments: that although it might be true that some, who qualified, were ill-informed, or, as had been alledged, perhaps even incapable of writing, they were still competent to give some instruction to their neighbours who could not read, and who were in other respects still more ignorant than themselves: and that, in short, the degree of learning which Dissenting teachers possessed was not an object that deserved the attention of the legislature: that to require a testimonial, would sometimes prove very inconvenient and vexatious: that where it did not degenerate into an empty form, it would confer upon ministers, if *they* were to grant it, a new and obnoxious authority; or, if to be granted by a man's neighbours, would lay him at their mercy: that it might often be difficult for a man, before he could safely exercise his talents, to obtain a respectable testimonial that he possessed talents: that in case a man's views of religion should happen to be different from those of all existing sects, it would either bind him to silence, or expose him, if he preached, as he probably would, to all the severities of the penal laws: that it could scarcely fail of investing the Quarter Sessions with some discretionary authority, in judging of the sufficiency of the testimonial, and this would be to subvert the very basis of toleration: that any such regulation would be directly at variance with a leading

principle among the Dissenters, who held that every man had a right
to propagate what he himself believed to be truth, without craving
permission from others, and without being liable to any penalties,
unless he infringed upon the peace and good order of society: that, as
to limiting the age of preachers, so few persons, if any, were found to
qualify at an unsuitable age, that no legal provision was requisite, and
that some particular individuals might probably be capable of preaching
in certain situations, at an earlier age than it might be thought proper to
fix as a general standard.[1]

The phrase about conferring 'a new and obnoxious authority'
on the ministers in this passage may have a sidelong reference to
the Wesleyan Conference; but the Deputies nevertheless defended
the Methodists vigorously against Sidmouth's expressed desire to
impose some restriction on itinerant preaching.

On this point, the Sub-committee assured his lordship, the Dissenters
would feel particularly jealous: that though their own regular ministers
were in general stationary, most of them occasionally preached in
neighbouring villages, or distant parts of the country: that it would be
a serious grievance to the Wesleyan Methodists, whose ministers were
mostly itinerant, and would be strenuously opposed, upon principle,
by all the Dissenters, though not so liable to be affected by it themselves: that it would only have the effect of harrassing and irritating
itinerants, for they would not be prevented preaching when they
considered it their duty, except by being thrown into prison: that in
fact itinerant preachers were often the most useful ones; and that whatever their faults or defects might be, their labours were upon the whole
highly beneficial, in civilizing the lower ranks and rendering them
sober, industrious, and religious.[2]

Last came the question of evading parish offices and military
service. The Deputies' answer on this point is illuminated by an
anecdote related by the Lord Chancellor when the Bill came to
be debated in the House of Lords:[3]

A curious circumstance happened with regard to himself: when he
was drawn for the militia he was ashamed to avail himself of his degree
of Master of Arts, but he was gravely pressed to qualify himself, by the
payment of 6d., as a Dissenting teacher.

---

[1] *Sketch*, pp. 86-8.　　　[2] *Sketch*, p. 89.　　　[3] *Sketch*, p. 111.

A footnote to the *Sketch* exclaims against this:

It is not a little remarkable, that the first Law Officer of the state should be represented as relating an anecdote, which seems to imply the palpably erroneous opinion, that in order to obtain exemption from the militia it is *not* necessary to be *the minister of a congregation*.

The anecdote does, it is true, point to evasions of the law having occurred, but, as the Deputies told Lord Sidmouth, the legal position was clear enough:

none but ministers of congregations were intitled to these exemptions by the law as it now stood (1st W. and M. c. 18. s.11); that to suppose any person could gain exemption by merely qualifying as a preacher, without being *bona fide* the minister of a congregation, was an evident mistake, and consequently that no alteration in the law was necessary to preserve it from abuse: that in fact not a single instance had been made out, in which it had been so abused: that to take away the exemption from ministers of congregations who were engaged in trade, without which their scanty income would not suffice to keep their families from want, would be a most grievous hardship, and operate as a direct punishment for being poor and industrious: and that the number of persons who claimed exemptions under the act, appeared by the returns to be too inconsiderable, to produce any material inconvenience, or require the interference of Parliament.

But the representations of the Deputies' sub-committee 'did not induce him to abandon the whole of his designs', although from the subsequent measures of the noble viscount they flattered themselves that they had had 'a considerable effect on his mind'. On 9 May 1811 he rose to propose his Bill. His speech described (quoting the records of two Archdeaconries) the kind of persons who now obtained 'licences':

it appeared these persons consisted of tailors, pig-drovers, chimney-sweepers, &c. He did not object to their situation of life, if they were considered by Dissenters as fit and proper persons to preach and teach: but what he objected to was the self-election by which they chose to consider themselves as fit and proper persons for that purpose ... when it was considered that persons obtaining licences were exempt from serving upon juries, from serving parish offices, and other duties to which their fellow-subjects were liable, it was surely requisite that some caution and circumspection should be used.

But the sting of Lord Sidmouth's speech was in the tail, in a passage which might strictly be described as irrelevant, but which rather diminishes the effect of his disinterestedness:

It was highly important that some means should be taken to prevent us from having a nominal established church, and a sectarian people.

New churches were required; for want of them

many persons were driven to Dissenting meeting-houses, as the only places where they could receive religious instruction. . . . Grants should be made out of the public purse in aid of the exertions of individuals; and every measure adopted to support the established church, which was a part of the constitution, and upon which so greatly depended the sound morality of the country.

Lord Holland and Earl Stanhope spoke against the Bill, though Lord Holland said 'he would not act so irregularly as to oppose the first reading'. In an impressive phrase, regretting 'that his noble friend should have interfered with the subject at all', Holland also deplored

that the noble viscount had spoken invidiously of persons in inferior situations of life becoming preachers; for surely they were as much entitled to preach their own religious principles, as those who enjoyed the rich endowments of the church.

Nevertheless the Bill was read a first time, and the second reading fixed for 17 May. This gave the Deputies only a week to organize the opposition, but they proceeded with their accustomed vigour. A Committee meeting on the 13th summoned a General Meeting for the 15th; 2,000 copies of the Bill were printed and circulated by the Secretary; a joint meeting with the ministers was arranged; Lords favourable to religious liberty were interviewed; resolutions passed by the General Meeting, and a petition prepared, and copies of both printed for circulation; so that when a postponement of the second reading gave them a few extra days grace (until the 21 May) over 700 petitions were ready to be presented. This 'agitation and alarm' impressed the Government, and Liverpool called on Sidmouth to withdraw the Bill, but he refused. In moving the second reading, he protested that the Bill had been misinterpreted, misconceived, and misrepresented. He repeated his arguments in its favour, and gave examples of preachers who could neither read nor write, and 'instances of great depravity'. He proposed 'a certificate of six householders, of the sobriety of life and conversation of the person applying for a license' for itinerant preachers; and six members of the congregation to certify ministers of separate congregations. For probationers, the licence would be for a limited period, and three ministers might be substituted for the six householders. He thought this was so 'moderate a measure, that he had no idea it could be resisted'.

In the debate, only the Lord Chancellor and the Earl of Buckinghamshire gave a qualified support to the Bill, and it was lost without a division. The Deputies, in a General Meeting on May 28th, passed a comprehensive resolution of thanks, and drew up an address for circulation among the Dissenters of England and Wales, which concluded as follows:

On the prompt and unanimous feeling, so favourable to the maintenance and advancement of our common interests and liberties, which this attempt has excited, and on the success of our resistance, we most cordially congratulate our brethren: and we think we discover equal cause of satisfaction in those unequivocal declarations against every species and degree of persecution, against every intolerant principle, which in the course of this discussion, short as it as been, have been drawn from persons of the highest rank, the brightest talents, and the most efficient public stations in the country.

From symptoms so favourable, arising, in our opinion, not from any accidental circumstance, but from the gradual and silent increase of just and liberal sentiments, we cannot but augur the happiest results. We trust that the present laws will continue to be administered with that liberality which we have so generally and so long experienced. We cannot but anticipate the speedy approach of that fortunate period, when the legislature shall expunge from the Statute Book, which they now disgrace—all penalties, restrictions, and disabilities on account of Religion: and we earnestly hope that nothing will occur to defeat these expectations, or by exciting a hostile spirit even to postpone a consummation on every account so devoutly to be wished. (*Sketch*, p. 121).

The end of this address charmingly blends, with its Shakespearean quotation, exhortation to persevere in the campaign for repeal, with the Deputies' old fear of intemperate action, and the 'hostile spirit' which it might excite.

The anxiety of the Deputies about the status of Dissenting ministers did not end with the abandonment of Sidmouth's proposals. Quarter Sessions were left to interpret the Toleration Acts as before; but they shewed some tendency to be less liberal than formerly in granting certificates. For example, two Swansea ministers had their appeal against the militia ballot refused, as they were not ministers of any separate congregation; and the Deputies, consonant with the interpretation which they had stressed in their interview with Sidmouth, had to advise that the Deputy Lieutenant's decision was in accordance with the Act.[1] Such more severe interpretations, though technically more correct than the earlier liberality, became so general that Parliamentary interference appeared to be necessary to render former practice legal, and so maintain the extended toleration which had grown up. Early in 1812, William Smith, the Deputies' Chairman, appealed to Spencer Perceval, who shewed himself cautiously sympathetic. He thought it well to wait until a relevant decision by King's Bench had defined the problem, and he reserved judgment as to the manner in which relief from the new type of decision should be given. He understood that the Dissenters wished that penalties for preaching and the like acts should be removed from all who qualified under the Acts, but that exemption from civil and military duties should be granted only to those preachers who were ministers of congregations and made the ministry so completely their profession as to carry on no other business except that of a schoolmaster. The Committee thanked him, but disagreed; the Toleration Acts had been intended to include all *bona fide* ministers of congregations, not merely those whose secondary occupation (if they had one) was teaching; they hoped that Perceval would not feel it necessary to deprive a class of 'useful and honourable men' of the ministerial privilege; and affirmed their belief that the older liberal practice was 'perfectly conformable to the origin and spirit of the Toleration Laws'.[2]

The Committee authorized William Smith to introduce a Bill embodying their views, and began to consider with the Wesleyans the repeal of the Five Mile Act.[3] Perceval's death threw the nego-

---

[1] 11 Jan. 1811.　　　[2] 24 April 1812.　　　[3] 7 May 1812.

tiations into the hands of Lord Liverpool, who received the Deputies' representatives and the Wesleyans with the greatest attention, and heard a general statement of the Dissenters' grievances. The result was that the Five Mile Act and the Conventicle Act were repealed by the Act 52 Geo. III c. 155; the Methodists supplying the form of the Act. It legalized what had previously been the practice of the courts in most counties in granting certificates, and allowed no room for the extra demands which had been made in recent years; but it still restricted exemption from military and civic duties to those ministers without any other calling but that of schoolmaster.[1] Nevertheless the Deputies welcomed it as an 'important amelioration', although they declared that 'it is the natural right of men to worship God according to the dictates of their own consciences' and regretted the continued existence of penal laws.

This was the end of the 'novel and ingenious constructions' which had 'endangered the security long enjoyed under the Toleration Acts'.[2]

It was not, however, the end of problems about militia service. In the autumn of this same year students at Wrexham Academy were included in the ballot for the local militia. Were they not exempt by the recent Act? The Deputy Lieutenants were themselves not sure. They behaved with the greatest civility and recommended the students to take legal advice. The Deputies consulted three lawyers and got contradictory opinions. These they forwarded to Wrexham.[3]

On the eve of the negotiations which led to the passing of 52 Geo. III c. 155 the Deputies had occasion to exhibit their settled determination not to endanger a small gain within their reach for the same of a less practical, though ideally more satisfactory, programme. They declined to join in a general petition against all laws penalizing Dissent from the Established Church. Many Anglicans, Roman Catholics, and Dissenters had signed it,[4] but a General Meeting of the Deputies specially summoned to consider it took no action.[5] When 52 Geo. III c. 155 was safely on the

[1] 26 and 30 June, 31 July 1812.   [2] 11 Aug. 1812.
[3] 27 Nov. 1812.   [4] 28 Feb. 1812.   [5] 13 Mar. 1812.

Statute Book the Deputies, as we have observed, made clear that nothing short of religious equality would ultimately satisfy them, but an indiscreet agitation on far-reaching lines might well have wrecked negotiations with a Tory Government at a critical moment.

A year later the Deputies felt it not indiscreet to petition both Houses to break 'every remaining bond and abolish every shackle on the entire freedom of religious profession'. The terms of this petition, asserting men's 'inalienable right' to worship according to conscience, are more doctrinaire than most of the Deputies' pronouncements.[1] They were probably not unconnected with 'Mr William Smith's Act' of that year, which abolished penalties against Anti-Trinitarians.[2]

In the discussions with Spencer Perceval the liability of meeting-houses for poor rates had been mentioned. Perceval expressed his willingness to support proposals to put Dissenting chapels on the same footing as chapels belonging to the Establishment, if indeed they were not (as he believed) on the same footing already. The Committee said that it could wish nothing more than what was so 'handsomely proposed' by Perceval.[3]

---

[1] 23 Feb. and 26 Mar. 1813.   [2] *Sketch*, pp. 117-21.   [3] 24 April 1812.

CHAPTER 4

THE TEMPORALITIES OF DISSENT

(*Property, Trusts, and Legal Status*)

PROPERTY HAS always been for an Englishman a large part of his civil rights. 'Real property law has been the battle ground in most of the great struggles in our history.'[1] In their defence of the civil rights of Dissenters, the Deputies often found themselves concerned about the fabric and property of the Churches.

English law made it comparatively easy to endow meeting-houses, and Dissenters in the 18th century took full advantage of this; but the price was to be paid later in the tendency of the law and law-makers to regard Dissenting churches as so many private charities, neither more nor less. The minutes of the Deputies would suffice to prove the vast number of benefactions mainly by will, but partly by deed of gift. Many, probably most, of the benefactions were very small; many never reached the churches for which they were intended. The restrictions of the Mortmain Act of 1736 were often not noticed, and not a few bequests were therefore void, because they were made payable out of real estate or out of the rents of houses and lands. Difficulties about Mortmain would be avoided, as the Deputies pointed out in a paper of advice prepared in 1808, if legacies were charged wholly on personal estate.[2]

No small amount of property reverted on one plea or another, genuine or false, to secular uses. This will surprise no one who remembers the poverty and illiteracy of many rural Dissenters, and the many pitfalls of the laws affecting real property. The pious benefactor believed that he had made an effective gift, when he had only seemed to do so. Some estates were not large enough to

---

[1] T. F. T. Plucknett, *A Concise History of the Common Law*, 1936, p. 449.
[2] 24 June 1808: Draft of a form of Trust Deed for Meeting Houses.

pay the bequest. Relatives claimed to be too poor to forgo the income. Executors and heirs were unsympathetic or fraudulent. They diverted the property or refused to pay the charges on it. An immense amount of litigation resulted, but much property was stolen, or was allowed to slide,[1] because it was too inconsiderable to be worth fighting about. On the other hand many bequests were large and even princely; these did not always escape the attention of untrustworthy executors and trustees. Two legacies of £1200 each to two Norwich congregations were held for years on every imaginable and unimaginable plea by the executor.[2] Where it appeared worth while to pursue the defaulter the Deputies did so unrelentingly year after year, and were usually rewarded by success—but not always.

Not only property but even meeting-houses were filched. Not a few stood on privately owned land; still more stood on leasehold sites. The day came when a hostile or indifferent landlord excluded the congregation and demolished the meeting-house or adapted it as a dwelling-house. The *Sketch* describes a typical case:

On the 19th of January, 1776, a case of great oppression was brought before the Committee. At Hackleton, in Northamptonshire, there was a meeting-house, at which about two hundred persons, chiefly poor people and labourers, usually attended; who, on account of their poverty, had been obliged to mortgage the house for £40. The money had been called in on the preceding Christmas, and as they were unable to raise the sum, the lady of the manor, an enemy to the Dissenters, endeavoured to get the mortgage into her own hands, with a view to converting the place of worship to some other purpose. The same lady has already turned several poor families out of their dwellings for attending the meeting: had beat down a wall belonging to the meeting-house premises, grubbed up a hedge, and made a carriage road, where it could be proved there had been no road for eighty years. The Committee immediately directed their secretary to acquaint the lady that if she did not repair the damage done to the ground, and make satisfaction to the parties, an action would be commenced. It is probable that by this time she was aware of the impropriety of her

[1] E.g. 25 Oct. 1806.
[2] 1 Oct. 1774—28 August 1807; a favourable end of one case is in sight, the money is to be invested in accordance with terms of will.

conduct, and compromised the matter; as by the advice of the minister of that place, nothing further was done by the Committee.[1]

The Deputies examined dozens of such cases; sometimes the aggressor was within his legal right, sometimes he was not. Often a friendly appeal secured a settlement that could not have been enforced at law. The most frequent cause of trouble arose from conditions of trusteeship. Here is a typical example. At Ringwood (Glos.) in 1806 the friendly co-operation of the minister and the Deputies probably saved the meeting-house from lapsing to secular uses. The legal position was most unsatisfactory. There were no trustees—they had indeed all died before the minister was appointed fifty years before. It was urgent to save the property before the minister died. As the congregation was poor, the Deputies had new deeds drawn up and bore most of the expense.[2]

The Deputies did not content themselves by intervening as effectively as possible when trouble was reported to them. They knew that prevention was better than cure, and that, too often, cure was out of the question. They tried therefore, by disseminating accurate information and advice, to secure that donors made their gifts effective, and that trust deeds of meeting-houses, schools, and academies were properly drawn. In 1806 they agreed to print 2000 copies of a model trust deed for distribution.[3] In commending its use, they urged that care should be taken not only about the *form:* negligence in filling vacancies among the trustees caused much inconvenience and, as the Deputies saw only too often, resulted in the loss of no little property. Ministers ought not to be trustees: their appointment often proved unpleasant both for the minister and for the people. Nor ought surviving trustees to be able to fill vacancies: if they simply co-opted new members the body of trustees might lose all touch with the congregation.[4] If left to themselves, trustees could not even be relied on to appoint new trustees at all. When enquiries arose about the propriety of use to which property was being put, they often declined to produce deeds for the inspection of local people. Sometimes they acted in this way in collusion with a minister whom they supported

---

[1] *Sketch*, p. 43.   [2] 30 Oct. 1806.
[3] 28 Nov. 1806.   [4] 9 Dec. 1808.

against the whole or a part of the congregation. Sometimes they did so, withholding income, in order to exclude a minister of whom they disapproved. Sometimes their object was to appropriate the property of the income for themselves. On very many occasions the Deputies forced trustees to produce deeds, urged arbitration, or supported legal action if the deeds proved to be clear. A very great part of their energies in the 18th and early 19th century was devoted to the admonition, correction, and prosecution of trustees.

Very often controversies with trustees were simple attempts to prevent an individual from enriching himself at the expense of the church; but very often these controversies had another meaning, as we have seen in our discussion on Presbyterianism. The trustees might be Socinian, the congregation orthodox; the parts might be reversed; there might be a Socinian and an orthodox party in each body; a minister might, and as the century wore on often did, change his views. Who had the power to dismiss him? The Deputies declined to arbitrate between two parties when a church was divided on doctrinal lines;[1] indeed, they could not have done so, for they were themselves divided in this way.

We may ask why, if trustees were so troublesome, the Deputies did not support a measure of State regulation or control. They were resolved to maintain the status of Dissenting churches as independent communities with rights specifically guaranteed under the Act of Toleration. It is significant that the second case which ever came before the Committee concerned the proceeding of the Commissioners of Charitable Uses;[2] while at the end of the period covered by the *Sketch*, in 1809, a Bill to register and secure charitable donations for the benefit of poor persons attracted their wary attention. It was agreed that, if Mr William Smith thought it necessary, a petition for the exemption of the funds of Protestant Dissenters should be prepared.[3]

Many reasons combined to keep alive this dislike of State supervision; some were no doubt more powerful at one time than at another. Traditional hostility to State control and fear of extra

---

[1] E.g. Saffron Walden, 30 July 1824; Maryport, 13 Aug. 1824. See also *Sketch*, p. 40.
[2] 8 July 1735.   [3] 26 May 1809.

expense were constantly felt. The connexion of Church and State made the Deputies fear, with only too much reason, that State control meant control by the Established Church. A characteristic expression of the attitude appears in a petition to the House of Commons about a Charitable Trusts Bill in 1845. They 'remind' the Commons that

the independence of their Churches of all state patronage and control is a fundamental principle of their constitution and has been uniformly recognized by the law since the passing of the Act of Toleration.[1]

We shall find many examples of their rooted determination to prevent Dissenting property from passing under the control of an authority which might easily be totally ignorant of their needs and unsympathetic to their objects.

As we have seen, the registration of meeting-houses had been important ever since the passing of the Toleration Act. In the 18th century it secured the protection which the law afforded to public worship; but when the danger of disturbance had passed it again became important for different reasons. For instance, the validity of marriages celebrated under the new laws in Dissenting chapels depended on registration; so did exemption from the control of the Charity Commission.

The old machinery of registration, as we have seen, was through the bishop, the archdeacon, or Quarter Sessions. At the request of the bishops, the Government in revising the marriage law in 1852 transferred (or intended to transfer) the registration to the Registrar-General. By a technical error, however, this object was not attained; and when in the next year the Government introduced an amending Bill, the Deputies (in their own phrase) 'corrected' it.[2] The extent of their influence—as in all matters connected with the beginning of the modern registration system—was very great; the form of the Bill was practically settled by Mr Mann of the Registrar-General's Office and the Deputies' Secretary.[3] The amendments accepted by the Registrar lessened the trouble and expense of registration and protected worship more effectively.

But the Deputies' attitude to State intervention was not merely negative. They agitated to improve the legal position of religious

[1] 5 July 1845.   [2] Report for 1853.   [3] 8 April 1853.

148

trusts and make it easier for them to acquire property and cheaper
for them to deal with it. In the thirties they shared in the general
desire for legal reform. In 1839 they expressed the opinion that it
was highly desirable to adopt a simple, uniform, and cheap system
for perpetuating the trusts of chapels and charitable institutions.[1]
The rapid increase in the number of small chapels for poor congregations made the matter urgent. By February 1840 a scheme
had been worked out; it is noticeable that in it the Deputies
dropped their old opposition to the co-option of trustees. Property
was to be vested in (say) seven persons who would be a body
corporate. They would co-opt new members as death caused
vacancies, and the recurrent cost of new trust deeds would be
avoided. The scheme was recommended to all Dissenting bodies
for consideration but met with more distrust than co-operation.[2]
The Deputies did not give up hope of a scheme being worked out.
The Congregationalists wanted a plan to benefit all charities,[3] and
it was on this line that a solution came in the end; but the Deputies
had to fight hard to prevent Dissenting churches from being
absorbed in the general mass, and in the outcome were not wholly
satisfied.

In 1841 the Committee worked over the problem again. The
Commons passed, but the Lords rejected, a Bill which would at
least have lessened the costs of appointing trustees, by permitting
old trust deeds simply to be endorsed, not replaced, when new
trustees were appointed.[4]

In the same year the Deputies tried to persuade Lord Lansdowne
to enlarge the scope of a Bill to govern the acquisition of land for
schools, so that it would improve the facilities for acquiring land
for religious purposes generally. But Lord Lansdowne thought
this would prejudice the chances of the Bill (which as it stood
was very urgently needed); and, in the event, the Bill failed on a
technical point.[5]

The next decade saw a spate of legislation dealing with charities,
which ended in the statute of 1853, the definitive Act establishing
the Charity Commission. It is instructive to watch how clumsy,

---

[1] 28 June 1839.   [2] 12 Feb. 1840.   [3] Report for 1840.
[4] Report for 1841; 21 April 1841.   [5] 21 May 1841.

and often abortive, were the efforts of Government and Parliament to find a satisfactory basis for control.

It was in 1844 that the Lord Chancellor introduced a Bill to deal generally with charitable trusts. It proposed the appointment of stipendiary commissioners to control administration. It was characteristic of Peel's Government that whilst 'funds applicable to the benefit of Roman Catholics, Quakers, and persons of the Jewish persuasion which were under the superintendence and control of persons of such persuasions' were to be exempt, no such freedom was to be allowed to Protestant Dissenters. The Deputies saw no reason why their charities should not also be spared Government interference and the cost entailed. They applied to the Lord Chancellor. The Bill was withdrawn, to be re-introduced in 1845.[1]

When the Bill appeared in 1845 the Deputies, raw from their trouncing in the struggle over the Dissenters' Chapels Act,[2] set about the Government with boundless enthusiasm. They knew the small regard that Peel's Cabinet might be expected to pay to the wishes and traditions of Dissenters, and (as they remarked with some grimness) the Bill had been under the eye of the Committee since its re-introduction. In a letter to *The Times*, revised by the legal sub-committee, they analysed their objections to the Bill. They found it 'ill-contrived, arbitrary, and unconstitutional', containing 'provisions of a most unprecedented and dangerous character', which would create evils of a more extensive and fatal kind than those which it proposed to remedy. Its object, they admitted, was wholly unexceptionable. It was desirable that charitable trusts should be administered without the expense of proceedings in the courts of equity. The Deputies' many criticisms may be reduced to two. In the first place the Bill invented a new form of injustice to Dissenters. It made no provision for their representation. It thus departed from the principle of the Charitable Bequests Act, which specified representation of Roman Catholics and Protestant Dissenters. It nevertheless put Dissenting chapels and schools under the arbitrary and irresponsible control of the commissioners. It underlined this injustice to Dissenters by exempting some charities such as universities and public schools. In the second place the

---

[1] Report for 1844. [2] See Part I, Chapter 5.

charge of 'arbitrary and irresponsible control' was developed and proved. Trustees might be summoned and examined on oath, but there was no provision that this should be made in public; such secret proceedings were 'a principle wholly foreign to the practice of our courts of judicature since the abolition of the Court of Star Chamber'. There was no provision for examination of witnesses by the defence. Equally objectionable was the power of summary decision from which there was no appeal when large sums of money and the honour of individuals were at stake.

But the Deputies reserved their strongest language for the commissioners' power to make any order respecting the objects of the charities as should seem fit to them. This power was merely 'unconstitutional and intolerable'. It was greater than that of the Lord Chancellor himself; he, at least, regarded the doctrine *cy pres*.[1] There no doubt was the sting. The Government, having in the previous year defied the doctrine of *cy pres* in the Dissenters' Chapels' Act,[2] was now about to remove that same protection against injustice from yet another part of the Dissenters' lives. It would be better (argued the letter to *The Times*) if the present proceedings were cheapened and expedited by giving one of the Chancery judges exclusive jurisdiction in these cases. The Dissenters would oppose to the last this 'glaring outrage' on religious liberty, this 'attack on the independence of our Churches from all state patronage and control'.[3]

A brief petition to the Lords denounced the proposals of the Bill as 'secret and irresponsible'.[4] But the Lords passed it; and so a petition to the Commons (based on *The Times* letter) was prepared, and an interview sought with Peel and Graham. Peel declined when the Bill was withdrawn for the session; Graham agreed, but his letter missed the Deputies' representative and the appointment was not kept (the Deputies had the unusual pleasure of thanking him for his courtesy). The petition requested that Dissenters' chapels and schools should be excluded from a general scheme; that the procedure for trying trustees should be public

---

[1] I.e. the doctrine that if the trust cannot be applied in the manner specified by the donor, it shall be carried into effect in a manner 'as near as possible' (*cy pres*).
[2] The story is told in Chapter 5 of Part I, esp. pp. 87 ff.
[3] 30 May 1845.   [4] 4 June 1845.

and proper; that the commissioners should be bound by the wishes of the founders of charities and the doctrine of *cy pres*; and that there should be an appeal from their decisions. The petition emphatically asserted its approval of the object of the Bill, if it were fairly within the scope of legislative interference and if the independence of Dissenting churches (uniformly recognized by law since the Toleration Act) were respected.

Next session a new Bill open to the same objections was introduced, and again it was defeated; the Committee recording with some complacency that it 'participated in the general satisfaction'.[1]

Meanwhile the Unitarians had prepared a Bill, sponsored by Joseph Hume and Dr Bowring, embodying their suggestions; this the Deputies found 'as crude and inefficient . . . as the previous bill was arbitrary and oppressive'.[2] The annual publication of accounts from all chapels and perhaps 40,000 charities would be very expensive, produce no equivalent safeguards, and involve offensive and prejudicial Government intervention. The Bill was dropped.

The Charitable Trusts Bill, eventually passed in 1853, made its first appearance in 1849, and was reintroduced in 1850 and 1852 before it finally became law as the definitive Act establishing the Charity Commission. During this time there was much discussion between the Deputies and other Nonconformist bodies, as well as between the Deputies and the Government; part of it turning on the Deputies' wish to exclude manses and schools as well as chapels —a point on which the Wesleyans were less severe.[3] In 1852 the Deputies prepared a special clause to ensure that pew rents would not bring chapels under the Bill; and as the Government refused to the last to propose the exemption of chapels, the Deputies had to get Apsley Pellatt, M.P., to secure the addition of the decisive clause in the session of 1853.[4] The Deputies were interested also in getting exemption for the Colleges of London University.[5] They were able to congratulate themselves on having at last reaped the reward for untiring opposition to bad Bills. But the matured scheme did not remove all their difficulties.

---

[1] 17 July 1846.   [2] Report for 1846.   [3] 20 and 27 May 1850.
[4] 26 May, 27 June, 5 Aug. 1853.   [5] Report for 1853.

They had still two main wishes. In the first place, they wanted a cheap and effective way of perpetuating their trusts; they did not wish to go through the whole costly process of appointing new trustees whenever recruits were needed. In the second place, they did not wish to purchase this convenience by subjecting their church trusts, like private charities, to the Charity Commission; in effect, they wanted these trusts to be regarded as incorporated. The Act of 1853, though it exempted buildings for religious worship, did not exempt other buildings and lands held on similar trusts; it was not until 1894 that exemption was secured for these, with the provision that they may avail themselves, if they desire, of the Commissioners' supervision.[1]

Between 1850 and 1894 the Deputies found themselves in the quagmire of Property Law, and the guiding lights they saw before them proved will-o'-the-wisps. Several statutes were passed which seemed to secure improvements, but judicial and administrative rulings deprived them of their force. The first of these had been passed in 1850 at the height of the controversy. The Titles of Religious Congregations Act (known as Peto's Act)[2] had provided that if property was held for any religious or educational purpose, and if no mode of appointing trustees was prescribed, or if the prescribing power had lapsed, then the congregation or corresponding body could appoint trustees who would hold the property with the existing trustees. It was believed at first that this Act would cover almost all new appointments of trustees; but in fact it did not touch trustees who were absent or unwilling to act. In 1853 a decision of Vice-Chancellor Kindersley declared that it only applied where power to appoint new trustees had lapsed.[3]

In 1857, at the instance of the Congregational Union, the Deputies prepared a Bill to remedy the defects of Peto's Act, but it was thrown out at the second reading.[4] Next year, with immense pains, they prepared a wider Bill to incorporate trustees of charities, and persisted with it from 1858 to 1861, when it was decisively rejected. This Bill would have allowed trusteeships of chapels,

---

[1] Charitable Trusts Act, 1869 (exempt may come under scheme). Charitable Trusts (Plan of Religious Worship) Amendment Act 1894.
[2] The Deputies had some part in preparing it.
[3] 4 Nov. and 20 Dec. 1853.   [4] 6 Feb., 5 May, 29 July 1857.

schools, and public charities to be filled by election. No stamped deed would be needed, but a certificate issued by a County Court Judge, and registration by the court would make the property pass to new trustees jointly with the old.

It was ten years after the failure of their own Bill that the Deputies got some satisfaction from the passing of the Charitable Trustees Incorporation Act of 1872, after other Bills adversely affecting their position had been introduced in 1862 and 1869. But again their satisfaction was short-lived. The Act of 1872 provided that the Charity Commissioners might, on the application of any body of trustees, grant them certificates of incorporation. It was intended, and expected, that after it was passed all trustees of Dissenting places of worship who applied to the Commissioners would receive certificates. But, to the surprise of the Deputies, the Commissioners, relying on the permissive character of the legislation, declined on principle to issue certificates, stating as their reason that they objected to the multiplication of corporate bodies, their experience showing that individual responsibility was thereby diminished. The Act remained practically a dead-letter.

The Deputies' point of view might not be, and indeed was not, generally shared; but there was enough trouble over the working of the Charitable Trusts Act to warrant the appointment of a Select Committee in 1884. The Deputies saw that their views were put before it. The Commissioners were obstinately set on compelling charities to vest their property in the Official Trustee; the Deputies urged that a certificate under the Act of 1872 would suffice.[1]

To secure reform, the Deputies pursued tactics which they had found valuable on other occasions; they prepared a Bill of their own as a lever.[2] They had indeed some difficulty in getting an introducer who agreed with the whole of their Charitable Trusts Amendment Bill;[3] but the Charity Commissioners were anxious that they should not press for their Bill, and agreed to grant certificates of incorporation to trustees of chapels, though they still refused to include endowments and other buildings as the Deputies had always wished. The Deputies decided to keep their

---

[1] 6 Feb. 1885.   [2] 30 Sept. 1886.   [3] 20 Jan. and 17 Feb. 1887; 2 Jan. 1890.

own Bill alive, and in the event were able to congratulate themselves; for Fowler's Act, the Incorporation of Trustees Act of 1890, extended Peto's Act to almost any religious purpose, and (with the needs of the Methodists particularly in mind) made it apply not only to the trustees of one congregation but to a society comprehending several congregations. The Trustee Act of 1893 was a consolidating Act covering all the purposes of the various measures which had been passed since 1850 and making appointment easier. But the Deputies were still not wholly satisfied.

In 1905 (perhaps as a result of the Scottish Churches case) they supported the principle that power should be given to Free Churchmen to revise their religious trusts under proper safeguards[1] and in 1908 had in view a clause to exempt charities from the possible operation of the Land Tax.[2]

After the First World War they made another attempt to improve the general position of trustees of charities; they wished in particular to enlarge their powers of selling properties. The opportunity afforded in the years immediately following the war made this suggestion most proper, and the experience of such bodies as the Colleges of Oxford and Cambridge indicated the advantages which charities might have reaped. The Congregationalists, Wesleyans, and Baptists expressed their general agreement with the Deputies' views but thought the time inopportune; in February 1919 the Deputies learnt that the Charity Commissioners were opposed to change; and the suggestion fell through.

We must now examine in more detail the working of the laws affecting charities, and particularly the Charity Commissioners, and see whether the Deputies' vigilance and mistrust were justified.

Despite the number of Protestant Dissenters in England, it was impossible for very many years for them to get any representation on the body which had immense power in regulating their charities. Their first failure was with Mr Gladstone. They asked him to appoint a Dissenter as a Commissioner to fill a vacancy. He replied by return of post with characteristic promptness and vagueness that 'he had wished to take into consideration the desirability of such an appointment, but it did not appear that it would be

[1] 29 June 1905.   [2] 20 Mar. 1908.

necessary to make any new appointment'.[1] The Deputies could only express the hope that at the next appointment the claims of Dissent would be considered.

In 1874 the Deputies resolved that if the Endowed Schools Bill became law and additional Commissioners were appointed, they would press Disraeli to see that a Dissenter was included.[2] The extended powers of the Commission would make this piece of elementary justice even more necessary than before. It was naturally felt that only under pressure, if indeed then, would that professional renegade be likely to do even the minimum of justice to those Englishmen who did not share his convert-enthusiasm for Anglicanism. Their suspicion of Disraeli was of course justified. With unnecessary but characteristic ill-breeding he omitted even conventional thanks for the Deputies' letter, and ignored the suggestion.[3]

When one of the Commissioners, Sir J. Hill, died, the Deputies made an attempt to use the opportunity for getting a Dissenter nominated.[4]

They resolved to ask Disraeli to see a deputation and, if he refused, to write to him as they had written to Mr Gladstone on the subject in 1872. True to form, Disraeli refused to receive a deputation, did not acknowledge a second letter, and appointed an Anglican.[5] Even his repugnance to the Gladstone tradition could not make him just to Dissent. The attitude of the Charity Commission was one of the subjects discussed at a conference between the Liberation Society and the Deputies on 15 Feb. 1876.

In 1882 the ludicrous inadequacy of the Commission to deal with one side of its work came under discussion in two ways. First, the only Dissenter on the subordinate staff was leaving.[6] The Deputies pointed out to Mr Gladstone the inconvenience of having no official who understands the Dissenting point of view. Second, sixty Members of Parliament signed a memorial asking that a Dissenter should be appointed to fill an existing vacancy.[7] Mr Gladstone expressed sympathy, but showed none. In the event he answered both representations by announcing that Sir George Young, not a Dissenter, had been temporarily appointed as a

[1] 30 May 1872.   [2] 27 July 1874.   [3] 29 July 1874.   [4] 5 Nov. 1875.
[5] 9 Nov. 1875; 3 Dec. 1875.   [6] 18 July 1882.   [7] 21 Nov. 1882.

Commissioner, that the Commissioners appointed the assistant Commissioners, and that public competition determined the lower appointments. The Dissenters, therefore, got for the moment nothing, but shortly afterwards Mr Anstie, Q.C., was appointed a Commissioner, though technically not a full member, being allotted to a special part of the work, and retiring on its conclusion.

It is not surprising therefore that in Dec. 1892 the Deputies resolved in connexion with the Charitable Trusts Bill that they would support no extension of the Commissioners' powers as it was at present constituted.[1] The death of Mr Anstie in 1893 left the Dissenters once again unrepresented[2] and Mr Gladstone was pressed to appoint a Dissenter.[3] In the same year the Secretary of the Deputies prepared evidence for a Select Committee of the House of Commons.[4] The decisive question was whether the Charity Commissioners should be directly under Parliamentary control,[5] and the Committee recommended that the Commission should become a Government department. The Deputies, whose evidence on points of detail had not been required, welcomed the proposal, because it would mean public criticism and control.

The pettiness of the spirit against which the Deputies have contended for two hundred years could have no better illustration than this contemptuous flouting for a generation of a request for even one representative. How important in the interests of justice it was that the Dissenters should have some spokesman on the Commission appears when we consider examples of particular problems that came before it. These examples also illustrate the certainty that as between Anglicans and Dissenters the Commissioners could be confidently relied on to do injustice unless they were successfully challenged on each occasion.

In 1888 the Charity Commissioners appointed nine governors for Holloway College. Not one of them was a Dissenter, though the founder had expressly stated his wish that the College should be non-sectarian when he founded it only five years earlier. The Foundation Deed stated that governors should be supplied on the nomination of certain public bodies, but the founder did not nomi-

[1] 15 Dec. 1892. [2] 5 Oct. 1893. [3] 18 Jan. 1894.
[4] 23 April 1894. [5] 14 June 1894.

nate the first governors, and when appointed they were all of them Anglican. The Charity Commissioners appointed three holding official positions in the Church without consulting the bodies concerned. The Deputies had characteristically taken counsel's opinion before making a move, and were advised that the Commissioners' action was probably *ultra vires*.[1] They accordingly protested against the Commissioners' 'perversion of the Founder's wishes' (which they were of course specially appointed and paid to safeguard) and instructed their own Committee to see that his wishes were fulfilled.[2] The Deputies pressed the governors themselves to apply for an amended order; and for some years prickly negotiations went on. The Dean of Windsor was (not unnaturally) anxious to prevent any publicity in a matter so discreditable.[3] In 1891 the Annual Report tactfully 'touched on' the matter without details, and in 1892 came an offer to elect three honorary governors who should take the place of ordinary governors at the first opportunity.[4] Professor Bryce, M.P., the Rev. Dr W. F. Moulton, and Sir Henry Roscoe, M.P., were asked to serve. The Deputies, still properly dissatisfied, pointed out that the Congregationalists and Baptists even now had no representatives and that they expected this to be rectified at the first possible moment.[5] In the following year Mr Evan Spicer, who had had a prominent part in forcing the improved settlement, was made a governor.[6]

This was not all. In those years the Charity Commissioners left little undone which would shew how well founded was every Dissenting suspicion of them. The Rebecca Hussey Book Charity was founded in 1862 to distribute religious books to schools and libraries. The Deputies protested that the Charity Commissioners had appointed none but Anglicans to administer a non-sectarian trust.[7] After an argument, in which the Deputies pointed out that at least one of the original trustees was a Dissenter, and that at least one should still possess the confidence of Dissenters, the Deputies helpfully suggested that they were prepared to nominate a suitable person.[8] The Charity Commissioners ended by accepting the Deputies' offer.[9]

[1] 5 June 1888. [2] 13 June 1888. [3] 31 July and 10 Dec. 1890.
[4] 17 Mar. 1892. [5] 14 June 1892. [6] 5 Oct. 1893.
[7] 2 Jan. 1890. [8] 24 Jan. 1890. [9] 20 Mar. 1890.

There is little wonder that at times the Deputies' suspicions out-ran even the Charity Commissioners' partisanship. With Rebecca Hussey's Charity still fresh in mind, and Holloway College still in dispute in 1891, the Deputies had fears that the Charity Commissioners' scheme for a Stockport foundation named after Elizabeth Dobson was putting it wrongfully into Anglican control.[1] Enquiry shews that for once the suspected sectarian scheme was justified.[2]

But the most famous of these cases, though it was not settled until the 1890s, dated from a period antecedent to the Charity Commissioners, and had given trouble to the Deputies as long ago as 1771.

Lord Wharton, a zealous Puritan who had fought with Parliament against Charles I, and at the Restoration strenuously opposed the Penal Laws and sheltered many of the ejected ministers, had on 12 July 1692 conveyed property in trust (several eminent Nonconformists being named trustees), the income to be used in buying English Bibles and catechisms to be distributed yearly amongst poor children who could read, and also for the preaching of sermons. 'Instructions' dated 24 April 1693 specified that the catechism referred to was the Shorter Catechism framed by the Westminster Assembly.[3]

During the second half of the 18th century, the Trust came exclusively under Anglican control, and the Church Catechism was substituted for the Westminster Catechism; gradually gifts to Dissenting chapels were dropped, and Anglicans only profited. A piecemeal policy of change went on; and Dissenters whose suspicions were aroused were unable to get information about the provisions of the Trust. A very large sum of money was involved; in 1899 the fund consisted of over £50,000 Consols, and the annual income was about £1,300 a year.[4]

It was in 1771 that the difficulties came to the Deputies' ears. A Halifax minister complained that, although his predecessor had had Bibles and catechisms for distribution, he could not get them. The Deputies knew from the mention of the Westminster Catechism that Lord Wharton had had Dissenters in mind, and a suit

[1] 17 Mar. 1891.   [2] 20 April 1891.
[3] Report for 1897.   [4] Report for 1897 and 1899.

159

in Chancery was alleged to have been decided in favour of them.[1] When they made enquiries, the Deputies found that Dissenters were being cut out as changes of minister or other circumstances gave them opportunity: books were still being sent to Bradford though not to Halifax. The secretary of the Trust played a somewhat disingenuous game with a skilful, and possibly practised, hand. He asked for the number of books usually sent to Halifax, and held out hopes that the trustees would send books on receiving this information.[2] A year later, however, requests to the trustees had produced no books,[3] and the secretary was disclaiming knowledge of the Halifax minister or his list. He admitted that in the past Halifax had had books; but the trustees must approve the new minister, 'which seems unaccountable'. The Deputies asked the minister to send another list[4] and he did so.[5] Mr Lloyd promised to lay the list before the trustees at their next meeting, but 'could not exactly tell when that would be'. It does not appear whether the support of the Deputies prevented injustice being done on this occasion to the Halifax Dissenters. It is perfectly clear, however, that but for their intervention the trustees would have had an easy hand to play. This episode throws a little light on the management of the Trust during that dark period for which there are apparently no records and in which Anglican ascendancy was established.

Thirty years later the total exclusion of Dissenters from the benefit of a trust intended exclusively for them appears to have been happily completed. In 1804 the Deputies decided to seek information about the Bibles and the extent to which Dissenters were entitled to share them. Enquiries were made of the Rev. John Pye Smith, Tutor of Homerton,[6] and an attempt was made to get a copy of the Deed.[7] The Rev. Mr Wellbeloved of York provided much accurate information. The Trust was established, he reported, not by Lord Wharton's will, but by a deed of gift in his lifetime. Though Dissenters were not mentioned by name 'yet it is plain that the Gift was intended for them' for three reasons: (1) Only children who learnt the Assembly's catechism were to have Bibles; (2) the annual sermons provided for were to

[1] 8 Feb. 1771.   [2] 30 Nov. 1771.   [3] 21 Oct. 1772.   [4] 18 Nov. 1772.
[5] 27 Jan. 1773.   [6] 13 April 1804.   [7] 27 April 1804.

be preceded by *extempore* prayer; (3) Swaledale chapel had been endowed by Lord Wharton for Dissenters. Mr Wellbeloved had not seen the Deed but had learnt of it from Mr Wood of Leeds, who had seen a printed copy or abstract some years before.

The Committee ordered a search for more information to be made in Chancery and the Exchequer and in Dr Williams's Library.[1] Search in Dr Williams's Library produced nothing; and as the exact title of any relevant cause in Chancery or Exchequer was not known, it had been impossible to ascertain if any decree had been made.[2]

Mr Wellbeloved next reported that the Trust was in the Harley family and that the Bibles were taken away from the Dissenters when they succeeded to the Trust.[3] Through Mr Hugh Smith of Lincoln's Inn, who was concerned for Lord Oxford, the Deputies learnt at last who was secretary of the Trust.[4] The secretary, Mr Hugh Powell, gave them no satisfaction. When asked why the trustees had ceased to distribute Bibles and catechisms as they had formerly done amongst Dissenters' children, he replied that

The Trustees after distributing books agreeable to the Deed had full power to distribute the overplus books as they thought proper and that they had for sometime past and should in future send such overplus to the clergyman of the parish where they wished them to be distributed and that they should not send any to Dissenting ministers.[5]

This was not the idle threat of an ignorant and incompetent bully. It was the considered policy of a well informed and shameless man. Mr Powell was indeed a notable character. He well knew the terms of the Trust which he flouted. His use of the word 'overplus' reveals his familiarity with the actual wording of the 'Instructions'. He had cunning enough to mislead the public by printing and circulating such extracts from it as did not betray the flouting of Lord Wharton's wishes. He had shrewdness enough to suppress the clauses which would have given him away. To these agreeable qualities he added disingenuousness enough in his reply to the Deputies to refer to one clause about the overplus as

[1] 29 June 1804.   [2] 27 July 1804.
[3] 26 Oct. 1804. It was in 1781 that Rev. John Harley, Dean of Windsor, was appointed trustee; but trouble had started earlier, as we have seen.
[4] 2 and 30 Nov. 1804.   [5] 25 Oct. 1805 (Powell is here referred to as *Treasurer*).

if he made it his business in fact to carry out the 'Instructions'. The only thing that can be said in favour of Mr Powell is that he apparently did not charge for his misdeeds. For twenty years, 1801-21, he gratuitously assisted the trustees to pervert the Trust.

The Deputies' Minutes are of interest because they confirm the statement in the *Monthly Magazine* for June 1803[1] that, from about 1770, Anglican clergymen were used as distributors in place of the Dissenting ministers. Not one of the trustees appointed in 1782 by the sole surviving trustee, Lord Oxford, was a Dissenter; but this was not a sudden change. It had come gradually.

One question inevitably arises. Why did the Deputies who knew so many of the facts in 1804 leave the abuse undisturbed? Why was there no action in 1820, when the Charity Commissioners examined the affairs of the Charity, and the diversion from the Dissenters was commented on? The difficulty and expense of fighting a case in Chancery no doubt counted for much; but difficulty and expense did not deter the Deputies from other fights where far less was at stake. It is difficult not to believe that the influence of the Unitarians among the Deputies was not one of the forces at work. With the Test and Corporation Acts still unrepealed, what was wanted above all things was unity among the Dissenters. Among the Deputies at least Mr William Smith was happily able to secure it by avoiding controversial questions. The Lord Wharton Charity did not, it is true, raise questions between the orthodox and Unitarian Dissenters, but it did touch very definitely the question of the right administration of a Presbyterian's property. The Anglican Catechism did not indeed well represent the opinions of a 17th-century Presbyterian; but it was nearer to them than the Unitarian creed supported in most Presbyterian meeting-houses in 1804. Mr Wellbeloved himself was teaching Unitarian doctrine in an orthodox meeting-house well endowed by a pious benefactor whose opinions were very like Lord Wharton's. Mr Wellbeloved and his like were in no position to fight Mr Powell. It is difficult to believe that they were unaware of this. As long as the Deputation included Unitarians enjoying endowments on Trinitarian foundations it was not well

---

[1] *The Good Lord Wharton*, p. 87.

placed for enquiring too punctiliously into the intentions of 17th-century Presbyterians.

There the matter rested for almost a century. Early in the 1890s the Rev. Bryan Dale of Bradford began to investigate the history of the Trust, and soon enlisted the help of the Deputies. On 28 July 1892 they noted that all particulars were not yet ascertained. Five years later they were satisfied that the Charity had been intended for Dissenters. Evidently their previous interest in the case was unknown to the Committee of that time; but at last they were able to do what their predecessors had failed to do—that is, get sight of the original Deed and Instructions of Lord Wharton.

The Rev. Bryan Dale published a pamphlet setting out the circumstances; the Charity Commissioners were appealed to, and the Deputies urged them to act.[1] After an interview with the Chief Commissioner, the Deputies agreed to indemnify Dale (who was secretary of the Yorkshire Congregational Union) if he would allow his name to be used for legal intervention. In their Annual Report for 1898 the Deputies were able to announce that the High Court was framing a scheme for the future adminstration of the Charity, and that they had joined with the Congregational Union in making suggestions which had been invited for the assistance of the court. But the confident statement of the Report of 1898 'that before long a new and satisfactory scheme will be settled' had to be revised a year later. Though the Dissenters got a share of what should have been wholly theirs,[2] the doctrine of *beati possidentes* which gave orthodox endowments to Unitarians allowed the Anglicans to retain part of the Trust. After all, they had enjoyed the whole of it wrongfully for many years.

The Deputies complained that the Attorney-General's solicitors had not fulfilled a promise to inform the Deputies when the case was coming on so that they could be represented, and that the first they knew was the publication of a scheme which had been approved, dated 5 August 1898.[3] Briefly, the scheme left the Anglicans a majority of the trustees (five out of nine), and divided the income of the Fund in halves, one half to be distributed by the Anglicans, the other half by the Nonconformists. The Deputies

[1] Report for 1897, p. 14.   [2] Report for 1899.   [3] Report for 1899, p. 12.

very properly commented that this last provision was the most unsatisfactory of all, 'it being quite clear that whatever other views Lord Wharton held, there is no doubt that he did not wish any Denominational application of this trust-money'.[1]

The Deputies did not feel free to make any further application, however, though they announced their intention of doing so if the Fund were used 'in a sectarian spirit'. They were encouraged to think that the trustees would act harmoniously by the voluntary retirement of Col. Haygarth, one of six continuing Anglican trustees, so that the four Nonconformist trustees might be appointed immediately. The Congregationalists nominated Rev. Bryan Dale as their representative.[2]

Another 17th-century Charity, the New England Company, originally established in the time of the Long Parliament for the purpose of preaching the gospel among the Red Indians, also gave the Deputies trouble; long negotiations about it began in 1910. At the date of its foundation it was clearly Nonconformist; but in the reign of Charles II in 1662 a charter was obtained by which governors were appointed. There were to be 45 members, Churchmen and Dissenters, and they were to promote the spread of the gospel among the heathen tribes of Canada, and instruct them not only in 'the Protestant religion' but in English, the liberal arts and sciences, and 'some trade, craft, or lawful calling'. Their missionary activity had never been denominational, but the governors appointed had recently come to be almost entirely members of the Church of England. It was said that the Charity Commissioners themselves had suggested the appointment of Nonconformists. The Deputies first attempted direct negotiation with the Company. The governors declined to elect Dr Massie because he was president of the Liberation Society;[3] Mr Evan Spicer and Mr Early appeared acceptable but were unable to serve;[4] and the next nominee, Mr Hardy, was refused for no specified reason, but apparently because he was strongly in favour of Disestablishment.[5] The Deputies then appealed to the Charity Commissioners; but they, as the Deputies' experience would lead them to expect,

---

[1] Report for 1899, p. 13.   [2] Report for 1899, p. 15   [3] Feb. 1912.
[4] Dec. 1911.   [5] Report for 1914.

declined to interfere. They interpreted 'the Protestant Religion' in the Company's charter as meaning 'by law established', since in Charles II's time only the Established Church was recognized. Still persisting, the Deputies asked Mr Joseph King to raise the matter in Parliament. After notice of motion had been given,[1] an unofficial invitation was given to Mr Shepheard, the Deputies' Secretary, to serve on the Board.[2] But this again fell through; and when the motion came up in the House of Commons, it followed immediately after the passage of the Home Rule Bill, 'when the House was in no mood to consider a question such as this, and after a brief reply from the representative of the Commissioners in the House the motion was shelved'.[3] With the pressing preoccupations of the war, no further opportunity was found of raising the matter.

The cases we have discussed were representative; the Deputies took up others, such as Miss Hester Meyrick's Charity (1901) and a Broad Town (Wilts.) Charity reported to have been originally undenominational, but now used only for Anglican children (1907). Even when the Charity Commissioners shewed themselves ultimately in favour of equitable arrangements, the Deputies often deserved the credit for first prodding authority to take the action which it ought to have taken on its own initiative.

We leave now the unhappy relationships of the Deputies and the Charity Commissioners, and the whole question of misapplied trusts and unfaithful trustees, to turn to a very different aspect of the standing of Nonconformist property.

From time to time the law of England has conferred privileges on property held for religious or charitable purposes, or has exempted it from certain burdens (such as rates of various kinds) which normally fall on property. The Deputies, in their care for the temporalities of the churches, have not been slow to take advantage of such privileges or exemptions as could be claimed by Dissenters. These claims affected meeting-houses, schools, manses, and endowments at different times and in different ways; no clear-cut separation can conveniently be made. But it was not easy to make the claims good.

---

[1] Oct. 1913 and June 1914.   [2] Dec. 1915.   [3] Report for 1914.

The authorities who administered the law were often (in the early days more particularly) bitterly prejudiced. The privileges were easily jeopardized if care was not taken about the way in which moneys were collected. Where technical requirements had not been exactly complied with, or where there was any ambiguity, the benefit of the doubt was not likely to go to the Dissenters. Moreover, at a time when local Acts of Parliament were constantly being passed the Deputies had need of constant vigilance. Burdens from which meeting-houses were in general exempt might be placed on them by private Acts. The Deputies kept a wisely suspicious eye on even the most innocent-looking legislation and legislative proposal.

Towards the end of the 18th century, the Deputies codified the rulings they had obtained at various times, and the opinions given 'by four able lawyers, who afterwards rose to the most distinguished stations, viz. Messrs. Dunning, Wallace, Wedderburn, and Macdonald' and entered a summary on their minutes (1796):

1. As to the Land-Tax.—If the ground upon which the meeting-house is built was previous thereto subject to the Land-Tax, it is so still; but if it produces no profit to any person beyond the rent reserved in the lease of it, that rent ought to be the measure of the assessment. But where no rent is reserved, or the trustees have the inheritance of the meeting-house, and no profit is made of it by any person, it is not rateable at all.

2. As to Poor Rates.—This is a tax on the occupier; and if any profit is made of the meeting-house, by letting the seats or otherwise, whoever makes that profit, whether the trustees in whom the lease is vested, or the preacher, may be considered as the occupier, and rated as such. But if the meeting-house is only used as a place of meeting for religious worship, and no profit arises from it to any body, no one can be considered as having any such occupation of it as will subject it to the Poor Rate.

3. As to the Watch, Scavenger, Lamp, Sewer, or any other Parochial or Ward Taxes, these will depend upon the several laws under the authorities of which these taxes are collected: but if they are taxes upon the occupier they will fall under the same consideration as the Poor Laws.[1]

Examples will illustrate the situation. A meeting-house was

---

[1] *Sketch*, p. 58.

liable to be rated if it were a source of certain profit to anyone. Much therefore turned on the question whether seats were let for a definite sum. Seat rents, it was pointed out in the course of a discussion of the assessment of a Barnstaple meeting-house, constituted a definite rent, even if the sum produced were inadequate to pay all expenses, and for this reason the meeting-house was probably legally assessable.[1] The plan of letting seats was abandoned, and the meeting-house was removed from the assessment lists by Quarter Sessions.[2] At Stilton a meeting-house was not freehold, but rented. Here the Deputies were not optimistic about fighting for exemption. The payment of rent presupposed that someone derived financial profit from the house. It would not be discreet here to raise that general question, as the *onus probandi* would lie on the minister. The best plan was to get the amount of the assessment reduced as much as possible and then pay it.[3] At Chalfont, Gloucestershire, the Deputies considered that a cottage used as a vestry would be liable to rates if the minister lived in it.[4] The trustees of a house in Cotton Street, Poplar, were advised to resist a demand for poor rates. The seats, it was alleged, were let for a certain sum; but the Deputies urged a fight, since the seats were not rented or ticketed.[5] To the surprise of their counsel, the assessment was confirmed; and what was particularly annoying, no appeal was allowed because of a section in the Act.[6]

Experience had thus taught the Deputies the need for a restatement of the law to confirm the privilege and to free it from teasing exceptions. Immediately after Repeal had been secured they turned to this object; and in 1829 drafted (with the Protestant Society) a five-point programme of their next demands. Two of these points concerned meeting-houses. A Bill should be re-introduced to secure exemption of all places of worship from poor rates[7] and there ought to be such an amendment of the last Toleration Act as would prevent Dissenters suffering from the neglect of clerks of the peace or ecclesiastical registrars to enrol places of worship.[8]

[1] 26 Jan. 1816.   [2] 29 Nov. 1816.   [3] 25 and 28 June 1828.
[4] 28 April 1820.   [5] 23 Feb. 1816.   [6] 28 Nov. 1816.

[7] On 20 May 1814 the Committee were asked to consider a proposal that Mr Inshington (for the Chancellor of the Exchequer) should move a clause to exempt places of worship from poor rates.

[8] Other points in the programme concerned burial and the registration of births.

When the end of the struggle about the Reform Bill allowed a return to more normal interests, this same question found a place in the programme of the United Committee of 1833.[1] This part of the programme proved easiest to put into effect. The agitation bore fruit in the Act of 1833. This ended some of the tiresome restrictions on the privilege, and definitely exempted from church and poor rates all places of worship if used exclusively for religious worship and if duly registered. Moreover the use of a building as a Sunday School, an Infant School, or a school for the charitable education of the poor was not to make it rateable.[2]

The Highway Act of 1835 gave exemption from highway rates.

In 1842 a demand for property tax from Bishopsgate Street Chapel caused the Deputies to seek a more precise definition of the situation. They got an important opinion from the solicitor to the Board of Stamps and Taxes. The trustees of chapels were not entitled, it appeared, to the allowances for rents and profits in land which were granted to the trustees of charities. Income tax was due on pew rents, but the trustees might deduct the minister's salary and necessary expenses, as the minister paid tax separately. This opinion had the happy effect of completely relieving Bishopsgate Street Chapel. It showed beyond all reasonable dispute the soundness of the Deputies' general contention, that since chapels did not enjoy all the advantages of charities they could not with equity be put under the same public control.[3]

As the century passed, the activities of local authorities increased, and *ad hoc* bodies of several sorts were set up with power to raise money or exercise control. This meant fresh problems for the Deputies. Chapels were exempt from poor rates, but what about sewer rates? The chapels in Westminster were threatened with assessment for sewer rates in 1841 and the Deputies decided that they must press for an exempting clause in the Bill then before Parliament.[4] The Public Health Act of 1875 gave exemption from the general district rate, and the minister of a building appropriated to worship and exempt from poor rate was generally exempt from charges for paving and sewering. Trustees, however, might be

---

[1] 5 and 15 Mar. 1833.
[3] 11 Nov. and 15 Dec. 1842; Report for 1842.
[2] 31 July 1833.
[4] 21 May 1841.

charged, except where the Private Works Act of 1892 had been adopted, and exempted them as well as the minister.

There was constant fear that what was alleged to be public control would in truth prove to be a reduction of their traditional and hardly won liberty. In 1848 a clause in the Public Health Bill assumed control over the building of chapels. This, the Deputies complained, was interference without precedent, and, since there had been no complaints arising from the building of chapels it was also interference without excuse. It entailed expense; it 'may be employed as a fearful instrument of oppression by prejudice and ignorance'. Only those who have not followed the Deputies in their conflicts against every kind of petty and insolent injustice will accuse them of using the language of exaggeration or hysteria.[1]

Since a deputation to ask Lord Morpeth to exclude chapels from the operation of the Bill secured only an unsatisfactory interview,[2] a General Meeting of the Deputies met and petitioned the House of Lords. Success rewarded the Deputies. The clause about ventilation which would have put chapels under the control of local and general boards of health was withdrawn. It is easy a century later to sneer at the Deputies' hygienic views; but they knew, and we have forgotten, the type of mind they were up against. The chance that such a clause would be used to cripple and irritate the Dissenters was not a chance; it was a certainty. The clause ideally carried out would no doubt have conferred advantages on the public; the Deputies had unique opportunity for judging how it would be carried out, and the advantage to the public would have been bought, in 1848, at far too high a price.

A continuation of this same struggle may be followed in the later part of the century. Highbury Hill Chapel was assessed for making up an adjacent new road.[3] The Deputies took counsel's opinion. In being advised that this was a good test case for the metropolis they decided to carry it to Queen's Bench, but expected some help from the church in the expenses.[4] Queen's Bench dismissed the appeal with costs.[5] The Deputies did not accept the

---

[1] 12 June 1848. [2] 30 June 1848. [3] 11 Dec. 1880.
[4] 18 Jan. 1881. [5] 15 Mar. 1881.

decision; and when leave to appeal was surprisingly refused began to plan an alteration of the law.[1] It appeared later that leave to appeal had been refused because the chapel was not put on trust in perpetuity and so was not proper for a test case.[2] In consequence of the peculiar wording of the Metropolitan Acts it seemed unwise to contest the matter further in the courts. Everywhere, except in London, chapels were exempt from poor rates; and a Bill was considered, to assimilate the law in London with the rest of the country. It was then discovered that the London Congregational Chapel Building Society had decided to take action, and the matter was left to them.

In the next year, when a suitable example of rating had been found, the Deputies were ready to make a test case of it and to share the expense with the church itself and three denominational building societies. No case was fought, as the assessment was reduced to a quarter the original figure.[3] In 1889 the Deputies were still anxious for a test case[4] for a paving rate. In 1890 they expressed the opinion that all property, including Anglican churches, ought probably to be charged. In existing circumstances, however, it seemed a more practical policy to claim for the Free Churches the exemption enjoyed by the Anglicans. They continued, therefore, to watch legislation relating both to London and to County Councils.[5]

As late as 1905 the Deputies and the Free Church Council were considering an appeal against the rating of Dr Clifford's chapel (Westbourne Park); but in view of the doubtful chance of success took no action.[6] A distraint on the deacons for the payment of poor rate three years later left them unmoved. They had strong views on the education question, but did not concern themselves with the passive resistance movement.[7]

The question was intricate; and had to be fought in detail. The Deputies, though they did not get all they wanted, undoubtedly saved the churches from paying unjustly many thousands of pounds. The knowledge that they might have to fight a case as far as the

[1] 23 Mar. 1881. [2] 2 May 1881.
[3] 13 June and 11 and 17 July 1883 (Chatsworth Road). [4] 19 Feb. 1889 (Rishton).
[5] 20 Feb. and 24 April 1890. A case at Gosport 5 June 1888.
[6] 10 Nov. and 15 Dec. 1905. [7] 8 Dec. 1908.

High Courts clearly had a salutary influence on unscrupulous local authorities. The reduction of assessments by 75 per cent tells its own tale.

One odd set of problems connected with Parliamentary Elections finds an echo in the Deputies' Minutes. In some districts political prejudice made it hard or impossible for the Liberal party to hire halls or schoolrooms for political meetings. The close alliance of the Dissenting interest and Liberal party as well as a praiseworthy dislike of mere injustice led the trustees of some chapels to lend their property, sometimes a schoolroom or (where there was only a chapel) the chapel itself for a political meeting. The natural revenge of their political antagonists was to try to get the exemption from rating cancelled in consequence. The Deputies had their eye on such an incident at Walton in 1888. In the event the magistrates declined to issue a warrant in support of a changed assessment, holding that the non-exemption of the chapel had not been proved.[1]

On yet another line the Deputies busied themselves about the temporalities of the churches. Fabrics and sites concerned them fairly often, their aim being to secure an equal treatment for Anglican and Dissenting property.

In 1836 the Deputies suggested to the Chancellor of the Exchequer that the new Stamp Act might well exempt from Stamp Duty conveyances and trust deeds concerning chapels and schools built by voluntary contributions.[2] In an interview which is described as short and very cordial the Chancellor declined to accept the suggestion.[3] He disliked indirect subsidies of good causes, and preferred that help should be directly given. He would therefore oppose any relaxation of timber or other duties when churches or schools were built. The Chancellor denied that he was making an invidious distinction in favour of the Church of England. Anglican proprietary and private chapels were not exempt from Stamp Duty. He had to admit, however, that the law did recognize the corporate character of parish churches; and these, after all, provided the true parallel with most of the Dissenters' chapels.

The Deputies' programme for legislation about sites shewed

[1] 22 Mar. and 26 July 1888.   [2] 6 April 1836.   [3] 6 May 1836.

interesting development. In the early part of the century they were much concerned with the Mortmain laws. There were fears on the one hand lest these might endanger property held, and on the other complaints of the obstacles offered to obtaining fresh land.[1] The great multiplication of chapels and the provision of day schools by the religious societies gave urgency to these problems. The Wesleyans were always particularly ready to co-operate where property was concerned. Their very numerous small chapels made them specially anxious about any legal difficulties or fees which would increase the cost of erecting chapels.[2]

It appeared to the Deputies very unfair that owners of land held for instance in tail could not part with it as easily for the erection of a Dissenting chapel as for the erection of an Anglican building. Through Mr Osborne Morgan they kept the whole question of procuring land for chapel sites before Parliament; and when Mr Osborne Morgan and the Committee were disposed to think that for the moment no useful action could be taken,[3] the persistence of a Deputy named Bromhall set the wheels again in motion.[4] In the event the Deputies prepared their own Religious Sites Bill.[5] Introduced by Mr Morgan into the Commons, it got as far as the third reading in the Lords, but was withdrawn in the face of opposition.[6] In the next year, 1873, with a little amendment it passed into law.[7]

It was not enough, however, to be able to buy when the purchaser was willing to sell. There were flagrant abuses of landlord's rights. It appears as if in 1877 the action of a Welsh landlord provoked the Deputies in a manner which men of his calibre had cause to regret. A chapel and chapel yard were taken possession of by the landlord;[8] and almost at once the Deputies discussed the propriety of introducing a Bill to compel landlords to sell the sites of leasehold chapels.[9] The Deputies had at the moment a Burial Bill before Parliament, and probably to give it a clearer course

---

[1] E.g., 3 Dec. 1847, 26 May 1853, 20 Dec. 1853, and much discussion in 1854.

[2] E.g., 28 July 1853. Will Succession Duty Bill interfere with chapel building? Mr Hadfield is assured by the Government that it will not do so.

[3] 19 Jan. 1871.   [4] 19 June 1871.   [5] 7 Dec., 21 Dec. 1871; 17 Jan. 1872.

[6] 15 Feb., 4 July, 1 Aug. 1872.   [7] 2 May, 6 June and 3 Oct. 1873.

[8] 5 Jan. 1877.   [9] 19 Jan. 1877.

decided against action at that time.[1] A few years later, however, the difficulty of acquiring the famous Old Surrey Chapel and the site of Marlborough Chapel (from the Bridge House Committee) led the Deputies to prepare a Bill to extend the provisions of the Chapel Sites Act of 1873 to Corporations and Public Bodies.[2] In 1881 the Bill had no chance,[3] but in 1882 with the omission of one important clause it became law.[4] Introduced by Mr Summers (M.P. for Stalybridge), it gave the Corporation of London and other Corporations the power to make grants or sales of land as sites for Nonconformist places of worship.

The Bill was no sooner passed than its inadequacy appeared. In 1885 the Ecclesiastical Commissioners declared themselves (possibly with no deep regret) unable to grant a piece of waste land on a manor as a site for a chapel, despite the Acts of 1873 and 1882.[5] The Deputies pressed for legislation to give the Commissioners the same power of granting land for Dissenting Chapels as they had for Anglican buildings.[6]

The problem appeared next from another angle. In 1889 the Deputies considered what attitude they ought to take towards a Church Sites (Compulsory Powers Repeal) Bill then before Parliament. They expressed on that occasion an opinion which they had expressed on several previous occasions: instead of taking away from the Anglicans their power to acquire sites by compulsory sale these powers ought to be extended to all denominations.[7] A year later the same view was confirmed.[8]

To this opinion the Deputies steadily adhered and at long last, in 1920, carried their opinion into law. In 1891 a Places of Worship Enfranchisement Bill represented their views, but with their ancient wisdom they issued no whips at the second reading since they 'do not think it wise to appear in any way as the promoters of this Bill'.[9] In the following year they were gratified by a majority of 119 for the second reading and had evidence ready for a Select Committee.[10] But in 1894 they were still urging Mr Gladstone to pass the Bill.[11]

---

[1] 2 Feb. 1877.   [2] 15 and 23 Mar. 1881.   [3] 2 May and 21 June 1881.
[4] 21 April and 18 July 1882.   [5] 6 Feb. 1885.   [6] 9 June 1885.
[7] 19 Mar. 1889.   [8] 20 Mar. 1890.   [9] 20 April 1891.
[10] 17 Mar. and 28 April 1892.   [11] 18 Jan. 1894.

When the Liberals returned to power after the ten years in the wilderness the agitation began again. This time the Wesleyans took the initiative, but the terms of the Bill were settled by the Deputies and the Rev. J. Scott Lidgett, and promoted by them jointly.[1] Introduced and re-introduced, the Bill did not secure enough attention to succeed.[2] At last in 1920 the Places of Worship Enfranchisement Bill became law, and the Deputies were active in making its terms known to Free Churchmen.

[1] 18 Oct. and 13 Dec. 1907; 27 Jan. and 20 Mar. 1908.
[2] 22 May and 23 Oct. 1908.

CHURCH RATES AND CHURCH COURTS

'THE MISERABLE question of Church Rates', John Bright called it;[1] and it was a miserable question. We almost despair of persuading the reader not to skip the chapter which deals with it—the issues seem so remote, the details so petty. Yet in the middle of the 19th century nothing excited more bitter feeling than Church Rates; there must have been some occasion for the intense antagonisms, the disproportionate heroism of the struggle prolonged through a whole generation? Perhaps the effort of the historic imagination needed to recapture the circumstances is worth while?

Church Rates represented the traditional duty of all the parishioners to maintain the fabric of the parish church, and to provide what was necessary for the decent celebration of its services. A vestry meeting voted the rate annually and assessed the parishioners. Dissenters had to pay with the rest, and the rate was enforced by law. In Church Rates and the jurisdiction of Church Courts the privileged position of one Church above the rest was made more clear, perhaps, than in anything else.

But Church Rates and Church Courts did not figure prominently in Dissenting thought or the Deputies' deliberations until the 1830s. We may ask first why this was so. So long as the Test and Corporation Acts remained on the Statute Book all other grievances were subordinated to their Repeal. Once Repeal was achieved there was a new aggressive spirit, and the desire to sweep away every other anomaly. After the passing of the Reform Bill, a new United Committee appointed in 1833 'to consider the grievances under which Dissenters now labour with a view to their redress' placed Church Rates in its list, with the want of

---

[1] John Bright, *Speeches*, vol. I, p. 405 (edn. 1869).

legal registration of births, marriages and deaths; enforced marriage in church; denial of the right of burial by their own ministers according to their own forms; and exclusion from the Universities.[1] This place they held in all general statements of grievances until Mr Gladstone solved the problem in 1868. They were included in a five-point petition to both Houses, prepared in 1834 for the ensuing session.[2] But there was to be no quick solution of any of the problems mentioned.

It was not merely the aggressive spirit fostered by Repeal that suddenly made Church Rates important. These compulsory payments were felt as especially galling at a time when Dissenters were building hundreds of new chapels of their own. Not only were Dissenters paying to build their own chapels—they were also expected to contribute to new Anglican churches. The great increase of population and the growth of mushroom industrial towns made new churches necessary; the only question was—who was to pay for them? To Anglicans it appeared natural to use national funds for the State Church—to Dissenters it appeared an outrage: why should they pay twice, as churchmen for their own churches, as citizens for other men's?

In the earlier part of the century the Anglican view prevailed. It has been calculated that in the fifty years from 1801 to 1851 2,529 churches were built at a cost of £9,087,000. Of this, £1,663,429 came from public funds, £7,423,571 from private benefactions.[3] Whatever might be said about the origin of the old endowments, this direct subsidy from national funds was open to grave objections; it was gradually recognized that it was unfair to millions of taxpayers; in protests against the practice, in slowing it down, and at last in ending it, the Deputies had taken an important and indefatigable part.

Subsidies at first were occasional, but when in 1818 a systematic plan was put before Parliament the Deputies appointed a committee to watch the scheme.[4] It was of course not merely the original grant which affected Dissenters. When the new church was erected, and perhaps a new parish made, was the population

[1] 5 Mar. 1833. [2] 4 Feb. 1834.
[3] Erskine May, *Constitutional History*, 1882, vol. III, p. 216 n. [4] 6 Feb. 1818.

generally to be rated to maintain it like an old church? The legal position was not clear, but before the courts had determined the precise liability of Dissenters in such cases the Deputies had reason to fear that special legislation would confer on churchwardens wider powers of raising rates for new districts than they had possessed in the old parishes. In 1828 the Deputies petitioned against a Church Building Bill which had these objectionable features. It would end cases now pending, contrary to justice. It would give churchwardens new powers of rating. It would add immensely to the heavy burden of Church Rates, 'so long and so patiently borne' on behalf of Anglicans.[1] A Bill to enable Anglicans to build new churches at their own expense was passed without opposition from the Deputies in the next year, 1829. But the Church Building Bill—the first of several—was withdrawn after great excitement had been aroused. 'Should a like measure be proposed' the Deputies grimly assured their constituency, it 'will not fail to meet with all necessary observation'.[2]

While this attention was being given to legislation, the Deputies were assisting a Mr John Blackett to test the legality, under the existing law, of a rate made on him for new churches.[3] The case was removed from the Court of Arches to King's Bench, and Blackett got a favourable judgment because less than a majority of the select vestry had made the rate. The main question of the power of a majority to make such a rate (in theory for repairs, but in reality for other purposes) was undetermined.[4] A nice problem was put to the Deputies in 1832 from Aberystwyth. A new church was protected from the sea by a wall: was the wall a proper object for a church rate? The Deputies had no immediate answer for this conundrum.[5]

No inconsiderable help was given to church building by loans and remissions of duty on building materials. This was summarized in a report in 1839.[6] The Deputies petitioned against more grants of public money for the 147 new churches to be built. They also endeavoured, but in vain, to extend to all denominations the

---

[1] 30 Nov. 1827 and 25 June 1828.
[2] 7 July 1828 and Report for 1828.
[3] 7 and 11 Jan. 1828.
[4] 25 Jan. 1828 and 31 July 1828.
[5] 26 Oct. 1832.
[6] 6 Dec. 1839.

power retained by the Anglican Church to acquire sites compulsorily for the building of churches.[1]

In 1846 another Bill to provide and repair churches was rejected by Parliament; but the Report of a Commission on Church Extension led to renewed proposals for legislation in 1850.[2] Lord John Russell displayed some anxiety to learn the views of the Deputies; and early in 1851 he discussed the Church Building Acts Amendment Bill with their Chairman, John Remington Mills. He explained that a commission of enquiry about the best method of dividing parishes had been appointed with the support of all parties; but that he did not himself entirely agree with its proposals, and since the Government was not prepared with any comprehensive measure for dealing with the whole question of Church Rates, his colleagues had agreed to drop the clause about levying Church Rates for churches built under the provisions of the Bill. Lord John was afraid that this might mean that the Bill would not be proceeded with at all.

Mills expressed gratitude, but reminded Lord John that there would be a constitutional issue if a commission (consisting entirely of Anglicans) were to intervene in the taxation of the public at large; under the Act of 1829 no churches built had been made chargeable to Church Rates; the Deputies would not oppose such Bills if they were not made liable to contribute.

The Bill went forward, and was passed; but the Deputies' view on Church Rates prevailed, and the measure bore other marks of their criticisms, especially in its proposals about churchyards and burial fees.[3]

We must now look back and set these proposals for the building of churches against the background of the struggle for the souls of the new towns. Everyone who knows anything of the early Industrial Revolution is aware of the moral problem it created. The squalor, misery, and degradation of the new proletariat, uprooted from the soil and deprived of its traditional culture, threatened the obliteration of moral standards, at a time when the

[1] See Chapter on the Temporalities of Dissent.
[2] 4 Nov. 1850 and 20 Dec. 1850.
[3] Report for 1851. See also Chapter on Burials.

Church of England was least equipped to exercise pastoral care. The Church had let the Evangelicals go out and found new sects, when Wesley would gladly have remained within the Church. The Oxford Movement had not yet arisen. This was the moment when the Utilitarians proposed the dispossession of the Church, so that its buildings and endowments might be put to useful secular purposes. No wonder that Nonconformists, struggling with some success in their Little Bethels to make besotted miners and factory girls into respectable parents, devoted wives, class-leaders and eloquent local preachers, thought bitterly about Church Rates. No wonder either that the Church, feeling its power slipping, tried to hold on to privilege.

The feeling between the two sides was now fanned by a series of cases of individual resistance which brought the hatred to white heat. Perhaps the most famous was that of Childs of Bungay, who was sent to gaol in 1835 for refusal to pay a church rate of 17s. 6d; as the Deputies' Report for 1835 somewhat heavily expressed it:

The incarceration of so respectable an individual for the passive offence of not appearing to a citation in an Ecclesiastical Court for non-payment of an obnoxious impost deservedly attracted public attention and sympathy.

The whole mediaeval mechanism of penance, excommunication and imprisonment was employed against Childs; and the effect was to rivet on the Church the label of obscurantism, and to bind together as twin evils Church Rates and Church Courts. Cases went on occurring throughout the period. In 1839 John Thorogood spent many months in Chelmsford Gaol, sent there by an ecclesiastical court for not paying a church rate of 5s. 6d. After he had served six months the Commons resolved that it was the duty of Parliament next session to alter the law to prevent events of this kind.[1] But it was not done. In 1844 we find the Deputies again protesting against the imprisonment of 'certain respectable citizens' of Norwich for refusing Church Rates.[2]

Throughout the whole time of their existence, the Deputies had had considerable experience of the working of the ecclesiastical courts. For long they had contented themselves with trying to

[1] Report for 1839; 2 Jan. 1840. [1] 13 Mar. 1844.

secure from them in appropriate cases the nearest approach to justice which the law allowed. In the 18th century they had even won resounding victories in these courts; though the proceedings were as slow and protracted as those of a Dickensian Court of Chancery.

Legal reforms in the 19th century were to transfer the great mass of the business of ecclesiastical courts to civil courts. As early as 1832 the Ecclesiastical Commission had recommended the abolition of the criminal jurisdiction of Church Courts; but in 1844 these 'unconstitutional and universally stigmatized tribunals' were still committing Dissenters to prison. Nor was it only for non-payment of rates. In 1838 two almost melodramatic imprisonments had made it impossible to shirk raising the general issue.

John James of Llanelly, 'a respectable farmer' and formerly a churchwarden, had been admonished in a Consistory Court for not attending his parish church. He refused to pay costs, and was sent to gaol. The Deputies regretted that he had not made a stand when the charge was first instituted, but offered to contribute to expenses. They advised James to take the oaths of allegiance and supremacy, to make the declaration of transubstantiation, and to refer the justices to the Toleration Acts.[1] In the event, it appears, James gave way; for the Deputies learnt that he had been liberated on payment of costs.[2]

The incumbent who had acted against James also had cited David Jones as churchwarden of a neighbouring parish for not attending his parish church, and for not providing sacramental bread and wine. Jones was also in gaol for not paying costs.[3] Having procured details of the trial held on 14 March 1838 and a copy of the writ *De contumace capiendo*, and having heard legal opinion, the Deputies decided that they could not take up the case. Jones had omitted to appeal, and no important principle could be raised for decision. But they sent £20 towards Jones's costs, and mentioned technical points which might be used by the local people.[4] After spending more than six months in gaol, Jones secured release on a technical point: the writ had been illegally issued by the surrogate, not by the bishop himself. If he had

[1] 19 Dec. 1838.
[2] Report for 1838.
[3] *Ibid.* and 14 Dec. 1838.
[4] 7 Jan. 1839.

promised to bring no action, Jones might have received costs, but he was discharged without receiving them, and intended to bring an action unless a compromise were made.[1]

As soon as they learned of the first of these imprisonments, the Deputies had determined to see Lord Melbourne,[2] and had decided that the question of Church Rates and Church Courts had better be attacked as a whole; it would be a mistake to be side-tracked into a struggle about minor aspects of the questions, such as the liability of Dissenters to be churchwardens.[3] At the interview Lord Melbourne was not optimistic about any wholesale change. He thought that something might be done to suspend the operation of ecclesiastical courts, pending thorough reformation of them; but he could not carry the abolition of Church Rates.[4]

It was actually not until 1843 that a Bill to reform Church Courts came before Parliament. The Bill was introduced by Dr Nicholl, who met the legal sub-committee of the Deputies at their request and freely discussed the whole matter with them. The Bill, it was said, represented a compromise with the bishops, but the Deputies could not be satisfied with what was, despite its advantages, an anomalous and illogical proposal. The courts of one Church were to continue to deal with some national affairs. Were the officers of those courts to be necessarily Anglicans? The Dean of Arches, for instance, was to be always an Anglican, yet he dealt with matters not exclusively Anglican, and an appeal lay from him to the Privy Council, not all of whose members were Anglican.

Burial cases were still giving trouble, and the Deputies wished the Bill to declare it a civil right for a baptized person to be buried by an Anglican clergyman according to the rites of the Established Church. Dr Nicholl said he did not think it was, and declined to to introduce a declaration to that effect for fear of increasing opposition to the Bill. He agreed, however, to support other suggestions, such as the request that clerks of the peace, not justices at sessions, should register Dissenting chapels, and he thought that Dissenters would benefit from a competent Court of Arches to

[1] 31 July 1839. [2] 7 Dec. 1838.
[3] 7 Jan. 1839. [4] 31 May 1839.

try Church Rate cases, and from a provision which would send tithe cases to common law instead of ecclesiastical courts.[1]

In the light of this interview it is easy to see why the Deputies maintained a two-edged policy towards the Bill. On the one side they tried to make the best of a bad job by securing useful amendments, such as a penalty for registrars who neglected their duty in the registration of places of worship. But on the other side they still opposed the Bill as a whole.[2] Their petition summarized their opinions. Since the repeal of the Test and Corporation Acts and recent legislation about marriages had altered the relation of non-Anglicans to the State, many matters had become unfit for sectarian treatment in Anglican courts which excluded Dissenters from office. State courts recruited from all citizens should deal with cases concerning wills and marriages. Nevertheless, the Bill would make great improvements.[3]

In the following spring another petition re-stated the same general views about a Bill which again failed to go far enough. The Deputies rarely forgot to mention that a Royal Commission in George IV's time had recommended the abolition of the diocesan courts on account of the incompetence of judges and practitioners in them.[4]

It was inevitable in Victorian England that grievances about Church Courts should beget an *ad hoc* society, and in 1846 the Deputies were promising co-operation with the Society for the Abolition of Church Courts, whose secretary, the Rev. Edward Marriott, attended and explained its objects:[5]

As whether they consider the origin—the number—the jurisdiction —the judges—the proceedings—the patronage—the appellant tribunals —the expense—the enormous powers—or the intolerant nature, objects, and operations of those Courts . . . they must as ordinary members of the community and especially as Protestant Dissenters unite with many eminent Lawyers and distinguished Statesmen in regarding them as incompatible with any liberal and enlightened jurisprudence.

Church Courts figuring in the catechizing of candidates at the Middlesex election of 1847;[6] and the Deputies were pleased to find

[1] 13 Mar. 1843.   [2] 14 June 1843.   [3] 5 July 1843.
[4] 27 Feb. and 27 Mar. 1844.   [5] 7 Oct. 1846.   [6] 22 Jan. 1847.

that, though some of his religious views were regrettable, Lord Robert Grosvenor was sound on Church Courts, regarding them as 'relics of a superstitious age'.[1] In a short petition the Deputies pressed again for civil courts to replace Church Courts; and Lord John Russell presented the petition to the Commons.[2] Church Courts indeed figured with Church Rates in much of the agitation of this period.[3]

But while a few Dissenters were languishing in gaol from conscientious scruple about paying Church Rates, and while the Deputies were pressing their views by interview and petition on Parliament and statesmen, the struggle was carried to the parishes themselves. The Deputies had their part in putting the agitation on a national footing, but they did not engineer it; it was a spontaneous movement. In 1834 the United Committee's memorial on grievances was supported by petitions and memorials from Dissenting bodies and public meetings in Manchester, Leeds, Brighton, Bradford, Nottingham, Hull, Huddersfield, London, Leicester, Staines, Durham, Liverpool, Braintree, Blackburn, Bedford, Bath, Wellingborough, Cheltenham, Stroud, Kidderminster, Newport (I.o.W.), Coventry, Petersfield (Hampshire), Glasgow; forty-four pages of close double columns.[4] In 1840 we find the Deputies' Secretary writing to Dissenters throughout the nation in a flamboyant tone almost unexampled in the Deputies' history:

Address to the Protestant Dissenters of the United Kingdom from the Committee of Deputies. 1840.

You are again called to action. Your complaints are disregarded, your grievances unredressed.

The advocates of the State Church are labouring to perpetuate the ecclesiastical domination—they will concede nothing to equity, they insist on continuance of Church Rates and oppose abolition of Church Courts, wish to control education and are seeking additional grants for Church extension.

In the last point, more than 900 petitions with 60,000 signatures have been presented from the Church side. It is unjust to tax one man to support another man's religion. Church extension is not only unjust

---

[1] 19 Feb. 1847. [2] 24 Feb. and 5 Mar. 1847.
[3] E.g., 13 Mar. 1848: conference with the ministers and the Congregational Union.
[4] From a tract in Dr Williams's Library (12: 66: 18).

but rapacious (as the Church is immensely wealthy) and opposed to Holy Scripture. The Church has had its establishment for 300 years, and now complains of irreligion, infidelity, socialism, and popery.

You have struggled before, you must struggle again. Pour in petitions.[1]

But apart from supporting the London Committee, the local Dissenters were engaged in their own battles. They were using the theory, by which all citizens still belonged officially to the State Church, to combat the wishes of the Church. They carried democracy into the vestries. They began with discussions about the amount and nature of the expenses which might properly be charged to Church Rates. Already in 1820 the Deputies took legal opinion on the liability of Dissenters for such things as the introduction and fitting of a new organ, the part of the organist's salary not subscribed voluntarily, and candles for the evening service. Thirteen years later they advised enquirers at Haverford-west in a similar way, that *repairs* extended to the organ and ornamental parts, and that the rate is legal if made at a regular vestry; and that though 'expenses of candles at the evening lecture' are not legally included, the Deputies did not advise interference on that ground. The 19th-century enthusiasm for church restoration and decoration meant that far more was spent on fabrics than had been spent for many years.

From disputing the amount of repairs Dissenters went on to wreck the machinery by declining to impose the rate at all when they could get a majority in the vestry. The classic description of the process is John Bright's description of what happened in Rochdale:[2]

I live in a town in which contests about Church-rates have been carried on in past years with a vigour and determination, and, if you like it, with an animosity which has not been surpassed in any part of the kingdom. . . . The very last contest of this kind cost the Church party in the parish as much money as, if invested at the common rate of interest, would have supported the fabric of the church for ever. (A cry of 'How much?') I can tell the hon. Gentleman what was the estimate formed, which I believe was never disputed, and which,

---

[1] From a copy in Dr Williams's Library. Signed by Hull Terrell. (*ibid.*)
[2] Speech on the 'Church Rates Abolition Bill' 1860, *Speeches*, vol. II, 517.

judging from the expenditure on the other side, was not, I should say, very inaccurate. I believe that the expenditure would not be less than from £3,000 to £4,000. It is a large parish, probably ten miles square, and contains nearly 100,000 inhabitants; and I need not tell hon. Members that there is no class of people in England more determined and more unconquerable, whichever side they take, than are the people of the county from which I come.

What was the result of that struggle? The result was that the Church-rate was for ever entirely abolished in that parish. I have since seen several lists of candidates for the Church-wardenship put forth by Churchmen, each of which claimed support upon the ground that they would never consent to the reimposition of a Church-rate; and the parish has been for many years upon this question a model of tranquillity. . . . I will undertake to say that since that contest that venerable old parish church has had laid out upon it, in repairing and beautifying it, from money subscribed not altogether, but mainly by Churchmen, ten times, aye, twenty times as much as was ever expended upon it during a far longer period of time in which Church-rates were levied. During that period there were discussions about the graveyard, about the hearses, about the washing of surplices, about somebody who had to sweep out the Church. There were discussions of all kinds, of a most irritating and offensive character. The clock which was there for the benefit of the public no longer told the time, and, in fact, there was evidence of that sort of decay to which the learned Gentleman has pointed as the inevitable result of the abolition of Church-rates. Since the rate ceased to be levied the clock has kept time with admirable fidelity, and to such an extent has the liberality of Churchmen gone, that very lately they have put up another clock in a neighbouring Church. I believe that in the parish of Rochdale the Church people have received far more benefit from the abolition of Church-rates than the Dissenters have. They have found out, what they never knew before, that when placed upon the same platform as Dissenters, and obliged to depend upon their own resources, they are as liberal and zealous as other sects.

But of course, when the device of voting out the church rate was first discovered by enterprising Dissenters, the Church party was not prepared to acquiesce, and took the matter to law. In Braintree in 1837, when the imposition was postponed for twelve months, the churchwardens levied it on their own authority. Upheld in the Consistory Court, they were prohibited by Queen's

Bench from collecting the rate. The same view of their incapacity to act alone was taken by the Court of Exchequer Chamber. There, however, Chief Justice Tindal suggested that possibly the churchwardens and a minority of the vestry might make a rate legally, as the majority (it might be held) threw their votes away in refusing to perform their legal duty.

'This subtle and technical device' (as Erskine May calls it) caused a second set of Braintree cases, which did not end until the House of Lords declared the device bad in law; the majority could not be so set aside. The cases went on until 1853. The result of the Lords' decision was great. By 1859 there had been refusal to make Church Rates in 1525 areas. But even this did not end the struggle. It was nearly another ten years before a general solution was found. We must now summarize the stages by which this came about, sparing the reader the details of interview and petition, of Bill and amendment, with which the Deputies' Committee occupied themselves from 1834 to 1868.

'You have tried every kind of contrivance', John Bright reminded the House of Commons in 1860. They had indeed. An early one was Lord Althorp's proposal in 1834 for a grant of £250,000 a year from the Consolidated Fund. This pleased no one. The Anglicans said it represented only half the value of the rates; the Dissenters, that it merely disguised their grievance by substituting indirect for direct taxation; it made Scotland and Ireland pay for the English Establishment, and destroyed the power of local assessment.[1] The Deputies petitioned against the Bill, which was dropped.

Early in 1836 the United Committee put forward their own suggestion in the course of a petition. The total revenue of the Church of England amounted to £3,491,190 per annum; it would be easy to replace Church Rates by making a small assessment on this revenue; a plan which had already been followed in Ireland.[2] After all, the Dissenters had built 8,000 chapels for themselves at a cost of £1,500,000 and maintained their own ministers at an annual cost of about a million pounds. To tax such people for the benefit of another Church was 'a palpable injustice'.

[1] 29 April 1834.   [2] 3 and 4 Wm. IV, c. 37.

In the autumn of 1836 the United Committee and the Deputies found themselves joined by a new ally, the Church Rate Abolition Society,[1] which desired them to leave the field, but to give the Society financial support. With their customary prudence, the Deputies voted the Society twenty guineas, sent a deputation to a general meeting, and promised co-operation but not withdrawal. Nevertheless, there was friction; the Deputies' resolutions about the Society were published (against their wishes) in *The Patriot*; they did not attend when Lord Melbourne was interviewed, and they petitioned again on their own account against Church Rates.[2]

The new Government then proposed a settlement intended to meet the complaints. From an improved administration of land and from pew rents was to be provided a fund to repair churches and so to make Church Rates unnecessary. This suggestion commended itself to the Deputies. To use a surplus of Cathedral and Chapter property to replace Church Rates was already a favourite scheme of theirs.[3] The Deputies approved the Government's plan, expressed their gratitude and prepared petitions.[4] The Anglicans' criticism not unnaturally took the line that the fullest benefit that could be derived from Church lands already belonged to them, and that in merely earmarking a part of what was already their property the Government offered them no genuine compensation for the loss of Church Rates. In the event the Government did not persist with the scheme. It had indeed never had adequate Parliamentary support. The Commons had approved the principle by twenty-three on 15 March 1837, but at the second reading on 23 May there was a majority of five only. The Government announced its intention nevertheless of bringing the scheme forward in the next session, when it would be strengthened by the Report on Ecclesiastical Property.[5]

The Deputies at least had nothing for which to blame themselves, though the scheme did fail. This year, though they had their hands full of the struggle with the Unitarians, they had shewn their powers of agitation and propaganda at their best.

[1] 24 Feb. 1837.   [2] 28 Dec. 1836.
[3] They had feared that if the recommendations in the Fourth Report of the Commission on the State of the Church of England were adopted this use would be impossible. (Report for 1836.)   [4] 29 Mar. 1837.   [5] Report for 1837.

Not content with a petition from a special General Meeting, they appointed a sub-committee to meet at the King's Head three times a week.[1] Paid agents were employed throughout April and May to stimulate ministers and Deputies to organize petitions, to arrange meetings, and to collect money. Immense supplies of literature were ordered for publicity.[2] We hear of meetings in Southwark, St Pancras, Marylebone, Mile End, Tower Hamlets, Westminster, and Shoreditch.[3] At the end of the year in resolving to maintain the Church Rates agitation the Deputies could congratulate themselves that 'the country has been agitated upon it to a degree almost unprecedented'. The petitions prove it:

2328 petitions with 674,719 signatures for abolition.

3194 petitions with 330,123 signatures against abolition.

These figures were the more remarkable since their opponents, as the Deputies did not forget to point out, now found 'ample scope for intimidation and revenge in forms equally offensive but less capable of exposure or punishment'.

But the agitation did not prove that a solution was near; there came instead thirty years of abortive legislation. Successive Prime Ministers—Melbourne, Peel, Russell, Palmerston, Derby—were to listen to the Deputies' pleas and protests without being able to indicate a solution. Many M.P.s, especially Easthope (in 1840, 1842, 1844), Osborne (1848), Clay (1851, 1852, 1853, 1854, 1856), Phillimore (1853), Packe (1854), interested themselves in promoting Bills of one kind or another; often two were in the field at the same time. But the most persistent and indomitable was Sir J. J. Trelawney; from 1849 to 1863 he kept at it, supported and occasionally relieved at his post by Hardcastle. We will indicate only some of the more important stages of the struggle.

Easthope's suggestion in 1840 was that Dissenters should be exempt from Church Rates on declaring themselves Dissenters. This suggestion was to reappear later, but Dissenters would not return to religious tests even for immediate benefit. The Deputies always contended that Dissenters were not oddities to be treated as a class apart, but normal Englishmen and normal Christians, supporting their own churches as all men should.[4]

[1] 31 Mar. 1837.　[2] 3 April and 15 May 1837.　[3] 24 April 1837.　[4] 26 Mar. 1841.

A special United Committee was accordingly formed to secure 'the entire and unconditional abolition of the impost'. Besides the Church Rate Abolition Society and the Deputies, it included the Protestant Society, the Religious Freedom Society, the Ministers, the Baptist Union, the Congregational Union, and the Congregational Board. The absence of Quakers and Methodists is significant of their attitude. The United Committee got no adequate income and effected little.[1] Early in 1841 Easthope presented another Bill providing this time for total abolition, but it had no success.

Melbourne's Government went out and Peel's came in. The Deputies intervened in the Election, setting up committees in the boroughs and examining the M.P.s' voting on religious questions; but they did not prevent Peel's return. They expected 'fewer concessions, if not direct opposition' to their cause; and their unfavourable estimate was to be more than justified. It was at this unfortunate moment that Chief Justice Tindal's remarks about vestries threatened to put all parishioners at the mercy of churchwardens.[2]

In these depressing circumstances, on 7 March 1842, some friendly M.P.s met the interested bodies to consider policy. They decided to promote an Abolition Bill as soon as the obsession with the Corn Laws allowed it. The Deputies prepared a petition, assuming that Lord John Russell would present it; but he would not, considering it hopeless to expect the present Government to get an equivalent for Church Rates out of leases. The Deputies got Lord Howick to present the petition instead, and asked for an interview with Peel.

Peel, whose manners at least never failed, received them very courteously, but explained that the Government did not intend to abolish Church Rates; he received in return a lecture on the whole subject, including a tart reference to his own keenness to settle the question in 1835.[3] In such circumstances the rejection of Sir John Easthope's Bill by 162 to 80 caused no surprise.

But at least Easthope was able to get Parliament to order the preparation of statistics on the rates. In 1845 they had still not

[1] 20 Jan. 1841.   [2] Report for 1841. See also p. 186.   [3] 15 June 1842.

been published; Sir James Graham, the Home Secretary, said they could not be completed, but the Speaker promised they should be published as they stood.[1] It took another year and further pressure from Easthope before they were available;[2] they furnished much ammunition for the future.

Peel's Government, so disastrous for Dissenters in every way, was succeeded by that of Palmerston, and the Deputies took heart again after a period of acute depression reflected in their acid comments. Early in 1848 a conference with the ministers and the Congregational Union decided on a new application to Parliament.[3] The Deputies had recently had before them the case of a man imprisoned for not paying fivepence.[4] But it proved hard to find an M.P. with the requisite standing and legal knowledge to raise the question; Charles Lushington 'politely declined'; B. Osborne was primed with careful legal and historical information but then had to go to Ireland.[5] At last Trelawney, who was himself an Anglican, took it up, early in 1849. His motion was defeated by 119 to 84, which represented a genuine advance; the Deputies conferred with John Bright and others on the next step.

It was agreed that Trelawney should during the next session move two resolutions: one calling for the abolition of Church Rates, the other asking for a committee to consider the mode of supporting churches. The Deputies, on their part, organized propaganda on a large scale; 3,000 ministers received circulars; there were meetings, press articles, petitions, and a conference with friendly M.P.s at the Reform Club. Lord John Russell continued unfriendly. In the event, Trelawney did not succeed in moving his resolutions, but a Committee of the House on Church Rates was ordered later. Trelawney sought the Deputies' help in preparing evidence, and so gave them an opportunity of doing work at which they excelled. They appointed a sub-committee to co-operate with him, and suggested names of suitable members for the Committee of the House.

The sub-committee produced an immense scheme shewing the main points which the enquiry must cover.[6] In brief, these were:

[1] 5 July 1845.   [2] 24 June 1846.   [3] 13 Mar. 1848.
[4] 20 Dec. 1847.   [5] Report for 1848.   [6] 21 April 1851.

(1) The origin of the law relating to Church Rates.
(2) The points actually in litigation.
(3) The varieties of local practice.
(4) The several reasons for abolition.
(5) The amount of money raised.
(6) The substitutes proposed.

The sub-committee proposed, in effect, a national preliminary enquiry by the Deputies, supervised by a lawyer and specially financed. At this point the Deputies began to think that their sub-committee was becoming too zealous; the evidence was being collected by individuals and denominations through other channels.[1]

The House of Commons Committee met nineteen times under Trelawney's chairmanship and examined twenty-three witnesses, but it made no report. Trelawney prepared an analysis of the evidence, which the Deputies printed; and Sir Robert Inglis (M.P. for Oxford University) applied for returns which were to shew:

(1) The number of Church Rates made or refused.
(2) The amount in the £ of such rates.
(3) The legal proceedings which had followed refusal.
(4) Relevant facts concerning population and poor rate assessments.

The returns were to cover the period since the Reform Bill (Easter 1833 to Easter 1851).[2] The figures when published were remarkable as shewing how unsatisfactorily the rates were working. If all extra-parochial places, areas governed by local Acts and the like were omitted, there appeared in a population of 6,365,351 possible ratepayers 3,519,387 who did not pay, and only 2,845,945 who did.

The year 1852 saw another General Election, in which Trelawney lost his seat. It had been his intention to introduce a Bill substituting pew rents for Church Rates; a vestry of seat-holders was to assess itself for rates, whilst the Ecclesiastical Commissioners' revenues should be available to help in extreme need.[3] The Report for 1852 contains a just and generous estimate of Trelawney and and his work: 'a true and reforming member of the Church of England', they called him. His mantle fell upon another Anglican, Sir William Clay, who now began to voice the Deputies' views.

[1] 26 May 1851. [2] 15 Aug. 1851. [3] 15 Feb. 1852.

But Clay did not find himself alone in the field in this new House which, as the Deputies said, 'contained an unusual number of members entertaining opinions in accordance with those of this deputation.'[1] Besides his motion for abolition was another from Phillimore reviving Easthope's old plan allowing Dissenters to 'contract out' by stating in writing that they were Dissenters. Lord John Russell supported Phillimore's plan; and as Phillimore got precedence and declined to withdraw, Clay moved his plan as an amendment to Phillimore's motion. Both the motion and amendment were lost. Lord John declared that Clay's proposals would subvert the whole Church Establishment. Sir Robert Inglis, who had moved for the returns mentioned above, also supported Phillimore; the Deputies' Report commented: 'he is ever the faithful representative and consistent exponent of the sentiments of the University of Oxford'.[2]

In a memorial to Lord Aberdeen, the Deputies declared their adherence to Clay's scheme and their dislike of Phillimore's. They included statistics which shewed that according to the Registrar-General's returns in 1851 there were 20,400 Dissenting places of worship, 17,000 being in separate buildings. If the average cost of erection was taken at £400, seven millions had been spent on them; and the annual expenditure could not be less than an average of £80, or £1,136,000 in all.[3] Aberdeen, however, would not disclose the Government's plans, and referred the Deputies to Lord Palmerston. Indefatigably, the Deputies went off to see Palmerston. The interview (in February 1854) must have been a picturesque affair; the whole Committee, reinforced by some outsiders, attended. On some matters Palmerston was communicative, but on Church Rates he would only say that the Government would introduce 'such a measure as should appear practicable'.[4]

The Deputies did not wait to see what this would be; they drafted for Clay a fresh Bill, which would abolish all rates except those under local Acts; these latter would cease as soon as money borrowed under the Acts had been repaid. This was lost on the second reading (Lord John Russell still opposing) by 182 to 209.

[1] Report for 1852. [2] Report for 1853.
[3] *Ibid.* [4] 7 Feb. 1854.

The Government renewed its promise to bring in a Bill next session, but Palmerston expressed his desire to see no more deputations on the subject.[1]

In the same session the House also threw out another Bill, introduced by Packe, with a fresh variant of the contracting-out device for Dissenters. But the year 1855 brought the Deputies, it seemed, very close to victory. With Palmerston's approval, Clay reintroduced his Abolition Bill; to appease Palmerston, the clause about pew rents was dropped; the Bill passed the second reading by 217-189.[2] But 'by a manoeuvre of its opponents' the Bill failed on the third reading. In 1856 there was even less satisfaction. The Government's sympathy was tepid, and in spite of concessions by the Deputies it refused to grant a day for the Bill, which had to be withdrawn for the session.

Derby's Government replaced Palmerston's, and Trelawney reappeared in the House of Commons; however, he did not at once take up Church Rates, but asked Hardcastle to replace him. In 1858 an Abolition Bill for the first time passed the Commons and reached the Lords, crowning the struggle of a quarter of a century. In the Lords the Bill was defeated by 212 to 61. The Deputies found this encouraging.

But when Trelawney returned to the fray in 1859 he found himself confronted with a Government Bill which 'astonished' the Deputies. It would have substituted rent charges for rates (thus in fact making it possible to reintroduce rates in parishes which had ceased to pay them); and it would have required an invidious declaration from Dissenters.[3] Again neither scheme was passed, and again the Government fell; and again, under Palmerston's new Government, the Commons passed and the Lords rejected an Abolition Bill.

In 1861 there was an unusual attempt to find a working compromise; the third reading was delayed a fortnight for this purpose.[4] Trelawney himself thought a compromise necessary, and the Secretary of the Deputies prepared a scheme dividing the vestries into payers and non-payers—a solution which moderate opinion had long hankered for. But the body of Deputies were

---

[1] 14 July 1854.   [2] 18 May 1855.   [3] 4 Mar. 1859.   [4] 5 June 1851.

furious; they deplored the original delay, ordered the erasure of the Secretary's scheme from their Minute Book, and in its place voted an uncompromising resolution that Church Rates

foster a spirit of insolent intolerance on the part of those who claim to belong to a dominant sect.

In a slightly milder mood they later deleted the word 'insolent'. Trelawney's Bill was lost in the Commons by the Speaker's casting vote.

If they refused to compromise, they refused to despond. They advertised in *The Times* and other journals a call to the Government to treat the question as one of national importance and to settle it by total abolition; they denounced a new Bill (Mr Cross's) as 'an enormous aggravation of the evil', and they declared that

It becomes the duty of the Nonconformist bodies throughout the country to take steps in every election to procure the return to Parliament of Gentlemen who will more faithfully represent their views.[1]

To the Deputies, Church Rates had now become more important than the suffrage, the ballot, or any other issue.[2] Putting their doctrine into practice, they interviewed Mr Wood, a candidate for the City; the importance of this interview is that we hear the first mention of what was to prove the ultimate solution of the problem: Wood was asked if he would support Lord Ebury's or Mr Bright's suggestions. These were to make no change in Church Rates themselves, but to deprive the Church of the power of legally enforcing payment. The impossibility of finding any other way out became plainer and plainer; the chances that the fortune of war might change encouraged each side to fight on, and kept many parishes in a state of permanent controversy and rancour.

In 1863 there were three Bills about Church Rates in the field,[3] but all were overshadowed by the Government's Church Building and New Parishes Bill, which would have authorized Church Rates in new parishes. A conference to fight the Bill included even the Methodists and the Friends, and when the Bill was held over to the following session, Palmerston had to see a large deputation of twenty-seven M.P.s and twenty representatives of

[1] 25 July 1861. [2] *Ibid.* [3] 11 Mar. 1863.

religious bodies. He would give no pledge, but they felt they had impressed him; and the Bill was at last withdrawn, leaving the law in the same unsatisfactory state.

In the new Parliament of 1865 there were as usual a commutation and an abolition Bill. The Deputies petitioned of course for abolition, and the Liberal Government seemed inclined to adopt it, but they remained cautious to the end. In taking counsel's opinion they shewed proper anxiety to ensure that those parishioners who did not pay the voluntary rate should suffer no disqualification except for the making and spending of the rate.[1] It was in this session that Mr Gladstone, who was eventually to cut the knot, first voted for abolition.[2]

But the fall of the Liberal Government brought another check. In 1867 the Lords again rejected Hardcastle's Bill for abolition. But in the next year the uncomfortable situation of the Conservative Government made bargaining with the opposition necessary. Mr Gladstone, himself so recently converted to abolition, used the circumstances to 'extort one striking reform from the conservative party'.[3] He introduced and carried a Bill which maintained indeed the machinery for levying the rate, but made it irrecoverable except where it had been assigned as security for debt. The Deputies, having interviewed Mr Gladstone, petitioned in favour of his Bill; and at a General Meeting viewed its success with satisfaction, and in a comprehensive and resounding denunciation closed the fight of more than thirty years; the compulsory levy was declared opposed to the teaching of the New Testament, productive of injury to true religion and of great suffering to Nonconformists.[4]

There are a few appendices to the main story which ends with Mr Gladstone's success. Special local Acts still regulated some districts and provided opportunities for abuse; in 1884 the Deputies were calculating that hundreds of pounds per annum had been illegally raised since 1868.[5] The Deputies were sometimes successful and sometimes not in countering these local Acts.

In 1879 they took counsel's opinion because of proceedings in

[1] 30 April and 14 May 1866.
[2] Morley, *Life of Gladstone*, ed. 1908, vol. I, p. 595.
[3] Sir Spencer Walpole in *Cambridge Modern History*, vol. XI, p. 345.
[4] 29 July 1868. [5] Report of 1884.

Poplar, to decide whether the local Act of 1817 had been revoked wholly or in part by the general Act.[1] A scrutiny of the items on which the rate had been spent in 1878 and 1879 seemed to shew that the charges to be set legitimately against the rate required £450 to be raised, not £1200. As a result of the Deputies' action the illegal items were struck out of the account, and the amount to be raised was put at £600 instead of £1200. A compromise later allowed the figure to be raised to £750. 'Pour encourager les autres' the Deputies made the facts public.[2]

Nevertheless, in the following year the vestry decided to make a three-farthing rate although, according to the estimate of the Church Committee, a halfpenny rate would have sufficed. The Deputies suggested that payment at the halfpenny rate should be tendered, and promised support if legal action followed.[3] A special case was settled by counsel on both sides,[4] and each side retained a leader.[5] The decision on appeal was for the Deputies. This, it was thought, would stimulate action in other places where the situation appeared to be similar.[6]

Bethnal Green and Marylebone were two such places; and in consequence of the Poplar decision Bethnal Green knocked £500 off its church rate. Counsel's opinion was taken in Marylebone.[7] A writ of *mandamus* was issued against the Bethnal Green vestry to oblige the churchwardens to raise by a compulsory rate the full amount needed for ecclesiastical purposes.[8] Notice of appeal was given. In Marylebone over £5000 a year was levied. The situation was complicated by repayment of old debts and the expenses of chapels and district churches. The Deputies called the attention of the vestry to the Poplar case. The vestry suggested that a conference should be called at which representatives of Marylebone and other parishes where compulsory rates are levied might discuss the question generally.[9] The Deputies welcomed the suggestion.[10] They determined to encourage resistance to the Special Acts under which rates were still raised.[11] In these affairs the Deputies did not succeed so well. The Marylebone conference seemed likely to fall

[1] 18 Nov. 1879. [2] 4 May 1880. [3] 2 May 1881. [4] 20 Dec. 1881.
[5] 24 Jan. 1882. [6] 7 Mar. and 22 Mar. 1882; Annual Report for 1882.
[7] 21 Nov. 1882. [8] 20 Feb. and 13 Mar. 1883. [9] Report for 1883.
[10] 13 Mar. 1883. [11] 11 April 1883.

through on account of lack of interest and the Liberation Society was appealed to for help.[1]

At Bethnal Green the Court of Appeal upheld the legality of the rate. The case turned on extremely technical arguments and judgment was given only after five months had lapsed since the hearing.[2] The vestry was unwilling to incur more expense, but the Deputies offered to bear one-third of the expense of an appeal to the House of Lords;[3] and to the Lords in due time an appeal went.[4]

In St Saviour's, Southwark, and in Holy Trinity and St Michael's, Coventry, compromises were arranged. The rates were abolished and replaced by funds raised mainly by subscriptions but aided from local rates and the Ecclesiastical Commissioners.[5] The Deputies welcomed and encouraged these charges. They subscribed £10 to help agitation against a rate in Pontefract; but the case was lost in Queen's Bench on a small technical point of local importance only.[6]

Though it is long and even tedious, though there is little that is picturesque and something that is squalid in it, the story of the Deputies' fight against Church Rates is worth telling in some detail —for the sake of the Deputies, and for the understanding of English religious and political life.

On the one hand no part of the Deputies' story illustrates better their shrewdness, patience, and indomitable pertinacity, their power of concentrating their efforts on a particular and limited objective, their unsuspected importance in English politics and their essential English temper.

On the other hand, if we are to understand English religion and English society in the 19th century we must measure the cleavage between the Established Church and Dissent. That is a commonplace, but it is impossible to measure that cleavage without tracing step by step as they traced it the dreary path from 1834 when abolition was first mooted to 1868 when it was achieved. Church Rates came to have a symbolical value for the parties; this was

---

[1] 13 June 1883. [2] Report for 1884. [3] 22 Jan. 1884.
[4] 18 Nov. 1884. [5] 18 Dec. 1883 and Reports of 1884.
[6] 22 Jan. and 17 June 1884.

not a matter which concerned ecclesiastical leaders only—it concerned every parish and almost every parishioner. Few were indifferent or unaffected—the controversy came home to them as even the Corporation and Test Acts had not done. A little of the same feeling exists about the Trade Union political levy in our time; but to make it comparable we should have to imagine each Trade Union branch equally divided, with two parties ready to carry their opposition to martyrdom if necessary, and with the backing of hundreds of years of tradition. That certainly does not exist, but in 19th-century parishes it did. On the one hand there was a sense of accumulated and accumulating injustice felt more consciously, more acutely, more widely every year. On the other was a sense of irritation against the implacable assailants of traditional and well-established rights, and to this was added the infuriating knowledge that, whatever victories might be won in Parliament, the battle was slowly but surely being lost in every parish. More than a generation of sour struggle in vestry meetings, in the courts, in the Commons and in the Lords poisoned the relations of Anglicanism and Dissent. Not until a new generation had lived out its time and the memory of that struggle had died could the two parties begin to form an impartial judgment of one another.

CHAPTER 6

OATHS AND DECLARATIONS

THE DEPUTIES were for ever talking about their concern for the rights of conscience. It was not mere verbiage. On scores of occasions they proved the sincerity of their claim that they supported religious freedom for all men. In nothing did they shew a more disinterested public spirit than in their untiring efforts to abolish tests and oaths and to replace them by declarations. Inasmuch as most of the oaths which survived after 1828 presented no difficulty to orthodox Dissenters, the Deputies' energy is the more praiseworthy. The reform of municipal corporations in 1835 brought into prominence the declarations still required from office-holders.

Already in 1831 the Deputies had petitioned unsuccessfully that there might be such a modification in the declaration as would enable Jews to hold office.[1] In 1833 the old privilege of Quakers to substitute an affirmation for an oath was extended to Moravians and Separatists; the privilege was to be effective for all purposes. These concessions to limited classes did not go far enough for the Deputies. In 1836 they instructed their Committee to try to secure the complete abolition of the declaration about the Church of England required by the legislation of 1828 and by the recent statute for municipal reform. The declaration was 'founded on false principles and productive of practical inconvenience'.[2]

Next year they seized the opportunity of achieving at least a part of their object. They petitioned the Commons concerning a Bill then before the House. They pointed out that many persons had conscientious scruples about subscribing the declaration required. These were excluded or had to trust to an Indemnity Act in the same manner as Dissenters in general had to do before 1828.

[1] See p. 211.　　　　　　　　　　　　　　[2] 27 Jan. 1836.

Indemnity Acts to legalize the evasion of a known law were calculated to weaken respect for law. The Bill as it stood would relieve Quakers and Moravians but no others. If the mention of Quakers and Moravians had not been made, all conscientious objectors would have been relieved. The Deputies press for amendments to include 'all classes of religionists entertaining conscientious objections'.[1] The Bill in its final shape came nearer to the Deputies' wishes. It included ex-Quakers and ex-Moravians who, having abandoned their connexion with those sects, had carried over their objections to oaths.

The Deputies continued to urge that the privilege should not be confined to particular sects and their ex-members.

Mr Wood's Bill in 1850 to allow all who objected to oaths on religious grounds to substitute an affirmation was supported by a petition;[2] as was Mr Apsley Pellatt's Bill to the same effect in 1854.[3] Petitions asking for the relief of all who had conscientious objections were made in 1855[4] and 1856,[5] and 1857,[6] and 1858,[7] and 1859.[8]

In 1861 the Deputies moved a step farther, and struck out the word 'conscientious' from the prayer. They simply urged that the declarations were unnecessary and in fact often omitted without bad results.[9] Mr Hadfield's Office Qualification Bill, which went farther and would have abolished the declarations completely, was supported by the Deputies, but was thrown out by the Lords in 1862.[10] In the following year the Bill passed the Commons and the Deputies were willing to petition the Lords in its favour.[11] In 1865 the Deputies petitioned the Lords in favour of a similar Bill but the Lords rejected it.[12] Next year the Deputies petitioned the Lord again,[13] and at last had the satisfaction of congratulating Mr Hadfield on the passing of his Bill and of thanking him 'for his long and persevering efforts to get rid of those declarations'.[14] The Act makes declarations unnecessary as a qualification for

---

[1] 6 Dec. 1837.   [2] 15 Mar. 1850.
[3] 12 May 1854. Apsley Pellatt became the Deputies' Chairman in the following year.
[4] 2 Feb. 1855.   [5] 7 Feb. 1856.   [6] 9 Jan. 1857.
[7] 9 Feb. 1858.   [8] 10 Feb. 1859.   [9] 22 Feb. 1861.
[10] 18 June 1862.   [11] 11 Mar. 1863.   [12] 3 April and 3 May 1865.
[13] 14 Feb. and 15 Mar. 1866.   [14] 8 August 1866. 29 and 30 Vict. c.22.

municipal offices and employment or for accepting from the Crown any patent or commission.

The Deputies had always taken the view that religious tests, whether by oaths or declarations, were unnecessary for civil offices because they were irrelevant. They had stated this from the beginning; but if Parliament would only go step by step they would press for more exceptions till the list included all *conscientious* objectors, and finally, all objectors. Tests would then cease to be the rule, and privileges to be doled out to lists of people noted as freaks.

Your petitioners feel that all religious tests are repugnant to true Christianity, and that the evidence of a man's fitness for office should be his good conduct and the esteem of his fellow citizens.[1]

The integrity of their position may be verified from the Bradlaugh controversy,[2] in which the Deputies' principles over-rode their prejudices—for they detested his views. The Ministerial Body shared the same point of view:

Deeply regretting the personal associations which are at present connected with the subject, but separating itself entirely from them, the General Body regards itself bound in pursuance of its ancient and uniform principle to petition in favour of the Bill.[3]

The Bill referred to was that introduced by Gladstone in 1883, which would have cleared up the controversy by allowing Bradlaugh to enter Parliament by making an affirmation. The Deputies' petition stated that they regarded the Bill as simply an extension of the principle which had already given relief to Roman Catholics, Quakers and Jews; they hoped that liberty in civil matters should not be in any way affected by opinions on religious subjects.

The Bill was lost, but in 1885 another was introduced, with the general object of making a declaration alternative to an oath; and once more the Deputies gave 'hearty support', declaring that the occasions on which oaths were required were 'unnecessarily numerous' and that multiplication lessened solemnity.[4] But again

---

[1] Deputies' petition of 1837.

[2] See Francis Holland's continuation of Erskine May's *Constitutional History*, vol. III, pp. 222-8, for a useful summary.

[3] Ministers' Minutes, 10 April 1883.   [4] 15 April 1885.

the Bill failed, and it was not until 1888 that success came. The Deputies discussed with Bradlaugh the precise wording of his Oaths Bill,[1] and noted its success.[2]

---

[1] 22 Mar. and 5 April 1888. [2] 27 Sept. 1888.

CHAPTER 7

RELATIONS WITH OTHER NONCONFORMISTS

(a) Roman Catholics

THE DEPUTIES have to their credit a record of attempts to amend the law not merely for themselves but for others who suffered from Anglican privileges. It is noteworthy that quite often this generous attitude provoked no response in those whom the Deputies helped. They sometimes declined to help the Deputies in return. They sometimes worked against the Deputies if some narrower gain of their own was, or was fancied to be, affected.

The Deputies were warm friends of Roman Catholic Emancipation and shewed their colours vigorously.

In 1825, as part of the campaign against any relaxation of the penal laws, petitions purporting to be the petitions of Protestant Dissenters were presented in both Houses, praying that no concessions should be made. Hearing of this, the Deputies held a special General Meeting. The meeting, which was particularly large (being attended by over 130 Deputies), disavowed any concurrence in, or approval of, the petitions; the Deputies would continue as in the past, at all seasonable opportunities, to urge upon the legislature 'the impolicy and injustice of every sort of penalty or disability, civil or political, for conscience' sake'.[1] When later in the same year they heard of 'an intended meeting' on the same subject, the Deputies considered holding another special meeting of their own, but came to the conclusion that it would be inexpedient.[2]

No sooner had the Dissenters been relieved of their chief political disabilities by the repeal of the Test and Corporation Acts

[1] 29 April 1825.   [2] 21 June 1825

than they threw themselves again into the campaign for Roman Catholic Relief. In February 1829 they approved short petitions in the same words to both Houses. Declaring themselves 'fully sensible of the wise and conciliatory Policy of the Government and the Legislature towards the Protestant Dissenters', they lament 'to see the peace of Society still disturbed by the Divisions and Jealousies' arising out of a continuance of laws similar to the Test Act. They therefore declare their joy at the prospect of a removal of all civil disabilities on account of religious faith and worship.[1] Lord Holland agreed to present the petition to the Lords, William Smith presenting it to the Commons.[2] The Deputies also paid for and circulated a pamphlet by the Rev. William Orme containing Strictures on a petition in opposition to the Roman Catholic Relief Bill purporting to come from the Ministers of London.[3]

The Annual Report for 1829 contained some reflections on the Catholic Relief Act of that year.

It is well known that very great pains were taken to excite public alarm on this most interesting question, and endeavours were used to represent the Dissenters as joining in a clamour so inconsiderate as that, without attributing unworthy motives, it is scarcely too much to say that it was pushed to an extreme which seemed but too likely to endanger the tranquillity and even the safety of the Realm.

Your Committee have observed with much pleasure that since the measure was sanctioned by the Legislature the agitation of the Country has subsided, and the dreadful denunciations of injury to the Constitution and ruin to the Church have ceased to terrify, and they profess to think themselves highly favoured in having been permitted to witness an event so honorable to the present age, so auspicious of future peace and improvement, and in such perfect unison with those liberal and Christian principles to which they have ever appealed as the basis and justification of their dissent, and which increases tenfold their confidence in the complete and final separation of Religion and politics, leaving to each its own province, and consigning each to its own Judge.[4]

The relations of the Dissenters and the Roman Catholics were probably more friendly in these years than at any time before or

[1] 13 Feb. 1829
[2] 27 Feb. and 27 Mar. 1829
[3] 27 Nov. 1829
[4] Report for 1829

since. The presence of Roman Catholics at the dinner to celebrate the repeal of the Test and Corporation Acts symbolized the feeling.[1] To any limitations on the freedom of Roman Catholics the Deputies were always to shew themselves hostile. They did not attribute to Roman Catholics any belief in religious equality which Roman Catholics did not possess. History made them suspicious lest Roman Catholics should attempt to secure unfair privileges for themselves; but the Deputies contrived to be wary without being unjust. They could not persuade themselves that the exorbitant pretensions of Rome were a reason for giving Roman Catholics less than equality.

Those same convictions about the relation of Church and State which had made the Deputies support Roman Catholic Relief made them join in opposition to a Prisons Bill enabling Roman Catholic Prison chaplains to be paid out of county rates. In their petition, which was presented by Lord Shaftesbury, they asserted 'the inalienable right of every individual however humble may be his station in life whether in or out of gaol to avail himself of the instructions of such minister of religion as he prefers', but not at the expense of persons of different religious convictions. The Bill introduced a new principle into English legislation, namely the payment of ministers other than those of the Established Church. There was no reason to suppose that either the Roman Catholic or Protestant Dissenting ministers had been hitherto anything but indefatigable 'in their attentions to that unfortunate class of persons'. It was understood that the proposal came from the Roman Catholic side. What was now asked for in prisons would be speedily asked for in workhouses. The Bill failed by one vote.[2]

In 1846 the Annual Report mentions the passing into law of the Roman Catholic Relief Bill. It did not affect Dissenters, but it gratified the Deputies to see removed 'old accumulated restrictions against their fellow-subjects who differed widely in their religious opinion from themselves'.[3]

This expression of goodwill rings the more agreeably because at this time, as for the rest of the century, the Deputies had more

[1] See p. 248.   [2] 1 Aug. 1838.   [3] Report for 1846.

occasion to check Roman Catholic claims than to remove Roman Catholic grievances. England was about to be torn by the struggle over the grant of State funds to assist Maynooth College.[1]

The Papal Bull which asserted the Pope's ecclesiastical jurisdiction over England and the establishment of a Roman Catholic hierarchy with territorial titles presented a pretty puzzle to the Deputies. It was one of their fundamental principles that every Church was entitled to conduct its business in its own way without interference from the State. They were therefore naturally inclined to deprecate any protest or retaliation. But, though this clearly appears, it is also clear that a second set of considerations had influence with them. In these very years that same Roman Catholic Church which aggressively asserted its freedom from State control was pressing for State subvention. Moreover the Church of England was believed to be drifting under 'Puseyite' influences to Rome. These were the years of melodramatic conversions. The intimate association of the Anglican Church with the State and its suspected association with Rome served to confuse the issue. In the event the Deputies used the incident to point the favourite moral of which they were sure and about which they were united: the need to sever all connexions of State and Church and to end all subversion of religion in order that ecclesiastical affairs and civil politics might take their separate ways independently.

The record of the Deputies' actions illustrates these varied feelings. The sub-committee appointed on 15 Nov. 1850 to consider if the Pope's assumption of ecclesiastical dominion in England called for any statement by Dissenters reported promptly that 'our civil rights' were not so affected as to make a declaration desirable at present.[2] The Committee adopted the same view,[3] and probably included it in the Annual Report for 1850. That Report is unfortunately one of the few of this period not transcribed in the Minute Books. When the Deputies met to receive the Report, and the Chairman proposed its adoption, it was first moved that the resolution about papal aggression should be expunged; and then that consideration should be delayed for a week.[4] At the adjourned meeting, two Committee meetings having considered the matter

---

[1] See p. 444.   [2] 18 Nov. 1850.   [3] 22 Nov. 1850.   [4] 3 Jan. 1851.

meanwhile, the original resolution in favour of no action[1] was carried by a large majority, nine only voting for expunging it and a fresh amendment getting no seconder.

Yet the meeting was not satisfied. A small minority, as it proved, wished for some action. A resolution was therefore moved which began by recording the Deputies' 'continued and unmitigated opposition to all penal enactments on account of religious opinion'. It was nevertheless 'the bounden and especial duty of Protestant Dissenters to resist by every legitimate means the encroachments of the Papacy in this Country, believing it to be the sworn and determined foe of civil and religious liberty'. The Deputies ought therefore, when Parliament reassembled, to express their views 'on the present aspects of Popery especially its recent aggressive policy'. They ought to petition Parliament 'against any legislative encouragement of that system, and particularly against the continuance of any pecuniary grant towards its support either in the United Kingdom or its dependencies'.

This resolution was carried by 34 to 24, after the defeat by 23 to 34 of a milder amendment. The amendment regarded 'the rescript lately issued by the Pope of Rome' as 'an act of priestly assumption', but considered that 'it would be both impolitic and unjust to attempt by legal enactment to prevent any portion of Her Majesty's subjects from following out that form of religious worship or Church government which they may prefer'. The amendment ended with a similar moral: it is wrong for the State to foster any ecclesiastical body or institution by State connexion or State endowment. It is not difficult to discern Maynooth written between the lines both of the resolution and of the amendment.[2]

It proved difficult to get a suitable expression of the Deputies' views. At first the Committee tried to agree on a resolution in advance approving of the Ministers' statements in the House of Commons 'more especially as Her Majesty's Ministers have declared themselves decided friends of religious liberty'.[3] As the Government Bill had not been printed when the Deputies met two days later, the Committee thought it desirable not to offer any resolution and the Deputies adjourned their meeting for a

---

[1] So I read the minutes.   [2] 10 Jan. 1851.   [3] 12 Feb. 1851.

fortnight.[1] The political crisis and Lord John Russell's attempt to make a coalition with the Peelites led to more delay: 'under the peculiar circumstances of the Government', said the Committee on 25 February 1851, 'it is not desirable to canvass the merits of the Ecclesiastical Titles Bill at the present juncture'.

When the Deputies met on 31 March the same division of opinion remained. The resolution, which on a show of hands was declared carried, asserted that the conferring of territorial titles and a cardinalate on British subjects, considered as the acts of a temporal potentate, were aggressions on the Prerogative of the Crown, which is constitutionally the fountain of honour. They were aggressions too on the liberties of Her Majesty's subjects. Even in professedly popish countries this would not be permitted without the express sanction of the sovereign authority. These acts are the result of the disposition shewn by successive administrations to endow Romanism, to patronize and defer to Roman Catholic bishops in England, Ireland, and the colonies. Against this Protestant Dissenters have maintained a uniform testimony. While maintaining the principles of civil and religious liberty, the Deputies considered the Ecclesiastical Titles Bill, as modified, 'inadequate to vindicate the independence of the Crown and the honor of the Country'. Finally they would rejoice at the withdrawal of State patronage from every portion of the Church, Episcopalian, Presbyterian, Methodist, Roman Catholic or other in every part of the Empire. The establishment, support, or control of religion by the State is opposed to the principles of Christianity.

The still longer amendment was lost. It asserted the inalienable birthright of every human being to worship God according to his conscience; in this he is not accountable 'to any man or body of men whether called the Church or the State'. For the State to compel a man to support a religion which he holds untrue is contrary to the Word of God. The Deputies have taken every suitable opportunity to protest against the unrighteous claims of the Church of England; they have suffered less from the practical oppression of the Roman Church but they continue to feel their forefathers' 'abhorrence of popery' and are 'ready to oppose it

[1] 14 Feb. 1851.

with all the means which the Word of God and their own principles allow them to employ'. They fear the spread of popish principles in the Church of England and the consequent encouragement to Rome. They protest against the claims made in the Bull to the spiritual government of England, especially against the insolent and haughty manner of the claim.

They cannot however allow their hatred of popery and their indignation at its recent assumptions to cause them to forget those great principles of religious liberty of which they have always been the earnest advocates.

They therefore regret the attempt now making in the Commons House of Parliament to interfere by Legislative enactment with the discipline and organization of the Romish Church because they believe it to be a violation of religious liberty and because they are firmly convinced that there are many persons who will gladly avail themselves of this dangerous precedent to intermeddle with other non-established religious bodies in this country.

Finally they regard the present struggle of parties in relation to the recent papal aggression as affording another striking example of the social and political as well as religious evils attending the connection of Church and State and they earnestly call upon all Protestant Dissenters to renew their efforts to repeal this unhallowed alliance and not to compromise their principles by recognizing the right of the state to interfere with the organization of any religious body whatever.

Despite opposition to the end from the minority, it was resolved to petition Parliament and to advertise the resolutions.[1]

The minority resolution deserves attention. It is sufficient to give the lie to Hume, who told Gladstone that the Dissenters knew nothing about religious liberty and asked for his speech against the Bill to circulate among them. Hume was of course a bitter Unitarian opponent of the orthodox Dissenters.[2] That at such a moment among the sons of Calvin, the farthest removed from Rome, so noble a statement of ecclesiastical freedom should have been made is a memorial of great churchmanship. The resolution is noteworthy in a second way. It illustrates the constant fear of the Deputies that on some pretext or other (such as charitable

---

[1] 31 Mar. 1851.　　　　　　　　　[2] See p. 152.

trusts) the State would encroach on the traditional independence of the Dissenting Churches. Leviathan was a foe more dangerous even than the Scarlet Woman and the Man of Sin.

Three years later, a Parliamentary Committee consisting of about fifty members of Parliament interested in the promotion of religious liberty was organized to meet each Wednesday. When it was first under discussion the question of inviting Roman Catholics was considered, but it was decided to include only Protestant Dissenters and 'liberal Churchmen'. The Liberation Society and the so-called Presbyterian Divines as well as the Deputies had an official representative on the body, and the Deputies' Secretary acted as its secretary.[1]

In 1865 the Committee resolved by a vote of 5 to 2 to petition in favour of a Bill to relieve Roman Catholics of the oath which the legislation of 1829 had required of them, and to substitute a more palatable oath;[2] but though this passed the Commons, it was rejected by the Lords.[3]

In 1891 they regretted the defeat of Gladstone's attempt to remove the religious disabilities attached to the offices of Lord Chancellor of England and Lord Lieutenant of Ireland.[4]

It is difficult to measure the depth of anti-Roman feeling in England at this time, but it is important to do so in order to do justice to the Deputies. Feeling had hardened since 1829. The spectacular conversions from the Oxford Movement to Roman Catholicism on one side and the increasing influence of the Oxford Movement on the other combined to produce a feeling of immense and immeasurable danger from Rome. Gladstone said of Parliament in 1854: 'We have a parliament which, were the measure of 1829 not law at this moment, would I think probably refuse to make it law.'[5]

This reluctance to encourage Rome served also to strengthen the hands of those who wished to keep Dissenters out of Oxford and Cambridge: to abolish Anglican privilege was to open the doors to Roman Catholics as well as to Dissenters. And at the end of the century the wider education controversy made the fear

---

[1] 3 Mar. 1854.   [2] 3 April 1865.   [3] 5 July 1865.
[4] 17 Feb. 1891.   [5] Morley, *Life of Gladstone*, vol. 1, p. 506.

vocal. In 1898 the Deputies expressed the opinion that the spread of ritualism in the Church of England was an encouragement to Rome and a menace to civil and religious liberty:

> In reviewing the proceedings in Parliament since their last meeting, the Deputies feel bound to express deep dissatisfaction with the educational measures of the Government as well as with their willingness to accede to the revolutionary demands of the Roman Catholic hierarchy to create and endow a University in Ireland which will be more or less under their control.[1]

The last incident illustrating this suspicion occurred in 1908, when the Deputies investigated a rumour that the London County Council had included propagandist publications of the Catholic Truth Society on its prize list, and noted with satisfaction that there was no truth in it;[2] an incident typical of their vigilance.

(b) Jews and Quakers

To the Jews as to the Roman Catholics the Deputies gave such help as they could from time to time. The removal of most of the civil disabilities of Protestant and Roman Catholic Dissenters in 1828 and 1829 had the natural effect of drawing attention to the disabilities of the Jews. An unintended consequence of the Repeal of the Test Act in 1828 had been indeed to increase those disabilities. Until 1828 Jews had shared the benefits of the Indemnity Acts and had been admitted to forbidden offices; but the declaration 'on the true faith of a Christian', which had replaced the oath, still excluded Jews; and there was now no Indemnity Act. The Deputies had of course always protested on quite general grounds against the declaration. As a religious test for a civil office, it was objectionable, even though it did not exclude them.[3]

In 1831 they petitioned both Houses to repeal laws attaching any civil disqualifications to Jews, asking especially for an amendment of this declaration. They remarked that having themselves been recently relieved from such disabilities they felt most anxious that no class of their fellow-citizens should so suffer. Lord Holland and Lord John Russell were asked to present the Petition.[4] The

---

[1] 27 April 1898.   [2] 22 May 1908.   [3] See p. 237.   [4] 11 Feb. 1831.

Commons shewed signs of meeting these wishes, but the Lords were adamant.

Ten years later a Bill was before the Commons to allow Jews to take advantage of an Act passed in 1837 for the relief of Quakers, Moravians and Separatists elected to municipal offices. They were allowed to make a declaration,[1] and in petitioning that Jews should have the same privilege the Deputies quaintly plead that 'to exclude from civil offices believers in the Laws of Moses is to condemn those Laws as making men bad Citizens'.[2] Again the Commons passed and the Lords rejected the Bill.[3]

In 1845 the Committee petitioned in favour of another Bill to admit Jews to municipal offices, but added their opinion that Jews should be eligible also for seats in the legislature and for all civil offices.[4] The Bill passed, and municipal offices were opened.

Two years later the Deputies went a step farther. Baron Lionel Nathan de Rothschild had been elected with Lord John Russell to the Commons for the City of London. The occasion was too good to be lost. The Deputies petitioned the Lords and Commons to admit Jews to both Houses 'in accordance with the genius of Christianity and the free Spirit of the British Constitution'.[5]

'You are aware', the Committee reported in due time, 'that this Bill so consonant with Christian charity passed the House of Commons, but was rejected by the House in which Christian Bishops have a seat and voice'.[6]

In 1853, when the Bill for the Registration of Places of Worship was under consideration by the Deputies, the interests of the Jewish congregations were not overlooked. A clause was prepared with special reference to them. It was dropped, however, as the Jewish Deputies were content with the law as it stood.[7]

In some ways the Jews, like the Quakers, had been the spoilt children of a persecuting State. They had enjoyed, for instance, the privilege of celebrating marriage according to their own rites when orthodox Dissenters had been deprived of the privilege.

[1] See p. 200. [2] 26 Mar. 1841. [3] Annual Report for 1841.
[4] 28 April 1845. [5] 20 Dec. 1847 and 14 Feb. 1848. [6] Report for 1848.
[7] 27 June 1853.

They were therefore concerned that any general improvement of the marriage laws to give more justice to the orthodox Dissenters should not prejudice the specially favoured position already held by themselves. In outwitting or buying off the various possible opponents of the Dissenters Marriage Bill in 1855 the Deputies had to see that a special clause put Jews and Quakers outside the operation of the Bill.[1]

It has become a matter of convention, whenever the Quakers are mentioned in historical narrative, to pay a tribute to their liberal and generous support of all humanitarian and progressive measures. It is to be regretted that the records of the Deputies do not justify the observance of this convention. The relations of the Quakers and the Deputies provide little evidence of that rather romantic virtue with which it has become fashionable to endow the Quakers. They appear in their relations with the Deputies as willing indeed to co-operate when their own interests were at stake, but rather indisposed to join in struggles for justice when only other men were concerned. They contrast indeed unfavourably with the Wesleyan Methodists in this. Despite their conservative tendencies and their reputation for aloofness from the general interests of Dissent, the Wesleyans worked with Deputies more heartily than the Quakers did; and the Wesleyans gave the Deputies help on critical occasions when their own interests were already safeguarded.[2]

The Quakers were indeed the spoilt children of a persecuting State. At a comparatively early stage in their history they had secured special privileges for themselves. Unlike orthodox Dissenters, they might worship behind locked doors and celebrate marriages according to their own rites. Many statutes had confirmed their peculiar privilege of making declarations in place of oaths. They could sit in Parliament as a result of this privilege. They were not personally interested therefore in many of the Deputies' struggles. Where they were interested no other-worldly superiority to political methods prevented their taking an effective share in the struggles. They shewed, for instance, considerable interest in attempts to abolish Church Rates. The Deputies asked

---

[1] 18 May 1855.   [2] See p. 344.

for their co-operation by approaching their Yearly Meeting in 1837[1] and again in 1849;[2] and John Bright's interest in the later stages of the controversy was most valuable, but even in that matter they were in a favoured position. An act of 1836 provided special machinery for the collection of rates from Quakers who resisted. This did not escape the eye of the Deputies. In petitioning in 1840 about the general grievances of Dissenters they used the concession made to Quakers to bring out the grotesqueness of imprisoning Thorogood,[3] who had declined to pay a rate of 5s. 6d.

Your petitioners believe that by a recent Statute 5 and 6 William IV c. 74 no member of the Society of Friends can be incarcerated for like conduct by which Act an individual of that Society was released from Carlow jail where he had been imprisoned for his opposition to Church rates.[4]

In 1855 the Quakers, like the Jews, caused the Deputies some anxiety when a Dissenters Marriage Bill was before Parliament.[5]

The least agreeable incident in the relations of the Deputies and the Quakers was perhaps that which occurred in connexion with the attempt to save Bunhill Fields burial ground from desecration by the Ecclesiastical Commissioners. It was a historic occasion, and the deepest sentiments were outraged. If ever there was an occasion for a united expression of outraged piety, this was it. The Deputies invited eleven bodies representing all classes of Dissenters to join with them in a deputation to the Home Secretary. Even the Unitarians sank their traditional rancour against the Deputies. Only the Quakers declined the invitation.[6] Doubtless the Society of Friends has deserved many of the bouquets thrown to it by social and political historians, but the Deputies' records do not shew it in an amiable or generous light.

---

[1] 29 Mar. 1837.   [2] 9 Mar. 1849: a request to support Trelawney's motion.
[3] See p. 179.
[4] 2 Jan. 1840. The Statute should be quoted as 6 and 7 William IV c. 71.
[5] See p. 281.   [6] 1 Mar. 1867.

PART III

FROM TOLERATION TO RELIGIOUS EQUALITY

CHAPTER 1

THE REPEAL OF THE TEST AND CORPORATION ACTS

TO SECURE the repeal of the Corporation and Test Acts had always been the main object for which the Deputies existed; indeed, they had at first no other object. It was only the failure of their first efforts that made them conceive the expediency of continuing the Deputation 'as a permanent Guardian of the civil interests of the Dissenting Body to which recourse might be had for Assistance in procuring Redress of Grievances'.[1] They could not imagine, when they first made their application for relief to Walpole, that their descendants would have to wait for justice until the days of Wellington and Peel.

As early as 1736 and 1739 motions were unsuccessfully brought before the House of Commons for the Repeal of the Acts;[2] but after the 1745 Rebellion, Dissenters secured a partial relief. They had taken a prominent part in the defence measures against Prince Charles Edward; and to protect them from the consequences of their loyalty they had to be indemnified for their breaches of the Test Act. An Act of Indemnity passed in 1747 proved to be the first of a series passed each year for 85 years, to protect Dissenters from certain of the penalties which they had incurred by holding offices without being properly qualified under the Acts. These Indemnity Acts, however, did not in any degree diminish the hatred of the Dissenters for the penal laws. Other grievances might in practice be more onerous, but the penal laws carried the stigma of inferiority which bred the other grievances.

After half a century, another determined effort was made to get them repealed, with the help of Charles James Fox and Henry Beaufoy. A United Committee was set up to conduct the appeal,

[1] 17 Mar. 1823.   [2] See above, p. 28.

which was to be the model for all future campaigns of the Deputies.[1] The Deputies had since their inception had a Committee of Correspondence which kept in touch with every county through a list of leading Dissenters revised from time to time. Through this rudimentary organization local committees were formed to prepare petitions, pass resolutions, and collect subscriptions. The United Committee, consisting of London representatives, clerical and lay, of the various denominations, was temporarily enlarged to receive delegates from the country. In 1787, Beaufoy's motion in the Commons was easily defeated; but in 1789, with the support of Fox, William Smith and others, he came near to success, the House dividing 124 to 104 against the motion. The Dissenters felt that emancipation was at hand; but in 1790, when Fox himself proposed the motion, the opposition had rallied: the motion was defeated by 294 to 105 votes. The vote, 'combined with the events that very soon after happened'[2]—the French Revolution and the Napoleonic Wars—meant the postponement of Repeal for a generation. The United Committee lingered on until 1795, but by that date the futility of any immediate appeal to Parliament was clear.

The first sign of renewed hope for Dissenters was the defeat of Lord Sidmouth's attempt, in 1811, to limit the liberty enjoyed by Dissenters under the Toleration Acts of 1689 and 1779.[3] The struggle which defeated Sidmouth led straight into an agitation which procured almost immediately the repeal of the Five Mile and Conventicle Acts. Lord Liverpool, having received a Deputation from the Deputies 'with the greatest attention', brought in a Government Bill which passed the House of Lords on July 29th, 1812; besides the Five Mile and Conventicle Acts, it repealed also the Act of Charles II (13 & 14 C. II, c.1) against refusal to take oaths, and made new and more liberal provisions for the registration of Dissenting places of worship.

This success is remarkable for several things. It is the beginning of co-operation between the Deputies and the Methodists—'the General Committee of the late Rev. John Wesley's Societies'; and

---

[1] *Sketch*, pp. 46 ff.   [2] 7 Mar. 1823.
[3] See full account in Chapter 3 of Part II, and *Sketch*, pp. 82 ff.

also between the Deputies and the recently founded Protestant Society.[1] It is also the beginning of a new temper. As recently as February 1812, a petition of the Deputies had argued their rights in an academic way, mentioning no laws or proposals specifically. But a year later they are speaking of 'breaking every bond and abolishing any shackle';[2] and though they gratefully received the 1812 Acts as 'an instalment of religious liberty', within six months they were instructing the Committee to prepare a petition to Parliament that session, praying for the complete repeal of all such laws.[3] Yet when, in February 1812, they had considered whether to co-operate in a petition drawn in the widest terms, asking for complete abolition of all laws to the prejudice of any Dissenters from the Established Church, which was being signed by Anglicans and Roman Catholics as well as Protestant Dissenters,[4] they had decided at a special meeting to take no action.[5]

The next few years were full of such events as made any success unlikely, and it was not until 1817 that the General Meeting reminded itself that the repeal of the Corporation and Test Acts was the original object of the Deputation, and that 'it becomes our bounden duty to embrace every fair opportunity of promoting that desirable object'.[6] But no action seems to have followed, and more than a decade was in fact to elapse before the Acts were repealed. This period is full of abortive efforts like those of 1819, when the General Meeting again raised the question of repeal.[7] The Committee met, and then adjourned for a fortnight for 'Enquiry and Reflection'.[8] It later met and deliberated with a committee of the Dissenting ministers; but 'from the best information they are able to obtain as well as from the most mature consideration' the joint committee decided that the time was not propitious for an application. Being pressed at the next Annual General Meeting to re-examine the question, they still had to return the same answer; deciding that the King's death and the dissolution of Parliament necessitated postponement.[9]

---

[1] For Protestant Society, see p. 46.   [2] 23 Feb. 1813.
[3] 29 Jan. 1813.   [4] 28 Feb. 1812.   [5] 13 Mar. 1812.
[6] 31 Jan. 1817.   [7] 29 Jan. 1819.   [8] 26 Feb. 1819.
[9] 11 Feb. 1820.

Most of the history text-books give considerable attention to Roman Catholic Emancipation in 1829, but pass over the repeal of the Acts affecting Protestant Dissenters in a few words. The few words usually give the impression that the repeal of the Corporation and Test Acts happened almost automatically as a mere prelude to Roman Catholic Emancipation, without trouble to anyone. Only ignorance of the history of the Deputies can make this view tenable. What are the facts about the decade before 1828?

These years were in fact full of activity and agitation. The Dissenters were keenly anxious to secure Repeal and determined to lose no opportunity; but they judged the prospects of success in different ways. The Committee of Deputies, led by the sagacious William Smith, M.P., was probably the best informed group of Dissenters; and until the eve of the final campaign the Committee appears never to have thought the moment auspicious, or to have encouraged an attempt at a decisive action. The general body of the Deputies was much more impatient, more optimistic, and less well informed. It sometimes suspected the Committee of a lack of enthusiasm. The Ministers of the Three Denominations, the Unitarian Association, and the Protestant Society expressed different views, the Unitarians being more inclined to action than the Deputies' Committee, and the Protestant Society even less inclined. One thing, however, is clear. The restiveness of the rank and file provided sharp stimulus to action, and constant enquiries from the Deputies' Committee kept the subject of Repeal clearly before the Government and friendly members of both Houses. Opinion was being shaped in the country and in Westminster by persistent and competent men. The great emancipation of Dissenters from the last and worst legacy of the House of Stuart did not 'just happen' as part of a general and inevitable evolution of public opinion.

It would be tedious to record step by step the postponements of the decade; but it is necessary to notice some details of the petitions presented to Parliament, because, even if without apparent result, they shew the evolution of the Deputies' thought, and were without doubt instrumental in bringing about part of the change in opinion. It is also necessary to watch rather carefully the relations between the body of Deputies and their Committee; and the Deputies and other Nonconformist bodies, as well as the Dissenting community at large.

A well-reasoned petition prepared in the spring of 1820 was presented to the two Houses of Parliament by Lord Holland and William Smith.[1] It urged the

expedience of abolishing every remnant of that system of coercion and restraint on religious profession which had its origin in times of darkness and intolerance; and by which your Petitioners are to this day, severely, and as they presume to think, most injuriously affected.

Having recapitulated the Deputies' favourite historical argument about Dissenting loyalty to the House of Hanover, it passed to theory, asserting private judgment in religion to be one of the 'absolute natural rights'. It gratefully recorded that

those truths which but a few generations ago could not have been asserted but at the risque of Personal Liberty and even of Life are now almost completely and universally recognized in every Protestant State

and that more had been done to 'emancipate religion from the civil thraldom' under George III than under any monarch since William III. Freedom was nevertheless not complete as long as Nonconformity was attended by such 'Disabilities and consequent Degradation' as was otherwise known to the law only as the appropriate penalty for heinous crimes. The petition countered the argument that the Indemnity Acts did away with any real grievance (an argument still to be found in almost any text-book), by saying that 'a partial and discretional Indemnity . . . is neither constitutional Security nor Equal Justice'. The protection of Dissenters by the Acts is incidental, since 'for their ease or relief they never were intended'; and the injury felt is not that the number of Dissenters in office is perhaps less than it might be, but that all Dissenters, indiscrimately, are held up to public odium as persons unworthy of office.

Quoting King William's remark that 'granting ease to the Dissenters would contribute very much to the Establishment of

[1] 26 May 1820.

the Church', they argued that the disabilities, even if justified, would do less for the success of the Establishment than justice and liberality. Finally, the use of the sacrament as a test caused disgust to many religious persons and was a scandal to religion. It was more than useless: it deterred the conscientious but was no bar to the unprincipled and ambitious. . . . This, however, was not the business of the petitioners: they would be equally injured by any other impediment equally efficient (as against the conscientious) and 'for the impropriety of the Test, those who ordain it, and not those who suffer under it, are responsible'.

These main arguments, the historical, the theoretical, and the religious argument about the use of the test, were to form the basis of the case as it was argued all through the Repeal campaign. But the petition had no immediate result.

In 1823 the feeling of impatience in the body of the Deputation found active form. In January they asked for a special General Meeting to consider the expediency of application to Parliament, and coupled this in the same sentence with the consideration of an alteration in the method of electing the Committee.[1] The special General Meeting in three Resolutions expressed the opinion that

much more of the active and vigilant attention of this Deputation should be directed to the great object for which it was instituted and to which all other subjects of its attention, however useful, ought to be subordinated.

Parallel cases in history shewed the efficacy of unremitted attempts to enlighten the public; direction to one end of all the exertions of all who ought to co-operate; and applications to Parliament at every favourable opportunity. Reports, correspondence and appeals should point out to the public the actual state of religious toleration and the relief sought, and should establish constant communications between the Deputies and their constituents.

These resolutions, by an unusual direction, were to be printed at the head of the circular convening the first meeting of the Deputies in the current year. They can hardly be regarded as anything but a rebuke to a Committee which the Deputies (almost certainly without reason) thought a trifle dilatory. This attitude

[1] 3 Jan. 1823.

222

was emphasized by the decision to ensure new blood in the Committee. At least three members who had not served on any Committee during the past ten years were to be elected every year.

In accordance with this new spirit the Deputies next appointed expressed their pleasure in asking the Committee to proceed 'instantly, ardently, and prudently' to consider the measures recommended in the three resolutions. They based their confident optimism on the 'rapid progress of knowledge and just views of civil government' through all classes during the thirty years that had elapsed since the last appeal to Parliament; they counted on the 'candid attention of their countrymen' and the indication that the legislature participated in the 'increasing liberality of the times'.[1]

The action taken by the Committee was first to prepare the Deputies' own constituency. A statement was drawn up for general circulation among the Dissenters throughout the country.

The statement reiterated the history of the Deputies and of their attempts to get Repeal in 1736-9 and again in 1787-90. It explained the reasons for their lack of success then, and the futility of proceeding until 'some change in public opinion should be manifest'. It described how the Committee had filled the interval by preventing persecution and insult of Dissenters and asserting their claims to their property. It stated that signs of the desired change in public opinion were visible, and it enumerated amongst them 'the liberality of the present times' which had diminished the cases of persecution with which the Deputies had to deal: the Lords' decision of the Sheriff's Cause in 1767; the Act of 1779; the rejection of Sidmouth's Bill; and the repeal of the Statutes (called) against Blasphemy, but by which 'all discussion of very important disputed points was forbidden under dreadful penalties'.

It then proceeded to explain why, in spite of these encouraging signs, the Committee had refused to act as quickly as some had wished.

Since the discussions on the Catholic question the Committee, though aware of the broad distinction between that case and their own, yet seeing also in how many points they were connected and how great an

[1] 14 Feb. 1823.

influence the decision of the one might have on the other, have deliberately preferred to be vigilant rather than active.

The prejudices roused against Roman Catholics might only too easily be felt against all who were not members of the Establishment. The Committee, 'considering the great length into which that question has been, and may yet further be drawn, and sensible that many excellent and judicious persons are extremely anxious that the Dissenters should be fully prepared for another unanimous and energetic appeal' to Parliament at the first favourable moment, now sent out a copy of the 1820 petition and invited correspondence. It is not difficult to see that the Committee did not commit themselves even yet to the optimism of many 'excellent and judicious persons'.[1] A General Meeting approved the statement and asked for its circulation.

Another reason for caution and justification for delay at once appeared. The Protestant Society asked the Deputies to consider postponing all publications on the Test and Corporation Acts while the Marriage Bill was pending in Parliament. Any excitement on the general question might indispose Parliament to grant the very important relief sought by the Marriage Bill.[2] Accordingly the matter was postponed. By June it was thought safe to advertise the statement and petitions in religious magazines. Meanwhile one minister in each county was asked to help the Deputies to perfect their lists of congregations throughout the country.[3] With some trouble the lists were compiled and in November the Secretary was instructed to order 2,500 copies of the address and petition and circulate it among all Dissenting congregations 'either by the post or in parcels by coaches', as he shall think best.[4]

The body of the Deputation was still pressing the Committee. In January 1823 they asked for a special General Meeting to consider Repeal, and it was accordingly held on 19 March. The Deputies then, on the recommendation of the Committee, decided to renew the application to Parliament 'temperately but perseveringly' from time to time, to revive interest and to prepare the way for 'that gradual but ultimate success' which has attended similar exertions in truth and justice. All the many methods

[1] 7 Mar. 1823.   [2] 25 Mar. 1823.   [3] 24 June 1823.   [4] 28 Nov. 1823.

known to the Deputies were to be used: petitions to both Houses, followed by a motion in the Commons; lobbying both Houses; co-operation with the Dissenting Ministers and other Societies in London; circulation of statements of the case; 'temperate discussion' in periodicals or in 'useful and judicious tracts and addresses'; organization of Dissenters throughout the Kingdom in sending up petitions and approaching their own Members of Parliament.[1] These, plans, it appears, had been put to the Committee in the first instance by Mr Edgar Taylor, a leading Unitarian Deputy.[2]

At once the circulation of information and forms of petition began,[3] but the response from kindred Societies was not altogether encouraging. The Unitarians were anxious to co-operate, but the Protestant Society at once,[4] and the General Body of Ministers on consideration,[5] thought immediate action inexpedient. The Deputies, on hearing this, resolved not to press for a motion in Parliament in that session, but wished petitions now being signed by the London congregations to go forward.

Towards the end of the year[6] the Committee reopened the discussion with the Unitarian Association and the Ministers; and after consultation also with the Protestant Society it was decided to announce in the press that the Deputies and the Ministers had decided to apply to Parliament next session for the Repeal of the Corporation and Test Acts, but that they did not intend to invite congregational petitions on this occasion.[7] The Unitarians promised financial help; Mr Sergeant Heywood was asked to revise his pamphlet written for the 1789 campaign, 'The Right of Protestant Dissenters to a Complete Toleration Asserted', and to publish it or allow the Committee to do so. The Rev. Mr Aspland was asked to prepare for publication some address on Repeal. The Sergeant pleaded ill-health and declined; Mr Aspland assented.[8]

An illustration of the way in which the opinions of the Dissenters might be misrepresented and a justification of the caution of the Committee during the discussions about Roman Catholic Emancipation were provided in 1825. Smith reported that certain

---

[1] 19 Mar. 1824 (General Meeting).   [2] 19 Mar. 1824 (Committee Meeting).
[3] 26 Mar. 1824.   [4] 30 April.   [5] 28 May 1824.
[6] 29 Oct. and 12 Nov. 1824.   [7] 3 Dec. 1824.   26 Nov. and 3 Dec. 1824.

petitions 'purporting to be the Petitions of Protestant Dissenters' had been presented to both Houses against any concessions to Roman Catholics.[1] A special meeting of the Deputies, which was especially well attended—perhaps twice as large as the average at the period—was held four days later. A resolution prepared by the Committee was carried, disavowing any concurrence in or approval of the petition and asserting that

The Deputation will continue at all reasonable times to urge upon the Legislature (as it has hitherto done) the impolicy and injustice of every sort of penalty or disability civil or religious for conscience' sake.[2]

It is a measure of the Deputies' public spirit that they rallied at such short notice in such numbers to ally themselves with a cause more likely than not to increase their unpopularity at the very moment when they had a fight on their own to attend to.

Now came the last lull before the opening of what proved to be the final campaign. On 27 May 1825 William Smith reported to a General Meeting the result of conversations with members of the House of Commons, on the basis of which it was resolved that it would be inexpedient to take any measures in that session; and very little action was possible the following year.[3] During this delay one incident encouraged the Deputation: Gray's Inn spontaneously abrogated the sacramental test applied to those who wished to be called to the Bar, and thus brought itself into line with the other Inns of Court.[4]

When in February 1827 the Committee returned to the subject of appeal, they found the Unitarian Association and Board of Congregational Ministers interested in immediate action.[5] A conference was called by the Committee and attended by delegates from the Protestant Society, the Ministers, the Board of Congregational Ministers, and the Unitarian Association. This meeting decided for immediate action, and in effect opened the final campaign. Once they had decided to fight, it was not the habit of the Deputies to use half-measures. It was decided to interview several members of both Houses as soon as possible; and for the purpose seven Deputies, six ministers, and three representatives of

[1] 25 April 1825.   [2] 29 April 1825.   [3] 26 May 1826.
[4] 16 Dec. 1825.   [5] 9 and 17 Mar. 1827.

the Protestant Society and Unitarian Association were named. Meanwhile the various Societies were recommended to take all prudent measures to prepare for active co-operation.[1]

Within ten days the critical interview was held. Lord Holland, Lord John Russell, Lord Nugent, John Marshall Esq., M.P., John Smith Esq., M.P., the Hon. Robert Smith, M.P., Matthew Wood Esq., Alderman, M.P., Henry Warburton Esq., M.P., Thomas Spring Rice Esq., M.P., and John Easthope Esq. met the deputation at Brown's Hotel in Palace Yard, Westminster. They unanimously encouraged immediate application. Lord John Russell was asked to move for the Repeal in the Commons at such time in the present session as he should think proper.[2]

Notice was given that the motion for Repeal would be moved on May 31st, and in preparing for the struggle the Deputies took as their model the campaign of 1787. As then, so now (on 9 April 1827) a United Committee was constituted under the same name: 'The United Committee appointed to conduct the Application to Parliament for the Repeal of the Corporation and Test Acts'. Of this committee the Deputies' Committee provided the core. To it representatives of each Society and Body in London which was desirious of acting were added; but not more than six representatives of each Society should be sent. The United Committee might add to its number. The Deputies had the largest single representation and their Secretary, Robert Winter, was secretary of the United Committee.[3] The Deputies provided also the Chairman—William Smith, M.P. It is typical of the relationship of the two bodies that the Minutes of the United Committee, though kept in a separate volume, were also transcribed into the Deputies' Minute Book along with their own Minutes, and were read from time to time when the Committee met. The Deputies' Committee naturally did not concern itself as a rule at its private meetings with the Repeal.

Invitations to join the United Committee were addressed to the Ministers, the Protestant Society, the Unitarian Association, the Society of Friends, the Wesleyan Conference, the Presbytery of the Scots Church, and the Associated Presbytery of Seceders.[4]

[1] 28 Mar. 1827.   [2] 6 April 1827.   [3] 9 April 1827.   [4] *Ibid.*

The Ministers and the Unitarian Association made nominations at once. The Protestant Society, though it could not perceive that any benefits would result from joint deliberation, appointed representatives who would attend when summoned for a particular purpose. The Presbytery of the Scots Church declined the invitation. It is interesting that the letter was signed by the Rev. Edward Irving, with three years of Presbyterianism still before him, and then at the height of his fame, proposing, according to Carlyle, 'sons of Mammon, and high sons of Belial and Beelzebub, to become sons of God, and the gumflowers of Almack's to be made living roses in a new Eden'.[1] The Friends proposed to consult a meeting of the General Concerns of their Society. The President of the Wesleyan Conference in a friendly letter regretted that only Conference, not himself, could appoint representatives, and promised to point out at the next Conference how imperfect Wesleyan machinery was when speedy action was needed.[2] Later communications were sent to the Friends and the Wesleyans with the other Societies.[3] The London Associated Presbytery co-operated fully and made the practical suggestion that Scottish co-operation should be sought through the Associate Synod in Glasgow. The suggestion was acted on,[4] and correspondence with the Synod arranged.[5] The Protestant Society represented Independents, Baptists, Calvinistic Methodists and seceders from the Wesleyan Connexion (numbering several hundred congregations) as well as Unitarians. The United Committee was, therefore, in touch with the whole of Protestant Dissent and Methodism, though not all sections were officially represented. The Established Church of Scotland kept aloof, but other orthodox Presbyterians co-operated.

The United Committee met for the first time on 20 April 1827 and decided to meet each Monday, and instantly got in touch with Dissenters all over England. A statement of the case, a circular letter, and a short form of petition for use among Dissenting congregations were sent to ministers—1499 ministers were written to in May—and their opinions were canvassed. The petitions were to be addressed on this occasion only to the House of

[1] T. Carlyle, 'Death of Edward Irving' in *Critical and Miscellaneous Essays*, vol. III, p. 298. [2] 20 April 1827. [3] 21 May 1827. [4] 30 April 1827. [5] 11 June 1827.

Commons; and the congregations were reminded in the letter that in their 'united and temperate' petitions 'it would of course be desirable to avoid every expression calculated to excite hostile feelings in their opponents'; and that the petitions should be signed by 'competent and suitable' male persons. It was decided that the statement of the case, which had been prepared by Edgar Taylor, should be sent to the magazines and all daily papers.

But once again, it seemed, enthusiasm had outrun prudence. After a vigorous May campaign and consideration of a great correspondence,[1] the position was reviewed at a special meeting attended by some thirty members of the two Houses (about 105 had been invited), including Lord Holland, Lord Althorp, Lord Milton, as well as Lord John Russell, Brougham, Easthope, W. B. Baring and others.[2] A motion had been put down for 7 June; but there was some feeling that it ought to be postponed. No decision was reached, but it was decided to continue with the collection of petitions.

A General Meeting of the Deputies three days later[3] heard the report of this Parliamentary meeting, and affirmed its confidence in the discretion of the United Committee in deciding whether or not to proceed with Lord John Russell's motion; but urged their own representatives in that Committee to press that the application to Parliament should not be delayed beyond next session at latest and, if unsuccessful then, should be pressed session after session until it did succeed. The Deputies set out their views on the whole question in a series of resolutions and in a very long petition (close on 5,000 words in length) to the House of Commons. The petition covers generally the same ground as that of 1820, but it argues the case much more fully: the rights of man, the equality of all members of the State, the social stigma of Dissent, the weakness of the Indemnity Acts are set out in detail.[4]

Why was there hesitation about proceeding that session? It is clear that this hesitation was not confined to those at the centre of affairs, for some of the correspondents of the United Committee, for instance in Suffolk, still doubted the expediency of the time. The Minutes of the United Committee on 28 May, which finally

---

[1] 21 May 1827.   [2] 22 May 1827.   [3] 25 May 1827.   [4] 25 May 1827.

decided to ask Lord John Russell to defer his appeal to next
session, give some explanation: the Dissenters themselves as well
as their Parliamentary friends remained divided on the propriety
of immediate action; the state of public affairs and the advanced
period of the session, as well as their unwillingness to embarrass
a Ministry from which liberal consideration was hoped, were all
questions which weighed in the decision. The United Committee
thanked those Members of Parliament who 'under the difficulties
of their situation had given this Committee the strongest assurances
of support', and urged them to continue their help next session.
From the rather apologetic turn of the phrase, it seems clear that
the delicate question of Catholic Emancipation was that most
prominently present in the minds, if not on the lips, of the United
Committee and their friends. One sign of the deep division of
opinion was that the Protestant Society, which was later to give
most active support, still maintained at this time the attitude which
had characterized its reply when invited to join the United Committee: it could see no immediate justification for an appeal to
Parliament.

Activity now slackened; the United Committee held monthly,
not weekly, meetings.[1] In January 1828, however, the Deputies
prepared with special care a new petition to Parliament.[2] They
were much encouraged by the news that the Corporation of the
City of London had agreed to petition Parliament for the Repeal
of the Corporation and Test Acts; it is a sign of the changed relation
between the Deputies and the City since the 18th century, and of
the Deputies' skill for having their members in key positions, that
the motion was brought forward in the Court of Common
Council by Samuel Favell, who had been a member of the Deputies' Committee since 1816.[3]

The United Committee used the interval profitably. First it
concerned itself with publications, a special sub-committee being
appointed. Thousands of copies of the statement and petitions
were circulated. 'A select number of the most respectable Ministers

[1] 4 June 1827.
[2] 11 Jan. 1828 and following. This year they petitioned Lords as well as Commons.
[3] 28 Jan. 1828.

and Lay Dissenters in the country' was compiled. The editors of the *Quarterly* and the *Edinburgh*, the all-powerful periodicals of the day, stitched in 12,000 and 10,000 copies respectively of the Dissenters' case. Further, a periodical devoted to the proceedings of the Committee, to be edited by Mr Aspland, was suggested; it appeared as the *Test Act Reporter*.[1]

Two points of interest arose incidentally. First, a courteous episode. Some copies of the statement were sent to the offices of the British Catholic Association, and a friendly acknowledgement was sent. The sub-committee explained that they were not responsible—the copies had probably been sent by Alexander Dawson, M.P.—but they sent their cordial thanks 'for the kind and liberal expression of their wishes in favour of the great cause of civil and religious liberty'.[2]

A problem arose when one of the members of the Committee, a Mr Bowring, published a letter to Canning. He offered to append a declaration that it was his individual opinion. The sub-committee thought that members of the Committee who published anything ought to do so anonymously unless they had the Committee's sanction.[3] This resolution was rescinded by the United Committee as imposing a restraint: individuals might publish and sign their individual views.[4]

The United Committee made further attempts this year to gain Scottish Presbyterian support.[5] Having failed with Irving, it was suggested by the Associate Presbytery in London that an approach might be made to the General Assembly of the Church of Scotland through the Rev. Dr Thomson.[6] In a long and interesting letter, dated 3 Dec. 1827, Dr Thomson advised no application to the Assembly. He himself and not a few able and influential men would support the abolition of all proscription on account of religious faith, whether Protestant or Catholic, but the question had been often discussed, and always settled in such a way as to shew that a new discussion would mean a new defeat. This would provide the High Church party with an argument against Repeal that

---

[1] 11 and 14 June 1827.   [2] 5 July 1827.   [3] *Ibid.*
[4] 30 July 1827.   [5] 30 July and 22 Oct. 1827.
[6] 30 July and 22 Oct. 1827.

would 'more than counterbalance the local advantage to be derived from the constitutional statement and sound reasonings of your friends as contrasted with the slavish doctrines and plausible sophistry of your opponents in our great ecclesiastical meeting'. Dr Thomson also mentioned the fear that was felt in Scotland of embarrassing or dividing the present Administration. Scotland, therefore, took no part in the Deputies' struggle: but the candid and competent opinion of Dr Thomson goes far to explode the common theory that Repeal just happened, that there was no opposition to it.

As the autumn of 1827 came on, the pace began to quicken with preparations for the renewal of the campaign. The Rev. Mr Pearce's sermon on the Test Act, with notes, was prepared for a new edition; 2,000 copies were printed and 1,000 circulated to ministers in the country, the remainder to be disposed of in various ways in London. The *Test Act Reporter* was to appear on 1 Jan 1828; 2,000 copies went to press under Mr Aspland's direction. Drafts of petitions were revised; and as the year was ending negotiations were reopened with Lord John Russell and Mr John Smith asking for a renewal of the application to Parliament; and the Marquess of Landsdowne, Lord Holland and Lord Dacre were to be seen.[1]

The United Committee were busy, too, marshalling their own forces. A circular letter to ministers informed them of the renewed application, thanked them for their zeal earlier in the year, when over 1,200 petitions had been presented in a few days' time, but urged that fresh petitions should now be sent. The Lords as well as the Commons were now to be petitioned, and a new petition would have more influence than reference to an old one. It ought to be possible to get fresh signatures, for instance from Anglicans who 'from motives of pious regard to the sacred Institution which is continually dishonoured by the operation of these Acts' would be willing to sign in favour of Repeal. The Committee, however, recommended the exercise of a 'proper degree of caution against the use of any undue influence in obtaining signatures' from Anglicans. Special forms for Anglican petitioners

[1] 17 Dec. 1827.

were enclosed, but the Committee did not wish to tie the petitioners to the forms: they could easily be modified—for instance, Dissenters and Anglicans might like to use a joint form. 'The Committee again earnestly caution their more zealous friends against the use of any intemperate or offensive expressions.' Practical instructions about signing and addressing were added—for the last batch had cost the Committee over £60 from being misdirected—and the letter concluded with a financial appeal and an advertisement of Dr Pearce's sermon and the *Test Act Reporter*.

As the Parliamentary campaign began, relations with the Catholics again came under discussion. Lord John Russell informed the Committee that he had seen in the newspapers that the Roman Catholics of Ireland were to seek the co-operation of Dissenters 'in their mutual objects'. Lord John expressed his private opinion against 'any formal junction of the kind proposed' though it might be right to thank the Catholics for their votes in favour of Repeal. The Committee replied that it had adopted and acted on the principle of not forming a union with the Roman Catholics, and that when it had official news of the resolutions referred to it would send thanks as suggested.[1]

The care which the United Committee took to ensure that nothing was published without its express sanction if there was the remotest chance of its being thought affected sometimes seemed fussy. Not only individuals but even the component bodies were discouraged from acting separately. The Deputies' gratification at the City of London's action was therefore translated into a special resolution of thanks passed by the United Committee and so advertised.[2]

An incident in January 1828 shewed how necessary was this vigilance. On the afternoon of 29 January Mr Winter[3] had a visit from a Mr Northhouse, who enquired on behalf of the British Catholic Association if the Protestant Dissenters were disposed to join with the Roman Catholics in a public meeting to aid the applications to Parliament for relief now being made for each body. Winter said he had no authority to do anything, but would put any proposal made in writing before the Committee. On the

[1] 7 Jan. 1828.   [2] 28 Jan., 30 Jan. and 4 Feb. 1828.   [3] The Deputies' Secretary.

evening of the same day he received from Mr Blount, the secretary, a resolution that, in response to 'an overture on the part of the Dissenters' the Association had requested a deputation to discuss the matter with Winter. Mr Winter promptly replied, on the 30th, that there had been no overtures, but only his conversation with Mr Northhouse; he must decline the interview as it appeared to have been suggested by a misapprehension. Mr Blount, acknowledging, admitted the misconception; and it seemed that the incident was at an end.

But the next day, 31 January, two papers, the *New Times* and the *Courier*, had a paragraph headed: 'Union between the Dissenters and the Catholics.' The paragraph began:

The British Catholic Association have received communications from some Committees of some Dissenting Communities inviting them to co-operate in their future exertions for the attainment of their common object—relief by the Legislature from the Civil disqualifications under which they mutually labour.

This brought a double danger: the United Committee were equally anxious to avoid the impression that they were caballing with the Catholics, and the impression that Dissenters were hostile to the Catholics, denying them rights which they claimed themselves. Winter wrote to the papers denying the paragraph; he and Waymouth interviewed Mr Blount, who disavowed all knowledge of it; he thought probably Mr Northhouse was the author (but this suggestion is deleted in pencil in the United Committee's Minutes). Though he approved of the Committee's letter, Mr Blount did not himself wish to contradict an anonymous paragraph.

Warned by the incident, the Committee sent to Lord John Russell and Mr John Smith a resolution stating that they had not thought it expedient to unite their application with that of the Roman Catholics, but that 'they heartily disavow the inference that their acting separately proceeds from any hostility to the claims of that numerous and respectable body of petitioners.'[1]

The 1828 campaign opened with a change of heart on the part of the Protestant Society, 'as the United Committee and this Committee now entertain the same sentiment and desire the same

[1] 4 Feb. 1828.

object with similar fervour and intenseness'.[1] Six representatives of the Protestant Society were accordingly received on the United Committee, and a financial arrangement was come to, which stipulated for the establishment of a special fund for the appeal, separate from the Deputies' funds. Out of this fund the expenses of the last session's activities should be paid; at the end of the campaign the Protestant Society would contribute one-fifth to any deficit, and expect to receive one-fifth if any funds were left from the contributions being raised throughout the country.[2]

The motion this year was to be moved earlier in the session, on 21 February, and during the early part of that month precise plans were discussed with Lord John Russell. He proposed to move a resolution in exactly the same terms as those adopted by Fox on 2 March 1790, viz:

That this House will immediately resolve itself into a Committee of the whole House to consider so much of former Acts as requires persons, before any admission into Office Civil or Military or of any place of trust under the Crown to receive the Sacrament of the Lord's Supper according to the rites of the Church of England.

Russell asked the Committee to provide statistics of the number of Dissenters in the Kingdom, and to send a statement of the case to all M.P.s; the Committee arranged for both of these. The report, prepared by Benjamin Hanbury, was perhaps hardly on a scientifically statistical basis, but it is of considerable interest.[3] It is based on two assumptions: that 300 is a reasonable estimate for a congregation assembled on the two parts of the day at Sunday worship, and that three-fifths of the Dissenting population attend service each Sunday. This gave the United Committee, who claimed to represent 2,324 congregations, a constituency of just under a million (976,080), while the Wesleyans, Quakers and other smaller sects not represented by the Committee (excluding the Catholics and Jews) made another two million: altogether about a quarter of the population. Hanbury's figures give the Wesleyans 2,597 congregations, or rather more than all the older Dissenting bodies put together.

The week before the date of the motion was spent in daily

[1] 14 Jan. 1828.   [2] 16 and 21 Jan. 1828.   [3] 13 Feb. 1828.

conferences: on Feb. 18th, deputations saw Lord Althorp, Tierney, Byng, Calcroft, and Dennison; on the 19th, Lord Milton, Lord Nugent, and Spring-Rice; on the 20th, Lord Brougham had the day to himself; on the 21st, the Deputation saw Alex. Baring, Sir Robert Wilson, Brownlow, Sir Francis Burdett, Lord Ebrington; on the 22nd, Abercromby, Sergeant Onslow, Hume, Bennett, Sir James Mackintosh; on the 23rd, Ward and Sir John Newport—and from all but one of this impressive list they received strong assurances of support.

On the night of 26 February, Lord John Russell's motion was carried by 237-193. No time was lost in drafting a resolution to be moved forthwith in the Committee of the House calling for the Repeal of parts of the Corporation and Test Acts: this resolution was carried without a division on 28 February. Meanwhile the United Committee had put the drafting of a Bill into the hands of a sub-committee; and having considered the heads, the sub-committee put the Bill in charge of Christopher Richmond of the Middle Temple, one of its Unitarian members.[1] By 31 March Lord John Russell had received the draft Bill. He intended immediately to ask leave to introduce it.

It appeared clear that a substantial majority of the Lower House was willing to remove the sacramental test; but it did not follow that there would be no religious test. The Committee learnt from the Marquess of Lansdowne that the majority might replace the test by oaths or declarations: and Lord John Russell was anxious that the Dissenters should not shew themselves unwilling to consider proposals that did not compromise their principles. Mr Peel, Home Secretary of State, was understood to be anxious to proceed in such a way as to conciliate the whole legislature. The Committee resolved that they were ready to consider any proposal, but declared unreservedly that they could not be satisfied with any measure which would make necessary further application to the legislature for Repeal. They appointed a special deputation to watch Parliamentary proceedings.[2]

On the following day, 4 March, the Committee's Bill, introduced by Lord John Russell, was read a first time; the second

[1] 27 Feb. 1828.   [2] 3 Mar. 1828.

reading being down for the 14th. On 5 March Sir Thomas Acland gave notice of an instruction to the Committee on the Bill to replace the sacramental test by an oath or declaration. The Committee immediately set to work, both publicly and behind the scenes, to meet this new danger. There was much conversation between the Chairman and influential politicians. Mr Edgar Taylor published a letter to Sir Thomas Acland, the Committee bearing the expense. Peel, interviewed by William Smith, was told that the Dissenters would not consent to anything like a religious test for civil office; he had no proposal to make, but declared that he did not intend to oppose the Bill at the present stage. Acland himself was not clear about his intentions; in reply to questions 'he begged not to be hurried'. He had not yet got a defined plan: he wanted to find out what would please all parties. Lord Althorp thought that if a 'plausible and reasonable proposal' were rejected, many in the majority would not be sorry to be able to say: 'These Dissenters are unreasonable, and we will not now vote for them'. He thought it would be politic to accept e.g. a moderate declaration not to use power obtained by office to subvert the Established Church.

While concerned with great issues, the Committee found time to provide publicity in the Commons for information likely to undercut what purported to be a petition against Repeal from the Mayor and Corporation of Colchester. In fact, the Mayor had opposed it, and only 22 out of 48 members of the Corporation were present when it was agreed upon.[1]

The progress of events now became dramatic; the Committee met almost daily. The Bill was read a second time with few observations on 14 March, debate being reserved for the committee stage. It was clear that everything would turn on the proposed declaration; Sir Thomas Acland suggested a form of words:

I, A. B., do solemnly declare that I will never exercise any privilege to which I am or may become entitled to subvert or disturb the present Church Establishment of the United Kingdom or either of them, and this I declare on the faith of a Christian.

[1] 14 Mar. 1828.

237

Later, Acland's friends suggested the insertion after 'entitled' of 'in virtue of the office'.

The Committee heartily disliked any declaration, but Lord John Russell made it clear that whilst a moderate declaration would ensure success in both Houses, without it the Lords would almost certainly throw the Bill out. Only after 'long conference' with Lord John, and 'lengthened conversation' in Committee, did the Committee take the modified line which ultimately ensured success. In a series of resolutions unanimously passed, the Committee recorded its opinion that any plan of a new declaration was unnecessary, impolitic, inconsistent with the course taken as to the Protestant Dissenters in Ireland, and objectionable in principle. If a declaration was necessary to pass the Bill, and if there was reasonable assurance that a declaration would facilitate its progress, the Committee thought the following form the least objectionable yet seen:

I, A. B., being about to enter upon the office of......do solemnly and sincerely affirm and declare that I will not exercise any power or authority to be vested in me by virtue of such office for the subversion of the legal rights and privileges of the United Church of England and Ireland or of the Church of Scotland as such Churches are established by law.

The declaration should be (1) applicable to all persons taking office, (2) imperative only on requisition, and (3) the penalty to be loss of office only.

Throughout the later discussions the Deputies continued to drive as hard a bargain as they could in two ways: (1) by attenuating the declaration as far as possible; and (2) by securing every possible assurance that success in both Houses would in fact follow. Their unanimity on such a matter indicates how certain their failure would have been without some concession.[1] Having swallowed the pill, the Committee ordered additional draft clauses to be prepared to incorporate the declaration.

A series of interviews followed to ensure that as many people as possible were in line before the critical debate; but they were unable to get Acland to tie himself to a form of words. On the

[1] 15 Mar. 1828.

day before the debate they set out in reasoned and lengthy resolutions their case against any declaration, which they felt was unnecessary and offensive in principle. They thought that the record of Dissenters since 1688 was proof that they would not act illegally or with violence. If the declaration were shaped so as to be least injurious and offensive they would accept it to save the Bill; if it could not be made 'innoxious' the Committee's duty to the trust confided in them, to their country and to posterity obliged them to declare that 'the interests of truth and liberty required the Bill to be abandoned.' The declaration must not restrict the freedom of action which the law already secured to Dissenters; and it must not be imposed on Dissenters as such, so fixing on them a new stigma of the sort which was one of their chief objections to the present law—it must apply to the whole community. These concessions should be made on the full understanding that they were the price of success.[1]

A satisfactory bargain was struck with Peel. He insisted on a declaration, but if the declaration satisfied him 'it would be distinctly understood that no difficulty would be raised in the Upper House'. Peel wished the declaration to be given on admission to office and not merely on requisition. He went into no more detail, but wished whatever either side proposed to come up in the House and not privately. In view of this, the Committee's deputation did not try to see Peel or Sturges Bourne (representing Acland) but reminded those who had voted in the majority for Repeal of the forthcoming debate.[2]

The debate on the committee stage went well on the 18th. Lord John Russell, Lord Althorp, William Smith and others spoke against any declaration; and it was in a conciliatory speech that Sturges Bourne proposed the declaration to which the Committee had provisionally agreed on 15 March. Peel's speech also was calculated to conciliate all parties: he wanted the declaration modified a little and after the debate explained that he particularly wanted to leave the Lords no inducement to meddle with it. 'If the Bill should pass the House of Lords without much observation there would be no ill-feeling in the country excited'; the words as

[1] 17 Mar. 1828. [2] 18 Mar. 1828.

amended, he thought, would satisfy the leaders in the Upper House, but 'he could not be answerable for the consequences if those words were altered'.[1]

When the Committee considered the Parliamentary debate it was not ill-pleased. It was a great point that no declaration was imposed on Dissenters which was not equally imposed on all other subjects. They thought it would be 'highly inexpedient to attempt any resistance to the form of Declaration proposed in so truly conciliatory a manner by the Right Hon. the Secretary of State for the Home Department'. They stated, however, that it must be understood in Parliament that the declaration would not lessen the present legal freedom of Dissenters in the expression of their opinions as individuals and in measures to support their own faith.[2] The lawyers associated with the Committee made a number of technical suggestions for the improvement of the Bill, and these were afterwards submitted to a barrister. Most of these concerned the public generally, not the Dissenters particularly; and though little came of them, they indicate the care taken in co-operation with Peel to present the Bill in as good a shape as possible.

One point of special interest arose: was not the word 'influence' in the declaration too vague, or admitting of misconstruction? Were not the determinate words 'power' and 'authority' enough? Peel would not agree to the omission, yet he expressly stated that

he considered that word as only applicable to the influence to be derived from office, and added that were he (Mr Peel) a Dissenter of large landed property, and were he to make the Declaration on entering into office, he should consider himself as much at liberty to use his influence on the minds of his tenantry and otherwise in support of his principles as a Dissenter as he had done previously to making the Declaration.[3]

On 31 March the Bill, with the amendments satisfactory to Peel and to the Committee, passed the third reading. On 1 April the Lords gave it a first reading and appointed the 17th for the second.[4] There had already at an earlier stage been rumours conveyed by Tierney that the Bill would meet with opposition from 'a certain high quarter'; but these had proved baseless and indeed had not

[1] 19 Mar. 1828.   [2] 21 Mar. 1828.   [3] 21 and 31 Mar. 1828.   [4] 14 April 1828.

greatly perturbed the Committee.[1] As the critical days in the Lords drew on, the chance that things might not go as smoothly as Peel had predicted had to be reckoned with.

Two days after the first reading Lord Holland reported to the Secretary his suspicion that there would be in the Lords formidable opposition, not merely to the declaration but to the repealing part. Lord Eldon threatened to find such important omissions in the Bill as would produce contradictions and incongruities without end. 'This sort of warfare is, I know by experience', wrote Holland, 'very formidable in the Lords, especially under so able a Guerilla Chief as the ex-Chancellor'. It was necessary to forestall him by announcing an intention to supply the omissions. Lord Holland asked that professional advice might be obtained on the extent to which later legislation (including Indemnity Acts) had re-enacted or altered provisions concerning the sacramental test. He urged that whatever petitions could be obtained 'without resorting to any questionable or obnoxious means' should be 'poured in' on the first day of the House's meeting. The clergy would probably provide more counter-petitions than the friends of the Bill had heard of.

Several conferences between Winter, Richmond, Holland and others followed. Richmond admitted the intricacy of the matter and Lord Eldon's extensive knowledge, but confessed that he had not discovered 'the assailable point in our repealing clause which the astuteness of the Ex-Chancellor professes to leave unmarked'. He had himself anticipated several of the points but had not pressed for amendments in the clauses settled by Peel and the Solicitor-General. He thought that it would be a mistake to try and annul the very complicated relations of the Indemnity Acts to the new declaration in the main Act. Points raised by Lord Plunkett were embodied in other additional clauses.[2] Some trouble arose about the precise way in which the declaration should be made in the City of London, but the City was anxious to co-operate, and in the end did not press for a clause which seemed not necessary and was objected to by Lord Holland.[3]

In the course of these conferences spirits rose, and Lord Holland

[1] 17 Mar. 1828.   [2] 18 April 1828.   [3] 14 April and 18 April 1828.

expressed the view that he expected so considerable a majority as to be able to give up the 50 votes which he had thought doubtful. On 17 April the Bill was read a second time without a division, and William Smith was able to report a personal conversation with the Duke of Wellington and the Marquess of Lansdowne after it: both expressed full satisfaction with the Bill and the declaration.[1]

It was decided after consulting friendly Peers that no amendment should be proposed by supporters of the Bill on the committee stage; care being taken to see that the clause affecting the City was brought forward. In a lively and animated debate various amendments were proposed and divisions taken; but all the clauses were agreed to except those relating to persons required by His Majesty to make the declaration. The declaration itself was very considerably modified into a form almost identical with that of the final Act: the words 'on the true faith of a Christian' were introduced, making it a religious test, even though it was one with which Dissenters could conscientiously comply. The report stage was fixed for the 28th.[2]

Nothing could have been greater than Lord Holland's care about every detail of the legal language of the Bill itself and about the tactics of the struggle at every stage. He was in touch with the Committee and Mr Richmond almost every day until the Bill passed the Lords. He was confident that the Bill would pass, though 'not without some unseemly incumbrances, yet without any that can practically aggrieve any Protestant Dissenter or indeed anyone else in the present state of the law'. Though the special arrangement desired by the City of London caused more anxiety, the main discussions concerned the wording of the declaration, and the introduction of the phrase: 'on the true faith of a Christian' or 'of a Protestant Christian'. The Deputies disliked the declaration, and disliked even more these additions to it, though not themselves affected. They struggled to reduce the limitations as far as possible; Roman Catholics and Jews were likely to be affected. Would the insertion of the word 'Protestant' adversely affect Roman Catholics, or were they in any event excluded by the need to take the Oath of Supremacy on entering

[1] 18 April 1828. [2] 22 April 1828.

corporate offices? The Roman Catholics consulted replied that the Oath of Supremacy itself excluded them; they never took it, nor could, unless it were altered or received a satisfactory legislative interpretation. The Government was informed of this. There was some fear that the Bishop of Llandaff might move an amendment requiring that the declaration should be made by Dissenters only; Lord Holland was sure that the House of Lords would not entertain this. One complication Lord Holland did avoid. Mr Lyon Goldsmid, on behalf of his brethren of the Jewish persuasion, took a petition to Lord Holland, but after a long discussion with him Holland declined to present it. Throughout all Lord Holland's remarks there was a lightness of touch and a good-humoured shrewdness which are most attractive. It was characteristic of him that he provided a paragraph to be inserted in 'some newspaper of general circulation in order to make known a fact which would soften the prejudices of many Churchmen and academical persons to our measure'. Only full quotation can do justice to the tact, the delicacy, and the irony of the paragraph:

It is gratifying to reflect that such of our greatest Orators and Statesmen as were prevented by absence, illness, or accident, from taking a personal part in the late discussions on the Repeal of the Test Act, were nevertheless anxious to support that just and salutary measure. The proxies of Lord Grenville, the Marquis of Wellesley, and Lord Plunkett were given in favor of the Bill: and the two last-mentioned Noblemen had confided theirs to Lord Holland, the Mover of it. Thus the two late Representatives of the Universities of Cambridge and Dublin vizt the Lord Chancellor and Lord Plunkett voted for the Bill and the Chancellor of the University of Oxford Lord Grenville from his dignified and honourable Retreat sent the sanction of a name equally revered in Church and State to a work of Charity, Wisdom and Justice which has been long desired but till this propitious Year almost despaired of by the friends of Religious Freedom.

On 2 April the Bill as amended passed the Commons. The declaration in its final form retained the word 'influence' and the phrase 'upon the true faith of a Christian', but the word 'Protestant' did not appear. It had reference to the Church of England, and not, as at one time proposed, to the Church of Scotland as well; and it did not require the declaration from a good many people who had formerly been subject to the test.[1] The Royal Assent was given on 9 May.

Whatever its blemishes, the Act was the crown of the Deputies' work and it aroused enthusiastic gratitude. The first expression recorded came from the Lancashire Congregational Churches, who wrote on 10 April to thank Lord John Russell for getting the Bill through the Commons. A London layman wrote on 2 May that, in view of the probability of the Royal Assent, a day of Public Thanksgiving should be appointed: 'a measure of this kind', he wrote, 'so just, so proper, so incumbent would be most agreeable to us all'. These letters were referred to the sub-committee on publications with instructions to consider the proper way of thanking 'our Parliamentary friends' and generally celebrating the event.[2]

Three days after the Royal Assent a set of nine eloquent resolutions was passed expressing the thanks of the United Committee to all who had contributed by action or inaction to the triumph. Despite the declaration which marred this removal of the grievance of a century and a half, the Committee declared itself 'now bound with increased affection to the civil and political institutions of the Realm and to the Government happily established at the Revolution of 1688 and confirmed by the accession of the present august family to the throne'. In thanking Lord John Russell for the 'happy union of zeal and moderation' which he had shewn the Committee did not forget to mention the inseparable connection of the name of Russell with the cause of constitutional liberty. Lord Holland's services had reminded Dissenters of 'their never to be forgotten obligations to his Lordship's illustrious relative the Right Hon. Charles James Fox'; many other individuals were named, and a 'tribute of unfeigned respect' was paid to the 'liberal and conciliatory spirit' of the Archbishops and Bishops. 'Most cheerful and grateful testimony' was borne 'to the steadiness and consistency' with which His Majesty's Ministers had adhered to their friendly professions. The Committee recorded their thanks to Anglicans 'in so generally abstaining from opposition to the

[1] 5 May 1828.　　　　　　　　　　　　　　　　[2] Ibid.

relief sought by their fellow subjects and fellow Protestants' and to many individuals and collective bodies among English and Irish Roman Catholics. Three thousand copies of these resolutions were circulated.[1]

A number of interesting replies were received. The Duke of Wellington wrote with old-fashioned, non-committal courtesy, so appropriate in a wary and well-meaning politician:

It is very gratifying to me to find that the conduct of His Majesty's Servants in the recent discussions upon that subject has given satisfaction to those who were so much interested in the result.

Peel wrote with characteristic rather wooden honesty, simply expressing thanks for the communication. Lord John Russell agreed with the Committee in regretting the declaration, but felt that no better terms could have been got 'without a protracted struggle of many years'. Like the Bishop of St David's, he hoped that goodwill between the Established Church and Dissent would follow.[2] The Deputies were human, and may be forgiven for the charitable inconsistency with which, at such a moment, they gave to the Anglican body the complimentary title of the National Church.

Thanks, however, were not enough for the Dissenters in this exuberant mood; a sub-committee was set up to arrange for a Public Dinner to celebrate the triumph. With express speed arrangements went ahead, the sub-committee meeting almost daily. There was nothing modest about the plans: the great room at the Freemasons' Tavern was to be used; the Duke of Sussex was to preside; as applications were expected to exceed accommodation the price of tickets was fixed at £2 2s. Some 267 respectable and influential Dissenters from every part of the Kingdom were asked to be Stewards; their liability was not to exceed five guineas, and even if they could not attend they were urged to send their names.[3]

The list of Stewards, Members of both Houses of Parliament to be invited, complimentary tickets to be distributed to Ministers and others, and the design of the dinner ticket received great attention. It was decided to employ no professional singers, but a

[1] 13 May 1828. [2] 19 May 1828. [3] 15 May 1828.

'band of music' was engaged to attend during dinner only. The Minutes of the Committee and the sub-committee shew the care with which every detail was considered; they record also trials and worries very like those which still pursue dinner-secretaries. Circular letters intended to indicate that Stewards who could not attend should let other people use their tickets were misunderstood as a hint that the Committee was indifferent whether they came or not.[1] Complimentary tickets were claimed by one person as a member of a sub-committee of which it appeared that he was not a member.[2] The Dissenting ministers of London were either slack in claiming their complimentary tickets or else not much attracted by the festivity.[3] On the other hand, the Mexican and Russian Ambassadors indicated their desire to be present, and were supplied with tickets.[4]

Twenty-four toasts were suggested, and the precise list was revised more than once. The sub-committee, though it at once found eloquent words to describe the merits of the other persons in the list, could not at once find words to describe the merits of William Smith, and left the draft: 'Our Deputy Chairman, William Smith, Esqre., the. . . .' The implied compliment was well deserved.[5] A small sub-committee (on which no minister sat) was responsible for food and drink.[6] Its first proposal deserves record:

The Dinner to consist of Turtle, Turbots, Salmon, Salmon Trout, Stewed Eels, Fillet Mutton with Cucumber stewed, Stewed Rumps Beef, Roast and Boiled Lamb, Roast Beef, Chickens with white sauce, Hams, Tongues, Stewed Veal and Peas, Pigeon Pies, Giblet Pies, Raised French Pies, Pullets Roast, Turkey Poults, Guinea Fowls, Ducks, Geese, Jellies, Gooseberry Tarts, Tourtes, Pudding Peas, Cauliflowers, Potatoes, Salads, French Beans, Garden Beans.

Port Sherry Bucellas Moselle Champagne Hock Claret Burgundy Madeira

Waiters Lighting and Glass

At £1. 16. 6 per head.

If with Venison 8/- per head extra.

If Champagne be omitted 2/6 per head will be deducted.

Each servant to have Dinner and a Pint of Wine at 5/- per head.

[1] 6 June 1828. [2] 12 June 1828. [3] 27 May 1828.
[4] 27 May and 17 June 1828. [5] 4, 10 and 12 June 1828. [6] 3 June 1828.

Ladies Refreshments 2/- a head.

This sub-committee agreed to recommend that the proposal for the dinner at £1: 16: 6 pr head be adopted. They recommend that Venison be omitted because it appears that it is difficult to get a sufficient supply which can be fully depended upon, and that at large Dinners it frequently proves a source of dissatisfaction.[1]

The sub-committee's proposal was accepted on the understanding that the price should include Dessert Ices and Malt Liquor.[2] The ministerial functions at the Dinner were allotted to ministers who had worked on the Committee and who represented the several denominations: the Rev. Dr Winter, an Independent, was 'to offer prayer for a Blessing before Dinner'; the Rev. Mr Broadfoot, a Scots Presbyterian, to return thanks afterwards. The Rev. Dr Cox, a Baptist, was to propose the toast to the Archbishops, Bishops, and other members of the Established Church, and the Rev. Mr Aspland, Unitarian 'Presbyterian', was to respond to the toast of the Protestant Dissenting Ministers.[3]

It appeared that not more than 420 persons could be accommodated at dinner and the Committee was anxious that no place should be wasted, as applications exceeded seats. Seventy ladies could be accommodated in the gallery; and, perhaps shewing a knowledge of human nature, the Committee had 100 tickets printed, which were distributed by the Acting Stewards.

One hundred and thirty-three Stewards received the distinguished gathering who met on 18 June to do justice to the occasion. Soon after six o'clock His Royal Highness the Duke of Sussex entered the hall, accompanied by the guests, who included 9 Peers of the Realm, 43 M.P.s, and other notabilities.[4] The hall and galleries were completely full. The Duke of Sussex prefaced the first toast of the King with some remarks which were very much to the point: he told the audience that if they kept their seats they would hear better; and he reminded the speakers that as their cause was now triumphant they need not argue it all over again. He then gave the King's health with the comment that 'among

---

[1] 3 June 1828.   [2] 6 June 1828.   [3] 12 June 1828.
[4] The details which follow are from 'Proceedings at a Dinner to Commemorate the Abolition of the Sacramental Test', taken in shorthand by Mr Gurney, London, 1828.

the many distinguished events which will have to be recorded in future ages, none will tend so much to endear the name of George the Fourth as the peculiar event we are met to commemorate'. He did not feel it necessary to make a speech to introduce the next toast: 'Every man's right and every nation's best interest—Liberty of Conscience', or to indicate more than a sincere adherence to the one which followed: 'The event we are met to celebrate . . . the triumph of Religious Freedom and Christian Charity in the abolition of the Sacramental Test'. He was then granted a merciful respite while he listened to William Smith proposing his health; and having got his breath, he replied at length 'under feelings of considerable emotion'. He reminded his hearers that it was the anniversary of Waterloo, and he asked the veterans of that engagement who were present whether when the order to charge was given they had paused to ask their comrades of what religion they were. If their feelings were united at such a moment, ought they not to remain united afterwards? Passing from eloquence to humour, in the happiest vein of post-prandial oratory, the Royal Duke here held up a candle to read the next toast, and exclaimed: 'I have a candle in my hand, but I am not standing here to do penance, though if I could thus atone for the wrongs which have been done to our Catholic friends and restore them to their rights, I should be proud to do it'. He gracefully mentioned the presence of Lords Stourton, Clifford and Stafford, and proposed 'Speedy and effectual relief to all His Majesty's Subjects who still labour under any legal disabilities on account of their Religion'. 'The whole company rose and joined in repeated rounds of cheering, expressive of the most intense interest and sympathy' and it was long before Lord Stourton could reply.

The Duke of Sussex now proceeded to introduce a series of toasts in honour of those who had most contributed to the triumph; a list in which the 'Immortal memory of Charles James Fox and the enlightened Patriots who maintained our cause in less prosperous times' was by a touch of poetry introduced after the healths of Lord John Russell and Lord Holland, and just before those of John Smith, William Smith, Lord Lansdowne, Lord Althorp, and 'the brave and illustrious Field Marshal and those gallant Troops

whom he had the honour and Glory of leading on to Victory'.
Then came the turn of the Church—the Established Church, proposed by Dr Cox, and the Dissenting Ministers, 'the worthy
successors of the ever memorable two thousand who sacrificed
interest to conscience', to which Mr Aspland returned thanks in
perhaps the most moving speech of the evening, admirable in its
tone, truly eloquent in expression, and vibrant with feeling. He
began by alluding to the honour which Dissenting ministers, 'a
humble class of men', felt in being united with the 'memorable
two thousand'. 'We cannot pretend, Sir, to their profound and
varied learning, to their unspotted and exemplary manners, and
to their exquisite sense of religious honour; but we do share with
them . . . in their ardent love of liberty, civil and religious liberty.'
He claimed that in speaking with veneration of the two thousand,
he was not actuated by sectarian feeling, and he quoted the
remark of a bishop in the House of Lords when Dissenting claims
were argued in 1779: 'I am not afraid, My Lords, of men of
scrupulous consciences, but I will tell you what I am afraid of—
and they are the men that believe anything, that subscribe anything, and that vote for anything'. He alluded to the hope of
further reform, and particularly to the opening of the Universities;
and in conclusion he prayed for a 'still more Christian government', not sectarian, but (he explained, in a striking anticipation of
Lincoln's phrase) 'that the future government of this country, the
best and the greatest country on the face of the earth, will and
must be the government *of* the people, and *for* the people'.[1]

There were still nine toasts to come, but since we perhaps lack
the attention of our ancestors in as great a degree as we lack their
physical appetite, we may bid farewell to this 'Festival', as William
Smith called it, with the Duke of Sussex's last toast: 'A long pull,
and a strong pull, and a pull all together', with which he left the
room (it being about half-past one o'clock) amidst enthusiastic
cheers, followed by the whole party, 'which the intense interest of
the proceedings had kept in undiminished numbers to the last'.

There can be little to quarrel with in the resolution of the
Committee, which recorded appreciation not only of the Duke's

[1] 'Proceedings', p. 38.

principles 'but of the urbanity with which His Royal Highness so enlivened the festival'.[1] The speeches had lasted almost six hours, and during that time the Duke was on his feet for certainly more than half: it is a feat at which imagination boggles and before which comment is dumb.

The United Committee did not, however, at once disband; its final meeting was not held until 15 Dec. 1828. There was some thought of erecting a building as a permanent commemoration of the victory and to serve the common interests of Dissenters.[2] The idea was not pursued; but the Committee had still to face the question of paying, not merely for the Dinner but for the Application to Parliament. There was a deficit of £390 on the Dinner, out of a bill of £1,053; and the Stewards were called on for £3 10s. out of their deposit of £5 5s.; the balance to be repaid to them or transferred to the general expenses of the Appeal as they directed.[3]

The expenses of the United Committee were reported as follow:[4]

	£	s	d
Printing a new edition of Pearce's Sermon	15	14	3
Printing No 1 to 7 (inclusive) of *Test Act Reporter*	103	0	0
Paper for ditto	96	3	6
150 copies letter to Sir Thos Acland	11	5	0
Compensation to the Editors of *The Mirror of Parliament*	20	0	0
Subscription to ditto	5	5	0
Votes and Appendix of the House of Commons	6	5	6
Parliamentary Agent's Bill	23	4	4
Fauntleroy and Burton's Bill (Printers) .	376	18	6
Rooms for Meetings at the King's Head	54	8	5
Secretary's Bill relative to the Application to Parliament	1876	12	8
Do. relative to the Commemoration Dinner	121	7	0
	2710	4	2
Addition to the above mentioned Bills of the Secretary voted by the United Committee 7 July 1828 so as to make the Bills amount to 2000 guineas	102	0	4
	£2812	4	6

[1] 1 July 1828. [2] 23 June 1828. [3] 3 July 1828. [4] 4 July 1828.

It was at first proposed to ask Dissenting ministers throughout the country to make collections to help to defray expenses; some congregations and individuals had at various times sent contributions unasked. But whilst the United Committee was still considering finance, the Deputies and the Protestant Society took the matter out of their hands, resolving themselves to bear the whole expense, and making no special appeal to congregations but asking them to keep up their donations to the regular funds of the two bodies.

The initiative in this was taken by the Protestant Society, which had, when it joined the United Committee, made certain financial stipulations. Recalling these, its Committee mentioned that they had been made on the assumption that success would be distant and that the capital and permanent resources of the Society and the Deputies would be exhausted. 'Providence having granted earlier and immediate success' there was now no need for a collection. The Protestant Society would forgo its claim for its separate expenditure, amounting to £271 19s. 2d., and give £1,000 towards the general expenditure, leaving about £2,000 to the Deputies. It was calculated that this would leave the Protestant Society with £3,000 Stock and the Deputies £5,000. The Protestant Society made it a condition of this arrangement that the United Committee made no collection; and 'altho this Committee [i.e. of the Protestant Society] presume not to direct the important and venerable body of Deputies' they express the hope that the Deputies will abstain from a general application till it appears that their remaining capital of £5,000 needs augmentation.[1]

Having abandoned the idea of a permanent building, the United Committee were unable to resist the temptation to a last commemorative fling. They resolved upon the striking of a medal, and the publication of an account of the Dinner, from the verbatim report taken in shorthand by Mr Gurney. Mr Scipio Clint, an appropriately named medallist, offered at his own expense to prepare a medal: if not more than two or three figures were introduced it would cost 60 or 70 guineas. Specimens by Mr Voigt were also submitted by Mr Kreeft, but as Mr Voigt was in Rome it was

[1] 7 Nov. 1828.

thought best to proceed with Mr Clint. The design was settled between Mr Edgar Taylor and Mr Clint, and was drawn by Thomas Stothard: it shewed Britannia, under the aegis of religion, handing to a figure emblematic of the Dissenting Churches their charter of liberty; it fairly represents what the Committee hoped for: 'a classical and pleasing memorial of a happy event'[1]—but it cost the Deputies rather more than their seventy guineas.

At the last meeting of the United Committee it made its political testament: a resolution bearing obvious reference to the question of Roman Catholic Emancipation. Although the Committee had abstained in its own application from coalition with other applicants it could not separate without expressing its desire for the abolition of all laws interfering with the rights of conscience and attacking civil disabilities to religious faith and worship. After votes of thanks to all who had shared in the agitation and organization the Committee intrusted to the Deputies the task of preserving its records and completing any part of the work left undone; and with 'heartfelt expression of their gratitude to God for the speedy success which crowned their exertions' dissolved themselves.[2]

The Deputies' Committee, when the Act was passed, reported generally on the situation to the General Meeting of Deputies on 16 May. The report emphasized that the Repeal had come not only earlier but under more favourable circumstances than had been expected. The absence of opposition and the co-operation of the Government, mentioned by the United Committee, are mentioned here too. This harmony among those who 'on the most essential points hold the Common Faith of Christians' enhanced the value of what was gained. In a great sentence they wrote: 'We did not seek a triumph over enemies but an admission to the common advantages of Fellow Subjects and Friends'. The declaration did not indeed allow that complete separation of religion and politics, but the admission of all Christians without exception meant that the chief objects which the Deputies, as representing Dissenters, had been commissioned to achieve was achieved. They therefore repeated the resolutions, mainly of thanks, passed already by the United Committee. The General Meeting approved all

[1] 11 July 1828.　　　　　　　　　　　　　　[2] 15 Dec. 1828.

this, and declared that 'the emancipation of the Protestant Dissenters of England' had been achieved.

The Report of the Committee for 1828 embodied the report made immediately after the passing of the Act, relating as they confessed in one of their rare moments of self-revelation: 'the successful issue of that application of which, as your Committee may now acknowledge, they scarcely dared to flatter themselves with the hope'. Another sentence well describes their methods:[1]

By temper and perseverance—never deserting our principles or our profession, nor omitting to assert our rights, when a fit opportunity for exertion presented itself, nor affording to our adversaries the encouragement to be derived from repeated victories; we gave to the public mind time to undergo that change of which we have at length profited almost without exciting a hostile observation, and have fair ground for hope that by persisting with similar firmness and moderation, whatever objectionable may yet remain will ere long be removed, so that every impediment to the utmost freedom of thought or profession may be swept from the face of the land; religion and politics, the affair of two worlds, may be finally separated, and man may be left answerable for his religious opinions to his God alone.

[1] Report for 1828.

CHAPTER 2

BIRTHS, MARRIAGES, AND DEATHS

(a) The Register of Births

IT WAS Thomas Cromwell who, as Vicar-General to Henry VIII, first set up any general system of registration; but the parish registers, kept with varying degrees of accuracy and literacy, were never very satisfactory. They registered baptisms and not births, and there might be a considerable interval between one and the other. There was no proper machinery for preserving or consulting them. And if they had some value while everyone remained, at least nominally, a member of the National Church, they lost a great deal of this when the evolution of the sects made the Church of England only national in name. Infants baptized by Independent and Presbyterian ministers, and the children of Baptists (who of course were not baptized in infancy), were not included.

In a sporadic way, the Dissenters kept their own registers; but there was no general system; it was not always clear whether the register belonged to the meeting or the minister; and since these registers had not the legal validity of the parish records they were even more seriously defective than these. With the evolution of the machinery of the modern State, the registers acquired greater and greater legal and administrative importance, they were no longer mainly a matter of Church order; and it became a considerable disadvantage to Dissenters if they could not produce evidence of age as readily as Anglicans. It is therefore not surprising that soon after their inception the Deputies considered the question of an authoritative register for Dissenters. After a special sub-committee had several times considered the matter in the early months of 1742, a special meeting was called for 30 June, to which the ministers of congregations not sending Deputies were specially urged to send representatives. This meeting resolved that

if a General Register of the Births of the Children of Protestant Dissenters of the three Denominations could be kept where constant
recourse might be had it would be of great advantage to the Dissenting
Interest. In order to [sc. effect] this it is proposed that an Alphabetical
Book be kept at—[name left blank] under the Direction of the Committee of Deputies for the time being, where every person paying
Sixpence may Register the Birth of a Child, which is to be applied to
defray all necessary Expenses and particularly to pay the Clerk for his
Attendance.[1]

It was decided further to apply to the trustees of Dr Williams's
Library to keep the registers at Red Cross Street under the care
of the Librarian. Several things are to be noticed about these
resolutions. In the first place, the register was to be a register of
Births, and not of Baptisms; no doubt the presence of the Baptist
Deputies ensured this, though the original proposal had been for a
'Register of Christenings or Births'.[2] In the second place it was to
be a *public* register to be used by 'any person paying sixpence'; it
was not limited to Londoners or to Protestant Dissenters; and
during its existence it was used by many others, including Anglicans, as well as the Deputies' constituents; there were even entries
from outside the British Isles.[3]

In October 1742 the trustees of Dr Williams's Library agreed
to the keeping of the register at Red Cross Street for a year from
Christmas; and the Librarian consented to act as clerk for an
annual fee of £5. It is characteristic of the apparently casual way
in which the Deputies established semi-permanent institutions that
this arrangement was never put on a standing basis; although
the register remained at Dr Williams's Library until it was taken
over by the Registrar-General, it was always continued there by
an annual vote of the trustees,[4] and by an arrangement with each
Librarian as he was appointed. Yet a rival scheme, which the
Deputies note as having been established by Dr Mortimer at the
Herald's Office in 1748, was much less successful, and was 'nearly
abandoned' after 1783.[5]

A sub-committee of five was appointed to direct the affairs of

---

[1] 30 June 1742.   [2] 25 Mar. 1741.   [3] 15 May 1837: Report.
[4] *Sketch*, p. 21.   [5] *Ibid*. p. 21 n.

the Registry; their first duty was to make the register widely known, framing certificates, of which stocks were printed on parchment,[1] and drafting a letter to be sent with supplies of the certificate to Deputies and ministers. The sub-committee was also to inspect the register at regular intervals, for the Deputies were proud of its accuracy. In 1768 it was agreed that this Committee should consist of 'all the gentlemen of this Committee who are of Dr Williams's Trust' and three others. From January 1769, when the sub-committee reported having inspected the registers and found

the Register Book kept very regularly, as also the Certificates from No. 1 to No. 303, so that in searching for any name it is readily found,[2]

until January 1781 there was a quarterly inspection which was faithfully recorded in the Minutes. This usually gave simply the inclusive numbers of certificates examined, with a note that they were found perfect. It seems that this admirable regularity was largely due to the public spirit of one of the Committee, Mr Bowden, for on his his death in 1780 there is a note that 'for years he had examined the registers',[3] and shortly afterwards the regular quarterly examination was discontinued, although at intervals there is a note of further inspection. The necessity of this inspection is shown by two notes in the Minutes. When in 1800 the Minutes record (for the first time in 20 years, although it seems likely that inspections were made in the interval, though not recorded) the inspection of the registers, the examiners, Mr Smith and Mr Cotton, mentioned that

they think it but justice to Rev. Mr Joseph Towers the Register[4] to say that the Register has been much improved under his management.

But four years later Mr Towers had fallen from grace; he resigned at midsummer, leaving the Register imperfect, and the Committee were driven to withhold his salary 'until the Register is perfected'.[5] This was effective, for on 2 Nov. it was stated that he had now completed it. The next Registrar, Rev. Thomas Morgan, was so

---

[1] For specimens, see *Sketch*, p. 246.   [2] 13 Jan. 1769.   [3] Nov. 1780.
[4] 'Register' is the name habitually used for the superintendant of the Register until the early 19th century. Sometimes 'registerer' is used; but this is as ugly as the other is ambiguous.   [5] 26 Oct. 1804.

careful and assiduous that it became the practice to pass him an annual vote of thanks;[1] but on his death in 1821 the new Librarian, the Rev. John Coates, was not so exact; in 1826 the sub-committee reported that copies of the register were found incorrect, and Mr Coates was warned 'to be particular for the future'.[2]

Perhaps enough examples have been given to illustrate the scrupulous way in which the Deputies strove to make the register *exact* and *reliable*, and to counter the fallibility of the superintendent and of their own Committee. But we must now examine the measures which were taken to make the register *effective*, and the degree of success which the Deputies attained.

At first, the Deputies had in mind a system for the registration of Deaths as well as Births.[3] But after considering the idea, and a scheme which had been outlined to them in a letter from a Mr Baskerville,[4] the Committee concluded that while such a register might be of service to the Dissenting interest, 'attempting it at present might be some hindrance to the Registry of Births, and that future consideration be postponed for a year'. The scheme was not taken any further. There was, however, a good deal more discussion on the subject of registering baptisms. The Committee received letters criticizing the fact that this was omitted; and after interviewing one of the malcontents, a Mr Dove, announced that it would make the Register much more useful if such Ministers as baptize infants would in their Certificates of the Births of such Children also insert the time of their Baptism.

This informal notice, however, was not very effective, and as the demand persisted for some means of registering baptisms, the Deputies in 1768 printed a special issue of forms with 'D' in the corner for recording baptisms, and kept the returns in a special volume. In their report to the Registration Commission in 1837, the Deputies explained the reason for this as follows:

The Deputies having in the first instance contemplated the registration of Children's Baptisms (though afterwards more wisely resolved on recording their Births) it did not afterwards escape their observation that some parents neglected to record the births of their children and

[1] 28 Mar. 1806; 31 Jan. 1817, and afterwards annually.
[2] 7 April 1826. [3] 30 Dec. 1741.
[4] Just possibly the great printer, at that time an obscure writing master.

trusted to the Minister to record the religious rite performed by him. Provision was accordingly made for Ministers to give in records of Baptisms—these cover part of one volume and the whole of another.[1]

In December 1768 a case which was brought to their notice decided the Deputies to make themselves responsible for other baptismal registers. One of the Deputies from the church under the pastoral care of Rev. Mr Harris (late Dr Earl's) reported that Dr Earl's register of children baptized by him was not to be found, 'which is a matter of great concern to that Congregation'[2] and desired the Committee

> to prevent the like happening again with respect to such ancient Ministers as are living, by getting their Registers entered in the Register Book at the Library, and that those entries when made should be signed by the Ministers as a true Copy, or in any other more Legal method as the Committee shall see fit.[3]

As a result of this, 21 registers from ministers, some extensive, others fragmentary, were deposited and preserved with the Register of the Deputies.[4]

In spite of all this care and attention, the Deputies' register was slow in coming into favour. We have seen that, when the first inspection of entries was made twenty-five years after the establishment of the scheme, only 303 names had been entered. The Deputies were conscious that this was slow progress. In 1744 they informed ministers that they might register any children baptized before Christmas 1742 *gratis*.[5] In 1759 they ordered that notice should be sent to every congregation for the better making known the same;[6] and ten years later they included on the summonses to the Annual General Meeting a reminder to ministers to give notice of the register, 'as great inconveniences have arisen from want of attention to that Register'.[7] This note was repeated from time to time; and as a result of these efforts the number of registrations steadily increased. From 1770 to 1780 there were over a thousand registrations, the numbers rising from 383 in January

---

[1] Report to Registration Commission, 15 May 1837.
[2] 16 Dec. 1768.   [3] 16 Dec. 1768.
[4] Report to Registration Commissioners 15 May 1837.
[5] 4 April 1744.   [6] 14 Mar. 1759.   [7] 10 Nov. 1769.

1770 to 1,393 in April 1780.[1] This, however, is still only a trickle when compared with the total of 47,000 and upwards which the register comprised when it was handed over in 1837 to Somerset House. And that total is the more surprising when we remember that soon after 1780 the Deputies were to be mortified by watching their greatly treasured register receive the first series of legal setbacks.

This was the Act of 1783 imposing a stamp duty on all registers of baptism, or the Register to take out a licence. The Rev. Mr Aubery, the then Librarian, accordingly took out a licence;[2] but there was some doubt as to whether the Act (which had been designed for parochial registers) applied to Protestant Dissenters.[3] The Attorney-General, whose opinion was taken, said it did *not*;[4] but as he gave no reasons, the Deputies applied also to Mr Maddocks, who gave the same decision, adding that the certificates of Dissenting ministers, though upon stamps, would not be legal evidence, and advising an application to Parliament to amend the Act to include them, and to make the certificates legal evidence.[5]

The country Dissenters pressed the Deputies to take action[6] and a committee of ministers was set up to co-operate with them.[7] They succeeded and got the Act passed in 1785, extending the registering of Burials, Births, and Deaths to Protestant Dissenters.[8] Circular letters were sent to Dissenting ministers throughout the country with the forms of necessary registers;[9] and from that time until the repeal of the Stamp Act, the signatures of the Inspectors of the Stamp Office appeared regularly in the registers at Red Cross Street.[10] But those Deputies who hoped that by these measures they had ensured full legal validity to the register were to be disappointed. Neither the Act of 1785 nor the frequent attempts of the Committee and their legal advisers to improve the form of the certificate were to be adequate. An example of this care may be given. In 1805 the Deputies took fright at the possibility of abuse by registering persons 'at an advanced period of life'.[11] The sub-committee revised the form of certificate, but said that

---

[1] 19 Jan. 1770; 28 April 1780.   [2] 21 Nov. 1783.   [3] 4 June 1784.
[4] 1 Oct. 1784.   [5] *Ibid.*   [6] 19 Nov. 1784.
[7] 21 Jan. 1785.   [8] 17 Oct. 1785.   [9] *Ibid.*
[10] 15 May 1837: Report to Registration Commissioners.   [11] 31 May 1805.

no such abuse as had been apprehended was likely to occur, as the certificate when produced would shew at what time the birth had been registered.[1]

At this time 2,000 notices were printed for distribution to ministers throughout the kingdom.

In 1812, however, the Librarian reported that the Resident Admiralty Officer at Portsmouth, on application for passing a midshipman as a lieutenant, refused the Deputies' certificate unless it was accompanied by an affidavit verifying the age; this was not required for parish registrations.[2] The Deputies directed their Secretary to discover whether this was a new regulation, and the Admiralty replied that it was a regulation, but not a new one.[3]

Such an incident might be put down to Whitehall red tape or naval intransigence; but in 1821 came a more serious blow. The Master of the Rolls refused to accept a certificate in evidence on the ground of a defect in affidavit, there being not sufficient evidence of identity.[4] Though on further affidavit the order prayed for was obtained, and though the form of certificate was again altered,[5] the Deputies were never quite happy. They had always been aware that the register was private and had no public status; but like any other satisfactory evidence it was accepted as good evidence; for on occasion an entry in a family Bible, an inscription on a tombstone, or a pedigree hung up in the family mansion had been accepted as good evidence.[6]

Towards the end of 1823, however, further reports of the insufficiency of the register for legal purposes had come in, and it was decided to take counsel's opinion.[7] The Deputies went to James Stephen, who had been engaged in the case heard before the Master of the Rolls.

He was decidedly of opinion that the Register could not be made more available than a Family Register—he also stated that the only way of remedying the evil would be an application to Parliament, and suggested that Clergymen of Parishes should be compellable to register the Births and Baptisms of Children upon application being made to

[1] 13 June 1806.   [2] 30 Oct. 1812.   [3] 27 Nov. 1812.   [4] 21 Dec. 1821; 11 Jan. 1822.
[5] 22 Feb. 1822.   [6] 28 Oct. 1823.   [7] 28 Oct. 1823.

them for that purpose within some short period to be named after the Birth or Baptism . . . and thus place the Dissenters upon the same footing as members of the Established Church.

The matter was not taken further until three years later; the Protestant Society and the ministers approached the Deputies and a joint committee was set up by the ministers and Deputies to see what could be done, and to remove the erroneous impression that the register had 'by the late decision of the Master of the Rolls been rendered nugatory'. The Protestant Society reported that they had received some favourable communication from Government on the subject, but did not think it advisable to make any application until the meeting of the new Parliament.[1]

The joint committee thought it worth while to take legal advice once more on the legal form of the register; this time they went to Tindal (afterwards Chief Justice Tindal) and two others, but the reply was always the same: the system was as good as it could be made without Parliamentary authority, and 'admirably adapted to the great Majority of purposes'.[2] But while earnestly recommending the use of the Registry, and regretting

that any difficulty or defect in possible cases, which no voluntary Institutions can avoid, should diminish its universality and subsequently its usefulness

the Deputies went on to resolve

that the whole scheme of Registration of Births Marriages and Deaths in the country appears to be radically defective; not only as being identified with the Establishment, but as being in its details defective in many important particulars even for the limited purposes it is calculated to serve.

The Deputies pointed out that Churchmen as well as Catholics, Jews, and Nonconformists were affected by the evils complained of, but they felt that reform was only likely to spring

out of a more liberal policy on the part of the legislature with regard to the greater questions which affect the political situation of persons differing from the Establishment.

In other words, the Deputies felt that Repeal must come first, and

[1] 2 May 1826. [2] 1 Dec. 1826.

in a new atmosphere the remedying of other grievances would be possible. But the Dissenters in the country[1] continued to press the Deputies, and the Deputies to press their sub-committee[2] to take any possible steps in the matter, and 'to give early consideration to a general system of Registration of Births, Marriages, and Deaths'.[3]

One practical matter of value did occur to the Sub-Committee. There was no place of safety in which their now extensive registers could be kept at Dr Williams's Library. It was decided to procure a 'strong iron chest, similar to the one in use at the Thames Tunnel Office'.[4] Unfortunately the safes of those days were unwieldy articles, and so new-fangled that even the practical Deputies seem to have been at a little of a loss with them. When the chest had been installed at Dr Williams's Library—in the hall, for there was not room for it in the Librarian's office—a complaint was received from the house committee that it 'was useless for the purpose intended and as placed was insecure and dangerous to the Librarian in using it'.[5] The Deputies' sub-committee sent down to examine it reported that it was not as ordered: 'they recommended one of more convenient dimensions and of a different material'; nevertheless it seemed secure enough, and if there was no objection to its standing in the hall the size was not material. Unfortunately it had been placed upside down; the *lid* should open as a *door*, and if it was altered and shelves placed inside it should be practicable. The chest was altered, Dr Williams's trustees professed themselves satisfied, and the last we hear of the iron chest, after the Deputies' registers had been handed over to the Registrar-General, was that it was sold to Mr Jackson, the printer of Dr Wardlaw's Lectures, for two guineas, 'he taking it away'.[6]

The time had now arrived when, with the Test and Corporation Acts repealed, the Dissenters could bring forward the question of a general scheme of registration, and this was among the grievances which they regarded as most pressing.[7] The indefatigable Secretary, Robert Winter, turned from his daily wrestling with petitions

[1] E.g., 26 March: Rev. Mr Harris of Wallingford enquires whether there is any intention of applying to Parliament. [2] E.g., 26 Oct. 1827.
[3] 30 Jan. 1829: General Meeting to Committee. [4] 28 Nov. 1828.
[5] 30 Apr. 1830. [6] 27 Nov. 1840. [7] 30 Jan. 1829.

and deputations to the preparation of a 'Plan for a General Registration of Births, Marriages and Deaths throughout the Kingdom to be consolidated into one Metropolitan Registry', which he presented to the Committee on 27 Feb. 1829. It is a pity that the Minutes of the Deputies contain no further details of this, which might perhaps be claimed as the first detailed scheme on the lines which were seven years later to be adopted by Parliament. For the moment, though a sub-committee was appointed to consider it and to act jointly with the Protestant Society, who had been specially asked by the Wesleyans to exert themselves in this matter, the first step seemed to be to communicate with the Commissioners appointed to consider the laws of Real Property.[1] The Annual Meeting of 1829 agreed that it was wise to await the Commissioners' report before approaching Parliament; but in this, as in so many other matters, the Deputies had to submit to a long delay. In Nov. 1830 they noted that they were still waiting for the report, and in 1832 they were still waiting, while the Reform Bill agitation had come to sweep all other questions out of the public mind. The next move came not from the Deputies or the Protestant Society, but from Lord Nugent, who in April 1832 presented a Bill for the Registration of Births.[2] The Deputies suggested a number of amendments, most of which he adopted; they added that they would have preferred the whole question of Births, Marriages and Deaths to be treated together in the general measure 'which has so long been considered by the Real Property Commissioners'. Lord Nugent's Bill lapsed when he went to a foreign station.[3]

A new 'United Committee on Dissenting Grievances' was formed in 1833, and placed registration among the six grievances to be first remedied; but in spite of general encouragement by Grey and friendly advice from Lord John Russell, there was no progress; it was 1835 before the fraying temper of the Dissenters led them to threaten the Government with 'serious consequences in the event of a general election' if something was not done.[4]

Something *was* done. In March 1836 the Deputies were expressing their satisfaction at the Government's prompt honouring of its

[1] 27 Feb. 1829.   [2] 6 April 1832.   [3] Report for 1832.   [4] Report for 1835.

pledges about registration and confidence in the action of the United Committee:[1] 'the principles on which the Marriage and Registration Bills are founded appear to this Deputation to be just, comprehensive, and conciliatory'. They accordingly supported the Bill by petition to the Lords after it had passed the Commons, pointing out that Protestant Dissenters could get no registration without submitting to rites of Baptism and Burial of which they disapproved; and that the Bill would not only be a much valued concession to Dissenters but would confer extensive national benefit.[2] The Lords passed both the Marriage and Registration Bills, but with alterations which, the Deputies thought, would 'much impair their efficiency and render them in some instances inoperative'.[3]

A Commission was appointed to examine non-parochial registers with a view to giving legal effect to them;[4] and the Deputies, who in 1831 had already appointed a sub-committee to arrange for binding in books all the certificates at the Library,[5] now took seriously in hand the preparation of the registers for the inspection of the Commissioners.[6] The sub-committee were authorized to call in such assistance as they might think desirable, and in particular Mr Edgar Taylor, a leading Unitarian who had shown his expert knowledge in the evidence he gave to the Select Committee of the House of Commons on parochial registers in 1833, was asked to lend his 'valuable co-operation'.[7]

The sub-committee reported on 26 December 1836. In the six weeks since their appointment they had collected the 'ancient files and bundles of vouchers on parchment, of great extent and apparently in much confusion'; had arranged them perfectly and tied them up in bundles of 250 each, four bundles being placed in cases the size of large folio volumes. In all there were thirty volumes, containing a total of 30,065 entries, and these agreed so perfectly with the registers that only thirteen vouchers in all were missing. The registers themselves of the parchment series were large (some very large) folio volumes, lettered A to H.

After 1826, when the form of the certificates was altered in

---

[1] 4 Mar. 1836.   [2] 6 July 1836.   [3] 31 Aug. 1836.   [4] *Ibid.*
[5] 28 Jan. 1831.   [6] 16 Nov. 1836.   [7] *Ibid.*

accordance with the advice of Lord Chief Justice Tindal, parchment 'on which few people write well'[1] was abandoned, and paper substituted. The sub-committee arranged the vouchers of the paper series, which in number exceeded 6,000, and had them bound in twelve folio volumes, properly lettered. For the paper series a new system was adopted, by which the voucher itself became the principal record, and the register was merely a Calendar to the records, constructed in the form of an Alphabet of Surnames. Although the sub-committee found the new form of certificate vastly preferable, they thought the register not so good, for the whole information in the certificate was not entered; and, the entries not being made in series, an error in numbering could arise, and on one occasion had arisen.

The most laborious work of the Committee, which had required the personal exertions of its Members, consisted in the completion of what was formerly done year by year, under the direction of the Committee . . . that is, the checking of the Register by the collation of every entry with its corresponding Vouchers.

But at last all was done, and the Committee was ready to answer the enquiries which were addressed to them on 24 Feb. 1837 by Mr Burn, the secretary of the Registration Commission.

The Report of the Committee to the Registration Commissioners is admirably full and detailed, and it has been already drawn on largely in our account of the history of the registers, so that there is no need to recapitulate; it is necessary, however, to indicate its form. It answers a questionnaire submitted by the Registration Commissioners under eight heads.

(1) *When was the Registry established? By whom? and for whose use?*
The answer to this points out that the first entry in the register is dated 5 Jan. 1742-3 (old style); that it was established as a result of the deliberations of the Committee of Correspon-

---

[1] Report to the Commissioners, 15 May 1837. We may note also that parchment has long been expensive and difficult to obtain. As early as 22 March 1776, the Secretary had reported 'That he had not yet got the thousand Certificates printed for the Register, for that Mr Johnson the Printer told him Parchment was so exceeding dear that they would come to Twenty Guineas and therefore he did not chuse to have them done without further Orders.
Resolved that they be printed forthwith.'

dence; and was primarily for Protestant Dissenters, especially those residing in and within 10 miles of London—the ancient limit of the Deputation. As the Committee of Correspondence was the Deputies' link with country Dissenters, we may surmise that there was a demand for the Register outside London; and the Report indicates that 'persons of all classes, of all religious denominations, and natives of different countries have recorded the birth of their children in these books'.

(2) *Under whose superintendence is it kept, and in what manner is such superintendence exercised?*
This is answered by indicating the arrangements with Dr Williams's Library, the register being 'altogether the property of the Deputies' and kept at Red Cross Street as a place 'both safe and convenient for public resort'. The provision for checking is set out, including the recent collation of parts not verified —'the result has been in favour of their accuracy'.

(3) *The Commissioners desire to have a detailed account of the manner in which the register was originally kept, and on what document it was founded.*
The answer here gives details of the original certificate on parchment, of which a large edition was printed ('Dr Avery alone is stated in a contemporary memorandum to have had 1,400 at one time'); and points out that from the wording '*this* month' it was intended to be filled up at the very time of birth. It then describes later issues with different prefixes from B (1760) to the latest parchment issue, *H*.
It tells also of the registers into which the certificates were entered; from A, a thin folio volume bound in vellum, through B, a large folio ruled in columns, succeeded by others yet larger and thicker, down to G and H, which are of very great size. It explains the provision for the entry of births before 1743 (some as early as 1715); for baptisms; and for ministers' registers which were deposited separately.
It explains how the original parchments were preserved, on strong files of brass; and how they have now been transferred to cases containing 1,000 bound in bundles of 250. Thirteen

vouchers, of which details are given, are missing out of 30,000
—these were taken off for various purposes (one, for example
had been sent to the Watermen's Company), and not restored.
The answer concludes with statistics of the entries:

A. 5 Jan. 1743— 26 Sept. 1759—112		
19 Jan. 1759—181	total	329[1]
B. 28 Mar. 1759—11 June 1792		3509
C. 12 June 1792—24 May 1805		3860
D. 29 May 1805—15 April 1812		4429
E. 16 April 1812—31 Dec. 1816		4365
F. 3 Jan. 1817—29 Sept. 1820		4217
G. 3 Oct. 1820—8 Dec. 1824		5089
H. 9 Dec. 1824—28 Mar. 1837		4267
		30065

(4) *What forms are at present in use?*
The Committee describe the giving up of parchment in favour
of paper, which is almost as durable and easier to write on; the
changes in the certificate made by the highest legal advice,
especially Lord Chief Justice Tindal's in 1826; and the new
method of using the register itself as an Alphabetical Index.

(5) *Have the documents frequently or ever been called for in Courts of
Justice—in what way has proof been made, by producing the original
or an examined copy?*

(6) *Has the Registry been refused admission in evidence?*
The answers to these two questions are given together. The
registers are in daily use for various purposes—certificated or
examined copies either from the registers or the original are
demanded and given by the Registrar. The passing of the
Stamp Act and its extension to Dissenters are described. The
reply does not, however, go into details about the Admiralty
or Rolls cases.

(7) *Is there any objection to their transfer to the Registrar-General?*
The answer to this is polite but firm, in a vein of true Deputies'

---

[1] The original register, Volume A, had three parts; the first for births anterior to 1743
(112 entries); the second for births registered as they occurred (181 entries); the third for
baptisms (36 entries).

caution. There is no objection to the transfer of the registers, on condition that they become 'more accessible, useful, and authoritative by such transfer (and until such a measure is provided the public duty of the Deputies is to keep them in the well-known place where they have been conveniently and safely lodged for nearly 100 years)' and that they be given 'that force and validity as evidence in all courts' of which they are most worthy through 'their extent, their accuracy, and inviolability' and put 'on a perfect equality with any other registers, parochial or otherwise'.

The Committee ordered the deletion of a section speaking of the source of revenue which they are forgoing, and for which they might be entitled to seek compensation.

(8) The last section of the Report gives details of the chapel registers deposited with the Deputies; they will not part with these, any more than their own, until proper satisfaction is given of their validity.

On 5 July 1837, 'the Statute of the last Session of Parliament having now come into operation', the sub-committee recommended that the register 'shall terminate and be absolutely complete' on the last day of July, as the risk of concurrent registration was inadvisable.[1] The General Meeting, in even more haste, made the date 30 June.[2] But it was found advisable for the convenience of country Dissenters to register in a supplement children born before 1 July 1837 by reopening the register from 1 September to 31 December. To this the Commissioners agreed.[3] It was decided to charge 2s. 6d. for entries in the supplement, of which the Registrar was to keep 1s, the normal fee,[4] and hand to the Deputies 1s. 6d. to pay the expenses of the Committee, which had been very heavy—binding alone had cost £106 5s. in the last twelve months.

On 1 December the sub-committee reported that there were

---

[1] 5 July 1837.   [2] Ibid.   [3] 28 July and 3 Aug. 1837.
[4] The original fee had been 6d. At some time the fee was raised to 9d. (apparently without authority). In 1800 it was put down to 6d. again, the Register to have 10 guineas in lieu of the reduction. In 1805 the Register was to have 20 guineas and the 6d.'s. but not to charge more. Two years later, however, the General Meeting made the fee 1s.

17,022 certificates in the paper series when it closed at 31 July; 'which had come in so abundantly as to render it impossible to make the entries concurrently with the filing of the certificates'. The whole number of volumes would amount to 34. As for the supplement, 372 certificates had been received, yet the demand continued. Fifteen hundred new forms had been issued. 'The present existence and speedy close of this Supplemental Register should be extensively made known, especially in the provincial papers'. At the same time it was agreed to remit the 2s. 6d. fee to poor parents in cases of hardship. As it was announced on 17 Jan. 1838 that the Registrar had £90 as the Deputies' share of 2s. 6d. fees, it seems that 1,200 people paid for entries, with an unknown number of others whose fees were remitted.

The register closed in a blaze of glory with the visit of the Registrar-General and the Commissioners on 30 March 1838, when they 'expressed great satisfaction with the same'. Losing no time, the Deputies wrote to the Commissioners to convey the 'very great anxiety felt by Protestant Dissenters concerning the registers which have been placed in their custody as to the manner in which it is proposed to deal with them hereafter'. The Commissioners were pressed to complete their report so that a measure might be passed 'in the course of the present session'. Two months later the Deputies again showed their anxiety by enquiring about the progress of the report and asking for an interview; but Mr Burn, the secretary, was able to assure them that the report was completed and signed and only awaited a final interview with the Lord Chancellor.[1] By the end of the year it was published. The Commissioners mentioned that 'a great portion [of the non-parochial records] consists of the Deputies' Registers at Red Cross Street'. They recommended that all should be kept in some secure place under the care of the Registrar-General and declared to be in legal custody and receivable in evidence (with legitimate safe-guards). The Deputies were satisfied and pressed for a statutory embodiment of the report.[2]

So far, all was well; and it seemed that there would be no more trouble, for on 18 Feb. 1839, Lord John Russell gave notice of a

---

[1] 30 May 1838. [2] 14 Dec. 1838.

motion to legalize the non-parochial registers. But nothing was ever made easy for the Deputies. In May they were obliged to make a fresh application to Lord John, asking for 'as little delay as possible';[1] and at the end of the year they were obliged to record that the promised Bill, though it had passed the Commons, had been lost in the Lords.[2] Until it was passed the Committee 'do not feel justified in recommending you to place your invaluable registers under the care of the Commissioners'.

In March 1840 the Deputies sent a deputation to see Lord Normanby on the matter, and he promised that the Lord Chancellor would introduce a measure when he had seen the judges on their return from circuit.[3] But in April the Deputies were anxious again; they wrote three times (2 April, 29 May, 26 June) and at the end of July, having had no reply, they sought a Peer to ask the Government for its intentions. The end of the story is best told in the words of the Annual Report for 1840:

Mr Baines also, when all hope seemed about to expire, brought the subject at the instance of your Committee before the house of commons, and they now congratulate their constituents that a bill was introduced by her Majesty's Ministers at the close of the session which has passed into a law. By this means 7,000 books of registers belonging to foreign Protestant Churches in England, to the Presbyterians, Independents, and Baptists, to the Wesleyans in their several branches, to Calvinistic Methodists and Quakers and to Roman Catholics, including the valuable register lately kept at Dr Williams's Library, have been deposited . . . and are now equally valid in courts of Justice with parochial Registers.

The Deputies now made a return gesture. The Corporation of London had 27 volumes of the Bunhill Fields Register, recording interments there since 1713 and containing about 100,000 entries. The Corporation, when approached by the Commissioners, would only hand over the registers if a copy was made for them, an expense the Commissioners would not meet. After the passing of the Non-Parochial Registers Act, 1840, a deputation from the Deputies went to the Corporation and persuaded the City Lands

[1] 3 May 1839.   [2] Report for 1839.   [3] 11 Mar. 1840.

Committee to recommend handing over the Bunhill Registers, and it was done.[1]

On 14 October the Committee of Deputies learnt that their registers had been removed from Dr Williams's Library to Rolls Yard, Chancery Lane, the place of deposit. All that remained was the iron chest, which Mr Jackson was to get for two guineas, 'he taking it away'. No longer were the servants at Dr Williams's to spend their time answering the door to importunate parents; a service for which in late years they had received an annual gratuity of two, and sometimes three, guineas. The Library was left to the somnolent peace of the Nonconformist ministers, who, according to a London guide of the middle century, were its chief patrons.

(b) Marriage Laws

The history of the marriage ceremony among Dissenters since the Revolution falls into three main parts: from 1688 to 1753; from 1753 to 1836; and since 1836. During the first period Dissenting marriages were tolerated though not legalized as such; in the second period they were neither tolerated nor legalized; in the third they were legalized, but under conditions involving a series of stigmas and disabilities which were only removed piecemeal by steady pressure for more than half a century.

Until the passing of Lord Hardwicke's Act in 1753, marriage in meeting-houses was not uncommon; for the public contract made by the parties constituted a legal marriage, though validity of the ceremony itself was not recognized by the law. The Act, which was occasioned by the scandals of prison weddings and other irregularities, was aimed not at Dissenters' marriages but at clandestine marriages. However, by making all marriages illegal in England except those regularly celebrated by the clergy of the Established Church, it removed the old Common Law toleration of 'irregular' marriages, and gave the Dissenters a new grievance. By that whimsicality which we have noted elsewhere, Jews and Quakers fared better than the Three Dissenting Bodies: they alone

[1] This is an instance of the extraordinary influence the Deputies had with the City at this period.

had the privilege of marrying according to their own rites, where both parties belonged to their persuasion. The *Sketch*[1] records a case in which a couple who had been married in a meeting-house at Barton, Leicestershire, prior to the passing of Lord Hardwicke's act, had their marriage declared invalid and their children illegitimate after a period of twenty-five years, in 1777.

During the second period, then, Dissenters were compelled to go to church (or to take a trip to Scotland) if they wished to be married legally. But the clergy were not always willing to marry them, especially if they were brought up as Baptists and had not been baptized. The Deputies had to intervene in several cases of this nature, and were driven at last to take counsel's opinion, from which it appeared that clergymen could not refuse to marry those who applied to them, even if they were unbaptized.[2]

The extension of toleration to Unitarians in 1812 opened a new question. As long as they had retained other names (most English Presbyterians were by now Unitarian),[3] the special grievance which Unitarians felt against being married in the name of the Holy Trinity obviously could have no remedy. But as soon as Unitarians were legally free to declare themselves and to organize Unitarian societies, the question became practical. From 1819 a series of Bills were introduced on the subject; William Smith, the Deputies' Chairman, was very active in promoting these, and the Deputies naturally desired to co-operate.

At first it was suggested that the clergy, in performing Unitarian marriages, should omit the references to the Holy Trinity; but this would merely have transferred the grievance to the clergy, and it was seen that the solution was to permit marriages in meeting-houses. The Deputies, however, were not anxious at this time to raise the general question while they were occupied with Repeal.[4] In March 1829 a resolution of the Protestant Society, approved by the Deputies, urged definitely that no measure about Dissenters' marriages should be put up at present. The Unitarians should conduct their own case alone with such help as they might expect from all who respect rights of conscience.[5]

[1] P. 45.   [2] *Sketch*, pp. 45 and 165-6.
[3] See Part I, Chapter 5.   [4] 19 Dec. 1823; 27 Feb. 1824.   [5] 29 Mar. 1829.

But in fact, though the Unitarians went on with their plans, the only possible solution was a general one, and it could not be satisfactory apart from the complex question of registration. The long-sustained hopes of the Unitarians and the friendly support of the Deputies were only to be satisfied in the end by a general measure. As long ago as 1824, William Smith had reported to the Deputies' General Meeting that he had seen Lord Ellenborough on the Marriage Act, and that the Lords' Committee seemed favourable; but this mention is deleted in the Minutes, as though it were recognized as indiscreet. In 1831 the Deputies, when they conferred with Edgar Taylor (representing the Unitarian Association) on the subject, found him still sanguine.[1] The Government could not help at so busy a time, but Lord Holland would; and the Bishop of London had admitted the need for reform. With their support the Bill might succeed. But it did not; the Bishop of London being prevented by the opposition of his clergy, while the Government felt, as Lord Lansdowne explained, that it dared not in the middle of the Reform Bill crisis present its opponents with a rod for its own back.

Although Lord Grey refused to introduce a Bill for the relief of Unitarians at this time, he said he would welcome any statement of the Dissenters' case which might be sent to him. This seemed to point to a general measure, and in March the Deputies instructed their Committee to take every means in their power to get the law improved for Dissenters generally.[2] They waited until the Reform Bill had received the Royal Assent (7 June 1832) and then in the autumn returned to the charge[3] with a brief statement prepared for Lord Grey. The statement claimed that Lord Hardwicke, to effect a good reform, had worked a violent change inadvertently. It was an infringement of the Toleration Act (which, its conditions once complied with, allowed worship of God according to conscience) that all except Jews and Quakers should be compelled on a certain occasion to observe the episcopal forms. The Committee claimed only what their fellow-subjects in Ireland, Scotland and the colonies enjoyed. The Unitarians felt strong objections to particular portions of the service; the rest of the Dissenters, though

---

[1] 19 Jan. 1831. [2] 16 Dec. 1831. [3] 26 Oct, 1 Nov., 3 Nov. 1832.

they found some parts objectionable, preferred to base their case on the objection to compulsory uniformity; and they felt that their reasonable objections might be removed and the civil advantages of the Marriage Act retained.

Lord Grey, in a friendly but non-committal reply, promised to consult his colleagues.[1] The importance of common action was now clear; and by arrangement with the Unitarians their Bill was made over to the Deputies, who paid £50 to them in consideration of their expenses in the matter. To them the Congregationalists and the several London and County Associations sent information about their own plans and enquiries about their attitude.[2]

The necessary alterations in the Unitarian Bill were discussed, and as finally approved a Bill was printed.[3] To ninety-six letters sent out to influential ministers, fifty-one replies were received by 6 Feb. 1833, all except three favouring an application; but many suggested that at the same time relief from other grievances should also be sought.

In consultation with the Ministers of the Three Denominations a list of the grievances was prepared, and a new United Committee, similarly constituted to that which had conducted the Repeal campaign, was formed, the Wesleyans and Quakers refusing their adherence. The Deputies, on 15 March 1833, agreed on a list of six 'practical grievances' which were subsequently made the basis of a memorial by the United Committee. They were compulsory conformity to the Prayer Book in Marriage; the want of a legal registration of Dissenters' births and deaths; liability to Church Rates and other ecclesiastical demands; alleged liability of places of worship to poor rates; denial of the right of burial by their own ministers in parochial churchyards; and virtual exclusion from the benefits of Oxford and Cambridge.

Earl Grey was still friendly, but owing to the importance of other business before Parliament, he assured them that there would be no Church reform legislation that session. The United Committee decided therefore to wait a year, preparing petitions, organizing local committees, and diffusing relevant information about Dissenters, especially among M.P.s.

[1] 30 Nov. 1832. [2] 21 Dec. 1832. [3] 26 Dec. 1832.

In Feb. 1834 the Deputies approved a petition based on the earlier list. They stated their conviction that marriage ought to be a civil contract, that its legal validity should depend on registration after due publicity by a civil registrar, any religious ceremony being left to the discretion of the parties.[1] A copy of this was sent to Brougham, and at his suggestion a Marriage Bill was prepared for the Deputies, authorizing marriage by Justices of the Peace. This was approved by a large body of London ministers and by the Deputies, but Parliament was prorogued before it was introduced.[2] Meanwhile Lord John Russell brought forward another Bill which satisfied nobody: it would have retained the publication of banns in the parish church but allowed marriage and registration in the Dissenters' chapels.

It became clearer and clearer that no satisfactory Bill could be produced until the civil registration of births, marriages and deaths was introduced. To this, therefore, the United Committee decided to devote its immediate attention. This plan they adopted by the advice of Lord John Russell, who discussed the matter with them 'with his usual candour and ability'.[3]

The brief Ministry of Sir Robert Peel provided the first of his many attempts to deal with problems affecting religion. He proposed, for Nonconformists, marriage before a civil magistrate and registration by the parish authorities, to which a religious service might be added if desired. Marriages in England would thus have been of two kinds: a religious Anglican marriage for members of the Church of England, or an essentially secular marriage supervised by the poor law authorities to which any religious service might be added if anyone was so minded. This is the first mention of the poor law in connection with Dissenters' marriages; it was to recur in varying forms over a long period, always arousing the same bitterness; for in the eyes of the respectable country Dissenter even the most fleeting connection with the parish officers carried an ineradicable blot. The Board of Congregational Ministers hit the nail on the head when they declared that what was wanted was (1) a purely civil contract for those who wanted that, and (2) a religious service as an integral part of the ceremony for Dissenters

[1] 8 April 1834.   [2] 28 June 1834; Report for 1834.   [3] Report for 1835.

275

not less than for Anglicans. In dancing on the grave of the
Bill and the Ministry ('Fortunately the authors of this measure
were not in power long enough to enable them to carry or complete it'), the Deputies only welcomed the measure as 'the acknowledgement of a wrong and the concession of a remedy by a
party which has uniformly opposed both'.[1]

The Whigs again took office. As soon as it was clear that another
session would go by without any remedy of grievances, a deputation from the United Committee warned Lord Melbourne that
'unless there were an explicit declaration of the intention of the
government to introduce measures for the relief of the Dissenters
early next session, the present postponement might be attended
with serious consequences in the event of a general election'. This
declaration, made on 29 June 1835,[2] had its result; for by 4 March
1836 the Deputies were expressing their gratitude for Marriage and
Registration Bills on what appeared to be sound lines. Civil
marriage was now to be made possible because an effective system
of registration was set up at the same time. On 31 August 1836
the Deputies held a special meeting to celebrate the passing of the
Bills, but their rejoicing was not unmixed. The United Committee
had been in constant communication with the Government both
through deputation and by learned counsel, and though some only
of their proposed amendments had been acceded to, these had
greatly improved the measures.[3] In particular, the Deputies successfully opposed a proposal made in the House of Lords that before
a civil marriage a declaration should be made: 'I have a conscientious scruple against being married in Church or Chapel by a
religious ceremony'. This, the Deputies pointed out, was a religious
test 'both needless and mischievous'.[4] But the Marriage Act contained serious defects which the United Committee, its deputations
and learned counsel had not been able to eradicate. Fees for the
celebration of marriage under the Act were higher than those for
marriage in the Established Church, and notices of application for
marriage had to be read before the Guardians of the Poor. The extra
cost would be a serious consideration for many poor Dissenters

---

[1] See Report for 1835 and Resolution of the Board 14 April 1835.
[2] Report for 1835.   [3] Report for 1836.   [4] 6 July 1836.

and would, in the language of the Deputies, 'render the Bill in some instances inoperative for many of the parties for whose benefit it was designed'. The wanton introduction of the Guardians of the Poor gave a touch of degradation to a Dissenting marriage which could hardly have been unintended.

So, in a mood of mingled triumph and vexation, ended the second chapter of the marriage question. It was to be twenty years before any further instalment of reform was obtained; the heart-breaking procedure of delay, evasion and postponement had to be faced again and again. Stimulated by the Board of Congregational Ministers, the United Committee tried without success to get the Government to bring in a Bill to amend the Act before it began to operate. Lord John Russell thought that a private Bill should be promoted, and this was agreed on. In finally thanking 'His Majesty's liberal and enlightened Ministers' for the Act the United Committee put it on record that 'these invidious distinctions were not introduced by the Ministers'. The Ministry returned the compliment by producing an amending Bill which rendered the proposed private measure unnecessary—but it did not pass into law.[1]

From time to time references to marriage appeared in petitions about Dissenters' grievances, for instance in 1839 and 1849,[2] but except for some minor concessions in 1840 nothing was achieved. These concessions, which had been thoroughly discussed with the Deputies and in their final form had met their wishes, were included in the Act moved by Mr Langdale in that year. They allowed Dissenters to marry outside their own districts, if there was not in the district where they resided a chapel in which the particular rites desired could be used. After this it was twelve years before the marriage question was reopened on the initiative of the Congregational Union; for during Peel's Administration the Dissenters had little to hope for except trouble.

By this time the Registrar-General's office was functioning smoothly, and the Deputies were able to consult its secretary, Mr Mann, on the drafting of a new Bill. On this and many other occasions he proved a good friend to them, though his chief, Major Graham, was not always so co-operative.

[1] Report for 1836 and 1837.   [2] 8 Feb. 1839 and 7 Dec. 1849.

The way was prepared by a petition setting out the grievances remaining and praying that Dissenters might have the same marriage facilities as Anglicans. The grievances were that notification must be read before the Board of Guardians; that marriages by licence sometimes needed notice to be given unnecessarily in two places, and afterwards were sometimes unnecessarily delayed; fees were too high; marriages were celebrated sometimes before Registrars in chapels to which parties did not belong, at inconvenient hours, and without the permission of those interested in such chapels.[1] The Deputies had already asked Mr Mann, through their legal sub-committee, if he knew what the position would be of parties who wished to marry in a licensed chapel if the minister, proprietor, or trustees objected;[2] but no answer is recorded, and it is probable from the sequel that the Registrar-General would not commit himself, or that a legal right was presumed.

The Deputies had noted in their Annual Report for 1852 that 'the House of Commons recently elected happily contains an unusual number of members entertaining opinions in accordance with those of this Deputation', and they prepared to take advantage of the situation by promoting and supporting various measures. It is instructive to compare the pages of the Minute Books for the years following 1852 with the previous years under Peel. Now the Committee meetings are taken up with a perpetual activity of drafting and re-drafting, attempts at conciliation, interviews with Ministers and M.P.s, petitions, consultations with interested bodies, reports, and advertisements in the papers. It is at this period that a standing Parliamentary Committee is formed with friendly M.P.s.[3] This, too, is the date of the founding of the Liberation Society, which, having held its inaugural meeting at Radley's Hotel on 17 Feb. 1853, lost no time in sending a deputation to the Deputies (18 March). But in spite of this activity and these fair hopes, the Deputies' schemes did not go altogether smoothly. On

[1] 16 May 1853.　　　　　　　　　　　　　　　　　[2] 18 Feb. 1853.
[3] 7 Feb. 1854; after an interview with Palmerston attended by the Deputies' Committee and 9 M.P.s as well as representatives of the Congregational Union. It had first been suggested by Josiah Conder in 1844 as a necessary piece of machinery. In the second half of the 19th century it was regularly appointed, and in the nineties was actively considering many Bills.

the subject of the marriage laws and other matters they had to face the new Home Secretary, the redoubtable Lord Palmerston. They had to remember many technical points which were raised from time to time by the Registrar-General, Major Graham. They must not forget the special position of the Roman Catholics, the Quakers and the Jews. But perhaps even more difficulty was caused by a side-issue which raised the old animosity between the Deputies and the Unitarian-Presbyterians.

This was the question of the registration of chapels, a measure which was intimately bound up with the marriage question since this registration was necessary for obtaining a licence for marriage. The Government prepared in 1853 a 'Places of Public Worship Registration Bill' to transfer the registration of Dissenting meeting-houses to the Registrar-General (which by a technical error had been previously omitted); to procure returns of Registered Places; and to remove doubts as to the legality of licences granted by chapels which could not prove that they had been registered. In actual fact this Bill had been settled between Mr Mann and Mr Terrell, the Deputies' Secretary, and almost every point had been agreed between them; but just before the second reading the 'Presbyterian' Deputies had waited on Lord Palmerston with objections: they wished all Protestant Dissenters to be registered under that head, not by denominations because they feared to lose their title to chapels given in a recent Act.[1] This produced confusion and deadlock between all the parties. To begin with, Lord Palmerston, new to the bewildering forest of Dissenting politics, understood the *'Presbyterian'* delegates to represent the *'Three Denominations'*; Mr Mann asked the Deputies to give their formal approval of the Bill 'that he might disabuse Lord Palmerston as to the error entertained by him'. The Deputies of the Three Denominations 'preferred publicity' on the denominational point, especially as any congregation might, if it wished, be registered under the head of 'Protestant Dissenters' only. The Unitarian fears were therefore groundless. The Registrar-General equally would not submit to some of the Unitarians' amendments; but the Government would not proceed in opposition to their wishes,

---

[1] See section on Dissenters Chapels Act in Part I, Chapter 5 (p. 87).

which had the weighty support of Lord John Russell. Lord Palmerston said he wished to do only what was agreeable to Dissenters generally; and after some M.P.s had failed in an effort to mediate, the Bill was dropped, leaving the serious situation that it was legally doubtful whether any Dissenting place of worship could be legally registered—though this was necessary to obtain a licence for marriage. It was not until 24 August 1855 that the Deputies recorded that the Bill had received the Royal Assent, after the Unitarian objections had been met.

When it is considered that at this period the Church Rates agitation was at its height, and that Lord Palmerston with other members of the Government was hearing a good deal about other Dissenting grievances, it is hard to refrain from sympathizing with him when he let it be known to the Deputies through the Registrar-General that he would introduce the Chapels Registration Bill if the Dissenters were unanimous, 'but if he is again to be subjected to what took place last session I think you must prevail on some independent member to introduce it'.[1] Nor can he perhaps be blamed if in July he refused to see another deputation on Church Rates.[2]

But if all this had its comic, it had also its serious side; as Lord Palmerston's patience wore thin, the hopes of a quick and complete settlement of the marriage question wore thin also.

The first delay in the summer of 1853 was occasioned by the Registrar-General. He said that the Bill drafted by the Deputies would cause much trouble to the Registration Office, that it did not go far enough, and that an official Bill covering registration as well as marriage was being considered.[3] In the autumn, however, the Deputies learnt through Mr Mann that the Registrar-General was not in fact preparing a Bill.[4] But in spite of the fact that Palmerston had put them off, that their efforts to introduce a private Bill had been abortive,[5] and that the Registrar-General had misled them, the Deputies were still hopeful, and believed that all their objects would be embodied in a Government measure in the next session.[6]

---

[1] 29 April 1854.   [2] 14 July 1854. See Part II, Chap. 5.   [3] 4 July 1853
[4] 4 and 22 Nov. 1853.   [5] 5 Aug. 1853.   [6] Report for 1853.

Accordingly, on 7 Feb. 1854 the whole Committee headed by its Chairman and reinforced by Congregationalists and nine M.P.s waited on Lord Palmerston. After a discussion of the Church Rates question they came to the Marriage Acts. Palmerston was reminded that he had approved of the Deputies' Bill, and that it had been postponed at the wish of the Government in order that additions might be made. He was now urged to introduce it as a Government measure with such additions as he thought fit. Lord Palmerston said that he was in communication with the Registrar-General and would consider the Bill. The Deputies then decided to interview the Registrar-General[1] and a General Meeting petitioned in its favour.[2]

By the time that the Deputies got to the Registrar-General, the ball had been passed back to Lord Palmerston. Major Graham informed the Deputies that the replacing of the publication of marriage notices before the Boards of Guardians affected so many Acts that Lord Palmerston thought a Consolidating Bill would be best. This would, of course, have to go to all the parties concerned, including the Lord Chancellor, and could not therefore come up until the next session. The Deputies were not satisfied; they appealed to their Parliamentary Committee, and all through the spring, from April to June 1854, they were pressing hard for action.[3] At last the Bill was read a first time, on the understanding that it should not be proceeded with till next session.[4]

A petition on familiar lines opened the campaign of 1855.[5] The Bill was read a second time, but it was still not plain sailing: there was considerable opposition and many amendments. Opposition came from the Jews and the Quakers, who were jealous lest the removal of Dissenters' grievances should touch the specially privileged position that they had enjoyed for many years. They were therefore cut out of the operation of the Bill; but after their objections and those of the Catholics had been met, and further difficulties with the Government over the question of proper notice of marriage had been overcome, there was still another obstacle. The Bill was dropped in the Lords because the Lord Chancellor

---

[1] 7 Feb. 1854. [2] 17 Mar. 1854. [3] 29 April, 12 May, 2 June 1854.
[4] 18 Oct. 1854. [5] 2 Feb. 1855.

refused to accept a clause which would have given a clergyman power to refuse to marry parties who produced a Registrar's certificate instead of banns.[1] Palmerston nevertheless promised to assist the Bill in the next session, and the season ended with thanks to their helpers, and to the Government for its 'acquiescence' in the Bill.

But even in the next session there was grit in the wheels. The Superintendent Registrars, the Quakers, the Liberal Jews, and the Scots had all to be conciliated. One objectionable proposal, which was resisted, was to have notices of marriage posted outside the Registrars' offices. Some of the parties interested made a proposal which anticipated the Act of 1898: this would have made the Dissenting ministers themselves Registrars of marriages. But the Deputies shewed their usual caution; not knowing of any inconvenience arising from the appointment of Registrars, they did not approve any change in the law in that respect. So at last the Bill was passed in the summer of 1856.[2]

The main point had been won, but, as might be expected from so long and so exasperatingly complex a dispute, some grounds of trouble were left, and another half-century of effort was needed before Dissenters could feel that their marriages enjoyed equal status with those of the Anglican Church. During the fifties and sixties the trouble was chiefly with Anglican clergy who refused to accept the validity of Dissenters' marriages; and with Registrars unsympathetic to Dissent who lacked the decency to refrain from irreverent behaviour in chapel. But these were few and isolated cases. A more substantial matter was the system of registration itself, which had many disadvantages. Sometimes there were not enough assistant registrars; and though sometimes complaint secured redress, as at Swinton, Manchester, local feeling in remote country districts like Cerne Abbas was not always strong enough

[1] 24 Aug. 1855.
[2] A Royal Commission was appointed 'to enquire into the authenticity and custody of non-parochial registers of births, baptisms, deaths, burials, and marriages'; and the Deputies' standing may be judged from the fact that of the seven Commissioners, three were Deputies—Robert Lush (afterwards Lord Justice Lush), Samuel Gale, and Hull Terrell, their Secretary. The others were Major Graham and Horace Mann, John S. Burn and William Palmer Parker, who had been secretary of the Registration Commission of 1837.

to produce a memorial.[1] Even the ancient stigma of a poor law connexion was not easy to avoid at times. The appointment of Relieving Officers as Registrars was not unknown, and suitable personally as such men might well be, the objection to such appointments was decisive.[2] But more radical was the growing feeling against the presence of the Registrar at Nonconformist marriages at all. It seemed that the Deputies had been *too* cautious when they said in 1856 that they knew of no inconvenience arising from the appointment of Registrars. But they long maintained their objection to the alternative proposal to enable Dissenting ministers to register officially the marriages that they solemnized. In 1880, for instance, they passed a resolution objecting to Mr Blennerhasset's Bill on these lines, contending that the existing method secured accuracy better. But the main objection was that it would make the ministers State officials.[3]

This rather doctrinaire position, however it might be explained by the Deputies' long struggle with State interference in religious matters, was not shared by all. The Methodists especially felt the necessity of some change which should make the attendance of the Registrar unnecessary. The defects of the arrangement were many. The limited hours within which marriages could take place, and the often inadequate number of Registrars, made it not always easy to get a marriage celebrated at a time desired by the parties. If a Registrar was hostile to Dissent he could make the machinery work very stiffly, or he could degrade the ceremony by mis-behaving when he did arrive. Even in the most favourable condi-tions his presence was a stigma marking the inferior status of a Dissenting to an Established minister of religion.

In 1881 a representative conference called at the instance of the Congregationalists to discuss the marriage laws found the Non-conformists still deeply divided, and this division can be seen in all the deliberations of the next decade, even though feeling became clearer and clearer against the attendance of the Registrar. As late

---

[1] 21 April and 18 July 1882.
[2] E.g. at Northwich in 1897. The Registrar-General declared his intention of with-holding his consent to the appointment of Relieving Officers if unwelcome to Noncon-formists; but in this case it had been strongly urged by local ministers (18 Feb. 1897).
[3] 25 Feb. 1880.

as 1892, when a joint consultative committee was appointed at the instance of the Wesleyans to assist with a Marriage Bill, the Deputies displayed great anxiety to keep control of their representatives on the committee; they could only give a binding vote when instructed in advance by the Deputies.[1]

Under these circumstances the only thing was to proceed stage by stage. The conference of 1881 had discussed three proposals: the equalization of cost for marriage in the parish church and elsewhere; the extension of hours from 8 to 12 to 8 to 6; and the abolition of the Registrar's attendance by making the minister or other 'leading person' responsible for legal formalities and certification.[2] No decision had been reached at the conference; and though by keeping up their presssure for a year the Liberation Society and the Congregational and Baptist Unions had prevailed on the Deputies to sponsor a Bill,[3] the Bill was first restricted to an extension of hours to 6 p.m,[4] and then dropped altogether.[5] It was not until 1886, after several attempts, that a partial extension of the hours, to 3 p.m., was at last obtained.[6]

Meanwhile, feeling about the Registrar's attendance had not abated. In 1883 the Wesleyan Committee of Privilege had consulted the Deputies about a general alteration of the law on the basis of Scotch law.[7] Three years later Sir Richard Webster, on behalf of the Government, introduced a Bill to abolish the Registrar's attendance. The Deputies helped to draw up resolutions, which were considered by a representative conference—and passed practically unanimously. They gratefully recognized that the Bill was an honest attempt to remedy an admitted grievance. But they were not satisfied with some of the clauses, such as those which made only ministers legal witnesses of marriage; required registration of ministers with unnecessary frequency; and paid Registrars for attendance though they did not attend. The Deputies hoped to see the Bill withdrawn and a more carefully considered measure introduced.[8] These critical resolutions were repeated by the Deputies at their Annual Meeting the following

---

[1] 17 Nov. and 15 Dec. 1892.   [2] 1 April 1881.   [3] 6 Jan. 1882.
[4] 3 Feb. 1882.   [5] 18 July 1882.   [6] 2 June 1886.
[7] 20 Feb. 1883.   [8] 2 June 1886.

year (1887) after another representative conference in the spring
had confirmed that Nonconformist feeling rejected Sir Richard
Webster's Bill.[1]

Early in 1888 something like a delimitation of spheres of influence
occurred. The Wesleyans, who for some time had been keenest
about marriage law reform, were to proceed with that, leaving
burial law reform to the Deputies and the Liberation Society. On
the basis of this the Methodists prepared a Bill, which was introduced by Mr Fowler in 1888, and re-introduced by Mr Waddy
in 1891. The Deputies supported this, in spite of the objections
which some Nonconformists still felt; though they suggested some
alterations, which were accepted. However, seven more years
were to pass before an alteration of the law was secured, largely
because general political conditions were unfavourable at the end
of Mr Gladstone's career and of the Liberal Government. In 1893
a Select Committee of the House of Commons had heard evidence;
the Secretary of the Deputies was the first witness after the
Registrar-General; and the committee's report was very much
in line with the Deputies' views.[2] The findings of the committee
were the basis of a Bill which reappeared in 1898, and was
supported, with reservations, by the Deputies.[3] The Bill became
law, and allowed an authorized person (who need not be the
minister) to take the Registrar's place, subject to somewhat burden-
some regulations about registers. The Deputies issued to the Three
Dissenting Bodies a statement on the use of the Act; and at the
request of the Wesleyans, they used it also.[4]

Dissenting opinion was still sharply divided about the measure.
In March 1889 the Deputies learnt that out of every five churches
which had communicated with their Secretary, three appeared to
favour and two to disapprove of the Act.[5] But by 1907, 2,398
churches had adopted the Act.[6] The English marriage laws will
always bear the mark of their mixed origin and their confused
upbringing, but with the many small adjustments that have been
made, all practical grievance may be said to have disappeared.

[1] 10 Mar. and 29 June 1887.   [2] 5 Oct. 1893.
[3] 27 April 1898.   [4] 22 Sept., 25 Nov., and 21 Dec. 1898.
[5] 20 Mar. 1899.   [6] 18 Oct. 1907.

(c) Burial Laws

The right of burial occupied the attention of the Deputies more frequently, and over a longer period, than any other. Burial cases were among the first which came before the Deputies on their formation[1] (Bideford, 1745, Watesfield, 1748) and a burial case is the most recent with which they have dealt (Chorley, Lancs., 1944).[2] For many years there were at least twice as many references to burial as to any other subject.

During the 18th century, in this matter as in others, the Deputies stood on the defensive, their main concern being to secure the recognition of the Common Law and Canon Law right of Dissenters to burial in parish churchyards by the clergymen of the parish. In the 19th century they passed to the offensive; a long agitation to allow burial *by their own ministers* in parish churchyards was at last successful with the passing of Mr Osborne Morgan's Act in 1880.[3] After 1880 they had a new task: that of seeing that the Act was obeyed by clergymen who detested it. Continuously, before and after 1880, they concerned themselves with the kindred but separate problem of securing religious equality in public cemeteries.

The problems were connected, but that of the parish churchyard was the most acute. The clergyman might with a good conscience decline to give Christian burial to anyone whose baptism was doubtful. He not only might refuse, it was his duty to refuse, to read the service over the unbaptized. There was, therefore, a large area for disputes about doubtful baptism; and there was the insoluble problem of providing Christian burial for the children of Baptists. Unbaptized children were sometimes denied not only Christian burial, but also interment. Action might lie against the incumbent, but the law was difficult to apply; and an application to Parliament for a change in the law was in the Deputies' minds long before the agitation seriously began.[4] Even with the greatest

---

[1] *Sketch*, pp. 13 and 134-5.　　　　　　　　　　　　　　[2] See below, p. 331.

[3] See below, p. 321, 43 and 44 Vict. c. 41.

[4] Shrewsbury: Deputies advise asking the Bishop of Hereford to prevent repetition, 29 July 1814.

charity and desire to understand another man's convictions the situation would have been difficult. When, as often, there was no charity and a readiness to misunderstand, the situation became tragic. What might be reported by solicitors and bishops as a clergyman's 'misapprehension' was known locally to be 'wilful misapprehension'.

The existence of a Dissenting burial ground lessened, but did not extinguish, the causes of trouble. Anglican officials claimed that, in whatever ground the burial might be, they ought not to be defrauded of their customary fees when funerals occurred in the parish: for example, when in 1806 the mother of a Dissenting minister at Godmanchester was buried in meeting-house ground, 'the Rev. Mr Harris, a Dissenting minister from Cambridge, delivering an oration at the grave', a fee was demanded by the clergyman, and refused by the Deputies' advice. Similar advice was given to the Rev. Mr Moy of Malden three years later. Mr Moy had also asked if the law requiring burial in woollens applied to Dissenters—the Minutes report that this question was answered, but, alas, provide no details.[1] Parish clerks claimed fees for tolling the bell and for grave-digging, even when the interment was not in the churchyard. When the mourners asked for the bell to be rung, of course they must pay for it,[2] but not otherwise. The Deputies had many cases of successful opposition to their credit.

In such cases, however vexatious, the law was clear. But a borderline case will illustrate the difficulties. In 1829, at Eatington in Warwickshire, the burial of a young married man by his wife's side in the churchyard was refused, on the ground that he had not been baptized. The Deputies referred the incumbent to the case of Kemp v. Wickes,[3] stating that the young man, whose name was Cakebread, had been baptized by immersion as an adult, and that burial could therefore not legally be refused. But the incumbent replied that he had good ground to know that Cakebread was dedicated, not baptized. The local Baptists, on the contrary, said they knew he had been baptized.[4] The correspondence was referred

---

[1] 24 Feb. 1809.
[2] As at Baldock, 27 Mar. 1833, or Tring, 18 Dec. 1829.
[3] Arches Court of Canterbury, 1809. See below, pp. 290 ff.
[4] 24 April 1829.

to the Bishop of Worcester, who expressed his regret at the 'misunderstanding'. The Deputies replied that unless a guarantee against future recurrence was given they would proceed in the ecclesiastical court. Several months later[1] the incumbent was still persisting in his statement that he was never positively told of the baptism (and he was still persuaded that Cakebread was not baptized), and he concluded:

I should feel it equally my duty to use the funeral service for anyone dying in my parish who had been baptized, whether by immersion or sprinkling, whether by a Dissenting minister or by a minister of the Church, but not for any who die unbaptized.

On this, the Deputies informed him they would not proceed with the case, as they were 'willing to believe' in his misapprehension.

But though burial was sometimes refused to adults for this reason, the bodies most often were the bodies of children. It was a matter of common knowledge in a village whether a child had been baptized by a Dissenting minister; no one had had time to forget. There was peculiar harshness in the refusal in most villages, for there was no burial ground except the parish churchyard; and if Christian burial could not be had there it could not be had anywhere. Even before the case of Kemp *v*. Wickes, these refusals were held by competent scholars to be unjustifiable; and when the Deputies appealed to the bishops (as in the case just cited), the bishops almost invariably responded in a way that made it plain that they had no sort of doubt about the validity of Dissenting baptism, and the right of burial with full Christian rites (that is, the Prayer Book service). Sometimes the bishop went beyond a reprimand: the Bishop of St Asaph on one occasion, having given 'such a reprimand that no such refusal would happen for the future by him or any other clergymen in his diocese', doubled the assurance by threatening to suspend any who should act similarly;[2] while the Archbishop of Canterbury threatened to leave a Margate clergyman to the legal consequences if he again refused burial to Dissenters.[3] The reprimand to the clergyman was sometimes accompanied by the request that the Dissenters will in future apply more 'decently' for the burial of their children, and give the

[1] 26 June 1829.   [2] 13 Mar. 1765.   [3] 26 Oct. 1792.

clergyman no reason to doubt that the child has in fact received baptism.[1]

Here is another borderline case, which shews the attitude of a very friendly bishop, and of a clergyman who, however sincerely perplexed, did not understand the law. In 1770 the Deputies laid before the Bishop of Llandaff a case in which the vicar of Marsh-fields refused to bury a child. The Chairman reported that:

The Bishop received them very politely, and said that he was very sorry that any clergyman in his diocese should be so little of the Gentleman and Christian and so ignorant of the Laws of his Country as to be guilty of such a piece of Misbehaviour. That he looked upon himself as greatly obliged to the Gentlemen concerned for not prosecuting Mr Evans without giving him [the Bishop] this notice, and since they had acted so genteelly, he begged they would grant him this further indulgence, not to commence any prosecution till he had wrote to him (which he said he would do forthwith) insisting on an acknowledgement of his Error to the Widow, and promising to bury all the Dissenters in his Parishes for the future, and that if he should then continue obstinate in his Refusal the Bishop said he should be prosecuted in his Court for such neglect of his duty.[2]

The offending vicar defended himself to the bishop. He had told the person who brought the child that

if it had been baptized by any regular Dissenting Minister he would bury it, but that he did not look upon the Gentleman who christened it as such, he not having been Ordained by any Regular Dissenting Minister only by one who was a Mason, and therefore desired they would bury the Child in their own Ground which they refused. The Bishop added that he could not say this was a sufficient excuse and that therefore he would write again to Mr Evans directing him for the future to bury all the Dissenters in his Parishes without asking any questions, and hoped the Committee would write to Mrs Daniel and her friends recommending Candor and Moderation to them.[3]

This was a Welsh case, and it is hard to resist the impression that Wales in the 18th century produced more than its fair share of outrages of all kinds. They seem to have increased as the Evangelical Movement disposed the people everywhere to practise

[1] 26 Oct. 1792: 'Woking near Ripley in Surrey'.
[2] 9 Mar. 1770.   [3] 11 May 1770.

their religion outside the Established Church, Welsh magistrates were more truculent than others in refusing to register meeting-houses and ministers under the Toleration Act; riots, insults, disturbance, and 'barbarous usage' were reported more frequently from Wales than from the rest of the Kingdom.

Of course it is possible to claim that the behaviour of the non-resident Whig prelates was less to be commended than that of the rustic Tory parson; that the parson, whatever might be said against his narrow mind and his heartless uncharity, had at least some understanding of the importance of the sacraments and the reality of Churchmanship, whereas the bishop, though nominally concerned with spiritual affairs, talked of the behaviour of gentle-men and an understanding of the law of England as decisive. This may be true, but it hardly tells against the Deputies; they would have been the first to see whatever truth there is in this way of representing the matter. It was their contention that the association of Church and State put the Church and its ministers in a false position, and caused spiritual to be sacrificed to temporal interests. It was to end this very arrangement, which provided the English Church with non-resident political bishops, that Dissenters fought against, and suffered under, the Tory parson in the village.

For, whatever may have been the reason, the Deputies were more and more busied by reports about refusals to bury Dissenters in the last years of the 18th century and the first years of the 19th —and not in Wales alone. The increase may have in part been apparent; perhaps the success of the Deputies in defending country Dissenters caused a larger proportion of the offences to be reported to them. In any event, on 5 October 1806 the Committee gave the Secretary a general instruction to write in their name to any clergyman who refused to bury a person because he had received baptism at the hands of a Dissenter; if the clergyman did not reply within a week, the bishop was to be informed. [1] It was in such an atmosphere that the Deputies at last instituted the proceedings in favour of Dissenters in the case of Kemp *v.* Wickes.

The Deputies did not go to court until they had explored every other avenue. In 1798 the Deputies had applied to the Judge

[1] 5 Oct. 1806.

Advocate, Sir William Scott, for an opinion on a case which arose at Woolston, near Coventry, in which a child, baptized by a Dissenting minister, had been refused burial by the curate of the parish. He had told the father:

'You may lay your child by the rest of your family, but I will not bury him, nor shall anyone else;—I will bury no Dissenter. I will only bury Roman Catholics and Churchmen.' The *Sketch* adds: 'The afflicted parent was obliged to make a grave in the churchyard, and bury his infant with his own hands.'[1]

The vicar having declined to intervene, saying that 'he paid the curate handsomely, that he was of such a violent temper that he did not know what to do with him, and that the laws were open', the Deputies asked Sir William Scott

Whether the curate has not acted improperly and illegally in refusing to bury the child? and whether he is not liable to a prosecution, and in what court, for so doing? and whether the vicar is in any, and in what degree implicated with him, in the impropriety of the transaction?

Before Sir William Scott gave his opinion, he asked a very sensible question:

Is there any form of baptism generally received among Protestant Dissenters? Some bodies of them (as Quakers) do not baptize at all and hold baptism to be unlawful and anti-Christian. I presume that there may be other Bodies of Dissenters who do not generally practise it. Among those who do practise it, is there any form so general as to be a proper subject of a general question?[2]

Instead of answering the question themselves, the Deputies referred the question to the local congregation ('the congregation of Woolston near Coventry of which the Revd. Baldwin is pastor'), and forwarded to Scott the reply which they received:

The Dissenters in general (except Socinians) who insist upon Infant Baptism have a form of baptism *generally* received amongst themselves and it is as follows and was used in the present case:

The infant (if its health admits), is brought to the Chapel, if not the Minister attends at the Father's house—an extempore prayer suited to the occasion is first used and the Minister then sprinkles the water and says: 'A. I baptize thee in the name of the Father, of the

---

[1] *Sketch*, p. 66.   [2] 27 April 1798.

Son, and of the Holy Ghost' The ceremony of the Cross is omitted and the Father and Mother attend instead of Godfathers and Godmothers and are charged and instructed by the Minister as to their duty to their Child. The words and form they consider as directed by Christ himself.

In the present case the Dissenters are a very numerous body calling themselves Independants and hold Baptism *essential* and the only ground of their dissent from the established church is their dislike to some of its ceremonies. They are firm Believers in all the doctrinal points contained in the thirty-nine articles and their catechism defines Baptism to be 'A Sacrament wherein the washing with water in the name of the Father and of the Son and of the Holy Ghost doth signify and seal etc.'

Satisfied with this answer, Sir William Scott gave his opinion in the following terms:

I am of opinion, that if reasonable proof was offered to the clergyman complained of that the child had been baptized in the manner described in the answer to the question proposed by me, he acted illegally and improperly in refusing to bury it, and that he might be prosecuted with effect in the ecclesiastical court for his refusal.—The vicar had no right to consider himself as totally discharged from the obligation of performing a parochial office, when applied to upon an illegal refusal of his own curate to perform it; it is a duty that must be done, and if it is a duty he could do, upon the refusal of the curate, properly signified to him, I think he had no right to leave it undone, and to refer the parties to their penal remedy against his curate; at the same time, I do not think that the refusal on his part was attended with such circumstances as would render him the proper object of a public prosecution, though liable to the just censure of his ordinary.—The ground upon which I hold the refusal of the curate to be unjustifiable is, that the child was *not unbaptized*, in the sense and intention of the compilers of our Litany and Rubric; what that sense and intention was, is very much a matter of fact and history:— and I think that that history has been collected by different writers, but particularly by Bishop Fleetwood, with sufficient accuracy to authorize the legal conclusion I draw.[1]

Sir William Scott's opinion fortified the Deputies in their intention to proceed; but 'though entitled to the highest respect, on account of his splendid talents and profound learning' it could not

[1] *Sketch*, p. 67.

be taken as final. Although they circulated the opinion among their constitutents and the clergy, cases came in as fast as before. 'The only competent mode of redress, was that of proceeding in the ecclesiastical court against some clergyman, whose persevering refusal might diminish the reluctance, the Committee naturally felt to adopt hostile measures.'[1]

The ideal opponent shortly presented himself. In 1808 the Rev. John Green, Independent minister of Rutland, reported to the Deputies that the Rev. John Wight Wickes, 'Rector of Wardley-cum-Belton, Rutland, and Chaplain to H.R.H. the Duke of Cumberland',[2] had refused to bury the infant child of John and Hannah Swingler, two of his parishioners. The Deputies wrote to the rector, but he paid no attention. They then applied to his Diocesan, the Bishop of Peterborough, enclosing a copy of Sir William Scott's opinion. The Bishop forwarded the opinion to the rector, but 'he did not seem satisfied'; the Bishop therefore replied to the Deputies, admitting the right of Dissenters to Christian burial according to the established forms, but stating that he should not further interfere in the business himself, and therefore that the Committee would proceed against Mr Wickes as they should think proper.

The rector did not stand on the defensive; he addressed an aggressive and vituperative pen to the composition of an open 'Letter to the Bishop of Peterborough in answer to an appeal made to the "Society for defending the civil rights of the Dissenters" relative to the important question of Church Burial by the established clergy'[3], with an epigraph which announces its tone:

'Sic notus Ulysses?   Virg. Aen.

Beware Ulysses and his artful guile,
His words are oily—though his passions boil;—
With specious lies he cloaks his foul pretence—
Trojans beware: and cry aloud—DEFENCE'

This pamphlet enables us to tell the story from the rector's point of view:

[1] *Sketch*, p. 67.   [2] His own description.
[3] Copy in Dr Williams's Library (Tracts 12:66:17).

John Swingler is a labourer of Belton, well versed in the manual uses of the spade, and not unacquainted with the properties of the soil. He had long been in the habit of keeping a private conventicle, or subscription pic-nic of theology, in his own cottage; occasionally illuminating the dear circle of his brother labourers, and spreading the light over this dark part of the kingdom, sometimes developing his own mystical lucubrations upon the new birth; and at other times stretching out his itching ears to the bagpipe melody of Huntingdonian stanzas.

Mr William Kemp opened a second shop of sanctity, gratuitously, in opposition to the pic-nic subscription house of Johnny Swingler. The chances were in favour of the former. Males that had transgressed, and those that wished to transgress, mixed in rapturous accord with females that had sinned, and females that wished to sin.

In view of this competition, the rector was astonished to find the Dissenters making common cause against him. It was John Green, the Independent minister, who reported the matter to the Deputies, and William Kemp in whose name the action was brought in the Arches Court of Canterbury. As for the London Committee, or 'as they are very pompously denominated, "the civil rights of the dissenters" '—did they act authoritatively for all the Dissenters?

I am at a loss to account for such a cordial agreement in this particular instance, when so much disunion generally prevails among them.

The rector was willing to grant the Dissenters their civil rights, but could not admit these to be infringed by a refusal of religious services which they had no particular or legal warranty to claim. He knew no injunction, statutable or canonical, which compelled a clergyman to read the burial service over those who had had no previous admission by Church baptism legally performed; especially where their opposition to the Establishment itself seemed ultimately to threaten its total subversion.

By the tenor of our ecclesiastical laws it is presumed that baptism performed by any other than the acknowledged, legal, and established clergy is invalid.

If the bishops have urged their clergy to comply with the wishes of dissenters on this head it must be from tenderness of disposition—but may not amiableness of mind descend into weakness, and ultimately produce danger? Quo plus habent, eo plus cupiunt.

I too well know the undermining principles of our adversaries—with butter in their mouths, they can scarcely conceal the overflowing gall near the heart.

Though I would not wish to force down the throats of the dissenters the strong meat of the established church; yet I see no fair reason why we should be so weak as to permit their triturated garbish to be thrust down our own throats. They have had most ample concessions granted them already and we have had many proper restrictions—but I know not any civil right of the dissenters which has been injured by the established clergy in refusing the performance of a religious service in such manner as is prescribed by the Book of Common Prayer.

One would imagine from such a passage that the rector knew nothing of the arguments for the validity of lay baptism, but to suppose this would do him an injustice. He admitted that much had been written on the subject, but thought it unnecessary to 'call the veterans of the contest from the quiet of their graves'.

I cannot suffer the Establishment to be progressively encroached upon in silence. . . . If the legislature concede them a further extension of rights in allowing full force to their congregational baptisms and immersions the established church would lose another of its props.

So much for the principles of the Rector of Belton. The most illuminating thing about the accusations brought against him is the tedium of their pettiness. According to the Rev. John Green, the rector had 'deprived Swingler of every privilege he could because he dared to be a dissenter'. The rector's reply was that he had never considered him as a Dissenter, but pitied him 'as a deluded, infatuated and ignorant disciple of the lowest description of Methodists'. According to Green, the rector had not only refused to read the burial service, he would not permit the bell to be tolled, nor the infant to be interred in the churchyard (without any ceremony) only on the condition of this poor man's paying five shillings for the breaking up of the ground and three and sixpence for the fees. The rector was surprised that they should want 'the steeple-house bell', or indeed the burial ground consecrated by episcopal forms; but he admitted taking the five shillings, and it was on this point that the Bishop specifically censured him:

One thing I am sorry you did, which was taking the fees as you refused to bury. This I am sorry you did.

The interment was eventually carried out on 29 August 1808, by William Billings the parish clerk and the man who made the coffin. The clerk expostulated with the rector, telling him that his predecessor had buried a child under similar circumstances—the minister replied that the clerk must be out of his head.

On 1 and 11 December 1809 the case came up at Doctors' Commons, and judgment was given for the Dissenters by the Official Principal, Sir John Nicholl. He began by noting that the rector accepted the fact that the child had been baptized by a Dissenting minister in the name of the Trinity but declared that he was not bound in law to bury a person of that description.

The 68th canon *prohibits* the refusal of burial in all cases except in the case of excommunicated persons, and *punishes* such refusal. The Rubric adds two other exceptions expressly, and forbids the office of burial 'to be used for any that die *unbaptized*, or excommunicate, or have laid violent hands on themselves'. But these are *exceptions*, and it is a rule of construction that the general law is to be construed favourably, and the exception strictly.

Here the general law is, that burial is to be refused to no person. This is the law not only of the English church; it is the law not only of all Christian churches; but it seems to be the law of common humanity, and the limitation of such a law must be considered *strictissimi juris*.

A decision, therefore, upon the validity of lay baptism is the crux of the matter. From a careful examination of all the authorities

the ancient general canon law,—from the particular constitutions made to regulate the English church,—from our own canons,—from the Rubric, and from any Acts of Parliament that may have been passed upon the subject

as well as the writings of eminent persons, it is clear that the Church of England has always considered *lay baptism as valid*, however *irregular*.

The old Canon Law expressly declares, 'Non reiteratur baptisma quod in nomine Sanctae Trinitatis ministratur'—'Valet baptisma etsi per laicos ministratur'. The character of the person who administered baptism had no effect upon its validity; the application of water and the invocation of the Trinity were considered as the substance of the rite; and baptism so administered, even by a heretic, a layman, or a woman, was received as valid, lest the invocation of the Holy Trinity should be treated as of no effect.

At the Reformation the law was not materially altered. Down to the time of James I all *private* baptisms were administered by the laity. The Rubrics of Edward VI and Elizabeth gave directions concerning private baptism:

Let *those that be present* call upon God for his grace, and say the Lord's Prayer if the time will suffer: and then *one of them* shall name the child and dip him in the water, or pour the water upon him, saying these words,—'I baptize thee in the name, &c.'

and although the Rubric enjoined people not to baptize their children at home, *except* in cases of necessity, it directed pastors to instruct their parishioners in the form of doing it. James I disliked lay baptism, and it was made irregular, but it never became invalid; King James himself said:

I utterly dislike all re-baptization on those whom women or laics have baptized.

The Rubric, even in its altered form, declared only two things essential—the use of water and the invocation of the Trinity.

The practice of the Church of England has been conformable to the law. Converts to the Church have never been re-baptized, if they had previously received baptism as Dissenters or Roman Catholics; and after the Commonwealth great numbers of persons baptized by Presbyterian ministers were confirmed, ordained, and buried, without any scruple by the bishops and ministers of the Establishment. The Toleration Act has given a further legal sanction to the status of Dissenting worship, and its form of baptism.

Such an interpretation of the law is supported by Hooker, Fleetwood, Burnet, Watson and the example of Bishop Warburton, who forbade the re-baptization of many in his diocese who had been baptized by an impostor falsely representing himself as in holy orders. On the other side the only authority is Wheatly; but his assertions are not only unsupported by authority, they would make it impossible for foreigners dying in this country to be buried, or Scots Presbyterians, or even visitors from a distant part of the country whose baptism by the Established Church could not be verified.

If the law has not excluded them from this ordinary right of Christianity and humanity, the ministers of the church will not surely be degraded by performing the office. On the contrary, the generality of the clergy, it may be presumed, will rejoice that in this last office of Christian charity there is no separation between the church and their Protestant Dissenting brethren. It is by a lenient and a liberal interpretation of the laws of disability and exclusion, and not by a captious and vexatious construction and application of them, that the true interests and the true dignity of the church establishment are best supported. Upon the whole of the case, and for the reasons assigned, the court is of opinion, that the minister, in refusing to bury this child in the manner pleaded in the articles, has acted illegally.[1]

By this judgment the Rector of Belton became liable to suspension for three months and to pay the costs of the action; but the Deputies were content with an admonition, which the court duly pronounced. It was like the Deputies to perceive that copies of the case 'taken in shorthand by Mr Gurney' would find many buyers among the Anglican clergy as well as among the Dissenters. The copies so sold would help to defray the cost of printing; and in order to avoid offending the judge or the clergy no animadversions whatever were to be added.[2]

But, alas, however authoritative the judgment in Kemp *v.* Wickes, however liberal the sentiments expressed by Sir John Nicholl, the Deputies were to find that it settled nothing. Several features of the case might give cause for anxiety. The first was that cases like this did not arise from ignorance or inadvertence—they arose from feud. To read the Rector of Belton's pamphlet, with its accusations and counter-recriminations, its disputes as to whether the rector did or did not deprive Swingler's little girl of a sixteen-shilling prize won in a school of industry, or as to whether the rector did or did not accept a fee of three-and-sixpence for reading the burial service—all this is like the nastiest kind of

---

[1] *Sketch*, p. 81.   [2] 15 Dec. 1809.

family quarrel, when the petty bitternesses of years of wrangling are brought out for an airing. Under such circumstances liberal sentiments may not prevail; and since bitterness breeds bitterness, the right is not likely to be all on one side.

The second disconcerting thing was the time and expense needed to obtain justice. This case had been almost two years before the court; other cases were to take longer. Clergymen reading the judgment in Kemp *v*. Wickes with an eye to making trouble lit upon a paragraph of Sir John Nicholl's remarks:

It has been asked,—if you do not require proof from the register, what other proof can you have? (of baptism, that is). How are the clergy to find out who are baptized, and who are not? To that it may be properly answered, they must be satisfied with reasonable evidence— with what a person acting fairly, and not captiously, would require.[1]

If we look on, thirty years after Kemp *v*. Wickes, to another remarkably similar and even more scandalous case, we shall see what dragon's teeth were sown here.

Jane Rumbold, a child of an Independent in Bassingbourne, Cambridgeshire, died on 16 February 1840. Mr Rumbold's wife and ten other children of his had been buried in the parish churchyard. Application was made to the Rev. William Herbert Chapman, the vicar, to have the bell tolled and the body buried. Chapman had buried some of the other children, but on this occasion he intervened at the last moment to have the bell stopped, and said to the father: 'There is the churchyard, and you may deposit the body if you please, but I shall not read the service over it'. He did not deny that the child had been baptized in the name of the Trinity by an Independent minister, the Rev. Mr Moase; but he denied that this was the baptism referred to in the Rubric. His attention was called to the decision in Kemp *v*. Wickes, which had stated authoritatively that it was; and the Bishop of Ely recommended him to act on it, but he did not do so.

The Deputies delayed action for a time until the result of a similar suit brought by the Methodists against the Vicar of Gedney was concluded;[2] but a year later the case was still undecided; and meanwhile the body of Jane Rumbold had been kept, unburied,

[1] *Sketch*, p. 78.   [2] Annual Report for 1840.

in her father's house, enclosed in a second coffin. The vicar a second time declined the 'performance of his legal duty' when the grave was re-opened;[1] but it was not until after a third refusal that the Deputies took proceedings.[2] Their slowness is partly to be explained by the fact that they were not happy about the adequacy of the information given or request made to the vicar.[3] It was more than six months before the Bishop of Ely could be got to take action in the case.[4]

The vicar now declined to bury a second Bassingbourne child, Esther Fisher.[5] The Deputies asked their legal sub-committee for a ruling on whether any penalties would attach to a Dissenting minister who conducted the service in a churchyard, but they were informed that this would be illegal.[6] So towards the end of 1843 the Deputies had to apply to the Bishop for similar proceedings in this case; they thought it prudent to secure a 'churchman' as the promoter on this occasion. But the Rumbold case was still going on, and proceedings in the Fisher case were delayed until the other decision was known.[7]

Chapman first raised technical objections to the proceedings in the Rumbold suit; these being overruled, he set up a defence that the child was baptized in heresy and schism. The Dean of Arches held, on 21 November 1844, that, as in Kemp v. Wickes, the baptism was valid and gave right of burial; but the Deputies' fears were realized: it was held that sufficient evidence had not been forthcoming to prove that convenient notice of burial had been given on 26 May 1841, and the vicar was dismissed with costs.[8]

It was true that the main decision of Kemp v. Wickes was re-asserted: the right of burial was valid. Yet the case might encourage other clergymen to refuse to do their duty; it confirmed the Deputies in their view that ecclesiastical courts ought to be abolished. It was on a defect of evidence that the suit had failed; but the practice of that court was to take evidence in private, and therefore all turned on the competence and integrity

[1] Report for 1841. [2] 13 and 29 July 1842. [3] 8 Mar. 1843.
[4] 24 Feb. 1843. [5] Ibid. [6] 8 Mar. 1843.
[7] 21 Feb. 1844. [8] 27 Nov. 1844.

of the examiner. With the best will in the world the examiner, being an Anglican, must find it hard to avoid bias; and open cross-examination would prevent this.[1] Meanwhile the Deputies could only recommend the giving of proper written notice about burials.

Esther Fisher's body lay still in the chimney of her aunt's house. On 28 January 1845 the Deputies applied for a *mandamus* to compel Chapman to bury it; and the court intimating that another application should first be made to Chapman, one was made the following day. After hesitation, he said that he would perform the service; but when, the day after, the body was carried from the chimney where it had lain for two years to the grave, Chapman did not appear; a neighbouring clergyman (at his request) read the service. His meanness was not exhausted after four years. The costs of the case were

Mandamus:	£ 17	
Chapman's costs:	47	17s. 2d.
Solicitor's costs:	167	12s. 1d.

$$£ \ 232 \ 9s. \ 3d.[2]$$

The Deputies asked the solicitors to be content with out-of-pocket expenses, as they had passed, as sufficient, evidence which proved to be insufficient, and so lost the case. The solicitors compromised for £150—so much had it cost the Deputies to secure for a child, two years after her death, the form of burial to which she was entitled by law.[3]

The Deputies now knew that nothing but Parliamentary action would settle the matter, and that, in fairness to the Church as well as Dissent, Nonconformist ministers should have the legal right to bury Dissenters in parochial grounds. The cases we have been describing concerned Independents, baptized in the name of the Trinity; but what of Socinians, and what of Baptists, who had no infant baptism? As early as 1814 a Baptist case at Shrewsbury had seemed insoluble except by application to Parliament.[4] Now

---

[1] Report for 1844.   [2] 5 Feb. 1845.   [3] 17 June 1846.
[4] 29 July and 25 Nov. 1814. It was first thought that an action would lie, as no service was required; but the law being difficult, the case was abandoned.

in 1846, after the Bassingbourne cases, the Deputies prepared a memorial to Sir James Graham (then Home Secretary) asking for relief.[1]

The memorial stated that the law caused 'serious inconvenience' to Dissenters and 'much scandal' to clergymen, Dissenters, who contributed rates to maintain parish churchyards, had a right to the use of them. Ecclesiastical law authorized the clergy to refuse to bury the unbaptized, so restricting the use by Baptists. It was, moreover, easy by false interpretation to deprive other Dissenters of the right of burial, notwithstanding a well-known decision of the Court of Arches, confirmed (for Ireland) by a recent decision.[2] What the Deputies desired in England was the burial of Dissenters by their own ministers in parish churchyards. The Bassingbourne cases were cited, and an Isle of Wight case in which, to the great scandal of Anglicans as well as Dissenters, a highly esteemed Dissenting minister was refused burial in a grave where two of his children already lay, because he had lived in an adjoining parish.[3]

Sir James Graham received courteously a deputation which presented the memorial, but in view of the difficulties he could not pledge himself to any action; though he expressed his regret that 'the remains of Churchmen and Dissenters were not allowed to rest quietly by the side of each other'. He sought further information as to the extent of the abuse; he was not aware that it existed 'to any extent', but if the refusals proved numerous 'he would consider the expediency of bringing it before his colleagues'. The Deputies in consequence asked for information from the Congregationalists, Baptists, and Wesleyans,[4] but they got incomplete returns.[5] The general issue was for long to remain unsettled, while attention shifted to another part of the field: the question of town cemeteries.

Everyone has seen those desolate town cemeteries with two chapels built near to one another, but apparently determined to be as unlike each other as the meagreness of their architects' imagination would permit them to be. One faces east and west; one north and south. One displays a cross, the other a dubious unmeaning

---

[1] 3 and 24 April 1846.   [2] Martin v. Escott.   [3] 24 April 1846.
[4] Ibid.   [5] Report for 1846.

ornament; one has elaborate Gothic windows, the other windows as little Gothic as the age of Ruskin would allow. As the decades passed, the chapels ceased to insult each other; they came under one roof as complementary parts of the same building. Finally, one chapel sufficed for Anglicans and Dissenters. The thing is an allegory; the public cemetary was the battlefield for the dreariest and most unedifying of all the campaigns in the long war between the Establishment and Dissent.

It is easy to dismiss the whole affair as too pitiable and degrading to examine; or to use it, with the insufferable insolence of the ignorant, as the final disproof of the Christian revelation; yet it had an important and an honourable meaning, even though the Anglicans proved unable to drop their assumption of superiority and privilege, or the Dissenters their obstructive tactics. The Church was determined that though the new burial grounds might lack the beauty and associations of the parish churchyard, they should lack nothing which the venerable rites of religion could confer on them. The Dissenters were resolved that the old inequality and injustice should not be repeated in the new setting.

The new industrial England had come into being without any of the amenities now considered essential. The towns had neither drains nor an adequate supply of clean water. Epidemics of cholera and typhus swept the country every few years, yet ignorance, indifference, and vested interest stood in the way of public services.[1]

Among the measures to combat this situation, a Health of Towns Bill, introduced in 1842 by Mackinnon (a Tory M.P.), aimed at preventing all interments within two miles of London and one mile of other large towns. A classic passage in *Bleak House* (1852) provides the best commentary on the Bill:

to a hemmed-in churchyard, pestiferous and obscene, whence malignant diseases are communicated to the bodies of our dear brothers and sisters who have not departed; while our dear brothers and sisters who hang about official back-stairs—would to Heaven they *had* departed!—are very complacent and agreeable. Into a beastly scrap of ground which a Turk would reject as a savage abomination, and a Caffre would shudder at, they bring our dear brother here departed, to receive

---

[1] G. M. Young, *Early Victorian England*.

Christian burial. With houses looking on, on every side, save where a reeking little tunnel of a court gives access to the iron gate . . . here, they lower our dear brother down a foot or two: here, sow him in corruption, to be raised in corruption: an avenging ghost at many a sick bedside: a shameful testimony to future ages, how civilization and barbarism walked this boastful island together.[1]

It is to be regretted that the Deputies may be counted among the forces which resisted this Bill; but there is little wonder that, with the Bassingbourne case on their hands, the Deputies narrowly scrutinized any burial proposals. They were convinced that episcopal influence had been 'eagerly exerted' to arrange the measure 'for the aggrandizement of the clergy and the discouragement of dissent'. They opposed the Bill 'in its present form'. They recognized that the health of towns might make legislation necessary, but they wished to secure an equal share of respect for the rights and religious feelings of all classes.

The Deputies considered that the evidence on which the Bill was founded was 'partial, limited, and inadequate'; for, though drawn only from London and the suburbs, it was applied to the whole of England. There had been no witness qualified to represent Dissenters and their claims, especially their proprietary rights in existing cemeteries: these had been dealt with in the 'most unceremonious and objectionable manner'.[2] Petitions were made to the House of Commons and to the Corporation of London against the Bill; to the latter, in particular, for those who had bought rights of sepulture in Bunhill Fields as late as 1836;[3] but the City did not intervene.[4]

The Deputies were on stronger ground in criticizing the machinery of the Bill than in trying to question the evidence on which it was founded. They told the promoters of the Bill, who consulted them on their objections, that there were two main grounds for dissatisfaction. The Bill proposed that cemeteries to be set up should be administered by a committee consisting of the clergy, churchwardens, and two inhabitants to be elected annually. The Deputies felt that this was not sufficiently popular, and suggested

---

[1] Charles Dickens, *Bleak House* (Everyman edn. p. 143).   [2] Report for 1842.
[3] 11 Jan. 1843.   [4] 3 April 1843.

a board of nine. The Bill also proposed a division of cemeteries into consecrated and unconsecrated parts, and the fixing of fees for services conducted in them. The Deputies criticized this; they felt that fees should be fixed for all *interments*, sufficient to maintain the cemetery; but that no fee should be fixed for *services*, at least in the unconsecrated part of the ground, although the committee might fix fees for Anglican services if that was desired. The Bill was amended in accordance with the Deputies' proposals, but they still would not pledge themselves to its support;[1] perhaps they were already nervous (although there is no specific mention) of the proposal to divide cemeteries, to which they took such strong objection later. The Bill did not pass, but it foreshadowed many aspects of the law to come.

In particular, the Cemeteries Clauses Act of 1847[2] followed it in general outline. This Act, to which there is no reference in the Deputies' Minutes, was a permissive measure to which companies could have recourse when they wished to establish cemeteries; and it was widely used, for in the hey-day of laisser-faire even burials were a subject for private enterprise. It empowered the division of cemeteries into consecrated and unconsecrated parts, and the building of an Anglican chapel on the consecrated part, at which an Anglican chaplain paid by the company and licensed by the bishop should officiate. In the unconsecrated part another chapel *might* be constructed in which Dissenting services could be held, but no payment was provided.

Next the Government took up the subject, introducing a Metropolitan Interments Bill (intended as a model for the whole country) in 1850. Once more the Deputies objected, in a petition to the House of Commons and an interview with Sir George Grey. There was now no argument about the need for the Bill:

This Deputation cheerfully admits the necessity for improved arrangements for the interment of the dead in the extended state of the metropolis,

but the Bill proposed to create a Board of Health with authority to close and open cemeteries, to divide and supervise them, to allot fees and rates. The Deputies felt that no Government commission

[1] 3 and 10 April 1843. [2] 10 and 11 Vict. c. 65.

whatever could be entrusted with such authority, involving the exercise of extended patronage, interference with private property, and the religious observance of bereaved families. The Bill proposed, further, that where the Anglican service was not used, a fee should nevertheless be paid. The general public, said the Deputies, would be taxed to provide perpetual annuities for the parish clergy, who would be relieved by the Bill of their duties, but not of their fees. The burden would be unfair to all, but especially to the Dissenters, who hitherto has used measures to exempt themselves from charges for services not enjoyed by them[1]. Amendments did not remove the grievances, and when the Commons passed the Bill, a similar petition was sent to the Lords.[2] The Deputies would hail with satisfaction a Bill to give relief through local authorities, if it respected private rights and constitutional principles in imposing fresh burdens on the people. They asked for a Select Committee to hear grievances, but, it seems, did not get their evidence heard.[3] The voice of the cholera was louder than the voice of the Deputies, and the Bill passed.[4]

But it was not effective in getting either the old churchyards closed or the new cemeteries opened. The Deputies next year noted with satisfaction that 'the government having at length discovered the impracticability of the Metropolitan Interments Act of 1850' were contemplating the introduction of a more comprehensive scheme.[5] They asked for an interview with Lord John Russell, but were referred to Lord Seymour. Their Chairman, John Remington Mills, pointed out to him that Dissenters had a Common Law right to burial in consecrated parochial burial ground. If they were to pay their share towards the new grounds, they claimed the right to burial in any part—not that they attached any importance to consecration, but they saw no necessity to separate members of the same family in burial. They ought to have the right, as Dissenters had in Ireland, to be buried by their own ministers. It had been legally decided long ago that the clergy had a right to fees for service only if they performed it; the Deputies objected to their claims for fees for breaking ground. The division

---

[1] 27 May 1850.   [2] 1 July 1850.   [3] 19 July 1850.
[4] Report for 1851.   [5] *Ibid.*

of cemeteries into consecrated and unconsecrated parts, and the compensation allowed to the parish clergy under Acts for cemetery companies (such as the Cemeteries Clauses Act), provided no principles proper for general policy—they were mere bargains with bishops, entered into in order to get the Acts through.

Lord Seymour expected that the clergy would probably want the same rights as before; and on asking what was the least the Dissenters would take, was told:

they could be satisfied with no arrangement that did not admit of their having service in some part of the parochial ground, and of being interred in any part of it.[1]

The Burial Act, the foundation of our modern funeral legislation, was passed without any further communication between the Government and the Deputies; but it did not become law until 1852, and in the meanwhile the Deputies found themselves faced with another Company Bill: the London Necropolis and Mausoleum Bill, to provide extra-mural interments at Woking. It was important not only as forming a weighty precedent, but as preparatory to making extra-mural interments compulsory.

First the Deputies tried to come to a friendly agreement with the promoters. They objected to a scale of fees by which, in effect, they would have to pay the Established clergy whose services they did not require; it was unreasonable to charge the same fee for consecrated and unconsecrated ground, but they did not wish the Company to pay Dissenting ministers—the payment for a voluntary service should be left, as in the past, to arrangement between the parties themselves. The promoters tried to justify certain clauses by quoting the Cemeteries Clauses Act as binding; but the Deputies argued that there was power to vary the clauses, and that what might be tolerable, though wrong, in a cemetery which was used by people who chose to use it was intolerable where use was compulsory.[2]

Negotiation failed, and the Deputies prepared a petition to Parliament, which marks an important stage in the development of their views about public cemeteries. The Bill provided for a fee of 6s. 2d. to be paid by the Company to the clergymen from

[1] 23 Dec. 1851 and Report for 1851.   [2] 9 Mar. and 6 April 1852.

whose parishes bodies might be removed for interment in consecrated ground. The implication of this was that the Dissenters would lose their Common Law right, for by charging the same fee in consecrated and unconsecrated ground the Company would impose on Dissenters part of this payment made to clergymen who performed no service. The Deputies in a cutting phrase humbly submitted that

the clergy of the Established Church have no vested interest in the bodies of Her Majesty's subjects to entitle them to any remuneration for the Burial of the Dead out of the Parish Church Yards.[1]

But there was no need to present the petition. 'Your expressed wishes', the Committee reported, 'had the effect of procuring concessions from the promoters of the Bill'; and special gratitude was expressed to Sir James Duke, one of the trustees, for his statement that as a Member for the City, where he reckoned as his constituents many Dissenters, he should feel it his duty to pay attention to their wishes, though in opposition to the interests of any company with which he was associated.[2]

The more general legislation now came on: in 1852 for the metropolis, and in 1853 for the rest of the country. The Deputies had to deal with an unfriendly Government; they failed to get many of their opinions accepted; and public cemeteries have since been made and administered in a manner distasteful to Dissenters. Already, on 16 November 1852, the Committee were asked for advice about a public cemetery at Boston, Lincolnshire, intended to exclude Dissenters; and the local people were told to find out at a vestry meeting under which Act this was to be done.

Arguing that the proper development of English society was not to assume that Anglicanism was the one normal expression of Christianity in England, and that outside it were groups of non-Christians and freakish Christians, who were all to be treated in the same way by watertight compartments marking them off from the normal life of the nation; but on the contrary, to equate the religious rights of Anglicans and Dissenters, recognizing each as a legitimate expression of Christian piety—the Deputies made it a main part of their argument that they had a legal right to burial

[1] 16 April 1852.   [1] Report for 1852.

in parish churchyards. Even the unbaptized had a right to burial, though not to service. In the new cemeteries, therefore, Dissenters ought to retain the right to be buried in any part of the ground, after service in any chapel on it. The fact that they wanted the new right of having the service read by their own ministers ought not to deprive them of their old right to be buried in any part of a parish ground.

The division of the cemeteries into consecrated and unconsecrated parts—'a new and invidious distinction'[1]—roused the keenest opposition of Dissenters; it was an evil legacy from the Joint Stock Companies, unworthy of incorporation into public policy. Such a provision 'would carry religious differences into the very grave', would hurt the feelings of survivors, and separate in death those who had lived in harmony despite theological differences. The Deputies deprecated 'that such a scandal should be attached to our common Christianity'.

During Lord Derby's short-lived Government of 1852, the Metropolitan Burials Bill was under the charge of Lord John Manners; he received a deputation, but 'the interview was not remarkable by any display of courtesy on the part of the representative of Lord Derby's government, and was highly unsatisfactory in its results'.[2] None of the great Tory statesmen of the past had ever treated the Deputies with personal discourtesy; it was left for a third-rate politician to invent that device, and the parvenu Disraeli to perfect it. The Government prevented the success of amendments to the London Act to secure that the closed graveyards should not be desecrated by buildings, and that any minister might conduct burial services in any part of the cemetery.[3]

The Deputies fared better the following year in amending the Bills for the country at large; they could not get rid of the division of the cemeteries, but they removed provisions compelling public authorities to provide a chapel and keep a register for Anglicans, but not for Dissenters.[4]

The new laws did not work smoothly, and by the end of 1854 the Deputies were considering the need for revision. Apsley

[1] 18 June 1852.   [2] Report for 1852.
[3] 25 July and 16 Nov. 1852.   [4] 4 and 28 July 1853, and Report for 1853.

Pellatt, M.P., who became their Chairman, asked in Parliament for a comprehensive enquiry, and the Deputies advertised for evidence, and even sought information about the new cemetery laws in France.[1] The law of 1852 had not succeeded in closing the London graveyards any more than that of 1850; it was not until 1855 that, with few exceptions, interments ceased in them. A petition to Parliament urged, among other points, that popular Boards should replace the clerical control of cemeteries.[2]

An amendment carried by Pellatt in the Act of 1855 gave the Home Secretary power to review the fees of all Burial Boards.[3] The Deputies lost no time in seeing that Sir George Grey (the Home Secretary under Palmerston) used his new powers, and put before him the unsatisfactory medley of charges as then made, especially in their hard bearing on Dissenters. Sometimes there were equal fees for clergy and ministers; sometimes no fees for either; sometimes there were fees for clergy, but none for ministers; sometimes less for ministers than for the clergy; while in some instances, again, unconsecrated burial was dearer than consecrated. Grey was clearly intending to be fair, but doubted if he had retrospective powers to amend scales already made.[4]

Further attempts were made, successfully in 1857, to remedy some of the grievances: in that year a Government Bill made fees equal for the consecrated and unconsecrated parts of the cemeteries, and made unnecessary the division of the two parts by a fence. When the Bill became law, the Deputies reviewed their tactics with some complacency. By introducing a separate Bill of their own, by keeping it afoot, and by dropping it at the appropriate moment, they had, they believed, secured the incorporation of some of their policy in the Government Bill.[5]

For the next few years there was little more Parliamentary activity about the cemeteries, and attention turned again to the parish churchyards. But before the remainder of the general problem engages us, one incidental result of importance which followed the closing of the London graveyards must be described: the agitation over Bunhill Fields.

---

[1] 8 Dec. 1854 and 21 Jan. 1855.　　　　　　　　　　[2] 2 Feb. 1855.
[3] 24 Aug. 1855.　　　　　[4] 30 Nov. 1855.　　　　　[5] 20 Nov. 1857.

Bunhill Fields is the Westminster Abbey—or, as Southey called it, the 'Campo Santo'—of Dissenting England: the resting place of Bunyan and Defoe; of Isaac Watts; of Daniel Neal the historian; of John Owen, Cromwell's chaplain; of Dr Daniel Williams, founder of the Library which bears his name; of Ritson, the antiquary, Joseph Hughes, founder of the Bible Society, William Blake, and Thomas Stothard. Distinguished Anglicans lie side by side with the saints and fathers of the heroic age of Nonconformity, and with them thousands of the nameless dead whose interment here in years of Tudor plague had begun the use of these fields for burial.[1]

It was consecrated ground. Strype's *Stow* records that in 1549 more than a thousand cart-loads of human remains were removed from the charnel of St Paul's Cathedral and deposited here. The ground formed part of the prebendal estate of Finsbury; the City was granted a lease in the 16th century, and in 1665-6 (at the time of the Great Plague) the Fields were enclosed with a brick wall and gates 'at the sole charge of the City of London'. Maitland in his *Survey* (1739) states expressly that the ground had been *consecrated* as a relief for the parochial burial grounds during the plague. Tillotson and Stillingfleet had attended funerals there; bishops had officiated; and the number of episcopalian burials had justified the appointment of an Anglican clergyman as permanent salaried chaplain.

As early as 1767 the Deputies had concerned themselves about the tenure under which the ground was held. They learnt that the City's lease from the Prebend of Finsbury had still sixteen years to run; Sir Matthew Featherston-Haugh held an underlease, and expected for a fine to get a renewal—provided the amount of the fine was reasonable.[2] To make the position more secure, a private Act was passed through Parliament in 1768. Under its terms, a ninety-nine year lease of the Finsbury estate was prepared, and the income divided into sixths. Three sixths went to the Corporation of London; two-sixths to the Bishop of Bristol, Dr Wilson,

---

[1] 'Proceedings in reference to the Preservation of the Bunhill Fields Burial Ground. Printed by order of the Corporation of London, 1867'.
[2] 13 May 1767.

who was then Prebendary of Finsbury, as his personal share; while the remaining sixth continued in possession of the Church. The City, as possessing the largest share, received the management of the estate, and in 1801, by purchase from the Wilson family, acquired five-sixths of the rents for the duration of the lease.

It is not clear what part the Deputies had in this arrangement, for they acted with more than their usual reticence in dealings with the City at this period. But that they had a considerable share is clear from the behaviour of Dr Wilson in 1786. He had not been very satisfied with the City's management; the number of burials was rapidly decreasing and the condition of the ground was unsatisfactory, for the wall and gates built a hundred years before had fallen into disrepair. Dr Wilson came to the Deputies to ask them to enclose the ground with iron rails 'which he thinks would make it look handsomer and prevent the dead bodies being stolen'. It was resolved 'that the Committee have nothing to do with this matter';[1] evidently it was considered the City's business. Two years later the City appointed a sub-committee to confer with Dr Wilson; they brought in their report on 1 Feb. 1788.[2] They considered that the decrease in burials was occasioned by two causes:

first, by the making of improvements on the Finsbury estate, from which an idea has arisen that these grounds may at some future time be built upon, or converted to other uses; and secondly, from the opening of several new burial-grounds in which the charges of interment are less than in Bunhill-fields.

To remedy this, the sub-committee recommended the advertising of a resolution that building on the ground would not be allowed,

but that the same and every part thereof shall at all times hereafter remain for the purpose of burials,

and it was decided also that the ground should no longer be farmed out to a keeper, but brought under the direct control of the City, with a new scheme of regulations to 'restore the confidence of the public'. These measures succeeded, and no further trouble arose until the closing of the metropolitan burial grounds in the

[1] 28 April 1786.   [2] 'Proceedings', p. 46.

1850s. In 1846 the Deputies were already discussing the perpetuation of Bunhill Fields;[1] twenty years later their fears were realized, for in 1865 the Ecclesiastical Commissioners took over the rights of the Finsbury prebend in Bunhill Fields, and the Deputies learnt that when the ground reverted to them on the expiry of the City's lease, they proposed to sell it for building. They addressed a 'respectful remonstrance' to the Commissioners, but it was ignored.[2]

A year later, in December 1866, the Deputies gathered the forces of protest, and presented a memorial to the City.[3] The inhabitants of St Luke's parish, in which the ground stood, headed by their churchwardens, associated themselves with the Deputies' action. The Corporation was sympathetic, and appointed a Bunhill Fields Committee with Charles Reed as its chairman. Reed was a Deputy who sat on the Common Council, and was later to be Sir Charles Reed, M.P. for Hackney, Chairman of the Deputies, and Chairman of the London School Board.

The City opened negotiations with the Commissioners for the transfer of the ground, so that it might be maintained as an open space for ever. The Commissioners refused a conveyance, except on payment of £10,000.[4] They stated that they had been approached in 1863 by a Mr Ivimey on behalf of parties possessing vaults and burying-places, with a conditional offer to purchase the ground, and they still adhered to the terms which they had stated on that occasion. The correspondence began bleakly and grew bleaker, but it has a rewarding side for those who appreciate irony. The City heard so much of Mr Ivimey and his bargain that it was at last constrained to direct the Town Clerk to add a postscript to a lengthy communication addressed to the Commissioners:

You will notice that in the foregoing letter all allusions which occur in the course of the correspondence to Mr Ivimey are advisedly avoided, inasmuch as the Corporation has no knowledge of or connection with that gentleman, or of negotiations entered upon, or now pending with him.

[1] 8 May 1846.   [2] 6 Dec. 1865.
[3] Text in 'Proceedings', p. 33   [4] 'Proceedings', p. 6.

The Commissioners varied their references to Mr Ivimey and his £10,000 by offering to accept

five-sixths of the purchase monies which had been paid to the Corporation for the sale of vaults, etc in perpetuity.[1]

Basing their claim upon the Corporation's statement that 'the total net proceeds of the burial ground during the period of the current lease amounted to £24,001 7s. 1d.', the Commissioners claimed £20,000. The City had to point out to them that only £1,168 19s. 6d. of the total was derived from sales, and that this included the bricklayers' charges. They solemnly offered the Commissioners five-sixths of this amount, adding:

It appears to the Committee that the great and important religious interests which the Commissioners represent would be impaired rather than promoted by accepting so inconsiderable a sum as that to which the consideration is now reduced; and the Committee desire me to suggest whether it would not be desirable, under all the circumstances, to make a free grant of this ground to the public.[2]

The Commissioners ignored both the offer and the advice. There is no wonder that the negotiations broke down; but one of the City members procured the publication of the correspondence, and the world was able to enjoy the spectacle of the two august bodies at fisticuffs.

The Deputies resolved now to carry the matter to Parliament. They noted that the Commissioners, while claiming their rights as freeholder, recognized the moral right of the representatives of those buried there to have the ground undisturbed. They urged the Commissioners to allay the anxiety, not merely of relatives, but of

all who revered it as a place of sepulture of great and good men of various sections of Christians in past ages.

They decided that if a deputation to the Home Secretary did not produce Government action, a private Bill should be introduced.[3]

To secure an adequate deputation, representatives were invited from a much longer list than usual: eleven in all. Only the Quakers refused to help. The vestry of St Luke's appointed a churchwarden to attend the conferences. The City also asked for

---

[1] 'Proceedings', p. 13. [2] 'Proceedings,' p. 20. [3] 20 Feb. 1867.

an interview with the Home Secretary. Leaving nothing to chance, the Deputies approved in draft a Bill which they sent to the Chamberlain of the City,[1] and later, on request, to the Home Secretary.[2] But in fact, the struggle was over. The Bill, when introduced into the Commons by R. W. Crawford, M.P. for the City, and later into the Lords by Lord Shaftesbury, had a very favourable reception; it became law by mid-July.[3]

The Corporation lost no time in improving the appearance of the ground, and after two years the Lord Mayor formally opened Bunhill Fields as an open space to be preserved for ever. At the request of the Corporation, the Deputies were represented at the ceremony, and at the Mansion House Dinner which followed.[4] It is natural that the Deputies should have since maintained a special interest in Bunhill Fields; in 1924, for instance, and again in 1951 they had the tombs of Bunyan and Watts there renovated.

The story of the Fields illustrates the bitterness, not to say venom, which marked the relations between the Established Church and Dissent at this time; and the Ecclesiastical Commissioners so far shared these feelings as to put themselves in a hopeless position. The proposal of the Commissioners was in itself an outrage, but the Deputies showed perhaps exceptional skill in making the most of the advantages which the ill-judgment of their opponents had given them: it was their own triumph to which the Lord Mayor invited them. The open space opposite Wesley's Chapel is a memorial not only of the heroic dead, but of the skilful defeat of a sectarian bigotry scarcely to be distinguished from malice.

The same bigotry, with less disguise, was shown in the country at large. Burial by the Anglican clergyman was still the only permitted form in parish churchyards, and petty intolerance of various kinds is reflected in the Deputies' Minutes. In Wales one clergyman refused to allow an inscription on the tomb of an Independent minister;[5] another refused to allow the repair of a tombstone.[6] The churchwardens in one parish refused to allow burial on Sunday till forced by the Deputies.[7]

[1] 1 Mar. 1867. [2] 13 Mar. 1867. [3] 17 July 1867. [4] 5 Oct. and 18 Nov. 1869.
[5] Tenby, 12 Mar. 1849. [6] Holyhead, 6 April 1852. [7] Creaton, 13 April 1852.

A distressing incident in Norfolk was the signal for a new campaign which did not end until, twenty years later, the Dissenters secured the right to burial by their own ministers in parish churchyards. In 1861 the Deputies learnt that at Hersey a parishioner, Joseph Fish, had been fined for singing on the way to and at the grave of an unbaptized child. The vicar, the Rev. Edward Pole Neale, informed against him for indecent behaviour, he being the only person authorized to perform the burial service there. The Deputies petitioned both Houses of Parliament that parishioners should be allowed burial with the rites of their own denomination, and that only riotous, violent, and indecent behaviour should be penalized. Learning that Sir Samuel Morton Peto intended introducing a Bill, the Deputies promised support, though he thought it best to confine his Bill to unbaptized persons; they supported him by petition, but in 1862 and again in 1863 he met with no success.

In 1864 the Deputies' attention was again called to the state of the law by the refusal of the Vicar of Colyton to read the service at the burial of a parishioner, on the ground that he was a Unitarian;[1] another variety of trouble occurred at Peterborough,[2] where the vicar would not let a body be interred unless he read the service.

Having once more failed in their support of a Burials Bill, which was withdrawn in 1869, the Deputies and the Liberation Society decided to prepare their own Bill, and persuaded Mr Osborne Morgan to introduce it in 1870. His and their persistence for ten years at last brought the needed reform. In 1871 the Deputies deplored the 'pertinacious opposition' which defeated the Bill, and urged Morgan to persevere.[3] Even the House of Lords seemed to admit the need for some change, for it passed a Bill of Earl Beauchamp's which would have permitted burials without a Church of England service, but forbade any other service. This the Deputies denounced as 'inadequate'; it was indeed flatly opposed to their conception of the Dissenters' position as lawful Christian churches.

Meanwhile, cases still came in. At Gravesend a child of Wesleyan

---

[1] 2 Nov. 1864. [2] 7 Dec. 1864. [3] 14 July 1871.

parents who had been baptized was refused burial, and this encouraged co-operation with the Methodists, even though, as the parents wished for no action, none was taken.[1]

In 1872 both Beauchamp's and Morgan's Bills reappeared. Beauchamp's was ultimately withdrawn; Morgan's failed again in the Commons after two readings, in spite of the Deputies' hopes for its success in view of previous large majorities on the second readings in 1870 and 1871. With the Deputies' agreement, though they deplored further concessions, Morgan had accepted an amendment which provided that, in order to prevent disorderly services, if no published ritual were used, the service should consist only of prayer, Holy Scripture, or hymns. But this did not save the Bill.[2] Morgan now felt that it could only succeed if the Government would adopt it, and this Gladstone refused to do.[3] The Deputies had to content themselves with a special resolution of triumph over Disraeli, who had declared his opposition:

Notwithstanding all the efforts of the Conservative Party, headed by the Leader of the Opposition himself, the Second Reading of the Bill was carried by the large majority of 63 in a House of 500.[4]

The Deputies' determination was unwearied. They wanted the Bill brought in again in 1874.[5] Morgan, however, was 'decidedly' of opinion that this would be undesirable. Neither the Deputies nor the Liberation Society wished to have the Bill introduced against his wish, and he was asked to embody his reasons in a letter which could be published.[6]

In 1875, however, after the Election which brought the Conservatives into power, the Deputies proposed a new Bill of 'a more decisive character' than that introduced into the last Parliament. Osborne agreed to introduce one giving parishioners generally the right to use churchyards without the Prayer Book or the clergy of the Established Church.[7] Though this Bill was lost on the second reading by 14 the Deputies felt confident that a settlement was at hand. Bright made a notable speech in the debate; and conferences between Dissenting ministers and Anglican clergy

[1] 15 Feb. 1872. [2] 4 July 1872. [3] 24 Dec. 1872.
[4] 5 Dec. 1873. [5] 2 Jan. 1874. [6] 23 Jan. 1874.
[7] 4 Dec. 1874 and 29 Jan. 1875.

occurred. The Government, Morgan thought, was not behind these.[1]

In 1876 Morgan got a late position in the ballot for the Burials Bill,[2] so he put forward instead a resolution, which was lost by 31.[3] There was still in some quarters a fear that a change in the law might result in unseemly burials. There was talk of adding a clause to make all services held under the Bill 'religious'. The Deputies would accept this, though they preferred to leave the question open.[4] They were emphatic in declaring that Dissenters' grievances would not be remedied by the purchase of additional grounds, or by permission to bury the dead in silence.[5] In the Lords a resolution of Lord Glanville was lost by 56, but gratified the Deputies by producing an 'interesting and instructive debate'. Opinion was taking shape. Something would have to be done; even the Dissenters' opponents could not hope that a policy of mere inaction would succeed: their problem was to find the minimum of concession that would suffice.

This was not lost on the Deputies, who resolved that in 1877 their Bill should be re-introduced, whatever steps the Government might take.[6] Morgan accordingly re-introduced it. Disraeli also announced a Government Bill, though with characteristically cheap and heartless cynicism he suggested that 'the difficulty is chiefly a sanitary one': this the Deputies exposed as an attempt to withdraw the public notice from the real grievance. They would have nothing to do with the Government Bill.[7] They met Disraeli's sneers by advertising some petulant arguments which were none the less effective for being slightly unreasonable in places. The Bill might be useful in consolidating earlier Acts, but its two contributions to the main problem were merely two methods of insulting the Dissenters. To provide new burial places where there was still room in parish churchyards was to cast odium on Nonconformists and to perpetuate sectarian distinctions. To allow burials in churchyards without any service put Nonconformists in a position of degradation which they could not accept.[8]

[1] 4 June 1875.   [2] 10 Feb. 1876.   [3] 10 May 1876.
[4] 31 Jan. 1876.   [5] 23 Feb. 1876.   [6] 5 Jan. 1877.
[7] 2 Mar. 1877.   [8] 14 and 27 Mar. 1877.

Lord Glanville was thanked for his protest against the Bill, and for endeavouring to amend it.[1] They pursued the Bill to the death, presenting four hostile petitions against it, and had the satisfaction of seeing the Government abandon it, while Osborne Morgan again urged a settlement on the lines he had advocated.[2]

In consultation with the Deputies and the Liberation Society, he renewed his resolution of 1876 in the session of 1878. The Deputies took the usual steps to support him, but the importance they attached to the occasion is shown by their postponement of the Annual Meeting until after the vote; in a House of 473 it was lost by only 15. The Deputies were jubilant, feeling that all the signs showed that moderate Conservatives were anxious to end the controversy. Among these signs was the dropping of a Bill introduced by Mr Balfour, which the Deputies had proposed to attack with amendments at the committee stage.[3]

A certain number of incidents continued to give colour to the campaign. The Committee had given instructions that all cases of refusal to bury were to be watched with a view to prosecuting.[4] A case at Tetbury was mentioned in the Commons, and ended with an apology from the vicar.[5] The Vicar of Winchcombe was more ingenious than most offenders: his plan was to omit part of the burial service when he buried Dissenters.[6] The Deputies collected names of people who could prove the offence, but before action was taken the vicar

announced publicly that in consequence of having been informed by the Bishop that the words 'sure and certain' do not apply to the 'individual body' about to be buried, but simply that there will be a general resurrection, he the Vicar was prepared to and accordingly should read the whole service over all persons buried by him.[7]

In 1879 a plethora of Burial Bills (most of which were dismissed by the Deputies as objectionable and insufficient) showed that settlement was near. The serious challenge to Osborne Morgan's Bill came from Balfour, who introduced his own Bill, virtually conceding the principle of Morgan's Bill, but burdening it with objectionable restrictions. The Deputies saw no hope of a united

[1] 4 May 1877.   [2] 8 June 1877.   [3] 14 May and 14 June 1878.
[4] 2 April 1875.   [5] 12 Feb. 1878.   [6] 25 June 1878.   [7] 29 Nov. 1878.

Liberal vote against it; they therefore advised that Morgan should support the second reading, that he should then specify the objectionable clauses, and make it clear that unless by amendment Balfour's Bill was equated with his, he would then oppose it.[1] The Bill was, however, talked out by Conservatives.[2] Nevertheless, the Deputies were still sanguine, regarding the existence of Balfour's Bill as evidence of the weakness of the opposition.[3] Their hopes were justified; success was not far away, but before it came Disraeli's Government had still a shock for them. Late in the session an Interment Bill to amend the Public Health Act of 1875 came on rather unexpectedly, and passed the Commons with almost no discussion. The Deputies petitioned the Lords against it, discovering that it destroyed features of the existing law which were valuable to Dissenters. Hitherto, fees for the Anglican clergy had not been exacted from the unconsecrated ground in public cemeteries; but sanitary authorities under the new Bill would provide grounds for Church of England burials only at public expense.[4] In spite of protests, the Bill passed.[5]

In planning the next session's campaign, the Deputies and the Liberation Society considered that a resolution, rather than a Bill, should be produced. The advance of public opinion and the passing of the Public Health Act made it necessary to have a more comprehensive resolution than on former occasions. It should include consolidation of burial laws and cemeteries as well as churchyards. It should demand that such form of service as the relatives prefer should be permitted in both sorts of parochial burying-grounds, without reference to any distinction between consecrated and unconsecrated ground.[6] Among the questions put to candidates at the General Election was one which tested them on this subject.[7]

The Deputies were now to reap the reward of many years' hard work. There was a Liberal Government again, and Gladstone no longer ignored their claims. A Government Bill, authorizing other services than the Church of England in churchyards, was introduced as soon as the Liberals took office. It won the general

---

[1] 31 Jan. 1879. [2] 21 Feb. 1879. [3] 25 Feb. 1879. [4] 4 July 1879.
[5] 29 July 1879. [6] 20 Nov. 1879. [7] 2 Jan. 1880.

approval of the Deputies, but did not go far enough for them. They objected to the classification of the unbaptized with criminals and the excommunicated, and would have liked all distinctions between consecrated and unconsecrated ground abolished.[1] They did not like the clause restricting services to Christian services.[2] Conferences with members of the Government made it clear that, whilst the Government would urge in the Commons the rejection of most of the Lords' amendments, they would support the clause authorizing only a 'Christian and orderly service'.[3] This view prevailed, and the Burial Laws Amendment Act made it possible, after notice given to the incumbent, for burials to take place in any parish churchyard or graveyard with any Christian and orderly service, or without any service at all. No anti-Christian or anti-religious addresses were to be permitted. The Anglican clergy might, if they wished, use parts only of the Prayer Book service, and might perform Church of England services in unconsecrated ground, but they were withheld from the unbaptized and the excommunicated.

The Deputies congratulated Morgan on the measure of success which had at last rewarded him, although the Act (43 and 44 Vict. c. 41) was confessedly imperfect, and it was still necessary to consolidate and harmonize the clauses.[4]

The Act of 1880 not only gave the Deputies what they had sought for half a century, it gave them a new task: to see that the new law was obeyed. At once they charged themselves with the duty of acting when they learnt of infringements of the law, and began to discuss the many problems that might arise.[5] What about tolling the bell for funerals under the new Act?[6] Could the clergy allot one part of the churchyard specially for Dissenters?[7] Could the clergy insist that, whatever the rights of parishioners might be, non-parishioners must be buried by them or refused burial?[8] Counsel advised that it would be best to wait for particular cases before seeking a decision; and the Deputies, with

---

[1] 1 June 1880. [2] 22 June 1880. [3] 6 July and 11 Aug. 1880.
[4] 28 Feb. 1881. [5] 18 and 22 Oct. 1880. [6] 9 Nov. 1880.
[7] 16 Nov. 1880. [8] 21 Dec. 1880.

their usual preference for action in individual cases rather than for general statements, at once decided not even to advertise their interest in the general observance of the Act, but from time to time to advertise the relevant facts which might emerge as particular cases were settled.[1] The ten years that followed were full of attempts to evade or make the working of the Act as unpleasant as possible for Dissenters; and later years provided enough problems to keep the Deputies well exercised. It is unnecessary to specify all; but specimen cases illustrate the slowness with which every approach to religious equality has been won in practice, even after it has been conceded in theory.

Two cases reported to the Deputies almost immediately after the passing of the Act led them to formulate the policy just described, and show their firmness and moderation. At Teddington, Bishop Sugden of the Free Church and a Mr Hoare reported that burial was refused to Mr Hoare's child 'on alleged sanitary grounds'.[2] Immediate action was needed: counsel was consulted; and, under pressure, the rector allowed the burial, and the tolling of the bell.[3] So far the Deputies would go, but when Hoare sued the rector for £20 damages, they advised against the plan and decided to take no further action.[4] Hoare lost his case, and despite appeals from Bishop Sugden and others, the Deputies would not assist in an appeal against the decision.[5]

At Shirland the refusal was not to bury, but to register burial. The Deputies tried to force registration of the burial certificate by *mandamus*[6] and to get costs from the rector if they succeeded.[7] The Lord Chief Justice and two judges first decided against the rector on the legal points and he was condemned in costs.[8] When the main case came before the Derby Assizes he lost it. Game to the last, the rector enquired if an entry by his curate would suffice. It was answered that as long as the certificate was duly entered, there would be no enquiry about the person entering it.[9] Even so the Deputies had to pay £29 7s. 9d. out-of-pocket costs. The rector's solicitors asked to be spared the expense of making a formal return to the writ of *mandamus:* but the Deputies insisted

---

[1] 22 Oct. 1880.   [2] 18 Oct. 1880.   [3] 22 Oct. 1880.
[4] 18 Jan. 1881.   [5] 27 Jan. 1881.   [6] 22 Oct. and 16 Nov. 1880.
[7] 18 Jan. 1881.   [8] 21 June 1881.   [9] 15 Nov. 1881.

on a formal return and on being satisfied that the entry, alleged
to have been made by the curate of Stonebroom, had been made
according to law.[1] A General Meeting was triumphant about the
complete success of the endeavour to vindicate the law, and condemned in the strongest terms Mr Hall's refusal to perform his
official duty.[2] Only a month later, however, the Deputies learnt
that they had not reached the end of the trouble with Mr Hall.
A burial under the Act, it was said, had not been registered. Hall
refused to allow the registers to be inspected, though the legal
fee of 1s. had been tendered, but said that if the relatives would
apply he would satisfy them. As the relatives concerned had
apparently left the county, the Deputies prepared to act.[3] Hall
himself then died, and his solicitors asked to be allowed to pay
the costs of the last motion without going to court.[4] On being
told that Hall had died in poor circumstances and had left his
wife poor, the Deputies pressed no more.[5]

At Harlow there was a picturesque as well as a petty element
in the story. The clergyman's action was more maddening than
often, but not so clearly illegal. The Deputies showed an unwillingness to compromise which was unusual and in the circumstances
unfortunate. The vicar locked the churchyard gates against a
funeral procession and forced it to go in and out another way.
Subsequently the gates were lifted off their hinges, and four persons were to be indicted. The Deputies agreed to defend them,
and enquired if an action could be taken against the vicar for
contravening the Burial Acts unless he expressed regret and promised 'not to commit a similar indecency again'.[6] The vicar made
no reply to letters, but it was learnt that, with a certain sardonic
ingenuity, he had caused the grave to be dug like a Dissenting
cemetery chapel, from north to south not from east to west; and
that he refused to produce the registers. The Committee was first
advised that the vicar's action was a misdemeanour, and they
indicted him, applying for *mandamus* to make him produce the
registers.[7] Later the Committee was advised to reconsider the plan
of legal proceedings, as there seemed to be no clear infringement of

[1] 20 Dec. 1881.   [2] 22 Mar. 1882.   [3] 21 April 1882.   [4] 18 July 1882.
[5] 27 Oct. 1882.   [6] 30 Nov. 1882.   [7] 19 Dec. 1882.

the Act of 1880. For once the Deputies set aside their legal adviser and decided to proceed, as they regarded the vicar's action as 'contrary to the spirit of the law of equity'.[1] At first all went well; the vicar was found guilty of a misdemeanour and sent to the Assizes. A form of apology was offered, but was deemed inadequate.[2] The Deputies considered proceedings in the ecclesiastical court also, to compel the vicar to close the new gate which had been made in the burial ground, to adjust the position of the grave, and to remove certain black posts that had given offence.[3]

Despite the Deputies' protests, the vicar got the case removed from Chelmsford to London, to avoid the prejudices of a local jury.[4] The judge's charge being adverse to the Bill of Indictment, the Grand Jury threw it out.[5] Not to be deprived of their prey, the Deputies next considered going to Quarter Sessions. At first they were told that it was probable that the Chairman would oppose the judge's view. The Deputies were most reluctant to abandon the case; and counsel finally advised that the vicar should be charged under the Act of 1880 with wilfully endeavouring to bring into contempt or obloquy the belief of a denomination of Christians and the members and minister.[6]

The vicar's solicitors retorted that these vexatious proceedings could only be actuated by malice; the promoters must be civilly and criminally responsible: they demanded the names of the promoters.[7] The Deputies explained the true reasons for their proceedings, said that of course a member of the Committee would give his name as responsible, and asked for suggestions to avoid the necessity of proceeding.[8] The vicar's solicitors said that the vicar always had disclaimed and again disclaimed any idea of throwing contempt on a Nonconformist funeral or of giving pain to the family. He was not responsible for an advertisement in *The Guardian* to which the Deputies had referred, nor did he know of it. On this, the Deputies allowed the matter to drop;[9] it was not one of their happiest encounters, for the grievance, though great in fact, was less in law than many.

---

[1] 12 Jan. 1883. [2] 13 Mar. 1883. [3] 20 Feb. 1883.
[4] 13 June 1883. [5] 11 July 1883. [6] 21 Sept. 1883.
[7] 1 Oct. 1883. [8] *Ibid.* [9] 15 Oct. 1883.

Yet the battle was not, it seems, without effect. Next year at Maidenhead (Bryn Hill) there was no need to fight when a vicar tried to prevent funerals using the ordinary way. The vicar promised to abandon his plan.[1]

Other complaints considered by the Deputies included a fee improperly demanded and paid under protest;[2] an 'exorbitant fee' demanded because the parishioner had died outside the parish;[3] attempts to impose fees, contrary to immemorial custom, for gravestones;[4] forbidding an inscription on the grave of an unbaptized child;[5] entering the burial of Nonconformists, not in the register, but in another book;[6] stopping a Nonconformist funeral on Sunday and alleging that Sunday was a day specially exempted by the Act of 1880[7] (Mr Osborne Morgan's opinion to the contrary was published); refusing a Baptist funeral because deceased lived a few yards beyond the parish boundary, although he had purchased a grave.[8]

At Gwinear the burial of an unbaptized child by a Wesleyan minister was interrupted by the sexton on the orders of the vicar. The Deputies resolved to prosecute if neither the Home Secretary nor the Wesleyans did so. A threat from the Wesleyans produced an ample apology from the sexton, and all that was left for the Deputies to do was to advertise the incident.[9]

An amusing example of Welsh adroitness occurred at Rhos (Ruabon). The Burial Board had provided a new cemetery, and the vicar got half of it consecrated surreptitiously by the bishop. The bishop himself was believed to have been ignorant of the holy duplicity to which he was party.[10] The papers were laid before the House of Commons.[11]

At Ebbw Vale a curate would not permit the Dissenting minister to read the service, but took it over himself.[12] When asked to apologize and to promise not to repeat the action, he said that the facts were misinterpreted. The vicar condemned his action.[13] The

---

[1] 2 May 1884. [2] Bronygraig, 9 Nov. 1880; cf. Llanaber, 7 Sept. 1880.
[3] Stapleford, 21 June 1881. [4] 15 Nov. 1881: Wales (several cases).
[5] Chislehurst, 3 Nov. 1882. [6] Earl's Barton, 19 Dec. 1882 and 20 Feb. 1883.
[7] Haverfordwest, 9 Dec. 1884. [8] Ruthin, 2 May 1884.
[9] 29 May and 13 June 1883. [10] 29 May 1883. [11] 21 Sept. 1883.
[12] 5 Aug. 1884. [13] 24 Sept. 1884.

Deputies procured corroborative action and decided to prosecute, unless the curate admitted his error; there were odd features in the course of events.[1] The Deputies' letter was returned marked 'not known' and 'insufficiently addressed', and the local M.P. strongly urged that a London, not a local, solicitor should be employed.[2] A registered letter extracted the necessary admission of error and promise for the future, though the curate pleaded ignorance and stuck to his account of what had occurred. At the request of the local minister, and so as not to seem vindictive, the Deputies accepted the apology and published the correspondence.[3]

At Hathern, as late as 1890, the incumbent stopped a funeral procession, though due notice had been given, and before admitting it to the churchyard demanded fees and a certificate. An apology being refused, a summons was issued.[4] The case got into court, but the summons was withdrawn when the incumbent's legal representative expressed 'unfeigned regret' and apologies for the breach of the law and pain caused to the relatives of the deceased. To their expressions of gratification about the legal proceedings, the Deputies added that they had learnt 'with astonishment' of the 'most offensive letters' written by the Rev. E. Smythies to their Secretary and to the minister who officiated. He had grossly misrepresented the proceedings in court and made defamatory statements declared by his Diocesan to be 'altogether unfounded'. The Deputies drew the moral: burial grounds ought not to be left in the care of clergymen 'who are subject to no authority which can effectually restrain them from the commission of acts of illegality and intolerance'.[5]

The clergy were not the only offenders. A peculiarly rank offence deserves to be recorded to the discredit of the clerk of the Ilminster Burial Board. He refused to grant a burial certificate to a Congregational minister for a child that had not been baptized. He next granted one as for any still-born child. The Deputies asked that the funeral should be delayed until they got *mandamus*. The Burial Board at a special meeting disowned the clerk's action, made him give an ordinary certificate, and an apology, and a

---

[1] 9 Dec. 1884.   [2] 16 Dec. 1884.   [3] 30 Dec. 1884.
[4] 30 Oct. 1890.   [5] 17 Feb. 1891.

promise for his future behaviour. The Deputies contented themselves by advertising the incident.[1]

At Pinner the clerk was made to refund £2 17s. 6d. illegal fees.[2]
At Hounslow the Board, which refused to alter its fees on representations made by the Deputies, was forced by the Home Office
to give way on the main point.[3] By means of trust deeds it was
found possible to make additions to parish grounds in such a way
as to avoid the Act of 1880.[4] At Ringmore (Devon) the incumbent refused to bury Dissenters in one part of the churchyard. The
Deputies advised a protest and he withdrew his refusal.[5]

The Deputies found their clients at times more trying than
their opponents. They would not produce evidence promptly;
they would not get the Deputies' authority before they started
proceedings, but they rarely failed to appeal for help when
defeated in actions which should never have been started. Many
complaints the Deputies did not take up; they were sometimes
ill-founded, and sometimes it was doubtful if the action reported
was illegal, however uncharitable or inequitable it might be. It
was sometimes of no public interest.[6] The Deputies must not be
represented as seeking trouble, or as ready to make wanton strife
about trifles.

Such being the background of the working of the Act of 1880,
we may examine the twenty years struggle which led to its
revision in 1900 on lines desired by the Deputies. No time was
lost in pressing for improvements of the measure. The Deputies
and the Liberation Society sought an interview with Sir William
Harcourt. The Government, he said, could not introduce another
Bill so soon after the last, unless it were a mere Consolidating
Act. He would not oppose a private Bill to secure that those who
wanted cemeteries consecrated should themselves arrange and pay
for consecration.[7] Accordingly, the two Societies prepared a Bill,
but limited it to cemeteries only. In particular, it abolished the
legal division of cemeteries and made consecration a religious act
only, of which the State took no cognizance. It provided for the

---

[1] 5 May 1885.   [2] 28 April, 15 June, 5 Oct. 1893.   [3] 7 Dec. 1893 to 14 June 1894.
[4] 31 July 1891.   [5] 30 June and 17 Oct. 1895.
[6] E.g. Ashton-on-Mersey, 27 Sept. 1888.   [7] 20 Dec. 1881.

extinction of certain rights and pecuniary claims at the death of the present holders.[1] The Deputies petitioned in favour of the Bill; but it was not reached.[2] A Select Committee of the House of Commons, however, considered the whole subject of ecclesiastical and mortuary fees.[3]

In the following year a large deputation, representing almost all the Nonconformists except the Wesleyans and Quakers, interviewed Harcourt and Chamberlain, and urged the need for consolidating and improving the law. Much publicity was given to the deputation, and as a precautionary measure Richard brought in again his Bill of 1882.[4] The Bill was talked out; but the Deputies were encouraged by the Select Committee's recommendations concerning the abolition of burial and mortuary fees. Public opinion was demanding popular control of burial grounds.[5]

At the next Annual Meeting the Deputies called attention to the Select Committee's recommendations, to the constant difficulties and injustices under the present law, and called on the Government to make good its promise of a Bill.[6] But another year went by, and though the Government did prepare a Bill, a General Election came before it was passed. The Deputies hoped that after the Election Mr Osborne Morgan would introduce a more comprehensive measure, ending the distinction of consecrated and unconsecrated ground, revising fees, and transferring control from the clergy to an elected authority.[7] As Morgan took office he was unable to bring in a private Bill, but the Government accepted his Bill with modifications,[8] and the Deputies thought it would go far to remove invidious distinctions in public burial grounds.[9]

The reality of this distinction had been illustrated quite recently. A Bill of 1884 had proposed to prevent building in disused burial grounds. For consecrated ground the prohibition was to be absolute; on unconsecrated ground burial might take place with the Home Secretary's permission. The Deputies agreed with the object but resented the distinction, and got the promoter to strike it out.[10]

[1] 6 and 20 Jan. 1882. [2] 4 April 1882. [3] 21 April 1882.
[4] 5 and 12 Jan., 14 Feb. 1883. [5] 11 April 1883. [6] 2 April 1884.
[7] 20 Jan. 1886. [8] 8 Mar. 1886. [9] 2 June 1886.
[10] 18 Mar. and 1 April 1884.

Another situation which the Deputies hoped to see ended by the Government Bill was illustrated at Attleborough. A majority of the inhabitants did not wish to consecrate part of the burial ground; other burial authorities were unwilling as long as consecration involved disabilities and unjust exactions. But the Home Secretary brought pressure to bear;[1] a case at North Kelsey a little earlier made it clear that burial authorities were under an obligation to consecrate the ground. (R. *v*. N. Kelsey Burial Board, 1892.)

Morgan's Bill, which he thoroughly discussed with the Deputies and the Liberation Society, covered a great many of the points that had been in dispute since 1880; though mainly connected with detail it would have had a great effect in sum and would have made most of the outrages impossible.[2] But in a time of political agitation it did not get a chance; and renewed efforts after Gladstone's return in 1892 and again in 1895 after his retirement met with no better success. It was not until 1898 that a Burials Bill got as far as a second reading, when it was rejected after an interesting and good-toned debate. The story of 1880 was about to be repeated. The opponents of the Bill admitted the grievances; a Select Committee was again appointed to examine the working of the laws, and the Deputies' Secretary gave evidence to it, and there was still hope of a measure to end the 'painful controversy'.[3] The Committee reported at the end of 1898; its report justified the Deputies' contentions, and its proposals satisfied them well in the main. They disliked the continuance of the allotment of the ground for separate denominations, and thought the proposals about the payment of fees recognized that the Church and not merely individual clergymen had a vested interest in them.

The Deputies proposed to press the Government to bring in a Bill, and not to re-introduce their own unless the Government were inactive.[4] It was not until the summer of 1900, however, that the Government Bill came on; it was supported, subject to a few amendments,[5] and passed. The Deputies, noting the fact with special thanks to Mr Carvell Williams, M.P., who had taken

---

[1] 29 June 1887. [2] 18 Jan. 1888. [3] 27 April and 15 June 1898.
[4] 17 May 1899. [5] 25 April 1900.

charge of the Burial Bills in the later period as Mr Morgan had in the earlier, expressed satisfaction that 'the long, anxious and strenuous efforts of this body and of the Liberation Society to secure religious equality in public cemeteries has thus been brought to a successful conclusion'.[1]

This Act, with the Marriage Act of 1898, marked in theory the end of a large section of Dissenting grievances, and made a good ending of the century for the Deputies. The Act provides that tables of fees must be submitted to the Secretary of State, and approved with or without alteration. Fees must be the same in the consecrated and unconsecrated parts of the ground. An incumbent, though exclusively entitled to perform the service in the consecrated part, is not entitled to fees unless he actually conducts the service, personally or by deputy. With temporary exceptions, no other fees are payable to the incumbent or churchwardens except for services rendered. The Act maintains the distinction between consecrated and unconsecrated ground; no fence is needed for the consecrated part, though its extent must be indicated. But consecration is no longer obligatory, as it had been until 1900, the duty being enforced by *mandamus*.[2] Now it is voluntary; the Board may act if it sees fit; if it does not, and the Secretary of State is satisfied that there is a reasonable number of persons who desire consecration, he may apply to the bishop. The fees due to the bishop will be the responsibility of those who apply for consecration. The Secretary of State may allot parts of the unconsecrated ground for the exclusive use of particular denominations. But if chapels are built on the unconsecrated part of the cemetery, they must not be consecrated or reserved for a particular denomination.

Even since the Act of 1900 the Deputies have had occasion to intervene in controversies. In Burslem in 1904 they were interested in securing and advertising a decision that no fee was payable to the incumbent when a burial in consecrated ground is performed by another minister.[3]

It was due to the changing temper of the age that cases of

[1] 12 July 1901. [2] R. *v.* North Kelsey Burial Board, 1892, see p. 329.
[3] 24 Mar. 1904 and 29 June 1905.

difficulty became fewer and fewer. A good illustration of this change in temper is seen in the settlement of difficulties which have arisen very recently over graveyards established under trusts in the period following the Act of 1880. An instance of this practice has been mentioned already; there was another at Christian Malford,[1] and these are representative of a considerable number. In 1944, on the initiative of the Liberation Society, action was taken over the burial ground at Chorley, Lancs. The churchyard of St Peter's, Chorley, had been consecrated in 1851, and in 1885, when it was nearly full, it was decided not to extend it, but to convey about three-quarters of an acre of land adjoining to the vicar, the two churchwardens, and others as trustees, with a proviso that only the burial service of the Church of England should be used and that only the vicar of the parish and authorized clergymen of the Church of England should conduct the services. The land was then consecrated.

But consecration carries with it public rights and public protection, for consecration is an ecclesiastical act, exercised by the bishop on behalf of the nation and not on behalf of a religious denomination. The trust deed in this case attempted to place the monuments in the burial ground under the authority of the trustees—but this is *ultra vires*, for the monuments in all consecrated ground come under the jurisdiction of the ordinary. It was evident that this ground was not in any legitimate sense a private burial ground.

After submitting a case to counsel and considering legal action, the Liberation Society and the Deputies decided instead to appeal in general terms to the diocesan bishops to put an end to difficulties of this kind. A letter was drafted which did not refer to the specific case but set out in detail the kind of grievance and the moral and legal objections to it. A prompt reply came from the Archbishop of York.[2] He consulted the Legal Board of the Church Assembly, whose reply was in the following terms:

It seems clear that any provision in a deed granting land as an addition to a churchyard, purporting to restrict the parishioner's rights, whether such right be the common law right to interment so long as the ground

---

[1] 26 Nov. and 18 Dec. 1908. [2] 16 Feb. 1945.

is not 'closed', or the statutory right to burial without the Church of England Burial Service, must be void.

A burial place must either be (1) a churchyard or an addition thereto, or (2) a private cemetery, or (3) a public combination of (1) and (2).

If the conveyance referred to in para (4) of a letter from the Liberation Society purports to grant an addition to a churchyard, it clearly does not comply with the Consecration of Churchyards Act 1867, and may be void altogether as an infringement of the Mortmain Acts.

In conveying this reply, the Archbishop said: 'I hope that this reply makes the position clear, and that any difficulties which have arisen in the past may cease'.

That is perhaps the best note on which to end this chapter. It might still be held that the burial laws are not fully satisfactory; it is certainly true that they are incomprehensible apart from a knowledge of their long and tortuous evolution. In watching that evolution we have been watching, from an unusual standpoint, the kind of complex operation which has created the machinery of our modern world.

CHAPTER 3

EDUCATION

(a) Elementary

IT IS NO PART of this history to retell the story of elementary education in the 19th century.[1] We have only to observe the place of the Deputies in the confused and acrimonious struggle. In the later stages of it their part was not very prominent or decisive; but in the earlier stages it was prominent, and perhaps at one crisis decisive.

The development of a national scheme of education provides one example of the many problems offered to Dissenters by the gradual extension of State activities. The field in which the State interfered grew wider and wider. This is the main thing. To most people in the early 19th century it appeared natural and indeed inevitable that as a fresh area of life fell under State control it should also fall under the influence of the State Church. Education had a traditional and inherent connexion with religion. Of all the areas newly claimed for State action in the 19th century, there was none in which it was so easy to foresee possibilities of conflict between religious parties. An attempt to make a profit for Anglicanism from national activities was particularly likely here; and in no other field in fact has State action so richly benefited Anglicanism.

This history records many successes for the Deputies, but in education it records at least partial failure. Until we have measured the menace which they withstood we cannot value at their true worth such partial successes as the Deputies did win. Moreover as we contrast the still smaller successes of the Dissenting interest

[1] Those to whom it is unfamiliar will find a good account in E. S. Woodward, *The Age of Reform, 1815-1870*. The reader is reminded that this chapter was written before the passing of the Education Act of 1944.

333

when it had other leaders and other methods we may wonder if, left to themselves, the Deputies might not have done better than their successors.

What was the attitude of the Deputies to education? It developed, and in developing it was completely transformed. The ecclesiastical principles of the Deputies remained the same and made some things always clear to them. Their political principles underwent considerable change, however, with the disintegration of the old individualistic political philosophy. The result was that any particular generation of Deputies might not always agree with one another or with their predecessors in the application of their ecclesiastical principles to a particular political situation.

It is clear to all but those who consciously and professionally misrepresent them that the Deputies, like other Dissenters, cared greatly about education for its own sake. They wanted more education for the mass of the people. The Industrial Revolution was increasing and was redistributing the population. The old provision for educating children had never been adequate, but every year made it less satisfactory. It is conventional to emit cheap sneers at Dissenting mill-owners and to depict their reluctance to see children educated. Such sneers miss the Deputies. The Dissenters in the North may (or may not) have been less enlightened than the Deputies. The Deputies' Minutes do not touch the problem. What they do make clear is the Deputies' own urgent concern for more education. Who, in their view, ought to provide it? And of what sort was it to be?

In the early part of the century the Deputies, like the majority of their countrymen, were under the spell of political individualism. They thought it no business of the State to educate children. That was the business of parents. If parents were poor, it was the duty of the Churches and philanthropic societies to help them. Side by side with this political conviction was a religious conviction: education must include religious teaching. If the parents, the Churches, or religious societies provided the money for education there was no insurmountable difficulty. The State must see that everyone had a fair chance to procure or to provide the religious teaching in which he believed.

334

Without any weakening of their ecclesiastical principles the Deputies moved to a very different opinion. The national situation changed, and was seen to have changed, in the middle of the century. At last men had to confess that, contrary to what they had expected, the activity of individuals, of Churches, of private societies had proved inadequate. The Deputies came to favour State education. They were determined nevertheless that this must not mean State Church education. But if education were to remain religious, as they wished, what could be done? Two main alternatives were produced: the first, to separate the religious element from the rest of education and to leave it to private or ecclesiastical agencies; the second, to find a religious element common to all Christians and to have that taught by the State. The supporters of each alternative asserted that it was perfectly easy to carry out the particular plan that commended itself to them. In truth it was not easy; and that is why the Deputies had a divided mind. In the event a peculiarly English compromise, the dual system, was worked out. In so far, however, as the dual system has defied the principles of the Deputies it has heaped up trouble for the nation slowly but very surely. When the crash comes, as come it must, the folly of those who defeated the Deputies' cause at this point will be apparent and will be admitted. The folly was not confined to ecclesiastics. The educational purists and administrators have an even more sorry record. With this preamble we may look at the detail of the story where, but only where, it touches the Deputies.

The story falls into three sections, sharply divided by the years 1843 and 1870. In 1843 the Deputies played a most important part in a great victory. In 1870 they had to lament a partial defeat. Since 1870 they have been powerless to avert the steadily accumulating evils which come from that defeat and which prepare an inescapable catastrophe.

In the first period, the Deputies' Minutes reveal two main anxieties. First, and governing all, is the anxiety to see schools multiplied by voluntary means. Multiplication of schools was not part of the duty specifically committed to them as defenders of the civil rights of Dissenters, but it is an object never far from their minds. The second anxiety sprang directly from their commission. The State might well attempt to make good the deficiencies of the voluntary system. This attempt must not be controlled by the State Church. If any Government presented elementary education to the Anglicans as an instrument for their sectarian propaganda, a quite new encroachment on the rights of Dissenters would have been achieved. Accordingly the Deputies shew themselves vigilant to the point of suspicion.

In the early years of the century, proposals for State control and support of elementary education had not yet become the marrow of the controversy. The two great voluntary societies were at work. 'The National Society for the Promotion of the Education of the poor in the principles of the Established Church' was founded in 1811. The undenominational kind of Christian education was already represented by the Royal Lancasterian Society, founded in 1808. This Society was the nucleus of the British and Foreign School Society. Established in 1814, it became the mainstay of the Lancaster ideals: 'with the Bible as the sole text-book the schoolmaster could teach the many great truths on which Christians are agreed'.[1]

As early as 1820 a proposal of Brougham's caused the Deputies alarm. The result of evidence which he had caused to be collected about the education of the London poor,[2] and about the use of endowments,[3] the Bill provided the first comprehensive plan for the education of the whole people of England and Wales. All teachers were to be members of the Established Church and to hold a certificate from the incumbent of the parish. He was to determine the teaching. No religious book except the Bible was to be used in the schools. The Deputies pronounced the Bill laudable in its objects and excellent in its designs, but they doubted if its method would achieve the object aimed at; and they feared that it would have an unfavourable effect on the liberties of Dissenters.[4] The Protestant Society and the Ministers had approached the Deputies in alarm; and the Deputies promised to act.[5]

[1] Quoted in F. Warre Cornish, *The English Church in the Nineteenth Century*, I, 96.
[2] Select Committee of 1816.   [3] Committee of 1818.
[4] 8 Dec. 1820.   [5] 28 July 1820.

The tactics used by the Deputies foreshadowed those which they were to develop in later stages of the controversy. First they had two private interviews with Brougham before Parliament met.[1] Then followed conference with other bodies interested,[2] and a publication appeared entitled 'An Enquiry into the operation of Mr Brougham's Education Bill as far as it concerns the Protestant Dissenters'. No hasty action followed: the Bill was in part good.[3] Anglicans found its exclusion of distinctive catechisms less satisfactory than the National Society's more complete Anglicanism; and the Bill was dropped. For many years State support of education, when given at all, would be given through the private societies.[4] The first national scheme had been ruined because it was too closely associated with the State Church to please the Dissenters and not closely enough associated with it to please the Anglicans.

During the next twenty years the Deputies remained anxious to spread education and at the same time not to allow the largest sect to turn the general desire for religious education to its own advantage. This double concern was illustrated by their petition in 1832 in favour of a Government plan for a national scheme of education in Ireland,[5] and by their resolve in the next year to watch in the interests of Dissenters any plan for general education.[6]

If the Deputies had not forgotten education, neither had Brougham (now Lord Brougham). In 1837 he introduced a Bill embodying the principles of his campaign. A Board of Commissioners was to distribute grants from the Treasury; parishes might levy rates for schools; religious teaching was to be unsectarian. The Deputies considered whether they ought not to publish a general statement on education.[7] Their sub-committee agreed with Brougham in regretting that, despite the efforts made, provision for education was still inadequate. It appeared to them, however, that his Bill gave such unrestricted powers to the commissioners that the rights of conscience and the just claims of Dissenters would not be sufficiently protected. They were

---

[1] 12 and 26 Jan. 1821.   [2] 23 Feb. 1821.   [3] 30 Mar. 1831.
[4] The first Parliamentary grant, £20,000 for building schoolrooms, was distributed by the National and British Societies in 1833.
[5] 24 May 1832.   [6] 30 Oct. 1833.   [7] 13 Dec. 1837.

x   337

unwilling to block any just and satisfactory plan for national education; but they confessed that the obstacles seemed almost insuperable.[1]

These apprehensions, however, did not prevent the Deputies from welcoming a national scheme which gave promise of being fair to all Churches. In 1839 Melbourne's Government increased the grant of £20,000 to £30,000 and set up a special Committee of the Privy Council to deal with education. This committee, which was to develop into the Board of Education, issued a scheme on 3 June 1839. The two great Societies, the National and the British, were to be assisted, not replaced, by the State. The State, since it provided money, was to inspect schools.

The prompt and enthusiastic welcome which the Deputies gave to this scheme disposes of the charge that Dissenters were unwilling to consider anything but a voluntary system, or that they were narrow individualists unable to recognize the function of the State in education. Until experience had convinced them that the State were not impartial in education, they had no reluctance to work with it. The report of the Privy Council Committee had been out only a week when the Deputies' Committee, after studying it clause by clause, expressed their gratitude to the Government for 'so liberal and comprehensive a scheme'. Though a General Meeting of the Deputies to petition Parliament was called for a few days later, the Committee took the first opportunity of declaring unanimously that the recommendations 'eminently deserve the approbation and support of all friends of national education on principles consistent with a due regard to the rights of conscience'.[2]

The General Meeting a week later had more to say, but it was to the same effect. Its pronouncements may be taken to represent Dissenting opinion before the ineptness of Sir James Graham had given it an unfortunate twist. The Deputies' petition recognized first that the State must intervene in education. The 'benevolent efforts of individuals and associations' had proved themselves inadequate; nor do the Deputies expect the deficiency to be met without Parliamentary help. The next put on record their 'surprise

[1] 18 Dec. 1837.   [2] 10 June 1839.

and alarm at the unjustifiable claims put forth by and for the clergy of the Established Church to the paramount and exclusive control over the education of the poorer classes' and over all money grants for it.

If such trust had ever been devolved by the legislature on the Established Clergy, they have for so long and to so fearful an extent neglected its duties as to render it inexpedient and unjust to have it confided to them now.

In a rich phrase they denounced any national sectarian system which defied the rights of parents to direct the education of their children and imposed the Anglican catechism on children not baptized in the Church of England. That would be 'not more repugnant to every feeling of enlightened benevolence than awfully offensive to the God of Truth, and fatal to the formation of moral principles'. Deep gratitude was felt for the Queen's double wish: first, that the youth of the kingdom should be 'religiously brought up', and second, that 'the rights of conscience should be respected'. In particular the Deputies were glad to perceive the Government's intention to encourage voluntary exertions, to extend the benefit of national grants to poor and populous districts, and ensure efficient teaching in secular subjects by inspectors who (it was understood) were to be laymen. In concluding the petition the Deputies hailed the scheme as

the most unexceptionable measure for national instruction, as regards the rights of conscience, which has ever been suggested by any body of advisers of the Crown.

In view of the change which was soon to come over the Deputies' opinions one incident at the meeting is of particular importance. One Deputy did not welcome State action. He wished to move an amendment stating that

national education or, to speak more correctly, education of the lower classes of society at the public expense is not a legitimate function of the government, which is constituted for the sole purpose of dispensing justice and of securing to the whole community without distinction the fullest enjoyment of liberty and property.

Only criminals and paupers, for whom the Government had a

special responsibility, should the Government educate. For this die-hard individualistic view of the functions of the State no seconder could be found among the Deputies of 1839. The malignant shadow of Sir James Graham had not yet fallen across English education.[1]

The Deputies' petition contained in embryo the Free Church case in the later education controversy. Had the lines indicated here been followed, the subsequent trouble would never have arisen.

But the struggle over the educational clauses of the Factory Bill of 1843 was at hand. No incident better illustrates the effectiveness of the Deputies in action; but it is important because of the unfortunate bias which it gave to Dissenters' opinions about educational policy. The bias was new, but it lasted for more than a generation. When the unhappy effects of the struggle of 1843 had at last spent themselves, it was too late to settle the problem in an amicable spirit. Sir James Graham had roused among Dissenters such suspicion of the State that they were far removed from the conciliatory opinions which they held in 1839. Graham was doubtless well-meaning: but his capacity for failing to see the obvious features of a situation was equalled only by his mulish self-conceit in clinging to an exploded policy. After all, the man whose main achievement was to divide Scottish Presbyterians who were agreed on essentials was not the man to unite Anglicans and Dissenters whose disagreements were almost fundamental. He has been deservedly pilloried as the person mainly responsible for the muddle which rent the Church of Scotland for most of a century. His vast contribution to the educational difficulties of his time has been less generously recognized. It is time to pay the debt.

Lord Brougham despite many rebuffs had remained undaunted in his enthusiasm for Educational Bills. In 1841 he urged Graham, the Home Secretary, to patronize 'a general parish plan' of education, 'permissive if you will'. Brougham recognized that the Tory Government must be expected 'to give the Church more sway in it than I should be expected or inclined to give it'. But Brougham would put up with that. He believed too that all would put up

[1] 17 June 1839.

with it, except 'those who hate the Established Church and love their sects more than they love education'.[1] This genial rhetoric which wrote off passionate devotion to a historic form of Church-manship as likely to be less substantial than interest in one particular way of educating people was characteristic of Brougham. He aspired nobly, but he understood nothing and nobody—least of all his Dissenting allies.

Graham was not hopeful. The dilemma was permanent. National education must be religious in order to work well; but England, unlike Scotland, had no common creed. The State could not teach 'the established creed' from public money without rousing the Dissenters.[2] Peel was even less hopeful than Graham.[3]

Lord Ashley, afterwards Earl of Shaftesbury, set the ball rolling by his eloquent plea early in 1843 for the education of the working classes. He contemplated that the religious teaching of factory children should be given by the clergy of all denominations. Sir James Graham's Factory Bill, which followed the appeal, was on very different lines. 'The most important feature was the introduc-tion of compulsory education for factory children under the direction of the Church.'[4] Factory schools were to be established under the management of the parish clergyman, churchwardens, and four persons elected by J.P.s in Petty Sessions. 'The Church', as Graham himself assured Gladstone, 'has ample security that every master in the new schools will be a Churchman, and that the teaching of the Holy Scriptures, as far as the limited exposition may be carried, will necessarily be in conformity with his creed'.[5]

What did the Deputies think of the scheme? It roused them and all the Dissenters to instant and unrelenting opposition. Here was the first national scheme for compulsory education; and it was placed under the control of the Anglican Church. To have allowed the educational clauses of the Bill to go unchallenged would have been to accept the general principle that compulsory State educa-tion must be State Church education. This was not the natural development of the principles of the Education Committee's

[1] C. S. Parker, *Life and Letters of Sir James Graham*, vol. I, p. 337.
[2] *Ibid.* p. 338.   [3] *Ibid.* p. 339.
[4] J. L. and B. Hammond, *Lord Shaftesbury*, 1923, p. 87.
[5] C. S. Parker, *Life and Letters of Sir James Graham*, vol. I, p. 344.

Report of 1839. It would have placed the Dissenters at a completely new disadvantage, whatever securities and safeguards Graham might offer. The danger was the more insidious because the educational proposals appeared as an incidental part of an excellent reform of the Factory Laws. The storm that followed provoked, and has continued to provoke, many cheap sneers. If it be assumed that ecclesiastical principles and practices are of no consequence even to those who pay and suffer for them, the opposition to Graham was indeed wantonly organized by bigots among fools. In order to take this view it is only necessary to ignore the facts. The Dissenters had in fact suffered some persecution and much inconvenience during more than two centuries for the sake of those same ecclesiastical principles and practices. It requires a mind anachronistic as well as ungenerous to blame them for refusing to think as lightly of religious differences as Mr and Mrs Hammond may think. It was not worth while to accept the wrong sort of religious education in order to get some sort of secular education a little quicker than one would otherwise have got it. That was the problem, from the Dissenters' point of view; and it is merely malicious ignorance to represent them as caring little for education because they cared much for religion.

Graham introduced the Bill on 8 March 1843. Only a week later the Deputies had condemned the educational clauses and established machinery to seek the co-operation of the Wesleyans, the Friends, and others. All M.P.s and Nonconformist bodies were informed of their resolutions. The Deputies now made their first open invasion of the field of Parliamentary politics. They rallied all their forces and they were to score a smashing victory. They secured it only by the hardest work.

They organized a United Conference of bodies interested[1] and a committee of this conference bore the brunt of the struggle. The campaign lacked nothing in the way of a plainly expressed programme. Even when Graham had made his concessions the Deputies considered that substantial objections would remain. The Bill would aggrandize the Established Church and degrade others; it would 'afford means for diffusing Puseyite errors'; it would

[1] March 1843.

increase poor rates; it would begin a course of oppressive interference by the Privy Council, by school inspectors, and by the
clergy. It was 'a severer blow at religious liberty than has been
aimed at it since the rejection of Lord Sidmouth's bill in 1811'.
In short it was the greatest legislative evil that 'inherited intolerance
could have devised or clerical tyranny in dark and barbarous ages
might have gloried to impose'.[1]

The Deputies did not forget to supplement their rhetoric by an
oidered list of objections. There was to be general taxation for
schools where religious teaching was to be under the exclusive
guidance of a clergyman. Since the bishops were to approve all
schoolmasters, Dissenters would be in practice excluded. There
was no provision for popular control over the clerical trustee.
Sunday Schools and British Schools would be destroyed, for
people would not subscribe to one school whilst they were rated
for another in the same place. A new religious test would be
introduced, for conscientious objectors to the payment of the poor
rate for this purpose would lose the franchise. Lastly it was
contended that the regulation of employment and the improvement of education, being separate subjects, ought to be treated in
separate Bills.

The campaign to secure petitions from congregations had striking results: 13,360 petitions with 2,068,059 signatures went in
against the original form of the educational clauses. Against the
amended version there were 6,200 petitions.[2] The Government
declared that it would not withdraw the clauses; the Home
Secretary had no power to suggest more alterations.

The Deputies continued the campaign. In an eloquent statement
prepared by John Wilks, they declared that

Notwithstanding all the calumnies . . . representing the opponents
to the clauses as enemies to the education of the industrious and poorer
classes . . . this Deputation reiterate their entire and unqualified condemnation of the clauses in their altered state.

All means of defeating the Government were to be used: more
petitions, lobbying, publication of divisions, pressure on M.P.s by
constituents, and the like. In the event the Deputies won.

[1] April 1843. [2] 14 June 1843.

'The Dissenters', wrote Graham whilst the campaign was undecided, 'will be too much for us. They will convert my measure of peace into a firebrand and a sword, and if we attempt to force it we shall do more harm than good.'[1] As was to happen on more than one occasion, the Deputies received more co-operation from the Wesleyan Methodists than their opponents had believed possible. Graham reported to Peel early in the fight that he had received a communication from the Wesleyan body with great regret:

It is more hostile than I had anticipated, and marks distinctly a wide estrangement from the Church. It is quite clear that the Pusey tendencies of the Established Church have operated powerfully on the Wesleyans, and are converting them rapidly into enemies.[2]

The Deputies, as has appeared, had not forgotten to wave Dr Pusey as a means of exciting the vigour of their adherents.

The United Committee had sat daily for ten weeks. On two occasions it had issued nine thousand circulars, including a Welsh version. It had dealt with 2,000 letters and 800 petitions. One member of the committee had visited fifteen counties and had formed daily committees in most of them. At the end of it all their chairman wrote: 'The Committee have closed their pleasant labours with esteem for each other and gratitude to Divine Providence'.[3]

The United Committee proposed to hold a public meeting to express their thankfulness for the withdrawal of the educational clauses and to urge on all denominations the duty of making exertions to promote the daily instruction of children. This the Deputies approved; but with their customary desire to improve an occasion they wished to add the 'practical object of raising a large fund for the promotion of education throughout the country'.[4] Such being the attitude of the Dissenters, there is little sting in the sneer of the Hammonds taken second-hand from Graham. When a Factory Bill was introduced in 1844, we read

No attempt was made to improve the education in factory schools, Graham observing grimly that he hoped that the rivalry of Church

[1] C. S. Parker, *op. cit.* p. 344.   [2] C. S. Parker, *op. cit.* p. 345.
[3] 14 June 1843.   [4] 5 July 1843.

and Chapel, which had made any State scheme impossible, would stimulate the supply of voluntary schools.[1]

To which sneer there is one adequate reply: it did.

Some of the criticisms of the Bill made by the Deputies may appear fiddling: almost any stick was good enough to beat it with. There is some petulant individualism, not worthy of the Deputies at their best, in the arguments that the Committee of the Privy Council would be a permanent board of control for children who were still under the natural guardianship of their parents; that this State body would have inquisitorial and severely punitive powers over schoolmasters whom the State did not pay; and that the inspection of schools and examination of children would lead children to disesteem and condemn their masters. There was more reason in the comment that the clergy were exempt from inspection under the Bill; but it was hardly a practical criticism.

When all allowance has been made, the Deputies' victory was both decisive and useful. Never again was so complete a capture of education by the dominant religious party threatened. The Deputies had not indeed been able to prevent the unfair subsidy of certain religious opinions, but they did secure in 1843 that this should not happen in State schools. Their later defeats, deplorable as they have been, have not reversed the victory won in 1843: State education has not been identified, as was then proposed, with Anglican education.

Enthusiasts for any sort of education on any terms continue to repeat with parrot-like accuracy the gibes of Sir James Graham. Considering it beneath their intellectual dignity to understand a major part of the problem before them, they lament with pious gestures the delay in educational advance caused by the rivalry of 'Church and Chapel'. The delay was indeed deplorable; but it would have been more deplorable to lay the foundations of compulsory national education as badly as Graham proposed on the shoddy foundations of his choosing. Some delay was not too high a price to pay for the national compulsory settlement of 1870, which, if not just, was at least less flagrantly unjust.

Between 1843 and the next important fight in 1870 a great

[1] J. L. and Barbara Hammond, *Lord Shaftesbury*, p. 89.

change came over the ecclesiastical scene. The primary responsibility of fighting the battle for religious equality in education passed from the Deputies to the national organizations of the Free Churches. The denominational unions, almost untried in 1843, were in 1870 able to assert themselves (the Congregational and Baptist Unions, for example, date from 1832).

The years 1843 to 1870 are the period of the experiment that failed. Since Dissent was strong enough to resist a scheme for Anglican national education, and Graham and his successors were unwilling or unable to provide an equitable scheme, it only remained to see if voluntary efforts could solve the problem. It cannot be too often or too emphatically said, however, that it was the failure of Graham in 1843 which drove the Deputies to a policy of rather rigid voluntaryism.

When the Factory Bill of 1844 was under discussion a hardening in the Deputies' tone was already to be noted. They opposed any interference of the Government in education. Inspectors ought indeed to refuse to allow children who could not read or write to work in factories,[1] but with that the Government's work ended and other people's began.

This was not a formula to cover inactivity. The years that followed 1843 saw Anglicans and Dissenters alike redoubling their efforts to spread education. They collected thousands upon thousands of pounds. They built schools by the score and hundred. They founded training colleges. The Committee of the Privy Council assisted the Societies by grants, but devoted its own efforts mainly to ensuring efficiency through its inspectors.

Nevertheless by these means the influence of the Government in education perceptibly increased. The famous Minutes of 1846 indicated how much the Committee of Council could do by skilful use of its money and inspectors. Lord Lansdowne plainly pointed out that the Minutes of the committee did not need confirmation in Parliament in order to become effective.

The Minutes of 1846 provided for an increase in the number of the committee's inspectors in order to secure more frequent inspections. A scheme was outlined for apprenticing pupil teachers

[1] 20 Mar. 1844.

to selected schoolmasters, making extra payments to such masters. Plans for pensions and gratuities were foreshadowed. Payments would be made according to the results reported by inspectors.[1] Here, it was clear, the committee had an instrument which might be made very effective for influencing both teachers and managers.

In their report for 1846 the Deputies had already noted that Lord John Russell intended to introduce an improvement in public education whilst at the same time maintaining religious liberty. The Deputies were now much more sceptical than they had been in 1839. 'Whether the legislature can interfere at all with public education without at the same time interfering with religious liberty has been doubted.'[2] The discussions in Parliament in the following year gave the Deputies an occasion for reviewing the whole situation and restating their views.

In unanimous resolutions they asserted, first of all, that they were active friends of the cause of education and that they had been so at times when others were suspicious of the cause or inactive about it. All parties and denominations were now exerting themselves with the happiest effects in multiplying the means and improving the character of popular education by voluntary zeal. The Government scheme would destroy these voluntary efforts (including Sunday Schools), would harm private teachers, and would destroy the spirit of self-reliance. The scheme must at least be fully discussed by Parliament. It could not be constitutionally set up on the authority of the Privy Council alone. The Deputies were of opinion that information was inadequate about the existing means of popular education. The magnificent educational endowments already in existence were misappropriated: they ought to be made available for the general advantage. The Government scheme would extend Government patronage by creating an army of functionaries and their families dependent on the executive for their support. It would thus tend to make people look rather to the favour of the State than to their own industry.

[1] Committee of Education: Minutes of 25 Aug. and 21 Dec. 1846. The later Minutes provide detail for the general plans sketched in the earlier Minutes.
[2] Report for 1846.

Apart from these general objections, the Deputies found in the newer developments of policy an obvious partiality for the Established Church. Funds to which all contributed were to be used to maintain schools and schoolmasters identified with one Church. The clergy of the Establishment were to have co-ordinate authority with the Government in administering the scheme. For the first time the Anglican catechism was to be constituted a lesson-book in schools which, since they were supported by public funds, ought to be open to all poor children without distinction of creed and worship. The plan in short tended to confirm the Deputies in their opposition to Government interference with the general education of the people.[1]

Within two days a memorial based on these resolutions was prepared. All the other chief organizations of Dissenters were approached, but not all responded. Lord John Russell interviewed representatives of the Deputies and the Congregational Board of Education. He gave no satisfaction. Despite his great courtesy of manner it was clear that he intended to go on with his plans. He could not accept as facts the statements contained in the memorial. In particular he jibbed at the word 'unconstitutional' when applied to the proceedings of the Committee on Education.[2]

A Central Committee was set up to organize opposition.[3] The Deputies disclaimed responsibility for its expenses, but made it a grant of £100. At their own General Meeting the Deputies adopted a petition to both Houses. They did not shut their eyes to the change in their attitude since 1839. At the request of one of their number, their petition of 1839 was read before the new petition was approved. The new petition was much shorter but rather stronger than the memorial founded on the original resolutions. It expressed the Deputies' belief that the present scheme would eventually supersede all voluntary efforts in infant, day, and Sunday schools which were not Anglican and that it would inordinately increase the power of the clergy. It frankly admitted that in 1839 the Deputies had requested that Parliament should sanction proposals for Government action contained in the Privy Council Minutes of 3 June of that year. The experience of the

[1] 24 Feb. 1847.   [2] 26 Feb. 1847.   [3] 5 Mar. 1847.

past eight years, the unjust manner in which the system had worked in the distribution of money, the statistics concerning the increase of education, the altered and irresponsible nature of the inspection which was now claimed by the Government, and the official connection to be established between executive Government and various religious communities have convinced the Deputies that 'any interference on the part of the State with the general education of the people is uncalled for, inexpedient, necessarily unjust in its operation, and dangerous to public liberty'.[1] Lord Brougham of all people was asked to present the petition; and always interested in education from almost any angle, he obligingly consented to do so.[2]

The opinions of the Deputies about education at this time were very like those of the Congregationalists, who had repudiated any sort of Government help for their schools and before 1853 had established some 459 schools on a rigidly voluntary basis. It was a heroic but hopeless fight. It is possible, though improbable, that voluntary subscriptions might have produced an adequate supply of schools if all parties had worked in that way; but voluntaryism had no chance when its schools were in competition with schools supported by State grants. The Congregationalists recognized this by 1867.[3]

At the General Election in 1847 the Deputies submitted five questions to candidates for London and the Home Counties. The question on education reflects the same strong feeling: would the candidate oppose any system of general education which either directly or indirectly compelled the use of a catechism or creed or attendance at any particular form of Church worship? Even this was too weak; and it was later stiffened by the insertion of the words 'more particularly any which' after 'general education'.

Despite the Deputies and the petitions which they organized, Lord John Russell got the increased grant for education from Parliament. The Annual Report for 1847 could nevertheless record that pressure on the Government had produced 'a modification of the obnoxious minutes of Council'. This may have been

[1] 25 Mar. 1847. [2] 28 April and 26 May 1847.
[3] See A. Peel, *These Hundred Years*, pp. 176-185.

intended as conciliatory, but it left the objections untouched, made the principles of the scheme unintelligible and offered to Dissenters, even if they had been willing to accept it, a mere fraction of the public grant in aid of education.

In 1853 Lord John Russell introduced his so-called Borough Bill. Hitherto voluntary contributions and payments by parents had been supplemented by Parliamentary grants from national funds. The Borough Bill would have allowed corporate towns to provide a new revenue by levying a local rate for schools. The Deputies were not yet convinced that the voluntaryism into which Sir James Graham's ineptness had forced them would fail to meet the needs of the country. They promptly declared their opposition to the Bill. Their attachment to popular education, they said, was continued and increasing, but in view of the progress made on existing lines the introduction of rates appeared unnecessary. If unnecessary, it was certainly undesirable, for a rate for religious education would revive the 'exciting contests which under the name of Church Rates have long distracted the country'. The arguments about discouraging voluntary effort and extending Government patronage were also advanced.[1] A petition on these lines went to both Houses, and a General Committee of opposition received £50 from the Deputies.[2] Lord Aberdeen was interviewed. At the end of the year the Deputies noted with satisfaction that the Bill had been wisely abandoned by its authors because of public dislike for it. It was nevertheless regrettable that the Privy Council Committee's vote was increased to £200,000 without a discussion of the manner of distributing it.[3]

In 1856 a General Education Bill of which nothing came was condemned: 'it is obnoxious in principle and will be objectionable in practice'.[4] A few weeks later a General Meeting hailed with delight the Commons' rejection of Lord John Russell's twelve resolutions on education. These had suggested an increase in the activities of the Committee on Education and the appointment of numerous sub-inspectors. The committee were to have power to group parishes in districts, and in districts where means of educating

[1] 18 April 1853. [2] 16 May 1853.
[3] Report for 1853. [4] 7 Feb. 1856.

the poor were inadequate school rates might be levied to provide schools. School committees elected by ratepayers were to control the schools and provide such religious instruction as they thought fit. Everywhere the Bible was to be read, but nowhere were parents to be forced to send children to religious instruction of which they disapproved. Employers of children from 9 to 15 years old must send children for some instruction and must pay for it. To the Deputies the defeat of these resolutions meant that the 'powerful and extended action of the voluntary principle had been vindicated'.[1] Lord John's defeat was due, it seems, to a union of Tories and voluntaryists. The Deputies' old antagonist, Sir James Graham, delivered a characteristically sardonic speech, this time on their side.

The fourteen years which divided Lord John Russell's resolutions from Mr Forster's Bill of 1870 were full of educational experiments and developments. Lowe's Revised Code gave grim effect to the policy of payment by results; and the Government grants, which had risen from £100,000 in 1846 to £836,920 in 1859, were cut down to £636,806 in 1865.

Why is it that in these eventful fourteen years we find in the Deputies' Minutes comparatively little reference to elementary education? The Deputies, we may suspect, were learning the unpalatable truth that voluntaryism would not suffice to give England the educational system that was needed. Whether voluntaryism had failed or whether it had never been fairly tried might be disputed; but as the year 1870 came in sight, Dissenters, like people of most shades of thought, agreed that Parliament must make good the obvious deficiencies in the supply of education. The inadequacy of voluntaryism was for the Deputies a most unwelcome fact, but it is of the essence of Dissent to face a situation which is not approved of; and the Deputies sturdily prepared to demand a fair settlement in the altered situation.

The general story of the struggles over the Education Bill of 1870 need not be set out here. In the first place, it has often been told elsewhere. In the second place, the Deputies did not take a

[1] 21 April 1856.

particularly prominent or decisive part in it. It is enough to mention two main aspects of the question.

On the one side, the voluntary schools existed. They represented the ideal according to which the Deputies had been working since they had been taught to mistrust Government action in education. The nation was now to abandon this ideal, or at least to supplement it. The Deputies felt that there was therefore no longer the old case for State support of schools giving religious teaching. If the State were going to take over much of what voluntary effort had done hitherto, let it now leave voluntary schools entirely to those who wished to support them.

On the other side, new State schools were to come into existence. Three points arose. First, the Deputies' victory of 1843 must not be relinquished. There must be no sectarian teaching in the new State schools. Second, a majority of the Deputies in 1870 considered that their old principle of no alliance between the State and any Church led to the provision of secular education only in State schools by the State. Private persons might use the buildings out of school hours for religious teaching, but that was another matter. Third, there was a not inconsiderable minority of Deputies who wanted religious, though not sectarian, education in State schools: education in the Bible only as the common possession of all Christians.[1]

As it was only on the first point that the Deputies (in this, fair representatives of Dissenters generally) agreed, it was only in this that they succeeded. The ground won in 1843 was not lost in 1870: sectarian teaching did not appear in State schools. But the State continued to support schools which it did not control, and in them it helped to make possible sectarian teaching which half the nation disliked. On the other side, it might be said that the State schools, though secular in theory, in fact taught that Bible religion of which some of the Deputies approved. The Dissenters had every reason to feel bitterly against Gladstone and still more bitterly about Forster; but they had not suffered a hopeless defeat.

---

[1] The Ministerial Body, in a resolution of 12 April 1870, waived comment on State Education in general, and objected to 'the proposal to empower local Boards to authorize the teaching of creeds and formularies, permissive inspection, and the obligation of parents to claim exemption from religious instruction'.

It might have appeared as if voluntary schools were now to be on trial. If enough people wanted voluntary schools, they would have them: if not, voluntary schools would gradually disappear. This, however, would be an inadequate account of the situation. Although it now provided its own schools the State continued to subsidize the voluntary schools. This gave them a chance of an artificial prolongation of life. All would depend on the amount of help given by the State. How great that help would be no one in 1870 guessed; but the shrewd had fears.

The true reason for the Deputies' disgust was this: the State, undertaking compulsory and universal education, left in the new plan the old roots of bitterness. It gave a foothold for sectarianism. It provided funds by which that foothold could be enlarged. The immediate concern was mainly with the Anglican Church, but the future trouble was to be mainly with another body. Against the advice of its best friends—its generous friends, as the handing over of the British Schools proved—the State insisted on providing a stick for its own back. The woodenness of Gladstone and the maliciousness of Forster prevented either of them from seeing the weapon which they had designed and presented to Roman Catholic clericalism. After fifty years the shrewder Anglicans began to see it. In another fifty it will be visible even to the self-opinionated Gallios of the Board of Education. The seeds of clerical and anti-clerical struggles, hitherto unknown in England, were sown by the ex-Quaker Forster and watered by Whitehall agnostics.[1]

The Dissenters may have been narrow-minded sometimes and violent often; but their main contention that the State should either control education or not control it was sound. They had worked willingly from 1843 for one scheme. They offered to work willingly after 1870 for the other. They only declined to bless a policy of making the worst of both worlds. If anyone still thinks that this was the attitude of men without ecclesiastical convictions of their own who were not prepared to pay for

[1] It must be remembered that these comments were penned by the author before the outbreak of war in 1939. I have not dared to tamper with them in the light of the post-war situation in education.—Ed.

denominational schools, let him consider, for instance, the policy of the Congregational Board of Education.[1] No more complete control of schools by an ecclesiastical body could have existed; but the Dissenters were willing to pay for the control which they exercised.

The use of local rates for education had been foreshadowed by Lord John Russell's Borough Bill of 1853 and his resolutions of 1856.[2] In the sixties similar plans were discussed, and the Deputies' Committee kept in touch with developments.[3]

When the Government Bill appeared in the early part of 1870 both it and the Government amendments to it were carefully considered by the Committee. They did not circularize the Deputies nor call a General Meeting until they had done all in their power to put their minimum requirements forward by resolutions and a petition from the Committee to the Commons. They began by fully recognizing the Government's desire 'to settle the difficulties which appear to be inherent in the education question'. They were constrained to oppose the provision contemplated for religious teaching both in existing schools and in the new schools. They were not entirely obsessed by the religious problems: they therefore thought that the Education Department ought to have larger powers of interfering where the attendance was unsatisfactory, as well as where accommodation was inadequate.[4] Later they were satisfied by governments about inspection, but not about religious teaching either in existing or in new schools.[5]

A special meeting of the Deputies was held whilst the fate of the Bill was still uncertain; but the Deputies shewed plainly that division in Dissenting opinion which was the fatal flaw in their campaign. Two resolutions were proposed. The first condemned the Bill for leaving the religious teaching in the new board schools to be determined by each School Board, for perpetuating and extending denominational management and teaching, and for compelling rate-payers to support the teaching of contradictory religious beliefs. In short the Bill did not give a sufficiently uniform system. The second resolution accepted the 'present religious character' of

---

[1] See above, p. 349.　　　[2] See above, p. 350.　　　[3] 13 Nov. and 11 Dec. 1867.
[4] 10 and 16 Mar. and 21 April 1870.　　　[5] 8 June 1870.

existing schools, subject to an effective conscience clause, but asserted that in 'schools supported to some extent by local rates' religious teaching should be by voluntary effort and outside State arrangements. An amendment was moved to condemn denominational teaching in rate-aided schools but to assert that 'on no consideration should the Bible be excluded from the schools'. The amendment was lost and the original motions carried.[1] In view of the divided opinion, nevertheless, no public action was taken.[2]

In the event, the Act continued national grants to the denominational schools with their denominational teaching; it allowed no denominational teaching in the new board schools supported by new local rates. The local School Board might choose between Bible teaching or no religious teaching.

The somewhat confused reflections of the Deputies on the whole matter found expression at their General Meeting in August when the struggle was over. The official resolution in a scathing phrase 'viewed with satisfaction the attempt of the Government to deal with the difficult question of education', but regretted that so little regard had been paid to the views of Nonconformists and feared that the Bill would produce a great development of denominational education. This was countered by an amendment viewing with satisfaction the success of 'so excellent a Bill for the national education of the people'. After discussion the resolution and the amendment were both withdrawn.

The State having definitely undertaken the duty of educating the people, the Deputies urged that it should carry out its duty fully and effectively. They hoped for a time when only State schools would receive public money. At a conference arranged by the Deputies for themselves and their friends on 25 February 1874 a programme was enunciated:

That no system of Elementary Education will be satisfactory that does not provide for the compulsory Election of School Boards in all districts; and that all Schools connected therewith shall be purely secular, and that in future there shall be no application of public monies or local rates towards the support of any schools but Board Schools.

The first part of the resolution won general assent, but an amend-

[1] 14 June 1870. [2] 21 June 1870.

ment insisting on 'the use of the Bible in our Day Schools' was defeated by only 36 to 27.[1]

It was a corollary of their support of State education that the Deputies should wish to see it universal and compulsory. They found much to criticize nevertheless in the Bill of 1876, and petitioned the Commons to amend it. To introduce compulsion into the educational scheme set up in 1870 meant that many parents would be forced to send their children against their conscience to a denominational school. This would be an infringement of religious liberty because the conscience clause of the Act of 1870 'has been found to be practically valueless'. The proposal to make extra payments to existing schools in poor localities will postpone indefinitely the creation of a national system. The association of Town Councils and Boards of Guardians with education and their powers to delegate their authority to nominees are very objectionable. The use of Boards of Guardians will suggest a connection between education and pauperism. Persons elected *ad hoc* should manage education.[2] The Deputies joined with the Liberation Society in organizing a general conference on the subject.[3]

The Bill became law, and the Deputies, practical as ever, at once used it to sound the alarm about the London School Board. At the meeting at which the passing of the Bill was reported to them, they immediately issued an appeal for the support of the right sort of candidates in the approaching School Board elections. With their customary promptness in detecting the far-reaching malice of their opponents they declared that they

cannot but remember that the Education Act of last session has given great encouragement to those who are desirous of hindering the work which up to this time has been carried on so successfully by the London School Board.

Supporters of denominational schools were trying to elect candidates

whose avowed object is to make the work of the School Board

---

[1] 25 Feb. 1874 and 5 Dec. 1873.   [2] 2 June 1876.
[3] 31 May and 9 June 1876.

supplementary only to that of the Voluntary Schools, thus subordinating the work of National Education to sectarian purposes.[1]

The election provided an impressive triumph for the Deputies' principles; and they permitted themselves a certain truculence in recording their satisfaction.

The Deputies are gratified at the defeat of the clerical party in their attempt to enlist the ratepayers on their side by alleging that the supporters of the policy of the School Board were altogether unmindful of expense. It is a source of great gratification to the Deputies to know that the intelligence of the electors enabled them to see through so transparent a device.[2]

For many years the Deputies' effective support contributed to the remarkable success of the London School Board; and chairmanship of the Board was undertaken by the Deputies' Vice-Chairman, Charles Reed; they followed its activities with vigilance, and for its excellent work they deserve no small credit.

Some examples of their action may be cited. In 1893 the Deputies submitted a memorial to the London School Board which was courteously received and referred to a committee.[3] In December 1893 they were asked to send representatives to a joint committee to secure the election of progressive candidates.[4]

In 1894 they were concerned about movements to disturb the Board's religious compromise of 1871. They believed it to be 'the best practicable basis upon which a State-aided system of elementary education can rest'.[5] Their concern is no doubt reflected in their activity in preparation for the next School Board election. A somewhat elaborate plan for a committee to represent the London Nonconformists generally came to little.[6] The Deputies later had representatives on the Nonconformist Joint Consultative Committee.[7] On their own account, the Deputies' Committee urged Deputies to support progressive candidates as the question at issue was religious. They prepared a pamphlet and 'disseminated' 7,000 copies.[8]

The results of the election (29 Moderates, 26 Progressives) gave

---

[4] 3 Nov. 1876.   [2] 29 Jan. 1877.   [3] 28 April and 15 June 1893.
[4] 7 Dec. 1893.   [5] 8 Mar. 1894.   [6] 5 April, 23 April, 3 May and 4 June 1894.
[7] 8 Nov. and 13 Dec. 1894; 17 Jan. 1895.   [8] 4 Oct. and 8 Nov. 1894.

the Deputies satisfaction. They regretted that the 'Reactionary Party have still a small majority', but more votes had been cast for the progressive candidates than for their opponents. This, the Deputies hoped, would mean the end of attempts to force denominational teaching on board schools or theological tests on teachers.[1]

Their hopes were premature, for at the end of the same year they had a brush with Mr Athelstan Riley. Certain teachers had addressed a memorial to the Board in answer to a circular about religious teaching. Mr Athelstan Riley was said to have threatened, at a Board meeting on 3 October, to oppose the promotion of these teachers, though the circular itself had stated that the religious opinion of teachers should not prejudice their position. The Deputies, after correspondence with him, by resolution condemned his action as a distinct breach of faith and unworthy of one holding a public position of trust and responsibility.[2] Mr Riley's reply is noted, but not described in the Minutes.[3]

Two years later we find the Deputies repeating their earlier activities in the School Board election and issuing another pamphlet.[4] The same thing happened in 1900,[5] when 6,000 pamphlets were distributed.[6] In 1907 the Deputies made a special appeal for the election of candidates who would not represent the denominational interests of non-provided schools, at the time when the requirements of the Education Acts of 1902 and 1903 as to sanitary and structural efficiency of those schools would have to be enforced.[7] Again in 1919, when educational changes were much discussed, the Deputies prepared questions for candidates for the London County Council, and urged the support of those who favoured religious equality.[8]

But to return to the general field of education. The next decade showed that the fears of 1870 had been well founded. The ancient contention of the Deputies had been sound: State support was certain in the long run to dry up the sources of private contributions. The voluntary schools were not securing adequate support from those who believed in them; nor were they dying. Their

---

[1] 28 Jan. 1895.   [2] 17 Oct. 1895.   [3] 19 Dec. 1895.   [4] 26 Oct. 1897.
[5] 16 Nov. 1900.   [6] 25 Jan. 1901.   [7] 11 Jan. 1907.   [8] Feb. 1919.

supporters were demanding more State help. They wanted local rates as well as national grants. Against this, and against any removal of the ban on sectarian teaching in board schools, the Deputies protested in 1888.[1] They had intervened at various times and places to prevent abuses of the dual system: the introduction of Anglican forms of worship into board schools;[2] the threat to expel pupils from a National Day School if they attended an Independent and not an Anglican Sunday School;[3] and the attempt to close the only undenominational school in a poor district.[4] There was only too much truth in their charge that the conscience clause of 1870 was often valueless. They kept a wary eye on all attempts to increase facilities for dissolving School Boards.[5]

In 1888 reports that the Royal Commission would recommend increased grants for denominational schools set the Deputies on their guard,[6] and when the Report appeared they had it analysed and published a pamphlet on the subject.[7] The condemnation by public opinion of the reactionary recommendation of the Royal Commission gave the Deputies satisfaction, but the success of the Anglicans in postponing the operation of the Revised Education Code distressed them. They welcomed as most timely the foundation of the National Education Association with the particular object of preventing educational interests being sacrificed to denominational interests.[8] They had subscribed £25 to the fund for its foundation,[9] but declined a later application for financial help.[10] They also shewed their customary caution in postponing *sine die* an invitation from the Association to co-operate in some unspecified agitation about the Apostles' Creed.[11]

In 1891 the Conservative Government introduced a Bill to replace fees from parents by increased grants. The attitude of the Deputies illustrated at once their magnanimity and the justice of their contention that they set educational interests first. The Bill had many defects. It proposed to increase the grants to voluntary schools without amending any of the proved faults of the 1870 system. There was to be no amelioration of the conscience clause,

[1] 24 Jan. 1888.   [2] Ditton March, 18 Jan. 1881.
[3] New Hampton, 21 April and 18 July 1882.   [4] Derby Street, 20 Jan. 1888.
[5] 20 June 1888.   [6] 13 June and 26 July 1888.   [7] 27 Sept. and 1 Nov. 1888.
[8] 10 July 1889.   [9] 19 Nov. 1888.   [10] 17 Mar. 1892.   [11] 14 June 1894.

'notwithstanding that it is generally admitted that in its working it has proved almost entirely useless'. There was to be no increased public control of voluntary schools, and no alteration of the arrangements by which Dissenters were 'practically excluded' from denominational schools and most training colleges. Nevertheless the Deputies would not urge the rejection of the Bill; for it was an admission of the necessity of free education, though not a step towards a national system.[1] The Anglican monopoly in thousands of parishes remained.[2]

The campaign to get more public money for the denominational schools and to get denominational teaching into the board schools gathered force with every year. 'The Deputies are not unobservant' (it is written in 1895) 'of the attempts which in certain influential quarters are being made to prepare the way for increased grants to voluntary schools from public funds.'[3] At the end of the year they repeat their opposition to such increases; they declare themselves ready to support 'any expenditure that may be necessary' to establish a complete system of public elementary education; and urge the establishment of School Boards in every part of the country.[4]

Soon after the return of the Conservative Government, the Deputies agreed to join in any action of the National Education Emergency Committee and the National Educational Committee of Evangelical Protestant Dissenters.[5]

They condemned as 'radically objectionable' the education policy of the Government as expressed in Bills and resolutions in 1896 and 1897.[6] It contained all the features which they had foreseen: no encouragement for board schools but increased grants to voluntary schools without any increase of public control or of religious equality in them. They noted also the first definite appearance of a new attack on the settlement of 1870, an attack which (had it been successful) would almost have reversed the Deputies' triumph of 1843. The possibility of sectarian religious instruction in board schools was now contemplated in legislative proposals for the first time. The Deputies organized and co-

[1] 19 June 1891.   [2] 8 July 1891.   [3] 28 Jan. 1895.
[4] 17 Oct. 1895.   [5] 19 Dec. 1895.   [6] 22 April 1896.

operated in agitation against the policy, and circulated 5,000 copies of a pamphlet specially written.[1] They protested against the manner in which the Government had forced the Bill through the Commons without assenting to amendments; and warned them that they might find their own precedent disastrous in future.[2]

The signs of the coming storm gathered. In 1900 the Deputies declared that the education question was becoming more important every day. Increased grants to voluntary schools had provided not more efficiency but simply relief to the private subscribers. A system had now grown up in which many schools were carried on chiefly or entirely at the public expense under private control. The Deputies were not merely critical. They demanded a complete system of secondary education, provided that denominationalism were excluded.[3] They were pressing greatly also for more unsectarian training colleges.[4]

A year later the Deputies' fears had changed into knowledge. They had had representatives in a deputation to the Duke of Devonshire, the President of the Board of Education.[5] He had told them 'it is almost a waste of time to go to a member of the present government and ask him to propose any radical alterations in the existing legal status of education'. Nothing remained therefore but to use every effort to get a House of Commons which would not unduly favour denominational education.[6] A circular shewing the religious questions at stake in the Election was prepared and circulated.[7] The Election of 1900 only ensured a development of the Government's recent policy.

The Education Bill of 1901 was denounced as 'incomplete and unsatisfactory', crippling School Boards and likely to provide doles to denominational colleges and schools. Withdrawal, not amendment, was asked for.[8] The Government was departing still further from the principles of the Act of 1870; the extinction of the School Boards appeared likely.[9] The Deputies condemned the use of the closure to prevent discussion of a measure which, if

[1] 30 April, 20 May, 23 July, 19 Nov. 1896; 28 Jan, 5 Feb., 24 Mar., 22 April 1897; 27 April 1898. [2] 24 Mar. 1897. [3] 17 May 1899.
[4] 17 May and 13 Dec. 1899; 29 Jan. and 25 April 1900.
[5] 25 April and 25 May 1900. [6] 30 May 1900. [7] 28 Sept. 1900.
[8] 17 May 1901. [9] 12 July 1901.

properly understood, would not have approved itself to the country.[1]

Rumours of a Bill definitely to abolish School Boards set the Deputies on the watch in the autumn of 1901.[2] On 4 April 1902 when the contents of the Bill were known 'the most strenuous resistance' was promised in a long and reasoned resolution. To support the denominational schools by local rates as well as national grants was to aggravate the very evil which the Deputies wished to remove.[3] Dr Fairbairn's address to Mr Balfour was circulated to Deputies.[4] Later in the summer, whilst admitting that amendments had improved the Bill, the Deputies found that its main defects remained. In particular they protested against the 'threatened destruction of that great educational agency the School Board for London'. The Deputies declined in advance to accept the measure as final or its provisions as binding on them.[5] The Bill of the next year, to extend the 1902 Act to London, naturally came under the same condemnation, 'radically bad in its conception and in its details'.[6] The Committee called on Free Churchmen in every constituency to require from every Parliamentary candidate seeking their votes 'a distinct pledge' that he would vote for the amendment of the Acts of 1902 and 1903. This must take precedence even of fiscal policy or War Office Reforms.[7] In this resolution we can foresee that Nonconformist rally to the Liberal party which brought the unprecedented success of the 1906 Election. The Deputies also urged the return of suitable candidates in Borough elections, but later on declined to assist in the Free Church Council Election Fund.[8]

In January 1905 the Deputies and the ministers put on record their opinion that the administration of the Act of 1902 inflicted special injustice on the Welsh and expressed sympathy with the attitude of the County Councils of Wales and Monmouthshire.[9]

The change of Government in 1906 gave hope of that change in educational policy which the Deputies had long desired. They left nothing to chance. Already by 2 February the issue of

---

[1] 29 July 1901.   [2] 29 Nov. 1901 and 14 Mar. 1902.   [3] 4 April 1902.
[4] 13 June 1902.   [5] 23 July 1902.   [6] 24 April 1903.
[7] 24 Sept. 1903.   [8] 23 Dec. 1903; 25 Mar. and 27 April 1904.   [9] 18 Jan. 1905.

'some document expressing their views' was mentioned.[1] Seven resolutions were sent to Mr Birrell, the President of the Board. These called for one system of elementary education controlled by local education authorities. Bible teaching should be allowed, but not other religious teaching in school hours. Voluntary school buildings should be taken over, if required, by local authorities, but the managers should be able to reserve times for religious teaching out of school hours. Council schools should also be available for the same purpose at the discretion of the local authorities. There should be no religious tests for teachers and no 'right of entry' into council schools. These preliminary motions were lost before the main resolutions were put. They measure the modifications of the Deputies' views since the middle of the 19th century. A motion excluding all religious teaching from schools under public control found no seconder. A motion calling for bodies elected *ad hoc* to control education in populous districts was defeated. Despite their affection for School Boards the Deputies were not blind to such merits as the Act of 1902 had had in unifying local government under County Councils.[2]

The Government Bill of 1906 did not satisfy these conditions, but the Deputies declared in May that they were prepared to support it as 'a compromise in the interests of peace', subject to the amendment of clause 4. This clause departed from the principles of the Bill, the freedom of all teachers from religious tests.[3]

In 1908 the Deputies, while re-affirming the same principles, welcomed the spirit of compromise recently shewn on each side and the attempts of the Government to end this 'protracted controversy' justly.[4] The same spirit governed their reception of the Bill of 1908. They pointed out that in two important matters it defied their principles: the introduction of denominational teaching into State schools for the first time, coupled with the 'right of entry' and the right of denominational schools to contract out of the national system. The Deputies (and they believed that they represented most Free Churchmen's views) had regarded freedom from religious dogma as a most valuable asset of public education.

[1] 2 Feb. 1906.   [2] 12 Feb. 1906.   [3] 18 May 1906.   [4] 29 May 1908.

They regarded its violation with 'the greatest repugnance'. Though 'contracting out' prevented the extinction of the dual system, it was a price worth paying to bring all the single-area schools under public authority, and so end what was practically the Anglican monopoly for 600,000 to 700,000 children.

The Bill did not satisfy the reasonable demands of Nonconformists, but in the interests of peace and education the Deputies would sacrifice reasonable views and rights. It must be understood that the Bill represented the utmost limit of concession.[1] These opinions were sent to the press, the Prime Minister, and the President of the Board of Education.

The failure of the 1908 Bill left the Deputies to record a year later that the educational problem was as pressing as ever it had been, and that those who are represented by the Deputies cannot be satisfied until a single system of public education has been established entirely under public control and free from all dogmatic religious teaching and doctrinal tests.[2]

All succeeding Governments failed to touch the sore. The Deputies did not play the leading part in the later negotiations, but from time to time they took a hand. In December 1910 they congratulated the Government on its success in the Election and pressed for an education settlement.[3] In 1917 they welcomed a Government Bill and regretted its delay, despite its failure to remove religious injustice.[4] By June 1918 they had to complain of the favour shewn to denominational education in the Bill which had at first had their approval.[5] In the following year a memorandum on national education was prepared for the Deputies by Dr Massie and sent to the President of the Board of Education.[6]

The proposals which Mr Fisher himself made for solving the religious difficulty met with the Deputies' strongest condemnation. To provide denominational education at the request of parents, to give the various denominations the right of entry into council schools would split the schools and foster strife.[7] The same condemnation naturally fell on the suggestion of the Archbishop of Canterbury that the denominational schools might be handed over

[1] 26 Nov. 1908.   [2] June 1909.   [3] Dec. 1910.   [4] Sept. and Dec. 1917.
[5] June 1918.   [6] Feb. 1919.   [7] May and June 1920.

to the public authorities subject to the provision of denominational teaching. On no consideration whatever would the Deputies agree to any right of entry to council schools,[1] whereas this seemed to Anglicans an essential part of any bargain.[2]

The syllabus for religious teaching proposed by the Board of Education was referred by the Deputies to the Congregational, Baptist, and Presbyterian Unions in 1924, and in subsequent discussions on 'agreed syllabuses' the Deputies did not figure. Such a matter was not, after all, entirely within the scope of their traditional duties. To protest when the Lord Chancellor asked a magistrate to resign because he was a passive resister was more obviously a relevant duty for the Deputies.

The most striking feature of the period since 1870 is the narrow limit within which the Deputies and those whom they represented scored any success. It is indeed a measure of their failure to convince public opinion, that the scheme which in 1870 they had bitterly denounced, they as bitterly fought for in 1902. This was not because they approved in 1902 of what they condemned in 1870; but because the direction of change in 1902 was even worse than anything suggested in 1870. In 1870 they had seen denominational education allowed to survive. In 1902 they were to see it still more richly endowed at public expense.

To what is the Deputies' failure and the failure of the Free Churches to be attributed? There were no doubt many reasons, of which the inherent strength of the Church of England was the chief. A second was this. Though the teachers were, as a class, sympathetic with the Deputies' views, those views clashed with the professional prejudices of the educational experts, paid and unpaid. And in the years since 1870 the educational expert came to loom larger and larger over the whole scene.

The educational system was becoming in many ways effectively unified. The old days of occasional inspection at long intervals were over. The immensely increased sums poured out for education had not gone only to the schools. Besides the teachers themselves, under the generous banner of administration a vast array of clerks, inspectors, secretaries, directors of education had come

---

[1] June and Dec. 1921.   [2] May 1923.

into being. To cynical eyes it appeared indeed that, even when money was not to be found for children or schools, it was easily to be had for typists and offices. By this vast and increasing machinery the Board of Education and the local authorities made themselves felt more decisively and more continuously each year. Outside all official circles stood an enthusiastic body of so-called 'educationalists' whose ideal was to give the State complete control of elementary and secondary education. These people inspired much of the legislation, and perhaps even more of the administra-tion, of the years since 1870. In such circumstances much depended on the attitude of administrators and publicists to religion.

Now in the critical years at the end of the 19th and the beginning of the 20th century it so happened that a number of key adminis-trative positions were held by Anglicans. But it was not only her own sons who served the Anglican Church. Many, perhaps most, of those who were concerned with administration regarded the whole religious controversy with cheap and bored cynicism. They found the Anglicans still in possession of a vast number of schools after 1870. The Anglicans were the strongest single party; and to people who regarded the religious question as of no importance in itself, it was mere common sense to placate the strongest party. By that method the way was easier for educational changes which were thought to be of genuine importance. It was for the mo-ment easier and cheaper to bolster up the denominational schools than to fight for their extinction. The Anglican who conscien-tiously cared for denominational education found an ally therefore in the cynic who thought one kind of religion as deplorable as another. To these were joined the educationalists of the Fabian type who wanted State control for its own sake at any price, and were prepared to sacrifice other men's religious scruples in order to get it. Only a little first-hand experience in dealing with Ministers of Education, Board of Education officials, and County Directors of Education is needed to provide abundant evidence of the dead weight of expert educational opinion against Dissent on any particular issue, however sincerely the general policy of Dissent might be applauded. To persons for whom religion matters little it is not worth while to give religious justice at the cost of hard cash or extra trouble. Such persons still regard the administrative progress made by the Act of 1902 with smug complacency. They treat the religious controversy as dead or dying. They have reckoned without their host. The Roman Church, once firmly entrenched in the dual system, will make the descendants of the Forsters and the Webbs see that it does matter whether religious justice is given or not. The privileged position of the denominational schools is introducing a clerical and anti-clerical struggle compared with which the old antagonisms of Church and Chapel will seem child's play. The supporters of a State-controlled education refused the help offered by the Deputies and Dissent generally: it is the supporters of a State-controlled education who will in the end most regret it.

(b) Secondary

The main concern of the Deputies was with elementary education; but they did not neglect secondary education. Their object was twofold: first to remove religious tests and sectarian domination from the older endowed schools, great and small; second, to ensure that, when secondary education was nationally organized as they desired, the elected and nominated authorities were not manipulated in favour of the dominant Church.

Religious tests in endowed schools which either excluded Dissenters or put them at a disadvantage the Deputies attacked as they attacked the Anglican privileges in Oxford and Cambridge. In the General Election of 1865 tests in universities and grammar schools ranked with Church Rates as the subjects about which it was essential that candidates should hold sound views.[1] In 1869 Parliament was petitioned in favour of the Endowed Schools Bill.[2] In 1873 they deplored that, as a result of a report on the working of that Act, the law was altered in such a way as to increase the advantages of the Established Church in endowed schools.[3] The success of Disraeli in 1874 ensured legislation of an even less pleasant kind. An attack was made on many of the results of the Act of 1869. The new Government Bill restored to the Church of

[1] 5 July 1865.　　　[2] 4 Mar. 1869.　　　[3] 4 July and 3 Oct. 1873.

England 'numerous schools in cases where the founder had recognized the authority of a bishop or had directed attendance in the service of that church or had required that the masters should be in holy orders'.[1] As finally passed, the Bill was greatly modified and weakened. The Deputies protested against the 'unprecedented and retrograde' policy of the Government Bill. It was abandoning the principle of recent legislation that the old endowed schools were to benefit all classes equally. Amendments to secure that there should be no religious tests for trustees, masters, parents, or children must be brought in.[2] If the Bill passed and additional Charity Commissioners were appointed the Deputies asked that a Nonconformist might be among them.[3] How Disraeli treated this very reasonable request is told elsewhere.[4] The Deputies again in 1875 protested against the attempt made in 1874 to upset the equitable principle of the Act of 1869, and undertook to oppose any other measure with a similar tendency.[5] The Endowed Schools Act and the action of the Charity Commissioners thereunder were among the subjects considered at a conference organized by the Deputies and the Liberation Society[6] on 15 February 1876. The enquiries put to Parliamentary candidates in 1880 included one about religious equality in universities and endowed schools.[7]

The Deputies came to include a national scheme of secondary education in their programme.[8] They were fearful lest in these, as in elementary schools, the State Church should secure unfair advantage from State help. In 1919 they protested against regulations made concerning the Governing Bodies of State-aided secondary schools. The representatives of public bodies were to be cut down from a majority to one-third, and a sectarian majority so became possible. This was a breach of the understanding of 1918 that there should be no interference with the religious teaching in schools.

It would have been contrary to the temper of the Deputies to content themselves with protests in general terms. They intervened or gave advice when particular abuses came before them. As far back as 1830 they co-operated in attempts to defeat a Bill

[1] Morley, *Life of Gladstone*, vol. 1, p. 709.   [2] 23 July 1874.
[3] 27 July 1874.   [4] See p. 156.   [5] 29 Jan. 1875.
[6] 7 Jan. and 25 Feb. 1876.   [7] 2 Jan. 1880.   [8] See above p. 361, n. 3.

which would have excluded Dissenters from any share in the control or the funds of Birmingham Free School. They had the satisfaction of seeing the Bill dropped.[1]

In 1871 the Special Commissioners under the Public Schools Act of 1868 approved a Statute establishing a new Governing Body for Harrow School. The Deputies protested against a clause which provided that in future all members of the Governing Body must be Anglicans. No such restriction, they argued, appeared in the will of the Founder or in the statutes made thereunder; nor had it been put in the statutes approved by the same commissioners on the same day for Rugby School. It was not in accordance with the liberal spirit of recent legislation for the universities, and it was 'unjust and most offensive to large bodies of the people'.[2]

In 1882 a scheme working unfairly for Wellingborough Endowed School was referred by the Deputies to the Congregational Union, who had an enquiry on hand.[3] In 1884 the Deputies had reason to complain of the action of the Charity Commissioners. The Anglicans were trying to get control of a school at Brassington, near Derby. It had been built for all parties. Two-thirds of the children were said to be Dissenters and the subscribers for the trust property were said to have been mainly Dissenters,[4] though the vicar in a letter to Henry Richard denied this. New trustees being needed, the Anglicans had at first 'by some means' procured an application for the appointment of three Anglicans which was signed by more of the existing trustees than were in favour of the appointment.[5]

Despite a subsequent protest by the majority of the existing trustees and seventy rate-payers, the Charity Commissioners at first declared their considered intention of proceeding as they had originally proposed.[6] Whether or not they were influenced by the Deputies' suggestion of putting the case to the Member for the Division, the Commissioners thought better of it. To be sure, they appointed the vicar and the vicar's churchwarden and another Anglican, but they added one nominee of the Dissenters. Though the Dissenters would have a slight majority and an appeal appeared

---

[1] 28 May 1830 and Report for 1830. [2] 15 June 1871. [3] 18 July 1882.
[4] 22 Jan. 1884 and 5 May 1885. [5] 2 May 1884. [6] 17 June 1884.

useless, the Deputies advised a public protest against the Charity Commissioners' order.[1] The incident well illustrates the reason for the Deputies' anxiety to have at least one Dissenter in the Commission; the risk that Dissenters ran of finding their property transferred by legal process to Anglicans; and the useful work of the Deputies in checking the cruder forms of official partiality for Anglicans even where they could not obtain full justice.

The Governors of Christ's Hospital provided the Deputies with a particularly interesting problem two years later. The Deputies scored no success in the first round, but in the end the Governors had reason to regret the incident. The Deputies enquired if the School would object to admitting a boy solely on the ground of his being unbaptized.[2] The inquiry was made because the father of an unbaptized boy, having been required to produce a certificate of his son's baptism, had consulted the Deputies. The Governors did their best to evade the question. In response to a request for the rules of the School, they referred the Deputies to a Scheme in course of preparation by the Charity Commissioners. The Scheme on examination was found to contain no clause concerning baptism.[3] When the Deputies enquired if there was any other Scheme which authorized the regulation about baptism, the School simply refused to recognize the right of the Deputies to interpose. The Deputies therefore obtained the father's consent to proceedings being taken in his name.[4] Four months later the Clerk to the School was still refusing to give any information about the authority for their action;[5] and when after more pressure the Deputies succeeded in getting their letters submitted to a meeting of the Governors, the Governors declined to reply until an actual presentation had been made.[6] Every month wasted was to the Governors' advantage, for the time for the boy's education was passing. By these not very creditable tactics the Governors secured more success than they deserved. They escaped from the unbaptized boy, for his father in the end decided not to try to get a presentation. It was then considerably more than twelve months since his son's entry had been planned.[7]

[1] 18 Nov. 1884.   [2] 15 Dec. 1885.   [3] 20 April 1886.   [4] 31 May 1886.
[5] 30 Sept. 1886.   [6] 21 Dec. 1886.   [7] 20 Jan. 1887.

It was not the Deputies' habit to forget old friends or old foes; and three years later they instructed their Secretary to place in their Minutes what may be called a record of the aftermath. The reluctance of the Governors to produce authority for their action was perhaps explained by the terms of the new Scheme which the Charity Commissioners were forcing upon them. This Scheme definitely brought the School under the conscience clauses of the Endowed Schools Act. The Governors had struggled to upset the Scheme on the ground that the School did not come under the Act. An appeal had gone to the Privy Council. Christ's Hospital, the Governors argued, was an eleemosynary, not an educational, charity and it was a Church of England charity. The Privy Council rejected both pleas, and upheld the scheme except in one particular. One small sop was thrown to intolerance. Boys taking advantage of the conscience clause might be refused places as boarders: they might be forced to be day boys. With this minor humiliation of Dissenters the unfortunate Governors of Christ's Hospital had in the event to content themselves.[1]

In 1890 and 1891 the Deputies were concerned with the education of blind and deaf children. They were anxious to see the position of these children improved, but demanded public control over schools which were helped by public money. In 1890 they helped to block an unsatisfactory Bill,[2] and early in 1891 were warned at the National Education Association Conference that a Bill 'of a most reactionary nature' was about to be introduced.[3]

The Deputies found themselves able nevertheless to welcome the Government's Bill to give greater facilities for special education for the blind and deaf. Two bad features called for amendment. The Bill in its present shape provided that School Boards should pay for the special education, but gave them no power to select the school, no share in the management of it, and no redress if the school managers refused to admit children. Moreover there was no adequate 'conscience clause' to protect parents who objected to the particular religious teaching in any school. The Deputies urged the alteration and the passing of the Bill.[4]

[1] 2 Jan. 1890.
[2] 31 July 1890
[3] 17 Feb. 1891.
[4] 6 and 17 Mar. and 19 June 1891.

(c) Oxford and Cambridge

In 1833, when the Deputies planned the formation of a United Committee to seek redress of grievances, the exclusion of Dissenters from the universities was one of the five matters mentioned in the preliminary discussions.[1] Before this time, it was little mentioned; not because the Deputies were unconscious of it, but because they saw no value in wasting time in assaults on impregnable positions.

At Oxford, subscription to the Thirty-Nine Articles had been required since 1581. At Cambridge, since 1616, subscription had been required at graduation. Dublin, however, had been open to Dissenters and Roman Catholics since 1793, and Scottish Universities did not exclude Dissenters.

In a general petition from the Deputies in 1834[2] the question therefore took the form as to whether it was right or politic that the Dissenter, whatever his intelligence or fortune, should be compelled to seek in the universities of the sister Kingdoms or of foreign lands those literary advantages which were denied to him at home. The pressure of the evil was more keenly felt from the want of a charter to the London University with authority to bestow such honours as Oxford and Cambridge bestowed.[3]

There were debates in both Houses; and a Bill to open the universities passed the Commons, but failed in the Lords.[4] The establishment of the University of London with full academic status was used as an argument against opening the older universities, and the Dissenters had to wait a generation before they got the full support of the Liberal party.

In 1843 Mr Hawes and Mr Christie asked the Deputies to petition Parliament for an enquiry into the universities, as it had been made an argument against granting an enquiry that no petitions had been received asking for one. Accordingly, a form

---

[1] 5 and 15 Mar. 1833. [2] 4 Feb. 1834. [3] 4 Feb. 1834.

[4] It was at this moment in 1834 that Macaulay, writing home from Calcutta, congratulated the Anglican, Thirlwall, on his expulsion from Trinity. He was expected to succeed Wordsworth as Master; but lost the job for writing a pamphlet advocating the admission of Dissenters to Cambridge. G. O. Trevelyan, *Life and Letters of Lord Macaulay*, vol. 1, p. 429 n. (edition of 1876.).

of petition was prepared in support of the motion in the following session.[1]

There was a repetition of the incident ten years later, when Mr Heywood asked the Deputies to support his University Oaths Abolition Bill. The Committee approved of the Bill, but thought it was too late to act that session.[2] Early in the following year, when the Committee of M.P.s favouring religious liberty was organized, one of its first acts was to prepare a memorial to Lord John Russell asking him to open Oxford and Cambridge to Dissenters: 86 M.P.s signed this.[3] 'A Bill for regulating the University of Oxford' was introduced, and one for Cambridge was expected. The Deputies petitioned the Commons that

these ancient institutions should be made conformable to their original intention as public schools for the instruction of the nation and also that they should be brought into accordance with the requirements of the present age.

The Deputies regretted that the universities existed only for the benefit of one section of the Church and were controlled in a great degree by its ecclesiastics.[4]

The legislation of 1854 made it possible to matriculate and to proceed to the degree of B.A. at Oxford without subscribing to the Thirty-Nine Articles.[5] Even this had been forced on the Government, which had angered the Dissenters by not including in its original Bill any provision to admit them. Dissenters were still shut out of Fellowships.

Two years later a Bill about Cambridge was under discussion. The Deputies sent a memorial to Mr E. P. Bouverie, M.P. They pointed out that as the recent Act concerning Oxford had not empowered Dissenters to proceed to degrees higher than B.A., greater precautions were needed in the intended legislation about Cambridge. As the charter of 1570 required no dogmatic religious instruction to be given to undergraduates it was inconsistent to require theological tests from laymen. The commission ought to include one member or more who would represent those who

[1] 19 April 1844.   [2] 28 July 1853.
[3] 3 Mar. 1854. The Parliamentary Committee had been convened on 4 Feb. 1854.
[4] 18 May 1854.   [5] 17 and 18 Vict. c. 81.

were not Anglicans. It should have 'ample powers' to bring Cambridge into accordance with the liberal spirit of the age.[1]

After another pause the Committee petitioned the Commons in 1864 in favour of a Bill to abolish certain tests at graduation in Oxford. The principle had been partially admitted by the Act of 17 & 18 Vict. c. 81 and ought to be applied to all degrees. Many Dissenters would gladly avail themselves of the great educational facilities at Oxford.[2] In the following year the Committee petitioned again in support of such a Bill.[3] This Bill got a majority of 16 at the second reading, but, as it had no prospect of passing, was withdrawn.[4] The Committee petitioned in the next year in favour of a Tests Abolition Oxford Bill and also for a Bill concerning the Declaration made by Fellows of Colleges.[5] In 1867 the Deputies petitioned for the Tests Abolition Oxford Bill.[6]

Early in 1868 the usual petition was ordered[7] and later in the year the Deputies congratulated Mr J. D. Coleridge on the large majority in its favour in the Commons, and urged him to continue his long struggle next session.[8]

In 1869 there was the usual petition.[9] The Bill again got large majorities in the Commons, but to the great wrath of the Deputies the Lords rejected it. With a mastery of the art of understatement they said that the Lords' action 'tends to shake their (Nonconformists') confidence in the impartiality of that House'. Sir John Duke Coleridge (as he had now become), the Solicitor-General, was urged to continued his exertions.[10] At a later meeting the Committee expressed the view that no measure short of compelling Colleges to open their Fellowships without regard to creed would be satisfactory. To the Parliamentary Committee the general Committee referred the delicate problem of deciding on 'the propriety of communicating this opinion to Sir John Duke Coleridge'.[11]

The situation in the Government was indeed not easy or simple. 'Coleridge, the solicitor-general', Morley tells us, 'was only

[1] 7 Feb. 1856. [2] 15 Mar. 1864. [3] 3 April 1865.
[4] 5 July 1865. [5] 18 Jan., 15 Mar., 4 July, 8 Aug. 1866. [6] 20 Feb. 1867.
[7] 11 Mar. 1868 [This is described as 'Tests Abolition Bill' and concerns Cambridge too].
[8] 29 July 1868. [9] 4 Mar. 1869. [10] 21 July 1869.
[11] 18 Nov. 1869.

allowed in a private capacity to introduce a bill removing the tests.' When he had been two years at the head of administration, Mr Gladstone warned Coleridge:

For me individually it would be beyond anything odious, I am almost tempted to say it would be impossible, after my long connection with Oxford, to go into a new controversy on the basis of what will be taken and alleged to be an absolute secularisation of the colleges; as well as a reversal of what was deliberately considered and sanctioned in the parliamentary legislation of 1854 and 1856. I incline to think that this work is for others, not for me.[1]

Despite these protestations, Mr Gladstone was (not for the first or the last time in his career) to do what a few months before he had pronounced odious.

During the winter, a joint deputation saw the Prime Minister on University Tests;[2] but he was not yet prepared to perform what was odious. The Deputies were represented both on the deputation and on the committee which was formed as a result of it. They were also in communication with an Association formed at Cambridge to work for the removal of religious disabilities.[3] The Bill, which Coleridge introduced privately, commended itself to the Parliamentary Committee as it stood. They therefore did not petition the Commons about it, especially as no serious opposition was expected in that House.[4]

The Lords this year did not reject the Bill as formerly had been their habit; but they kept it so long in Select Committee that it failed to become law. The Deputies, unable to agree a resolution on the Elementary Education Act,[5] agreed without difficulty about the Universities Tests Bill. They highly disapproved of the Lords' obstructiveness and earnestly invited the Government to bring the Bill forward early next session, and to press it forward vigorously.[6]

The Cambridge Association, the Deputies were informed, intended to urge that the Bill next session should deal with clerical Fellowships.[7] A deputation to Gladstone to discuss enlarging the scope of the Bill was being arranged when Gladstone himself,

---

[1] Morley, *Life of Gladstone*, vol. I, p. 710.
[2] 16 Dec. 1869. It was not until 1871 that Gladstone consented to make the Bill a Government measure. Morley, *op. cit.* [3] 21 April 1870.
[4] 12 May 1870. [5] See p. 355. [6] 10 Aug. 1870. [7] 15 Dec. 1870.

despite the violent language which he had lately used about Dissenters,[1] sought for a private interview. Representatives of the Deputies and the Cambridge Association together with Mr Miall met Gladstone. They learnt that he intended to introduce the Bill and that he hoped that it would become law before Easter.[2] The Minute records no thrill in the Deputies' Committee when they heard of the Prime Minister's change of front. They had taken Gladstone's measure. When the news of the interview was reported to them we read only

Resolved, That the consideration of the subject be adjourned until the Bill is introduced into the House of Commons.[3]

The Committee found Gladstone, though a late convert, as good as his word but they watched him warily. Their cautious attitude to their ally, so recently their bitter foe, is reflected in their calm record of the Bill's progress. On February 21st they note that the introduction of the Bill by the Prime Minister so early in the session affords 'a reasonable hope that the measure will shortly become law'. They went on:

The fact that Students at Cambridge who are Nonconformists have passed their examination so successfully this year as to take the position of Senior and Third Wranglers forcibly illustrates the grievance under which Dissenters labour. These gentlemen because they are Dissenters are unable to accept the Fellowships which, if they were members of the Established Church would be awarded to them.[4]

The Bill passed the Commons, and the Deputies' Committee petitioned the Lords in its favour.[5] The fate of the Bill in Committee[6] and the Lords' final acceptance of it were reported step by step.[7] Gladstone, as Morley justly says, having once adopted a project never loitered. 'He now resolutely refused the changes proposed by the Lords'.[8] The Act provided generally that subscription to religious declarations should not be required in Oxford, Cambridge, or Durham from the holders of lay degrees or of lay College or University offices. It left still closed against Dissenters

---

[1] Morley, *Life of Gladstone*, vol. I, pp. 703, 709. Dep. Minutes 19 Jan. 1871.
[2] 19 Jan. 1871.   [3] *Ibid.*   [4] 21 Feb. 1871.
[5] 16 Mar. 1871.   [6] 20 April 1871.   [7] 15 June 1871.
[8] Morley, *Life of Gladstone*, vol. I, p. 710.

a good many places: the Headships of Colleges, Divinity Professorships, and certain offices specially reserved for Anglican clergymen or laymen.

The Deputies wound up the chapter with a resolution even more interesting for what it omits (despite its length) than for what it contains.

The Deputies congratulate their constituents on the passing of this Bill by which the right of all students at the National Universities to participate in future in the honours and emoluments of those Institutions without enforcing invidious tests is recognized and secured.

The Deputies believe that the consistent conduct of those Nonconformists at the Universities who have in recent years taken honours but have refused Fellowships which they could not conscientiously accept has greatly aided the passing of this measure and deserves the grateful recognition of Dissenters and the public generally.

The Deputies return their cordial thanks to Sir John Duke Coleridge the Solicitor General who has of late years taken charge of the Bill in the House of Commons for his great services in passing the Bill as well as James Heywood Esquire, F.R.S., J. G. Dodson Esquire, M.P., The Right Honourable G. I. Goschen, M.P., The Right Honourable E. P. Bouverie, M.P., and H. Fawcett, Esquire M.P., who in previous years exerted themselves strenuously in favour of measures for extending the benefits of the universities to all students without respect to creed or churches.

The Committee regret that the Act just passed does not extend to all Fellowships, but they recognise the wisdom of the supporters of the measure in excluding clerical Fellowships from the present Bill and trust that the time is not distant when Parliament will give expression to the wish of the people that all the privileges of the Universities shall be open to all the members thereof.[1]

Only one name seemed missing: in the hour of triumph the Deputies had no bouquet for the Prime Minister. Though it was he who had introduced the Bill which succeeded, the Deputies did no injustice in omitting his name from the list of their friends.

The Deputies next concerned themselves with the reduction of the barriers that still remained against Dissenters. They joined with the Liberation Society in a conference on educational and burial

[1] 19 July 1871.

377

laws in February 1876.[1] In 1876 Lord Salisbury introduced a Bill concerning Oxford. The Deputies took the opportunity of asking that the good work begun in 1871 should be completed by the removal of tests for Headships and the abolition of clerical Fellowships. Knowing the tendencies of Disraeli's Government[2] in education and naturally distrusting its promises that 'no reactionary policy is contemplated', they demanded amendments to ensure that the commissioners to be appointed should not have it in their power to reimpose religious tests:[3] a Bill about Cambridge earned similar criticisms. The Joint Parliamentary Committee of the Liberation Society and the Deputies resolved that the opinion of the Commons on these questions ought to be taken by some amendment similar to that moved in the Lords.[4] The Deputies feared in particular the creation of new theological offices to which the Act of 1871 would not apply.[5] The Commons were petitioned,[6] the progress of the Bills very closely watched and the withdrawal of them duly noted.[7] The same procedure was followed when a Bill similar to the 1876 Bills was introduced in the next session.[8]

In the years 1876 to 1878 the Deputies were interested in a controversy about Hertford College, Oxford. A scholarship there had been announced as confined to persons signing the Thirty-Nine Articles and the Liberation Society had taken proceedings to determine if this was contrary to the Universities Test Act.[9] The Deputies promised a sum not exceeding £50 to enable the Liberation Society to continue litigation.[10] The first decision was against the College,[11] but on appeal the College view was upheld.[12] The Deputies learnt that the promoters did not intend to appeal to the House of Lords, but rather to seek an amendment of the law.[13] Of the £600 costs the Deputies gave £50[14], but after renewed hesitation, refused further grants. Without expressing an opinion about the wisdom of going to law about this matter, it is but fair to the Deputies to say that when they were the chief movers in a matter they rarely staked so large a sum and lost.

[1] 7 Jan. and 25 Feb. 1876.　　[2] Cf. p. 356.　　[3] 14 and 29 Mar. 1876.
[4] 31 May 1876.　　[5] 2 June 1876.　　[6] 28 June 1876.
[7] 7 and 26 July, 3 Nov. 1876.　　[8] 2, 8, and 23 Mar., 27 April, 4 May 1877.
[9] 7 July 1876.　　[10] 3 Nov. 1876.　　[11] 6 July 1877.
[12] 14 May 1878.　　[13] 21 May 1878.　　[14] 29 Nov. 1878.

Religious equality in the universities was one of the topics on which the Deputies recommended a test of Parliamentary candidates' views at the General Election in 1880.[1]

The Deputies in that year petitioned the Commons in support of Mr Roundell's proposals to remove clerical restrictions from all Headships save the Deanery of Christ Church and Mr James Bryce's proposals to remove them also from the Professorships of Hebrew and Ecclesiastical History,[2] but in vain; these restrictions still remain.

When the Rev. R. F. Horton, a Congregational minister, then a Fellow of New College, was rejected by Convocation at Oxford as an examiner in the Rudiments of Faith and Religion, the Deputies advertised a resolution of protest. They pointed out that as Mr Horton's suitability in every respect except his Nonconformity was 'distinctly admitted', it was 'beyond question that he has been rejected on religious grounds alone'. This was a direct infringement of the spirit of the Act of 1871. That Act provided that no person should be prevented from holding any post of honour or emolument, other than certain specified offices, on the ground of his religious belief.[3]

In spite of protests, Mr Horton was not admitted as an examiner. But this was the last matter, so far as the Minutes afford evidence, in which the Deputies felt called on to intervene in the conduct of the Older Universities.

(d) London and Provincial Universities

The part which Dissenters generally took in the foundation of the University of London and the reasons which led them to take this part do not come within our subject.[4] It is sufficient to say that University College was founded in 1828 on a completely undenominational basis and that theology formed no part of its curriculum. King's College, opened in 1831, represented a reaction against the undenominational plan and was designed to teach also 'the doctrines and duties of Christianity as the same are inculcated by the United Church of England and Ireland'. The

[1] 2 Jan. 1880   [2] 28 June and 6 July 1880.   [3] 18 Dec. 1883 and 29 Jan. 1884.
[4] University College was opened in Oct. 1828 as the University of London, the first Council having been appointed in 1825.

existence of two Colleges led to the separation of the University of London from University College. The University was constituted as an examining body to confer degrees on 28 Nov. 1836, University College and King's College being alike incorporated with it. The attempts to reduce Anglican exclusiveness at Oxford and Cambridge having failed immediately after the passing of the Reform Bill, the creation of a body from which Dissenters could obtain degrees was regarded by some as a useful argument against future assaults on the Older Universities.

Before the foundation of University College the Deputies figure among the persons who put up the funds necessary to start the new venture. On 15 December 1826 the Committee recommended that the Deputies should subscribe from their funds for ten shares of £100 each[1] in the 'University of London' as it was then described in inverted commas.[2] This was approved on consideration. It was thought better not to buy in the united names of the present trustees but in the name of ten Deputies, not already shareholders and chosen for the purpose. Four were to be Independents, three Presbyterians, and three Baptists. There were to be not less than three trustees for each share; and a declaration of trust was to secure control for the Deputation as a whole.[3] The form of declaration was approved eighteen months later.[4]

Despite the deliberation and discussion which had attended these decisions one Deputy named Tibbs maintained a running opposition.[5] Not being on the Committee, he did not appear in person, but sent a letter which was 'maturely considered'. The Committee supplied him with the names but ignored his protests.[6] He continued to sit as a Deputy.

The reason for the opposition does not appear. £1000 may well have been thought by some Deputies too large a drain on their resources. At a General Meeting of Deputies at the end of the year Mr Tibbs's motion to rescind the resolution was defeated by a large majority.[7] By a somewhat elaborate plan, which did credit to the sub-committee's calculating powers, 'the trustees are not the same to any two shares, each gentleman is a trustee for three

---

[1] See also above, p. 81.   [2] 15 Dec. 1826.   [3] 26 Jan. and 23 Feb. 1827.
[4] 14 Nov. 1828.   [5] 16 Feb. 1827.   [6] 23 Feb. 1827.   [7] 14 Dec. 1827.

and each has a vote as the first trustee of a share'. The immediate payment of £350, the first and second instalments, was recommended 'as most consistent with the character of this Deputation, and best calculated to promote the interests of the University'.[1]

The ten shares[2] held by the Deputies in the University of London entitled them to nominate ten students. It was at first suggested that the trustees should nominate. Their own sons were to be always ineligible and preference given to sons of Ministers of the Three Denominations.[3] After considerable delay and discussion nomination was put in the hands of the Committee, not of the trustees, in order to prevent anything like patronage. Students for the ministry were to receive preference; and only in default of such, whether sons of ministers or not, was preference to be given to ministers' sons.[4] The balance due for the shares was ordered to be paid at the same meeting.

On 11 July 1828 the Deputies authorized a statement about their financial position and an appeal for donations. A statement went out to all congregations in England and Wales on 11 Feb. 1829.

The Deputies were asked to help the University of London in another way. Could they furnish the names of 'respectable Dissenters in the country' who might act as its agents? The Deputies thought that suitable names might be chosen from the list of gentlemen who had been asked to be stewards at the Repeal Dinner.[5]

In describing the work which they had done in the general interest of Dissenters the Deputies mentioned their support of London University. They must have found peculiar pleasure in referring to the projected establishment of King's College as an Anglican imitation of their own undenominational College.

In 1827 the Committee felt themselves warranted by the state of the funds of the Deputation in recommending that assistance should be afforded to the projected London University by the purchase of some shares in that institution. They felt that next to the civil proscription inflicted by the Corporation and Test Acts, there is no badge of distinction more disgraceful, no greater hindrance to the spread of knowledge and of charitable feeling, than what results from that narrow-

[1] 9 Mar. 1827. [2] Numbers 841 to 850. 14 Nov. 1828.
[3] 7 July 1828. [4] 14 Nov. 1828. [5] 25 July 1828.

minded Policy which confines the means of liberal Education to the established Sect and perpetually places before the Minds of Youth the distressing and demoralizing alternative of either doing violence to their consciences or surrendering their fairest prospects of public or professional advancement. To obviate as far as they could the effects of such a system, or at least to bear their strongest practical protest against its continuance, the Committee recommended, and the general body of Deputies sanctioned, the investment of £1000 (part of the existing fund) in purchasing ten shares in the new institution; and they are happy to mark its rapid progress towards success, as to which the most decisive of all testimonies has lately been borne in the projected establishment, in almost every respect on the same principles, of a rival College, by those whose strenuous efforts were long directed to deprecate such attempts at increasing the means of knowledge and to deny their policy and even practicability. The Deputation have had great pleasure in rendering the Shares in the new university of which they have thus become proprietors subservient to providing the churches of the Dissenters with Men of sound Learning as their pastors, and in assisting those pastors to give to their children the advantages of what they confidently hope will soon be rendered as complete an Academical Education as this Country can afford, students for the Ministry and in default of a sufficient number of applications on their behalf, the Sons of Dissenting Ministers having by their regulations a decided preference in filling up the nominations at the disposal of the Deputation.[1]

In 1834 the United Committee pressed for a charter for London University.[2] In 1835 the Deputies' Committee welcomed the Government scheme for establishing a London University Board to confer degrees as being better than the grant of separate charters to different literary and scientific bodies empowering them to confer degrees. They made it a condition of their approval however that the plan would be carried into operation 'irrespective of religious persuasions'.[3] The General Meeting was more cautious and, declining to endorse the Committee's resolution, deferred consideration till the Government had explained the details of its plan.[4]

The view of the United Committee that one or more representatives of University College and King's College should always be on the Board of Examiners was not accepted by the Govern-

---

[1] 13 Feb. 1829.   [2] Report for 1834.   [3] 28 Oct. 1835.   [4] 11 Nov. 1835.

ment. In the discussion the Government was reminded 'that although the Dissenters were grateful for the measure proposed, they did not forego their claim to be admitted to all the privileges of the Ancient Universities'.[1]

In 1837 the Deputies protested against a proposal before the Senate that all candidates for the degree of B.A. should be examined either in one of the Gospels or in Acts in Greek and in Scripture History. This, they considered, would be an indirect violation of the understanding by which the proposal to give University College power to confer degrees was dropped and the University of London founded instead. The Deputies' nervousness about the introduction of religious knowledge is easily understood if it be remembered that in the thirties it was practically impossible to prevent any official recognition of religion from providing a vantage ground for the State representatives of religion, the Anglicans. The Deputies were jealous lest, after the Dissenters and their friends had founded an undenominational College, it should be merged in a University in which Anglicanism contrived to secure a privileged place. They recognized the advantages of making a united University, but the inclusion in it of a sectarian College, like King's, meant that there was need for constant vigilance. In 1846 a similar proposal that all candidates should be examined in one of the books of the Pentateuch in Hebrew or in one of the Gospels or Acts in Greek and in Scripture History attracted the Deputies' interest.[2]

As late as 1892 the Deputies showed the same fear lest London University should fall under sectarian influence. They urged that Parliament should condemn the draft charter founding a proposed Albert University. The Charter assigned a position of influence and authority to King's College; and since King's College rigidly excluded all but Anglicans from its offices, this proposal contravened the principle affirmed in the Act of 1871.[3]

The Deputies noted that as a result of opposition the Government had withdrawn the proposal to give a Gresham University charter. They gave £5 towards the expenses of the committee which conducted the opposition.[4]

[1] Report for 1836.   [2] 17 July 1846.   [3] 21 Jan. 1892.   [4] 17 Mar. 1892.

In 1838 financial difficulties caused the Deputies to agree to sell their shares in London University. The trustees who held them were to have the option of purchasing at the market price. It was easier to pass this resolution than to carry it out. The intricate arrangements originally made for the holding of the shares meant that a good many people or their executors were concerned. Some of these were Unitarians, and the Unitarians were not disposed easily to release their grasp of the Deputies' property.[1] Throughout the forties references to the sale of shares or to the difficulty of selling them appear;[2] and as late as 1864 a search was ordered for shares believed still to be unsold.[3] The Treasurers' books shewed that six of the ten shares had been sold but no trace could be found of the remaining four.[4] It was possibly part of the price paid by the orthodox Dissent to save the name Presbyterian from the Unitarians. It should be added, however, that the shares that had stood in the names of William Smith and Edgar Taylor, two of the most prominent Unitarians, had been sold without apparent difficulty, the Deputies' rights after the secession of the Unitarians not (it seems) having been challenged.[5] As the price mentioned for one share in 1843 was only £8 the matter was probably less serious than it might appear.[6]

In 1832 Oliver Cromwell's foundation of a University of Durham was revived. An estate of the Dean and Chapter was appropriated to found and maintain it. The Bill was introduced in June and the Deputies, with the object of preventing the exclusion of Dissenters, at once prepared a petition to Parliament.

The Bill was treated as a private Bill to enable the Dean and Chapter to deal with a part of their property in this particular way and passed rapidly without alteration, receiving the Royal Assent on 4 July 1832. The Dean and Chapter were made Governors, but the Deputies' Committee learnt that it was understood that Dissenters would be admitted to receive education. It was intended to confer divinity degrees only.[7]

[1] See p. 81.

[2] E.g. 10 Mar. and 29 Oct. 1841; 28 April and 15 Dec. 1842; 14 June and 29 Nov. 1843; 6 and 20 Mar. 1844; 24 April and 11 Dec. 1846.

[3] 15 Mar. 1864.   [4] 6 April 1864.   [5] Report for 1842.

[6] 29 Nov. 1843. Share No. 845 sold to Samuel Gale.

[7] 26 and 29 June 1832. Report for 1832.

CHAPTER 4

DISESTABLISHMENT AND DISENDOWMENT

THE DEPUTIES never forgot that they were laymen dealing with civil rights. They interfered not at all with theology, and rarely expressed views on religious questions, even those on which they felt strongly. Sunday observance, for instance, is rarely mentioned except where it involves some breach of liberty. Thus in 1849 there were alterations in the Post Office which would expose Dissenters and others either to labour on the Sabbath or dismissal; and on this the Deputies sent resolutions to Lord John Russell and the Post-master-General; while in 1899 the *Daily Mail* was congratulated on abandoning the Seven-Day Newspaper, and in 1923 the Deputies resolved to deplore Sunday games. In all such matters a definite question of personal liberty was involved, apart from the religious issue, on which the Deputies individually might have strong convictions.

Yet there was one general matter which loomed behind all the Deputies' grievances, behind the friction on burials, rates, education, and the like: Establishment. In the words of the Deputies, 'the dominant sect' was established; and because the law looked on it with partial eyes, the other sects had of necessity a sense of injustice. Whatever the original opinions of the Three Dissenting Bodies had been concerning the relations of Church and State (and the three had not thought alike) the Deputies at the beginning of the 19th century were fairly well agreed in condemning the existing arrangements in the United Kingdom.

They did not all condemn the Establishment with equal vigour. To the Congregationalists, the ending of the Establishment was, it seems, more a matter of principle than it was to the others. All, however, were more concerned to secure the immediate redress of urgent grievances than to refound English society on a plan theoretically correct.

The Deputies felt that they might well lose rather than gain from the broadcast of too sweeping and too logical a programme. It was at once their strength and their wisdom to appear what in fact they were: sober, respectable, loyal subjects with a stake in the country, anxious not to turn England into a pantisocracy or anything at all odd, but anxious to remove certain disabilities which were quite unnecessary for the security of society and were indeed alien from the spirit of English law and the constitution as settled in 1688.

Having achieved their main political object, the Repeal of the Test and Corporation Acts, in 1828, the Dissenting Bodies considered the next step. With the passing of the Reform Bill and the establishment of a Whig Government, time seemed ripe; and the first step of the United Committee on Grievances was to seek an interview with Earl Grey. On 25 May the deputation 'met with a very courteous reception and held a very long and interesting conversation with that liberal and enlightened statesman' on the list of subjects they had drawn up in the form of a memorial. Earl Grey intimated that the Government might be expected to sanction 'any reasonable measures', and it was upon this line that the United Committee wished to keep the Dissenters' agitation.[1]

The Deputies approved, but it is to be noticed that they had from the first urged on the United Committee vigilant attention to any measure of Church Reform that might be proposed. They did not presume to interfere in the internal regulation of the Established Church but were concerned to see that the interests and just claims of Dissenters were not compromised.[2]

At a General Meeting in December 1833 both notes, general and particular, were struck. The Committee was instructed to prepare petitions to both Houses, on the one hand praying for relief from grievances and on the other declaring 'unjust and unscriptural' the union of Church and State, however it may be modified.[3] In the petition the Deputies carried out the instruction.

[1] Report for 1833.   [2] 15 Mar. 1833.   [3] 27 Dec. 1833.

They first recorded as one of the fundamental principles of Non-conformity a decided and conscientious objection to any alliance of ecclesiastical systems with the civil power. But having briefly paid their homage to general principles they left the question of Disestablishment 'to the progress of Events and the determination of an enlightened Legislature under the providence of the Most High'. The petition then turned to what was evidently its true business and dealt in great detail with particular grievances: registration; marriages; burials; universities; Church Rates.[1]

The explanation of this attitude is to be found in negotiations which had been going on with the Government. The Deputies had been working in close association with the United Committee and a deputation on 15 January had interviewed Earl Grey. Earl Grey strongly expressed 'his disapprobation of any measure calculated to destroy the Established Church', but was ready to take into immediate consideration the practical grievances mentioned in the 'Brief Statement of the Case of Protestant Dissenters' which the United Committee had drawn up. The committee did not wish to lose what the Government might give them by irritating requests for what was certain to be refused. It met almost daily in February and was much in attendance upon Lord John Russell, Lord Holland, Lord Lansdowne and other Members of Parliament. It continued to press the Government for information about its intentions. Lord Grey's response, though friendly, 'could scarcely be considered satisfactory'. Meanwhile Dissenters less in touch with the Government were growing restive. Provincial Dissenters pressed for a national meeting. The United Committee on 24 March replied: 'they would respectfully deprecate such a meeting as unseasonable and undesirable'.[2]

As soon as an agitation for Disestablishment began, the Dissenters began to examine their own record, and at once became sensitive about the *regium donum*, which their ancestors had accepted without a qualm. We have already described the origin of this grant[3] which began as a charitable gift from the Royal purse to the families of poor Dissenting ministers. The Deputies had not

---

[1] 4 Feb. 1834. [2] Cf. Deputies' Minutes, 26 Mar. and 8 April 1834.
[3] See above, p. 22.

only no scruple about it at first, they had even, in 1753, helped to get an additional pension upon the Irish Establishment for Dissenting ministers in Northern Ireland. This Irish endowment was to prove a particular thorn in their flesh during the Maynooth agitation[1] and the campaign for Disestablishment of the Irish Church; and it was not in fact ended until Irish Disestablishment carried it away in 1869.

The English *regium donum* ended a little earlier, being withdrawn by the Chancellor of the Exchequer in 1851 in response to continued pressure. This had begun in 1833 as soon as the United Committee on Grievances was constituted. In December 1833 the Deputies condemned the 'Parliamentary Grant'[2] as a 'direct violation of the principles of Dissenters', and in January 1834 the Ministers passed a similar resolution.[3] But more than resolutions were needed; in 1835 we find the Deputies occupied with finding a practical scheme to abolish the grant; and ten years later the question of providing an alternative fund to avoid hardship, which fell particularly hard on the Baptists, was still causing trouble.

But we must now return to the general campaign against the Establishment. In April 1834 a group of Dissenters (presumably under Congregational leadership) met in the Congregational Library to urge that a public meeting to petition Parliament to dissolve the alliance of Church and State 'could not fail to strengthen the hands of His Majesty's Government'. That any men could dream of such a result of such a petition shewed how far they were from the facts of the situation. The enemies of the Government accused it of dark designs on the Established Church, and its friendly relations with the Dissenters might easily become a source of danger to it. The United Committee consulted the bodies represented on it. The Deputies, for their part, declared against such a meeting, as it would end the negotiations with Government for the redress of practical grievances.[4] The United Committee's view was the same. The line of action which it approved was shewn by its calling a General Meeting which sent

---

[1] See below, p. 444.

[2] It had for a long time been paid through Parliamentary channels, instead of through the Privy Purse, as at first.

[3] Ministers' Minutes, 28 Jan. 1834.   [4] 16 April 1834.

a deputation to protest against Lord Althorp's Church Rates proposals.

The United Committee feared that wild rumours about a Disestablishment and Disendowment campaign were being used to alarm opinion and to prevent any redress of grievances. Popular fears for the safety of the Church were shared by the King, who distrusted his Ministers. On 9 June the United Committee did a wise thing. They passed five resolutions to clear themselves of the charge of designing the destruction of the Episcopal Church and secular profit to themselves. They believed Christianity would flourish better when separated from the State. They would not accept any of the property for their own churches. To interfere in the internal reform of the worship or discipline of the Episcopal Church would be against their conviction that every section of the Church had the right to regulate its own affairs. They disclaimed all connexion with 'the intrigues of faction and the designs of infidelity' and wished to use only dispassionate argument and scriptural authority. On the other hand they were determined on the earliest possible relief from practical grievances.

These hopes were blasted by William IV's dismissal of the Whigs in 1834. When Melbourne returned to power in 1835 his Government had less power, even if it had the will, to carry any thorough-going redress of grievances.

The Deputies' part in opposing grants to the Church of Scotland is noticed elsewhere. The case for the grants and for Church Establishments generally had been presented in London in April 1838 by the Rev. Dr Chalmers, of Edinburgh. His course of lectures had obtained 'a large and respectable auditory' in Westminster. The Deputies promptly appointed a sub-committee to answer him and present the case for voluntaryism.[1] The Rev. Dr Wardlaw, of Glasgow, one of the representatives of the Scottish Dissenters in the 1838 agitation, was invited by the Deputies to prepare a course of lectures for the following spring.[2]

Dr Wardlaw consented, and in March and April 1839 the Deputies' Committee met no fewer than seven times to make arrangements concerning the place, advertisements, police, tickets

[1] 30 April 1838. [2] 18 May 1838.

and so on. It proved not very easy to find a minister to offer the prayer before the lectures, and in the end Dr Wardlaw was asked to do this himself for all the lectures except the first. A room at the Freemasons' Tavern holding 800 people was engaged. Arrangements were made to print each lecture as it was delivered in order to ensure prompt publication when the course ended. It is typical of the horse-sense of the Deputies in seeing the importance of detail that they wished the lectures to be printed 'in the same type as those delivered by Dr Chalmers last year and on equally good paper'. Several publishers' offers were considered. Messrs Jackson and Walford agreed to pay £150 for the first edition not exceeding 2000 copies, the price not to exceed 7s. and no cheap edition to be issued by the Deputies for at least nine months.

The care of the Deputies had its reward. The eight lectures were most successful.[1] 'Numerous, respectable, and most attentive assemblies' heard Dr Chalmers's arguments refuted; and the Deputies in a resolution ultimately prefixed to the lectures could scarcely find words to express their admiration of the accumulated information, the happy discrimination, the luminous and eloquent style, the scriptural basis on which the whole superstructure was reared, the courteous yet unflinching temper, the Christian charity blended with high and fixed determination.[2] The Doctor received also twelve copies of his book and an honorarium of £200.

Virtues of this order rarely win the financial success that they merit; but these lectures proved an exception. The first edition of 1000 was too highly priced for general circulation, and at the end of the year 400 copies of the lectures were unsold. The Deputies then took these over and arranged for a cheap edition of 10,000 copies to be sold at a shilling.[3] Twelve months later the profits to the Deputies on the cheap edition had reached £106; and only 135 copies of the first edition remained.[4] A year later the whole of the cheap edition was sold out and only 80 of the first edition were left. The cautious Deputies did not propose to risk another edition despite the demand.[5] In 1848, nevertheless, the Committee decided that a new edition was desirable[6] and Dr Wardlaw agreed

---

[1] 3 May 1839.   [2] Report for 1839.   [3] 18 Dec. 1839 and Report for 1848.
[4] 27 Nov. 1840.   [5] Report for 1841.   [6] 8 May 1848.

to bring the lectures up to date.[1] In 1863 the son of Dr Wardlaw wrote to the Deputies proposing republication of the lectures, but though some discussion took place it does not appear that action followed it.[2]

The later thirties and the forties abounded in talk of Disestablishment. Events in Scotland leading to the Disruption fanned the interest. A number of societies were born and died after longer or shorter lives. Voluntary Church Associations began in Scottish towns. The Evangelical Voluntary Church Association was intended to unite Evangelicals inside and outside the Church of England in a religious movement against Establishment. The Religious Freedom Society spread a wider net to compass Roman Catholics and Jews also: it proposed too to use political agitation. The Deputies themselves could not remain unaffected by this turmoil, but did not themselves move far from the course which experience and their peculiar constitution had made their own.

In the Report for 1839 the Deputies took a far-sighted as well as a penetrating view:

> The discussions carrying on at the present time amongst the members both of the English and Scottish Establishments are favourable to religious liberty. The friends of old and high Church doctrines at Oxford and of the low state doctrines now promulgated by the non-intrusionists of Scotland are alike loosening the connexion between the Civil and Ecclesiastical powers. Nor can the adherents of either establishment make any progress or attempt any alteration without feeling that their defences against Dissenters operate as a restraint on their own freedom and that the State whilst it is their patron assumes at the same time an imperious authority not consistent with the Christian liberty of the Church. The voluntary principle is alive both in the English and Scotch Churches and the work which your Committee have been so long endeavouring to effect from *without* is prosperously advancing from *within*.

The cautious attitude of the Deputies did not satisfy everyone. The representatives of Craven Chapel urged that the Deputies should be more numerous and more aggressive. The Committee replied that they had already a plan to increase numbers, but that

---

[1] 30 June 1848. [2] 29 Jan. and 11 Mar. 1863.

to be more aggressive would be inconsistent with their original constitution for the 'protection' of religious liberty.[1] At their next General Meeting the Deputies resolved to meet specially to consider the separation of Church and State.[2] The sub-committee which prepared resolutions met with little success. It met three times but its suggestions were referred back by the general Committee;[3] and only one member turned up to the next meeting. The truth was that the general Committee thought it 'highly inexpedient' to submit any resolutions on the subject to the Deputies.[4]

When the Deputies met as agreed and heard the Committee's opinion, Mr J. C. Evans, who had asked at the last meeting that resolutions should be prepared, himself moved six resolutions which amounted to a short treatise on the evils of Establishment and the way to end them. Concurrent endowment of a number of Churches was condemned and the State was called in to 'resume' possession of endowments for purposes not specifically religious.

The Deputies postponed consideration, some thinking the resolutions 'inexpedient', and the Committee was again instructed to prepare resolutions.[5] Meanwhile the urgent danger of the Dissenters' Chapels Bill[6] and the Norwich Church Rates case[7] engaged the Committee, and when the Deputies met the same division of opinion appeared. Some thought the resolutions inexpedient; some still wanted resolutions from the Committee; but a majority approved Mr Evans's resolutions in a slightly revised form. The Deputies added that they rejoiced to learn that an Anti-State Church Conference was about to be convened.[8] It may be surmised that they rejoiced for slightly different reasons.

The Committee must have welcomed any safety valve for the tiresome and untimely enthusiasm of the irresponsible. The Conference met in April and May and from it emerged the British Anti-State Church Association, known after 1853 as the Liberation Society.[9] The relations of the Deputies with this Society were always interesting, often intimate, and sometimes advantageous;

---

[1] 29 Nov. and 7 Dec. 1843.   [2] 17 Jan. 1844.   [3] 7 Feb. 1844.
[4] 14 Feb. 1844.   [5] 14 Feb. 1844.   [6] See p. 87.
[7] See p. 179.   [8] 13 Mar. 1844.
[9] An account of the Liberation Society is given above, p. 50.

but later history was to justify the cautious attitude of the Committee of 1844. The objects of the two societies were not quite the same and if the Liberation Society was sometimes a useful safety valve it was sometimes an embarrassing ally. The Unitarians undoubtedly knew how to contrast the political vigour of their orthodox opponents, especially the Congregationalists, with their own political opportunism and moderation. At the crisis of the struggle over the Dissenters' Chapels Bill it was all to the interests of the Unitarians that the orthodox Dissenters should be represented and should represent themselves as firebrands, the implacable and intemperate foes of the Established Church. Such considerations were unlikely to escape the notice of the Deputies' Committee.

In 1849 the Deputies presented a short general petition on Dissenters' grievances which put on record that the Dissenters' wrongs arose from the connexion of Church and State and that they hoped that the time was fast approaching when it would be dissolved.[1] In the actual petition the injustice of establishing one sect was mentioned, and it was lamented that Great Britain, after taking the lead for so long, was now left in the rear for religious liberty by the promulgated constitutions of France and Prussia; but particular attention was called to Church Courts and Church Rates. They were at a loss to understand why, when Church Rates were abolished in Ireland as unjust, similar relief was refused in England to

Protestant Nonconformists whose character for sincere attachment to the House of Brunswick and for cheerful obedience to the laws will bear comparison with that of any other body of their fellow subjects.[2]

For some years after its foundation the relation of the Anti-State Church or Liberation Society with the Deputies was not so close as it afterwards became. The Liberation Society was perhaps a little inclined to think that Parliamentary affairs might not be handed over to it by the Deputies. It was very anxious for united action. Mr Miall had proposed that the Liberation Society and the Deputies should finance the newly organized Committee of M.P.s but the Deputies' Secretary blocked the plan. The Deputies had a

[1] 19 Jan. 1849. [2] 19 Feb. 1849.

wider function than merely Parliamentary interests. In 1845 the Deputies decisively declined the Liberation Society's proposal for a union between the Parliamentary Committee of that Society and the Deputies.

The Deputies made it quite clear that they were not prepared to abandon their activities in Parliamentary affairs and that they saw no advantage to themselves in uniting with the Liberation Society. There was perhaps a touch of patronage in the Deputies' remark that the Liberation Society was 'likely to be very useful' as its representation extended to the provinces whereas the Deputies only represented the metropolis. The Liberation Society also might be useful in supplying Liberal candidates for Parliament. On particular occasions or in a crisis the Deputies would unite, as in 1828, with other bodies and free intercommunication was always desirable.[1]

The Liberation Society was apparently a little mortified, but dropped the plan. It corrected with slightly needless emphasis a possibly ambiguous phrase of the Deputies. The offending phrase (if the rest of the Deputies' letter were ignored) might have been understood to mean that the Liberation Society represented the provinces only.[2]

Three years later the Deputies reasserted their independent status. In making an appeal for funds they ordered that a statement of their work in the past year should be made showing the distinction between their 'objects and labours' and those of the Liberation Society.[3]

Ten years later the two societies had drawn together more definitely. Whether this close association with a Society of a different temper meant a gain in the effectiveness of the Deputies may be doubted. What cannot be doubted is the share of Mr Miall and Mr Carvell Williams in bringing it about. In 1866 the Deputies had a plan for holding a meeting early in the Parliamentary session for M.P.s and other public men interested in the Deputies' aims. The Deputies learnt from Mr Carvell Williams, himself a Deputy and secretary of the Liberation Society, that that Society had a similar plan.[4] The Liberation Society was unwilling to delay

[1] 2 June 1854.   [2] 14 July 1854.   [3] 27 May 1857.   [4] 3 Jan. 1866.

its meeting at the Deputies' request, but was willing that a joint meeting should be held.[1] The meeting took the form of a breakfast attended by seventy to eighty people.[2]

For many years similar joint meetings at breakfast were arranged, often early in the session. The change in habits since Victorian times is indicated by the fixing of the hour for breakfast in 1868 at 9.30 a.m.[3] At first the breakfast was an annual event, but at varying intervals breakfasts were held until well into the 20th century.[4]

The breakfast arrangements varied. Complimentary tickets were send to M.P.s and to some other people: 3s. 6d. or 5s. might be the ordinary charge. The cost was usually divided between the two societies. In 1884 the Deputies offered to pay the whole cost, £17 12s., as the Liberation Society had twice omitted to recover a half share from them.[5] In 1880 nearly 200 were present, including 30 to 40 M.P.s.[6] Numbers were not always as large as that.

Another sign of co-operation with the Liberation Society was the representation of the Deputies at the Triennial (and occasional) Conferences which it held for many years. When the invitation came in 1871 the Deputies cautiously thought that members of their Committee should attend in their individual capacity,[7] but later the officers of the Deputies were usually nominated as such to represent them.[8]

In the seventies and later there was much co-operation. Representative conferences were held at times.[9] The Parliamentary sub-committees frequently sat together to draft and amend and oppose Bills on many subjects of interest to Dissenters. They prepared lists of questions to be submitted to Parliamentary candidates. But the most notable change was the Deputies' open and unqualified campaign for Disestablishment. In place of the old detailed and more modest petitions which mentioned the connexion of Church and State in the preamble but addressed themselves mainly to particular grievances, the Deputies took to resolutions and petitions in favour of Disestablishment pure and simple. There followed a

[1] 18 Jan. 1866.   [2] 5 Mar. 1866. In 1868 120 attended, including 12 M.P.s.
[3] 26 Feb. 1868.   [4] 2 Feb. 1906.   [5] 1 Feb. and 18 Mar. 1884.
[6] 1 June 1880.   [7] 28 April 1871.   [8] E.g. 27 April 1877, 23 Oct. 1908.
[9] E.g. on University Education in Ireland, 5 Dec. 1872.

period of intense agitation for Disestablishment until about 1886, when the schism in the Liberal party over Home Rule altered the whole political scene. Moreover Mr Miall died in 1881, when the Liberals had just returned to power. No leader comparable to him took his place.

Something like a new chapter opened when in 1871 the Deputies resolved that the time had now come for Parliament to consider the separation of Church and State. They therefore welcomed Mr Miall's notice of a resolution in the House of Commons in favour of extending the policy of Disestablishment from Ireland to the rest of the United Kingdom.[1] When the Liberation Society asked for the co-operation of the Deputies over a public meeting of Nonconformists to support Mr Miall's resolution, the Deputies agreed;[2] and 'a large and influential meeting' was held at Cannon Street Hotel.[3] Mr Miall received the formal thanks of a General Meeting in 1872,[4] and later a special sub-committee was appointed to give assistance by petitions and meetings to his resolutions on English and Scottish Disestablishment in the next session.[5] A conference of 74 Deputies and 120 of their friends was held on 11 December 1872. Not only was general approval of Mr Miall's resolution given, but a 'resolute and systematic plan of action' was outlined: petitions; public meetings; correspondence with and deputations to local M.P.s who have not yet voted for Disestablishment; organization of electors for the next election.[6]

In 1873 Mr Miall's motion was defeated by a larger majority than in the preceding year. The Deputies ascertained, however, that this was simply due to its opponents forcing an early decision: the supporters of Disestablishment in Parliament had not diminished. The Deputies had written to all metropolitan and county Liberal Members urging them to vote for the motion. The Deputies, dissatisfied by the behaviour of metropolitan Members, urged Nonconformist voters to take appropriate steps to secure more faithful representation. These resolutions and a statement of metropolitan Members' votes were sent to the press and to metropolitan M.P.s.[7]

[1] 21 Feb. 1871. [2] 16 Mar. 1871. [3] 20 April 1871. [4] 25 July 1872.
[5] 7 Nov. 1872. [6] 11 Dec. 1872. [7] 6 June 1873.

In the following year a general resolution on Disestablishment reflected the ritual troubles of the time. The Deputies expressed the hope that the divisions in the Establishment and

the proved impossibility of securing uniformity of belief amongst its members upon the most important points of our common faith will lead earnest men in the Establishment to desire freedom from the trammels of the State.[1]

At the beginning of the next year the General Meeting resolved

That the Ecclesiastical Legislation of last Session has confirmed the Deputies in the opinion they have always held that Parliament is not fitted to deal with religious affairs.

They look forward to 'perfect religious equality', the freedom of religion from the State connexion.[2]

That Disestablishment was believed to be almost a practical question was indicated by an incident at the General Meeting in 1877. An unofficial resolution called on the Committee to prepare as soon as possible the outlines of a Bill for Disestablishment and 'dealing with' the endowments. The previous question was carried.[3] The Deputies maintained their cautious attitude when at the end of the year they learnt that the Liberation Society had done something like what they had themselves declined to do. The Liberation Society had published 'Practical Suggestions relative to the Disestablishment and Disendowment of the Church of England,' and 'The Property and Revenues of the English Church Establishment'. They circulated these works to all Deputies[4] and arranged for a special evening meeting to discuss them.[5] No reporters were invited; but a brief official report, after revision by the Committee, was sent to the press.[6] In 1880 a list of questions was prepared by the Deputies and the Liberation Society for Liberal candidates in metropolitan and adjacent constituencies. Disestablishment in Scotland and England had the first place, but the Deputies' caution may perhaps be traced in the qualifying phrases:

(1) 'Do you agree with Lord Hartington that when the time comes

[1] 21 May 1874.   [2] 29 Jan. 1875.   [3] 29 Jan. 1877.
[4] 2 Nov. 1877.   [5] 20 Feb. 1878.   [6] 26 Mar. and 2 April 1878.

that Scotch opinion shall be fully formed on the subject [of Disestablishment] the Liberal party in England will do its best to give effect to that opinion?'

(2) 'Are you in favour of a policy of Disestablishment *in England* so soon as public opinion is sufficiently advanced to justify such a change?'

The last of the questions also touched the same principles: the discontinuance of grants for religion in India, Ceylon, and the colonies.[1]

The education controversy had left the Deputies with no illusions about Mr Gladstone, and they had no reason to expect effective help from him. They kept the matter prominent by resolutions; and they linked it steadily with the problem caused by the ritual controversies. On the one side, only freedom could satisfy the Anglicans and the distraction and discontent now prevailing within the Church of England; on the other side illegal practices and ceremonies 'inconsistent with its Protestant character' could not be suffered to continue in an Established Church.[2]

In 1884 three motions to be moved in Parliament on Disestablishment concerning England, Wales, and Scotland were made the main business of the joint breakfast.[3] The Annual Meeting of Deputies united in urging that, when discussed, these resolutions should be given every possible support by their constituents, and found encouragement in the division on a recent motion concerning the right of bishops to sit in the House of Lords: 'The division which took place seems emphatically to suggest that opinion in favour of Disestablishment is rapidly ripening.'[4]

The approach of a General Election found the Deputies urging support at their General Meeting[5] for candidates pledged to defend religious equality; but the Committee decided 'in the present condition of this question' of Disestablishment not to interfere, and to defer action until after the Election.[6]

This apparently odd procedure corresponded to the odd condition of the Liberal party. Mr Chamberlain's unauthorized radical programme included, as an important feature, Disestablishment; but Mr Gladstone had to consider also those of his followers who

---

[1] 2 Jan. 1880. [2] 23 Feb. 1881. [3] 1 Feb. 1884.
[4] 2 April 1884. [5] 15 April 1885. [6] 3 Nov. 1885.

were not Whigs; and he had his customary and congenial success in enveloping with words and mystery his real intentions about that 'gigantic question' (and others). 374 Liberal candidates were said to be in favour of Disestablishment; when the Election was over and the Deputies examined the results they found with 'much satisfaction' that 'there are now a far larger number of members who are in favour of complete religious equality than has been the case in any previous Parliament, whilst again the number of Members actually pledged to vote for Disestablishment is also greatly increased'. This satisfaction was enhanced 'by the fact that at no previous election have such persevering efforts been put forth by the supporters of the Establishment to prevent the return of persons opposed to their views'. The Committee therefore felt encouraged to further measures for complete religious equality.[1] At the joint Parliamentary breakfast Disestablishment, and Disestablishment only, in many forms, was to be the bill of oratorical fare.[2] This agreeable prospect was, for all that, delusive. In fact the peak of the movement had been passed. Home Rule was about to fill and cloud the whole horizon; and Mr Chamberlain, the most prominent political agitator for Disestablishment, was to leave the Liberal party. In fact Disestablishment in England and Scotland had never been as near practical politics as it had seemed; and the agitation for it took a second place and died down gradually and imperceptibly. Resolutions were still moved and carried in many places; but the effective attention even of the Deputies turned in other directions.

It may indeed be argued that the influence of Mr Miall and the close alliance in the last two decades had not helped, had perhaps retarded, progress on the lines which the Deputies had made their own before the Liberation Society was born. The Deputies had long shrunk from the exciting platitudes of political campaigns. They had preferred detailed concessions to oratorical programmes. By not appearing too radical, by not exciting wild apprehensions, by not presenting unscrupulous opponents with weapons, they had won great triumphs. Mr Miall and the Disestablishment campaign had awakened new fears in the plain man's mind.

[1] 15 Dec. 1885.   [2] 20 Jan. 1886.

Liberal candidates could be caricatured as applying lighted faggots to parish churches. The conservatism that is near the heart of every Englishman was enlisted against the Deputies' cause, and the Deputies, it is likely, got a less favourable hearing when they pleaded for small but important redresses of grievances because they had been tarred with another Society's brush. Their business, as in the past they had not been shy of saying, was defence, not offence. This interpretation of the work of a heroic generation may be wrong; but it may be right.

It remains to observe the Deputies' attitude to Disestablishment after 1885. For a time the affairs of England, Wales and Scotland are all to the fore. From the mass of resolutions it gradually appears that Disestablishment in Wales and in Scotland take precedence as likely to happen before Disestablishment in England. In both of these, but especially in Wales, the argument that the Established Church was the Church of a minority could be used more effectively than in England. It was indeed by something like a return to the older tactics that progress was to be made. By concentrating finally on Wales the Disestablishment campaign was to achieve more than by all the larger schemes of the middle of the century.

In 1885 Mr Peddie's Bill for disestablishing and disendowing the Church of Scotland won the wholehearted support of the Deputies.[1] In 1886 they welcomed three motions concerning Welsh Disestablishment, the removal of bishops from the House of Lords, and the appointment of a Select Committee to enquire into the origin, nature, amount, application and distribution of the revenues of the Church of England.[2] The Welsh Disestablishment motion was lost only by 229 to 241,[3] and so on the eve of Mr Gladstone's defeat on Home Rule and the long period of Conservative dominance the Deputies conceived that they might draw renewed encouragement in demanding Disestablishment in England as well as in Wales and Scotland.[4]

In 1888 they expressed the hope that the entire Liberal party would support Dr Cameron's motion for Scottish Disestablishment and Disendowment. The Established Church comprised

[1] 15 April 1885. See above. [2] 8 Mar. 1886. [3] 22 Mar. 1886. [4] 2 June 1886.

only a minority of the population; and its Establishment involved a waste of public resources and discontent and division.[1]

In 1889 a motion in favour of Welsh Disestablishment, introduced by Mr Dillwyn, was lost in the Commons by 231 to 284.[2]

In 1889, nevertheless, the Deputies claimed to find marked progress in public opinion. Mr Gladstone's speech at St Austell meant that Welsh and Scottish Disestablishment must be taken to be items in any future Liberal programme.[3] This conversion of the official Liberal party was indeed something new, even though it occurred near the beginning of a period in which Liberal programmes were to have very little practical importance. In 1891 the Deputies supported Mr Pritchard Morgan's resolution in favour of Welsh Disestablishment.[4] In the following year they supported a similar motion which was lost by only 47 votes.[5]

In the brief interval of Liberal Government the Deputies urged that Scottish and Welsh Disestablishment should be undertaken at once. A majority of the House was in favour of Disestablishment generally.[6] A Welsh Church Bill was heartily approved in 1893.[7] When Lord Rosebery succeeded Mr Gladstone the Deputies 'confidently expected' the new Government to introduce Disestablishment measures for Scotland and Wales. They so far forgot their tradition indeed as to put Scottish and Welsh Disestablishment before 'other questions of secondary but practical importance' such as Bills concerning burial and marriage, sites, enfranchisement, and rating of places of worship. These latter they pressed for, but Disestablishment must demand primary consideration.[8] The attitude of Lord Rosebery's Government proved to be satisfactory; and in January 1895 the Deputies rejoiced at its pledge to introduce a Welsh Disestablishment Bill.[9] The Bill appeared, and in April at the second reading got a majority of 44.[10] The Government resigned, however, in June, and the long period of Conservative rule put an end to these hopes.

On the eve of the 1900 Election the Deputies urged that efforts should be made to secure for Disestablishment a prominent place

---

[1] 20 June 1888.　　[2] 29 April 1889.　　[3] 10 July 1889.　　[4] 17 Feb. 1891.
[5] 25 Feb. and 17 Mar. 1892.　　[6] 23 Nov. 1892.　　[7] 2 Mar. 1893.
[8] 8 Mar. 1894.　　[9] 28 Jan. 1895.　　[10] 25 April 1895.

in every Liberal candidate's programme. The unrest in the Established Church, the inability of Parliament to end it, and Liberal opinion generally warranted this.[1] The unjust Education Act of 1902, said the Deputies in 1903, 'has for its aim the strengthening of the Established Church: it is necessary therefore to make increased efforts for disestablishment'.[2]

The same notes were struck after the Liberal victory of 1906. The educational controversy and the Royal Commission on Ecclesiastical Disorders reinforced the old arguments against Establishment and Endowment. Not only was religious equality violated: the right of self-government was denied to the Anglican Church, and Parliament was given religious duties which it was incompetent to perform.[3] In the following year, in welcoming the Government's promise of Welsh Disestablishment, the Deputies reasserted their determination to work for Disestablishment everywhere. That alone could end religious struggles inside and outside the Anglican Church. The disabilities of Dissent, although lessened, still existed.[4] In 1912 Disestablishment figured with education as the subjects of speeches at a lunch held by the Deputies and the Liberation Society.

After the 1914-18 War the amalgamation of the Deputies with the Liberation Society was discussed; but the Deputies declined the suggestion. They showed their continued goodwill by subscribing at intervals to the funds of their old ally.[5] In 1929 the Deputies expressed the opinion that Disestablishment might be left to develop from the Anglican Church itself.[6]

The decline in the vigour of the campaign for Disestablishment is not difficult to understand. In Ireland and in Wales, where the Established Church had been the Church of a minority and in part a foreign Church, it had been disestablished. In England, though the Anglican Church was still established, Establishment meant something very different and something far smaller than at the beginning of the 19th century. Anglicanism was indeed still in a privileged position, but the efforts of the Deputies and others had

---

[1] 30 May 1900.   [2] 24 July 1903.   [3] 15 Mar. 1907.
[4] 29 May 1908.
[5] E.g. July 1924, £15; 1927, £10 10s.; 1928, £15 15s.; 1931, £15 15s.   [6] Nov. 1929.

diminished its privileges. Legislation about marriages, burials, Church Rates and the like had not only reduced the grievances of Dissenters. Looked at from the other side it had brought about a partial Disestablishment. Much still remained to be done before religious equality and justice were achieved; but an Englishman's interest in abstractions like equality and justice is tepid; and by removing many of the practical inconveniences of Establishment the Deputies may be held in fact to have postponed the date of Disestablishment.

PART IV

AMBASSADORS OF DISSENT

CHAPTER 1

THE AMERICAN COLONIES

A SHORT section of seven pages in the *Sketch*[1] gives only a hint of one of the most important chapters in the Deputies' early history. In it the claim is made that the

Committee of Deputies was now regarded [i.e. in 1740] as a body qualified, by its wisdom and experience, to give advice and assistance in every weighty affair among the Dissenters, in all parts of the British dominions.

This claim, which is not substantiated by the *Sketch*, is substantiated by the Minute Books. During the colonial period, it is clear, the Deputies acted as an unofficial legation for those American Colonies which derived from the Puritan exiles. Advice was asked and given on the most trivial as well as the weightiest matters which had any connection with religion; the Deputies were a regular channel of approach to the King and the Court, and Colonial Governors corresponded with them and received their encouragement, and sometimes their admonitions. Contact was maintained through the Deputies' 'Committee of Correspondence'; but it was a very informal and largely a personal correspondence.

For convenience, we will describe some of the smaller matters first and treat of the more important afterwards, although by doing so we may destroy the richness of the impression which comes from their being mingled indiscriminately in the Minutes.

The first incident, as described in the *Sketch*, arose in 1740, when 'Dr Coleman and his brethren in New England' applied to the Committee 'respecting some injurious claims set up against them with regard to their glebe lands'. Reference was made to the particular case of 'Mr Terry, a Congregational Minister at Kings

[1] *Sketch*, pp. 13-20.

Town in New England' who feared to be dispossessed. The Deputies sent advice, for which they were thanked, but the nature of it is not stated.

In 1746 Dr Avery, the Deputies' Chairman, and Mr Eliakim Palmer, apparently the colonists' official agent, presented an Address from the pastors of New England to George II. Dr Avery apologized to the Committee for not having

desired the Committee or a Competent Number of them to have gone with him [but the] Duke of Newcastle had told him that he had better present it alone or at most not bring more than One with him.[1]

This was the first of a number of such deputations, which reveal not only the relationship between the Deputies and the American Colonies, but also between the Deputies and the Court. For instance, in 1751

The Dr also read an address of Condolance to his Majesty on the death of the late prince of Wales from the Ministers at Connecticut, also another address upon the same Occasion to the princess Dowager of Wales which he had received from New England.[2]

In 1756 the Deputies promised their assistance in the choice of Governors for New York and New Jersey;[3] but when they saw Lord Halifax he would not commit himself further than to say

that the person the Colony feared would be made Governour of New Jersey was not at present thought of.

In 1762 they appointed a sub-committee to assist in getting the Royal Assent to an Act of the General Court of Massachusetts

for granting a charter to several persons there for Evangelising the Indians of North America;

but on this occasion, again, the Committee reported that they had not been able to succeed in their application.[4] Lord Halifax was equally guarded in his reply when in 1757 Dr Avery saw him 'to intercede that Mr Oliver might succeed' as 'secretary of the Massachusetts', but 'the Earl said he would not promise absolutely' (the word 'absolutely' being subsequently deleted in the Minutes).[5]

More than once the colonists tried to put this informal embassy

---

[1] 18 Oct. 1746.   [2] 23 Oct. 1751.   [3] 29 Sept. 1756.
[4] 30 Mar. 1763.   [5] 23 Feb. 1757.

on a more official footing. In 1749 Dr Avery was asked to become the London agent for Connecticut; he refused, but 'by the advice of the Committee' recommended them a Mr Storke. The Doctor told the Deputies that

the People at Massachusetts and Connecticut desire that if any of their body are here at the time of the Meeting of the Deputation or Committee they may attend at such Meeting to consult and advise with them.

The Deputies agreed.[1] A generation later, when the recently established General Convention of the New England Churches was considering appointing a London agent, the Deputies discouraged the idea, on the ground that the colonists would be better advised to work through the London Committee of Deputies (which they sometimes referred to as the 'General Meeting of the Deputies for managing the affairs of the Dissenters').[2] The Deputies could not be accused, as an agent might, of personal interest or bias.[3]

At times the attitude of the Deputies to the colonists was a little patronizing. There was a good deal of trouble in the early days about the licensing of meeting-houses,[4] and on one occasion, when complaints were received that a licence given by the County Court had been revoked by the Governor and Council, the colonists were told to 'be easy until fresh instructions were sent'.[5] In the tone of such letters we may understand how the 'Boston Tea Party' was provoked, although perhaps the patronizing tone is in part explained by the numerous appeals for financial and other assistance received from the colonists.

In Virginia the licensing question became so troublesome that a Mr Davies was sent specially to London to see the Deputies about it.[6] He appeared before the Committee and drafted a form of petition to the King in Council, which after being 'much shortened' by the Committee was approved of, and two parts of the petition were sent to Virginia for signature in 'two separate ships'.[7] At the end of 1754 many complaints from Virginia were still being received, and Dr Avery arranged to see the Earl of Halifax and the Duke of Newcastle about it. Halifax advised dropping the

---

[1] 14 Mar. 1749/50.   [2] 12 April 1768.   [3] 14 May 1771.   [4] E.g. 26 April 1751.
[5] 29 Jan. 1752.   [6] 27 Feb. 1754.   [7] 24 April 1754.

petition, and recommended that the ministers should preach without licence and, if prosecuted, appeal to the King and Council. Detailed instructions were sent to this effect.[1] There is no record that any of the ministers were prosecuted, but in 1756 letters from Virginia are again noticed in the Minutes, 'touching a new settlement in North America on the river Ohio', and the question of licensing meeting-houses in the newly-settled districts.[2]

The Deputies were lavish with advice and help in high places, but they were not so ready to assist financial appeals. In 1751 Dr Avery read a letter from Nova Scotia describing 'the growth of the Dissenting Interest and praying a supply of good books to give away to the poor'.[3] In 1753 he read

a Narration that he had received from Governor Belchier touching the erection of a Publick Seminary for Religious Literature in New Jersey.[4]

In 1754 the Committee felt that it did not fall within their province to recommend delegates appointed from New Jersey to collect in Great Britain for the College of New Jersey.[5] In 1756 came an appeal from three Methodist Ministers in Connecticut relating to a charter 'to erect a Charity School for the Instruction of Indian Children'.[6] In 1764 the Deputies earned the reproach of posterity by turning a deaf ear to the 'great loss Harvard College has sustained by fire'.[7]

But we must turn to the major question which concerned the Deputies and these their most distant constituents. This question was the relationship between the Three Denominations in America and other religious bodies. On the one hand there was in the minds of the Puritan colonists an irremovable fear of the claims of the Established Church; on the other hand the older Dissenting bodies were faced by the growth of Methodism and the first of those 'religious revivals' which have swept over America many times since. Nor did American Dissenters see the Establishment and Methodism as such widely opposed things. Had not John Wesley first appeared in Georgia in 1735 as a High Church agent of the Society for the Propagation of the Gospel? Did he not to the last assert that Methodists were 'no republicans', and sanction the

[1] 27 Nov. 1754.   [2] 25 Feb. 1756.   [3] 25 Sept. 1751.   [4] 28 Feb. 1753.
[5] 30 Jan. 1754.   [6] 25 Nov. 1756.   [7] 10 Oct. 1764.

appointment of bishops among American Methodists? So the Dissenting colonists were inclined to view High Churchmanship and Methodism as two prongs of a fork; and when the new Evangelical spirit spread in the 1740s, they were inclined to restrain this fervour by legal action. It is greatly to the Deputies' credit that, although they themselves had no liking at this period for Evangelical fervour, they were emphatic about the danger of persecuting it.

In 1743 we find Governor Jonathan Law of Connecticut defending himself volubly to the Deputies; and although indeed, as he says, it is not his talent 'to Comprize Multum in Parvo' the letter is an eloquent tribute to the intimacy of the links between the Deputies and the colonists as well as a graphic description of the phenomena of religious enthusiasm. The Mr Palmer referred to is doubtless the Mr Eliakim Palmer whom we have already met, accompanying Dr Avery in presenting Addresses to the Throne.

The Letter of the Govr. of Connecticutt in New England to Dr Avery

Milford, Nov. 1743.

Honble. Sir,

Yours of the 25th of Febry. I received and most thankfully observed your Readiness to assist Mr Palmer in Securing the Rights of our Churches and College as well as the Prosperity of our Civil State, and had we no Enemies to our Interest we should less need the Interposition of our able and faithfull friends, for I perceive by a Copy of a Letter said to be read publickly in our lower house or Assembly wherein you lament the Confusions and Disorders which have been the Product of Some Ecclesiastical laws lately made destructive of that Liberty by which wee Subsist and savour of the Leaven of Imposition and Persecution—That some have not been wanting in their Endeavours by their Misrepresentations to deprive us of that Help we relyed on with the greatest Assurance.

The Laws themselves you may see in our Law Book sent to Mr Palmer.

Those Laws which were represented as the Cause of those Confusions are of a later Date and so could not be the Cause but are the Effect and since those laws were made, those Confusions have very much subsided & now are Subsisted only or Chiefly by those (and some of your friends) who with Politick Views, use it only as an Handle for their Advancement as they did the Controversy for making a fflood of Paper Currency—

About two or three years agone our Confusions and Disorders began by a Number of our Ministers setting up Enthusiastical Principles and a Spirit of Discerning, leaving their own Parishes, became Itinerants and Crowded themselves into other Parishes everywhere proclaiming both Ministers and Magistrates and all others who did not give into their Schemes and Methods to be Carnal and unconverted, Pharisees and Hypocrites, going themselves and leading others to Hell and therefore unfitt for any Improvement in Church or State, and by setting up Illiterate and Ignorant Persons to be Exhorters they drew Multitudes together both Night and Day, where at their Meetings they and their Exhorters strook the People in Screamings, Screeches, Swoonings, Convulsions, Trances, Distractions, Visions and Revelations, on which followed Divisions and Separations in Churches and Societys and ffamilys. Children and Servants taught to disobey their Parents and Masters. The Common Affairs of life almost wholly laid aside in many places for a Considerable Length of time, introducing an Occasion for the Doctrine of Community of Goods which some began to advance.

In the College the Publick Exercises almost laid aside yea wholly for a time, Studies neglected. The Governours of the College insolently declared by the Youth (after the manner of those whom they followed) to be Carnal and unconverted men, old Pharisees. Humane Learning, exploded as a Useless thing in matters of Religion—many left the College and others went when and where and as they pleased, Setting up another College at New London called the Shepherd's Tent under the direction of One Allin, lately Minister of a parish in Newhaven, dismisst by a Council of Ministers and Messengers of the District to which he belonged for teaching among other heterodox principles that the Bible was but an Old Almanack, where he with others running into many wild Conceits, at length made a Sacrafice or Bonfire of such Books as they Condemned and could gett, and made Preparation for another of their Cloaths and other things which they said they had Idolized.

Whereupon the Governmt. thought it necessary to pass an Act for regulating Schools as you may see.—

And now those that went off from the College would and do return with their Acknowledgements of their Delusions and Misconduct, and more than forty of them have offered themselves for an Admission into the College, which seems to be restored to a flourishing and peacable state.

After reviewing the ecclesiastical regulations to shew that they did not affect settled ministers and congregations and were not persecuting established sects, the Governor continues:

Thus Sir I hope you will see that our Circumstances if what I have informed be true as to the facts, required a Remedy. That the Confusions and Disorders were not made but Suppressed by the laws, and that the Remedy provided can by no means deserve the Imputation of Persecution or Imposition, or be any ways inconsistant with Christian Liberty, and retain us in full Charity and do us all the good Offices you did intend and fall within your compass.

And he concludes:

Hoping you will excuse my Voluminous Way of writing it being not my talent to Comprize Multum in Parvo.
I subscribe
Yours much engaged ffriend
and most humble Servant
Jonth Law.

The Doctor replied on behalf of the Committee in the following terms:

Honoured Sir,

Your Letter of November, 1743, to Dr Avery, and the papers which accompanied it, have been imparted to us by the Dr and as wee all feel, so your Honor will allow us to express our Joint Concern and Sorrow, for undesirable Situation with respect to those Ecclesiastical and Religious Disputes which prevail among the Inhabitants of your Province.

Wee all of us have a great Dislike to those Principles which wee hear from other hands, as well as from your Honor's, have with too great Eagerness and Success been propagated in those parts. Wee see the Tendency of these Principles, and of the Way that is taken to spread them; they plainly tend to Create Feuds and Animosities, and to destroy that Peace, Unity, and mutual Good Will, so amiable among Neighbours, so essential among Christians. We fear that such Opinions and Practises, as you justly complain of, will not only lead many weak Persons into Enthusiastick Delusions, but will likewise much abate that

Spirit of Industry and Application to Business, which is well known to be absolutely necessary to the Prosperity of the Colony.

We are Sensible that by the Propagation of such Sentiments as have lately crept in among you, the Minds of many must be unhinged, endless Doubts and Perplexities will arise, and Scepticism and Infidelity seem likely to be the Unhappy Issue.

But great and manifest as these Mischiefs are, wee Cannot be of Opinion that the Magistrate has anything to do in this matter, but to see that the publick peace is preserved; that there are no Riots or Tumults; and that his Subjects are not allowed to assault, hurt, maim, wound, plunder, or kill one another in these Religious Contests.

Wee apprehend the making Laws against these Opinions, and those who avow them, can answer no Valuable Purpose. It is no way that God has appointed to inform the Judgements of men, or alter their Way of thinking. It will neither enlighten their Understanding, or procure their Esteem or good Will. It will exasperate them,—drive them to a greater Distance and Disaffection; and it will be apt to move Compassion in disinterested Bystanders, and thereby increase the number of those Eager Enthusiasts and ill-informed Zealots.

For such reasons as these, we imagine, it is, that both Church and State have Connived at the irregular, unseasonable, and perhaps Sometimes almost tumultuous Assemblys of the same kind of Mistaken Men in this Country. The Governours both of the State and Church well know, that not in minutes have laws in being, to the penalties of which these men make themselves daily obnoxious. But not one of these Laws has been putt in Execution against them. No attempt of that nature has been made. Nay, when any have offered to abuse or disturb them in their Assemblys for Worship, which possibly were not strictly legal, the Magistrate has interposed, and punish'd such who have presum'd to insult them. And it is visible that this Method of Connivance has had a very Desirable Effect. Expostulations and Entreaties, attended with strong Reasoning and a steady Persevering Lenity and fforbearance, promise great Good in Contests of this kind. Force can do nothing but Mischief.

Wee find, sir, it is apprehended to be injurious Treatment, when your Laws, particularly that act in May, 1742, is represented as of a Persecuting Nature.

Wee firmly believe that your Honor and the Majority of the Legislature, who enacted that law, did think it quite Consistent with all the Just Rights the Inhabitants of Connecticut had any Claim to, and that it was likely to be serviceable to the Country; or else wee cannot persuade ourselves that you would ever have propos'd, encourag'd, form'd and pass'd it.

But you must allow us to add, that this thing appears in a very different Light to us. The three penalties, of which you seem to think and speak so lightly, appear to us very grievous; Wee well know we should think them so, were the case our own. And the Instances of Conduct which are threaten'd with these Penalties, are not necessarily, and in their own nature, Violations of that public Peace and Tranquillity which the Magistrate is obliged or Concerned to preserve. Wee mean, that a Man, whether settled Minister, Inhabitant, or fforeigner, may, without any Breach of the publick peace, cognizable by the Civil Magistrate, at the request of any number of Inhabitants, preach in any Parish or Town to which he does not stand related as their Stated Minister.

And if this be not true, Wee Cannot see how Christianity at first, or the Reformation since, could have Claimed or obtained a fair Hearing.

It may possibly not appear to the Majority in Connecticutt any way hard or injurious, to lay a Restraint, by publick Authority, on Parents and Guardians in educating their Children. But we well know, and shall not easily forget, what wee felt on a like Occasion. Wee were greatly alarm'd and disquieted by an attempt made here about thirty years ago, to deprive us of the liberty of educating our Children in the way most agreeable to our Judgements and Consciences. Thro' the Goodness of God, the threaten'd Storm blew over. The Act, tho' passed, was never executed, and was soon repeal'd. And wee have lived to hear the Gentlemen of the most forward Zeal and greatest Bigotry, who were principally Concerned in making that Attempt, reflect upon their own Conduct in that affair and Censure it as unreasonable and not to be defended. And it can't fail of giving us great Uneasiness should wee hear it said, that what the most zealous high Church men profess now to be ashamed of here, should be Copied and imitated by our Presbyterian and Congregational Brethren abroad, in their Conduct to persons of their own, or indeed of any Denomination of Christians.

In short, whether Wee Consider this matter in a religious or Political Light, it seems every way most adviseable to let these men alone, how wildly Erroneous soever both you and wee may take their Sentiments to be. Any Penalties, Incapacitating, ffining, Imprisonments, Banishments, or Vexatious Prosecutions, will not fail of being represented here, to our, as well as to your, Disadvantage. And if on such Accounts as these any such Complaints should be made to the King and Council, Wee should not be able, and indeed it would but ill become us to endeavour, to vindicate such Proceedings. Perhaps wee don't know every Circumstance that attends your Situation distinctly enough, to take upon us to advise you what part it will be most prudent for you to act on this occasion. But wee think nothing can be more Clear, than that it is absolutely necessary you should avoid all kinds of Rigour and Severity in your Methods of Proceedure.

Wee heartily wish you, Sir, Health, Happiness, a lasting and growing Usefullness and Reputation. May you, Sir, your Council, and the house of Representatives, be directed from above how to behave in this arduous and Criticall Juncture.—Wee shall rejoyce to hear that the Province is settled on the Sure and lasting ffoundation of Truth, Righteousness, and Peace.—Signed in the name and by order of the Committee.—

B. AVERY, chairman.'

In spite of the tone of this reply, it appears that the Governor's earnestness had some effect on their views, for the Report to the General Meeting of 1744 speaks of

unhappy Differences which have arisen in the Collony of Connecticut; Differences which have taken their Rise, or gathered great Strength from some Religious Sentiments that have gained considerable Ground there and visibly endanger the publick Peace.[1]

But, however alarming, 'Enthusiastick Practices' were only an incident. The pressure of the Established Church to increase its authority in America was perennial. In 1749 Mr Palmer reported that Dr Avery and himself had seen the Duke of Bedford, the Duke of Newcastle, the Lord Chancellor and Mr Pelham about a proposal 'to make two new Bishops for the West Indies at Barbados and Virginia to confer orders on people without giving them the trouble to come to England'.[2]

They all Declared that the Affair was farr from being Concluded on, And that nothing would be done in it without the maturest Deliberation, and that they should be very willing to hear any Objections thereto from persons of any Consequence.[3]

[1] 10 Oct. 1744.   [2] 5 April 1749.   [3] 5 May 1749.

In fact, the introduction of bishops into the American Colonies never was 'concluded on', but the proposal in one form or another was being perpetually revived, and it developed in the 1760s into a bitter controversy which contributed greatly to the exacerbation of feeling which preceded the Declaration of Independence. The trouble was that the position of the Church of England in America was never clearly laid down, and its status varied in the different colonies. Theoretically, the colonies belonged to the diocese of London, and were ruled by commissaries appointed by the bishop. In the northern colonies the Church had little power; in the southern colonies (Maryland, Virginia, the Carolinas) it was established, but lacked leaders of weight and eminence. In the middle colonies, where many religious bodies had adherents but none was all-powerful, there was most controversy, and it was here that the Society for Propagating the Gospel (founded in 1701) was most active in the interests of episcopacy. It had been founded, its enemies said, to convert the Indians; but instead of that it was chiefly engaged as an instrument for the establishment of Anglican worship. The matter is thus stated in the Deputies' Minutes:

Dr Avery reported that he had found the Danger arises from the Society for Propagating the Gospel in fforeign Parts who are very intent upon having Bishops sent into those parts. That he had spoke to Mr Pelham about it who told him that there was a Talk afresh again about it, and that next Thursday there was to be a Meeting of some Lords about it, and that he had advised him to wait on the Lord Chancellor to Desire his Weight and Interest against it and he intended to wait upon him accordingly. (28 March 1750)

A month later the result of the interview is recorded:

The Lord Chancellor told him that he believed there was no Danger at present of such a Scheme taking place. (30 May 1750)

and an answer was returned to the gentlemen in New England to this effect. But although there was no danger at present, the gentlemen in New England were not satisfied; their enquiries were repeated at regular intervals, with reassurances from the Deputies' Committee which did not comfort them.

In such an atmosphere, it was inevitable that complaints from both sides of the conduct of the others should reach the ears of the Deputies. In 1753 Dr Avery reported that

A Gentleman of great consequence in the Church complained to him that an Account had been sent to the Society for Propagating the Gospel of a Man of the Episcopal perswasion in Connecticut being Whipt by Authority for not Attending the Presbyterian Worship.

We have seen often enough in our own time how such rumours are used to manufacture an atmosphere of crisis; it was one of the Deputies' functions to get the facts, and they sent at once to Connecticut for information, which was supplied by a Mr John Ledyard and by Governor Walcott himself. Here is Ledyard's letter:

HARTFORD. 13th *Augt.* 1753

A few days past his Hon^r. our Govr. was pleased to shew me your favour to him and an Enclosed Copy of a Letter wrote by the Revd. Mr Ebenezer Sanderson to the Society's Secretary. I was not without some surprize at the Contents of it, and Esteem it my duty to acquaint you with what I know thereabout on good information viz:

Ashford is a Town in the Colony lately settled. At such new places people of judgement in Matters of Law are often scarce, however the best to be found are put into Authority, one Mr Tiffany was a justice of the Peace at Ashford. Mr Jno. Pitts in full Comunion [?] with the Presbyterian Church in Ashford was presented for not Attending Publick Worship on the Lord's day and found Guilty by Justice Tiffany. By a law of this Colony he was liable in such case to be fined 3/- instead whereof the weak unhappy Justice sentenced him to be whipt which in a sort of a Ludicrous manner was really done, Pitts being well cloathed with his own and neighbours thick garments. Such a Scandalous Scene indeed I have not before known amongst us and for it the Justice's Commission was Stript over his Ears at the next Assembly and Pitts has an Action if he pleases against him—This Mr Pitts never was a Churchman but had he been one or indeed tho' he was a Presbyterian would he have proved he had attended Publick Worship at the Church of England or at a Baptist or at a Quaker's or at any other place of Publick Worship (allow'd of) it wo^d. as effectually have secured him from all legal Penalty as if he had proved that he attended publick Worship at the Presbyterian Church in Ashford.

How then can it be said he was Whipt notwithstanding his great Age and past Services for not Attending publick worship at their Meetings?

—I read several years past one of the Society's[1] Annual Sermons and I found therein when speaking of New England and as I remember particularly of Connecticut words to this purpose, viz[t]. 'They were advised that the Spirit of persecution run as high as ever against those of the Established Church in that Country.' Now I really believe there was no more of persecution at that time against any Churchman as such than there is in the Case of Pitts—Persecution I abhor in all its Shapes and Colours and it Troubles me to see this Colony without any just cause represented as persecutors and that by her own Children who have ever been treated with kindness and Love. I dare challenge Mr Sanderson to find anything that has been done here for many Years which the Bishop of London on having a thorough knowledge of the Case would say was persecution against a Churchman—It gives me great Satisfaction that what Mr Sanderson wrote is (thro' your goodness) known here. Could the Colony be informed of all that uneasy Gentlemen say to her hurt she would clear her Character where it now Suffers by misinformation, You Sir have the thanks of many for your care and kindness to the Colony and particularly the very hearty one of

Sr. Yr. m[t]. Ob[t]. & m[t]. hble. Servt.

JOHN LEDYARD[2]

A postscript continues the tone of indignant surprise: 'Who would have thought that Mr Sanderson on the desire of a superannuated person full of resentment would have made so injurious an information?'; and the Governor's letter takes the same tone, describing Mr Sanderson's letter to the Society for the Propagation of the Gospel as

Short, pungent and persuasive that there is such a Spirit of persecution against the Church in Our Authority that if a man holds Communion with the Church of England neither Age nor Merit can Excuse him from the whip unless he will joyn with the Dissenters.

I assure you there is no spirit of persecution here against the Church we bless God and the King we are allowed to worship according to our own Conscience and are willing the Church and all other Prostestants shd. Enjoy the same liberty and the truth of this I think is confirmed in that those that are the most Industrious to put the most infamous terms of persecution upon us can pick up nothing against us but such false and Triffling stuff as this.

The Law of the Colony is that all Persons attend the Publick Worship

---

[1] I.e. the S.P.G.   [2] 10 Oct. 1753.

on The Lordsday under the Penalty of three shillings for each offence unless hindered by some Lawfull cause no presentments to be made but within a Month after the Offence. This law is not made for any particular Sect—the Churchmen and Anabaptists have the same benefit by it as others and nobody is uneasy with it as I hear of unless Mr Sanderson. . . .

This has been a Law with us from the beginning and I hope has been a good means to promote Religion nor can I see any Tincture of Persecution in it since it has no respect to Sects in their different Modes of Worship but only to Oblige the worst of men to know what the Christian Religion is be happy and restrain them from profaning the Sabbath.

From New Hampshire, on the other hand, came accusations of

the Governor and Council being greatly bigotted to the Church of England and endeavouring to Discountenance the Dissenting Interest there [and of] the unjust Claims and Encroachments of the Episcopall party.[1]

while from New York came complaints that missionaries in that State had been obstructed on account of their not being episcopally ordained. Dr Avery was asked to speak to the Earl of Halifax to interpose his good offices with the Governor 'that the said missionaries might not be obstructed on that account'.[2]

As time went on, the Dissenters in the colonies became more alarmed. Their friends at home might endeavour to diminish their apprehensions, but they were not allayed. The 'Congregational Pastors of Massachusetts Bay', writing from Boston, 4 Jan. 1768, to Messrs. Mauduit,[3] Dean, and Crisp, 'the gentlemen of the Corresponding Committee', thought it necessary to defend themselves from accusations of being 'sunk in ignorance and infidelity and abandoned to the greatest profligacy of manners'. They were on the contrary, they said, 'a sober, Civilized and Industrious People' with 'decent structures for publick Worship, well qualified Persons set apart for the work of the Ministry, Numerous Assemblys attending the Instruction of Religion every Lord's Day, and Schools established for the Instruction of Youth in human and divine knowledge'.

---

[1] 25 Sept. 1751.   [2] 25 Sept. 1754.

[3] Mauduit, the Deputies' Chairman, was at this time official London agent for Massachusetts.

Let any impartial Stranger survey the state of Religion and Morality in those parts of this Continent where the Inhabitants are generally of the Presbyterian or Congregational persuasion, and compare it with those places where the Church of England is the publick Establishment, and we are sure we shall not suffer by the comparison.

We cannot therefore but be of the opinion that their grand aim in so earnestly desiring Bishops to be sent over into America is not to Christianize but to Episcopize the Plantations.

The pomp and splendor which Attend a Bishop might possibly dazzle the Eyes of some gay and thoughtless Youths, but would have no tendency to promote real Christianity. The interest a Bishop would naturally have with the Dignitaries on your side of the Atlantic would give him a prevailing Ascendant in almost all our civil affairs—The Governors would probably pay a submissive regard to his recommendations lest their Conduct should be placed in an unfavourable Light at home—Places of Honour and Profit would generally be distributed among those who should merit them by becoming proselytes to the Church of England—These things it is to be feared would be managed with such art and address as in a few years to produce an Establishment similar to that in South Britain—then the great design for which our heroic Ancestors transplanted themselves into the wilds of America would be entirely defeated, and their Posterity left to struggle with greater difficulties than those which banished them from their native country.

Your successful opposition to this imposition in the Plantations when proposed from time to time, We trust will encline you to appear with Zeal and Vigour now the attempt is renewed.[1]

On receipt of this letter, the Deputies' Committee once more renewed their enquiries, and on 1 April and again on 12 April 1768 wrote to reassure the colonists, saying that 'we verily believe they will never be able to accomplish any design to introduce Bishops'.

But the colonists were not reassured. In order to meet the danger, which was all the greater because of the theocratic element in the civil government of the New England Colonies, they set up the General Convention of Delegates from the Consociated Churches of Connecticut and from the Synod of New York and Philadelphia. This body, from its first meeting at Newhaven, 14

[1] Letter signed by Chas. Chaimey, C. Pemberton, Andrew Eliot, Saml. Cooper.

Sept. 1769, proceeded at once to establish contact with the Deputies. Their letter, signed by the Rev. Dr John Rogers, begins by explaining their reasons for calling the Convention, especially the threat of 'any attempt of any other Denominations of Christians to oppress us'.

Our fears would not be so much alarmed, could any rational Method be devised for sending over Bishops among us, stripped of every Degree of civil Power . . . and that the British Parliament would send them over thus limited, to gain a peaceable Settlement here, would never be induced by their Complaints for the Want of Power, to enlarge it at some future Period.

We well know the Jealousy of the Bishops in England concerning their own Power and Dignity suffering by the Example of such a mutilated Bishop in America; and we also know the Force of a british Act of Parliament; and we have Reason to dread the Establishment of Bishops Courts among us. Should they claim the Right of holding these Courts, and of exercising the Powers belonging to their Office by the common Law of England (which is esteemed the Birth-right of a British Subject) we could have no Counter-ballance to this enormous Power in our Colonies, where we have no Nobility or proper Courts to check the dangerous Exertion of their Authority, and where our Governors and Judges may be the needy Dependants of a prime Minister, and therefore afraid to disoblige a Person who is sure of being supported by the whole Bench of Bishops in England. So that our civil Liberties appear to us to be in eminent Danger from such an Establishment.

Besides, nothing seems to have a more direct Tendency to weaken the Dependance of the Colonies upon Great Britain and to separate them from her, an Event which would be ruinous and destructive to both, and which we therefore pray God long to avert.

As our Distance from the Throne and Parliament renders us unable to do anything to prevent it, untill it be too late, we are obliged to depend upon the Interest and Vigilance of our Friends in Great Britain who are engaged in the same common Cause with ourselves.[1]

We do not need to remind ourselves, as we read this letter, that we are in the age of Lord North; and so, however earnestly the 'Dissenting Committee in London' might insist that 'there is no such design on foot at present',[2] their correspondents would not

[1] 31 July 1770.   [2] 12 Oct. 1770.

be placated. In September 1771 the General Convention wrote to describe in detail the machinations of the Church party. 'The whole bench of Bishops, and many Bigots with you are constantly teized by our Missionaries to procure an American Episcopate.' Archbishop Secker had promised a bishop to any Province which petitioned for one; and the President of the College of William and Mary in Virginia, a clergyman named Horrax, had been sent to England with such a petition, though two of his professors who protested had been thanked *nem. con.* by the House of Burgesses for their 'seasonable stand for liberty'. In Maryland, too, petitions had been prepared addressed to the Throne, the Archbishop of Canterbury, the Bishop of London, and Lord Baltimore; but here again the Dissenters claimed that the Church party was far from unanimous, that ten of the clergy had protested, and that the Governor and Assembly had refused their approbation. 'Much more we have reason to suspect is done by them in other provinces which has not so fully come to our knowledge.'[1]

In February 1772 the Deputies learned that the petitions had indeed been presented,

yet we do not believe they will meet with any Success, and that however the Bishops and Clergy may labour the point the persons in power do not seem to be at all for it at present and we hope never will; but we must remind you that in our last we desired you, if you found any Petitions were handed in about to be signed, you would send over counter petitions signed by as many respectable persons as you could which we think you should do as soon as possible that they may be made use of if needful.

We may guess without much difficulty why 'the persons in power do not seem to be at all for it at present'. With the gathering clouds of the War of Independence the threats of episcopal domination are ended; and ended too is the intimate contact between New England and the 'Dissenting Committee in London'. But while the first Congress of the United States to be was meeting in 1774, the General Convention were still writing to London, assured that the design is not given up, though unaccomplished:

[1] 15 Jan. 1772.

We are taking all possible pains to ascertain the number of Episcopalians, and their proportion to the non-Episcopalians of different denominations in the several Colonies, and have made some progress in it, but we find it a work of no small labour and difficulty to do it with proper precision.

We find by a paper read before us at our present meeting that the Episcopalians in the Colony of New York bear the proportion of about one to twenty of its present inhabitants. By another of the same kind respecting the Colony of Connecticut it appears they do not bear a greater proportion. And in the provinces of New Jersey and Pennsylvania their proportionable numbers are less; and in the Massachusetts Government, Rhode Island, and Province of New Hampshire they are much less still. And in the Southern Colonies where Episcopacy is Established; vizt. Maryland, Virginia, North and South Carolina and Georgia, the non-Episcopalians are in some of them a majority and in the rest a large and growing proportion. We are pursuing this important design and promise ourselves the pleasure of Effecting it with a greater degree of Accuracy before our next Meeting, when you may expect to hear further from us on the subject.

What the Deputies heard further from their correspondents is a matter of history. The Declaration of Independence was signed in 1776.

The *Sketch*, however, adds a note:

Since the separation of the two countries, the introduction of Bishops has been partially carried into effect, but with an entire restriction of their authority to concerns purely ecclesiastical. The liberal and amicable reception they met with in America, may be considered as a proof that the resistance made by the Dissenters originated in no principles of intolerance towards episcopacy, but simply in a just fear of its influence when allied with temporal power.[1]

---

[1] *Sketch*, pp. 19-20.

CHAPTER 2

JAMAICA

THE EXISTENCE in Jamaica of slavery gave a peculiar character to the Deputies' work there. When they could, they avoided general discussions of slavery itself; but Dissenting missionaries had concerned themselves with the spiritual welfare of the coloured people, and it was the Deputies' task to ensure that freedom for the worship and teaching of the Church suffered no diminution. In times of political and social unrest this freedom was (and is) in desperate danger. The European settlers saw 'in the religious assemblies of the slaves an organization easily diverted to seditious activities. Moreover, sectarian animosity was not lacking: the majority of the settlers were Anglican—they did not favour, if they did not emulate, the Evangelical labours of the Dissenters among the slaves. The Dissenting missionaries naturally understood the grievances of their flocks, and to some extent shared in their political aspirations. The line between revolutionary propaganda and the cure of souls was not drawn by the settlers and the Dissenters in the same place; and if ignorance of local conditions limited the vision of the Deputies, self-interest warped the judgment of the settlers. The Minutes record many brisk clashes, and many appeals to the home Government, whose views seem usually to have resembled the Deputies' more than those of the settlers.

The beginning of the story is told in the *Sketch*.[1] In December 1802 the Assembly of Jamaica passed an Act introducing a licensing system for preachers and teachers. Two years later[2] the Deputies' Committee learnt that

with a single exception, the Toleration Act might be considered as totally suspended in that island; no public preaching, or even meeting for social prayer, among the Dissenters, being permitted; and that one

[1] pp. 61-4.   [2] 27 April 1804.

425

person, who, on being refused a license, had ventured to preach without one, had suffered a rigorous imprisonment.

A memorial presented by three Dissenting ministers to the Privy Council, and supported by the Deputies, had the effect of procuring the annulment of the Act, though the memorialists were informed

that a new law would be recommended to the legislature of Jamaica, to prevent designing men from collecting assemblies of blacks and people of colour, under pretence of religious worship, and concerting schemes of public mischief.

The Deputies asked for an opportunity of stating their objections before any instructions were sent to Jamaica 'which might have a tendency to abridge the Toleration Laws'. But they were relieved to hear from the island that the preachers in Jamaica had resumed their social gatherings.

The relief was of brief duration. In August 1807 the Chairman read an extract from a letter from a Baptist preacher in Jamaica (himself a person of colour) with a copy of an ordinance passed by the Common Council of Kingston, closing all the Dissenting meeting-houses there, except the Methodist chapel.

The Deputies took the ordinance to the Attorney-General, and on receiving his opinion that it was illegal, advised the preacher to re-open his meeting-house, promising him money and assistance in his defence, and an appeal to the Supreme Court of Jamaica if necessary.

In 1808 a new consolidated Slave Law forbade Dissenters of every denomination to preach to slaves. This was again disallowed; and not only so, but instructions were sent to the Governors of the West Indies in the following terms:

It is our will and pleasure, and we do hereby require and command, that you do not on any pretence whatever give your assent to any law or laws to be passed concerning religion, until you shall have first transmitted unto us, through our principal secretary of state, the draft of such bill or bills, and shall have received our royal pleasure thereupon; unless you take care, in passing such bill or bills, that a clause or clauses be inserted therein, suspending and deferring the execution thereof until our will and pleasure shall be known thereupon.

This, however, did not end the struggle; in 1811 the Deputies learnt of a new law which they considered objectionable. This time it was an annual measure, designed in the first instance to cover the period 31 December 1810 to 31 December 1811, and to prevent preaching and teaching by 'persons not duly qualified'; as well as to restrain dangerous meetings which might be held under religious pretexts.[1] The Deputies feared that the chance of Dissenters being approved by the courts in Jamaica as 'duly qualified' were small. The Deputies were already pressing for the Royal consent to be refused, when they learnt (on 8 November) that the Prince Regent had disallowed the Act.[2]

This time a much longer period elapsed before the colonists tried again. It was 1827 before the Deputies had again to appeal (to Lord Gooderich) against a Jamaican Act which by its regulations concerning missionaries and slaves infringed the rights of Dissenters under the Toleration Act. Having secured its annulment, the Deputies celebrated their victory with a tart gibe at the colonists:

The exercise of the Prerogative in favour of oppressed individuals and liberal principles excited great indignation in the colony, as might naturally have been expected, and much petulance was displayed on the occasion; which however your Committee trust will have no greater effect on the measures of Government at home than similar improprieties in former instances have produced.[3]

But at the end of 1829 the Jamaica legislature re-enacted the measure, with alterations which made it still more injurious and oppressive. All meetings between 6 p.m. and 6 a.m. were declared illegal, slaves were forbidden to teach each other, and Dissenting teachers were prohibited from receiving any pecuniary aid from slaves; in short, it would have made religious work among slaves impossible for Dissenters. Protests were made once more by the the Wesleyans and the Deputies, and once more the Act was disallowed.[4]

In 1832 the 'petulance' of the colonists found disgraceful expression. In April the Deputies learnt of riots, outrages on the persons

[1] 27 Sept. 1811. [2] 13 Dec. 1811.
[3] Report for 1828. [4] 19 Feb. 1830 and Report for 1830.

of missionaries, and destruction of meeting-houses; especially of Baptist meeting-houses. Insurrection of the negroes led to violent counter-measures. Missionaries who shewed sympathy with aggrieved slaves were misrepresented as fomenting civil strife; they were persecuted, arrested, and accused by false witnesses; and measures for expelling all 'sectaries' were demanded.[1]

The Baptists at once petitioned Gooderich for compensation; the Deputies, with their usual caution, awaited fuller information before they joined the Baptists in approaching the Government. Gooderich in his reply agreed that no charge of inciting or countenancing an insubordinate spirit among the slaves had been proved among the Baptists. Strict enquiry by the Governor was ordered; the Baptists should be indemnified out of general funds or special levies on the riotous districts.[2] The Deputies expressed gratification, and in July published a comprehensive set of resolutions.

Declaring that silence about the civil rights of Dissenters in Jamaica would be a dereliction of their duty, the Deputies asserted that magistrates and militia had led the riots, in which £23,000 worth of damage had been done to chapels erected for negroes; that one missionary had been imprisoned on bribed testimony, others had been cruelly handled, and a system organized to exclude all missionaries, even of the Established Church. Without approving of the negroes' insurrection, the Deputies reprobated the behaviour of the militia and the magistrates. From the incident they drew a practical lesson: at the General Election everyone should vote for the immediate extinction of slavery; nothing else would provide a remedy. The Deputies bought and circulated £200-worth of a pamphlet prepared by the Baptists: *Facts and Documents connected with the late insurrection in Jamaica*.[3]

In the autumn another outrage, and a demand for the forcible removal of the Dissenters made by a body calling itself 'The Colonial Church Union', occasioned another address from the Deputies asking for protection, but raising neither slavery nor political questions. They appointed a sub-committee to ascertain the actual state of the law in Jamaica, and consulted the former

[1] 27 April and 8 May 1832. [2] 12 June 1832. [3] 26 July 1832.

428

Advocate-General of Jamaica on the subject.[1] Gooderich replied that the Government's policy of protecting the missionaries was unchanged; and a Royal Proclamation was issued, declaring that toleration must be upheld, and warning the Colonial Church accordingly.[2]

By this time feeling was running high among the Deputies, and a General Meeting was summoned by special requisition, at which it was resolved to petition both Houses of Parliament in extremely strong language in favour of the immediate emancipation of slaves. The particular concern of the Deputies was with religious freedom, but this was irreconcilable with slavery—the extinction of the one was necessary for the existence of the other.

A separate and longer memorial to Earl Grey gave details of the outrages on which their case rested, and explained that, though the evils of the last revolt had in fact been mitigated by the Dissenting missionaries, the planters even denied the negroes rest on Sunday for religious teaching.[3]

The delay in restoring the wrecked chapels caused the business-like Deputies to enquire if the Baptists needed their help in pressing claims, but this was thought for the present unnecessary.[4]

Three years later the Deputies called attention to a renewed offence against religious liberty: the Rev. Henry Taylor, a Baptist missionary, was presented in a secular court for exercising church discipline in a sphere where secular and spiritual interests met. He had dismissed from church membership a negro apprentice who had taken on himself the office of constable, and had been employed to flog other negroes.[5] A reply from Downing Street said that a report had been demanded, and that instructions against the invasion of religious liberties had been given. In the following autumn the Deputies rejoiced to learn that a Society for the Protection of Religious Liberty had been founded in Spanish Town.[6]

But even the coming of emancipation did not mean the end of trouble; in 1851 the Deputies were again concerned about religious

---

[1] 30 Nov. 1832; 22 Feb. 1833.   [2] 27 Mar. 1833.   [3] 25 April and 2 May 1833.
[4] 26 June and 31 July 1833.   [5] 27 July 1836 and Report for 1836.
[6] 27 Oct. 1837.

conditions in Jamaica. For instance, a Cholera Orphans' Asylum had been established in which no proper provision was made for the religious liberty of the inmates.[1] So efficient were the Dissenters and their correspondents that their protests against the Bill reached Earl Grey before the Bill itself.[2] This protest did not succeed; Grey's view was that, though it might be well to amend the Bill if the Jamaica legislature consented, he did not see sufficient cause to prevent its confirmation.[3]

The Deputies took a similar interest in similar dangers to religious liberty elsewhere in the West Indies. In 1824 they petitioned Parliament against attempts to invade religious liberty in Demerara.[4] In 1841 they urged on Lord John Russell that local legislation in the Bahamas which infringed religious liberty there should be disallowed, pending enquiries: it excluded the agents of the Baptist Society from the influence which they had before possessed over public opinion, in favour of the clergy of the Established Church.[5]

---

[1] 30 June 1851.   [2] 25 July 1851.   [3] 5 Dec. 1851.
[4] 28 May 1824.   [5] 21 May 1841.

CHAPTER 3

INDIA

AT THE END of the 18th century the Churches were shewing a new enthusiasm for foreign missions. When the East India Company's privileged position was being reviewed in 1793 religious as well as economic considerations had now a place in the minds of some Englishmen. The Company's exclusive trade was again extended, though with modifications, Wilberforce failing to secure the insertion of a clause for the encouragement of schools and missions. But in 1793 Carey went to Calcutta, and when twenty years later the East India Company's status was again under discussion, vigorous missionary work was going on, in the face of many difficulties, of which not the least was their uncertain legal position. In April 1812, therefore, the Deputies' Committee considered whether in view of the opportunity afforded by the renewal of the Company's charter steps ought not to be taken to get legal security for Dissenting missionaries.[1] Apprehending that 'their exertions are not necessarily confined to this country' but may be extended to all British dependencies, the Deputies hoped to obtain security for 'every description of Christians engaged in the promulgation of our holy religion'.[2] A General Meeting authorized a memorial to His Majesty's Ministers asking for 'sufficient opportunity' for 'those benevolent persons who shall be desirous of going to India for the purpose of communicating to its population the benefits of Christian light and moral improvements'.[3]

The memorial was supported by an appeal to public opinion; the Deputies printed and circulated the Rev. Robert Hall's 'Address to the Public on the Renewal of the East India Company's Charter'. Petitions to both Houses were presented in April 1813 by Lord

[1] 24 April 1812.　　　[2] 1 May 1812.　　　[3] 7 May 1812.

431

Holland and William Smith. These petitions expressed with care the Deputies' desire to spread Christianity without using the civil power to promote it:

> Your petitioners venture to suggest it as their opinion that to represent a system of idolatry and superstition as equally tending to produce moral virtue and human happiness is no less contrary to the dictates of sound reason and philosophy than irreconcileable with the first principles on which our faith is built.

> That entertaining a directly opposite sentiment your petitioners are anxiously desirous that the light and blessings of Christianity should be gradually diffused over the immense empire of Great Britain in the east, which instead of being thereby endangered would, as they believe on the ground of fact and experience derive additional strength and stability from the spread of the Christian religion.

> That your petitioners are fully aware of the mass of ignorance and prejudice to be encountered, and that the progress of knowledge must be proportionately slow, but while the means of persuasion only are employed (and all others they utterly deprecate) they are at a loss to discover from whence any such apprehension of danger can arise as should induce any wise and good government to discountenance the attempt.

> That they desire not to embarrass the civil authority by any request for assistance but merely beg to express their prayer that in the arrangement for the new charter to be granted to the East India Company the wisdom of Parliament will be pleased to provide that such benevolent persons of the various professions of Christians as may be disposed to devote themselves to the promulgation of our holy religion in India may under certain regulations be permitted to enter that country and to remain there unmolested while they conduct themselves as orderly and peaceable subjects.

> Petition approved by General Meeting, April 12 1813.

Opinion had changed since 1793, and on 4 August 1813 the Deputies recorded their satisfaction at the passing of an Act which afforded 'sufficient facilities for the introduction of the Christian religion among our fellow subjects in India'; among those specially thanked were Liverpool, Castlereagh, and Wilberforce. Three weeks later the Deputies gave £100 to Zachary Macaulay, Treasurer of the General Committee in London for promoting the

Introduction of Christianity into India, towards the disbursements incurred in the agitation.[1]

The Deputies concerned themselves in several Indian problems in the course of the century. Their object was always to secure religious liberty and, as far as possible, religious equality; sometimes as between Christians and others, sometimes as between Christian and Christian.

The hardships which fell on converts to Christianity naturally interested them. In 1848 they considered the possibility of altering the law by which a Hindoo or a Mohammedan lost his property and status on becoming a Christian.[2] They prepared a Bill to remedy this. The East India Company professed sympathy but declared that they could not accept the scheme.[3] The Deputies hoped nevertheless to get their Bill introduced into the House of Lords. They had hopes of the Duke of Argyll, but he declined, asserting that the Bill would have little hope of success unless an older member of the House would sponsor it. The Deputies could not find a Peer who thought that his legal and practical knowledge would justify him in taking up the case.[4]

The Indian Mutiny gave to the Deputies an opportunity of reading some favourite lessons to the Government and to the East India Company. The principles which the Deputies had commended to the attention of the civil government had been flouted: what but disaster could be expected?

A petition to both Houses from the Deputies contains some vigorous and enlightened criticisms. The Deputies regretted that from time to time they heard of 'obstructions which had been raised by the traditional policy of the East India Company to the progress of Christianity amongst the nations under their control'. Any relaxation of this anti-Christian policy was to be attributed to the Imperial legislature and to conscientious parties in Great Britain and India: the Company's own policy was still uneradicated. It was not surprising that a Company originating in and carried on for commercial purposes should have had its attention too much fixed on gain and too little on the highest interest of the native races. The Mutiny, the petition optimistically asserted, would have

---

[1] 27 Aug. 1813.   [2] 8 May 1848.   [3] 12 June 1848.   [4] 28 Feb. 1849.

been prevented if Christian converts had not been dismissed from the ranks: the designs of the conspirators would have been known before they reached maturity.

The Deputies urged that the Government should take a completely neutral attitude in religion. All natives ought to have access to the sacred and civilizing truths of Christianity. All support and patronage ought to be withdrawn from their present false religions. 'All state interference with religion in India, whether by pecuniary grants or civil patronage, even in favour of Christianity' is inconsistent with the principles and prosperity of the Kingdom of God. To tax the heathen population for the support of any Christian Church Establishment was repugnant to common justice as well as to Christianity and was 'calculated effectually to retard the success of Christian missions'. The introduction of an Anglo-Episcopal Establishment had led to marriage and burial disputes which needed checking by the Imperial Parliament and the Governor-General in Council. The petition asked for such modification of the laws of India as would give 'free scope without state support to the labours of all Christians'.[1]

Twenty years later the Deputies took up the same argument. They had heard 'with great satisfaction' that the Cingalese had petitioned for the removal of the ecclesiastical endowments from the general revenues of the island. The charges amounted to Rs 140,000 a year: only 15,000 persons in a population of 2,405,287 benefited from them. All State grants in aid of religion are wrong in principle: circumstances make this injustice particularly great.[2] A resolution in support of the Cingalese petition was lost in the Commons by 26 votes.[3] One of the questions asked of candidates for Parliament in the 1880 General Election reflected these controversies. Candidates were asked if they favoured discontinuing annual grants for religion in India and Ceylon out of taxes paid by the heathen and of abolishing ecclesiastical grants in colonies.[4]

[1] 11 Dec. 1857.   [2] 8 Mar. 1877.   [3] 4 May 1877.   [4] 2 Jan. 1880.

CHAPTER 4

TAHITI

THE DEPUTIES touched at one point the tangled story of Tahiti, from which neither the French nor British Governments emerged with credit. The London Missionary Society had worked in Tahiti with dauntless heroism and considerable success since its pioneer vessel, the *Duff*, sailed thither in August 1796 under the mission flag, 'three white doves with olive branches on a purple field'.[1] Charles Darwin's well-known words in commendation of their labours after forty years were written after his visit in the *Beagle* in 1835.[2] Almost exactly at the time when Darwin visited Tahiti the Roman Catholic mission began its dubious work there. In 1836 two priests were expelled by the native Queen and her Council, who wished for no other religious teachers than those already in Tahiti. France took up the incident as an outrage on her citizens. In August 1838 a French frigate, the *Venus*, forced the Queen to apologize, to pay, and to procure protection for Frenchmen who wished to live in Tahiti. The Queen appealed to England, and a new law prohibited the teaching of new religious doctrine. The French Government again intervened and backed its demands in favour of Roman Catholic worship by a frigate; the resistance encouraged by an English missionary, Cunsul Pritchard, failed after a tussle; in 1842 the French declared a Protectorate, which nominally respected the authority of the Queen; but annexation followed, and Pritchard was expelled in 1844.

Feeling ran high in England: national feeling against France; Protestant feeling against Roman Catholic aggression; sympathy for a small power struggling to defend its independence; cynical wonder why Roman Catholic fervour should be turned to an island where Protestant missionaries had been at work for forty

[1] C. S. Hoare, *Story of the L.M.S.*, pp. 23 ff.   [2] *Ibid.* p. 55.

435

years rather than to one of the many where unbroken heathenism prevailed. The future of the work of the L.M.S. was threatened in the very island where it had won its earliest heroic triumphs. Subsequent events more than justified these fears.

By February 1844 the events in Tahiti had excited the 'astonishment and indignation' of the Deputies. They offered to assist the L.M.S. in redressing the 'infringement of the religious liberties of their fellow-Christians in that island'.[1] In August a special sub-committee held four meetings in five days.[2] A petition prepared for a special General Meeting stated that the Deputies

consider the conduct of the French naval commanders in forcing the reception of Roman Catholic Missionaries upon the Queen and Government of Tahiti by the threat of hostile proceedings as an unjust interference with the Government of those Islands and with the peaceful and exemplary labours of the British missionaries to which the islanders of the Pacific are indebted for their Christian civilization, literature, laws, and social institutions.

They called for reparation from the French Government and the restoration of Queen Pomare to independent and royal rank. Nothing had justified the withdrawal of the friendly protection promised to her by Britain in 1827; nor had the missionaries deserved this. It was 'a dishonourable sacrifice of British interests, commercial and religious, a breach of faith towards the Queen and people of Tahiti' and the result was the destruction of thirty years of missionary work.

The Deputies, like many of their successors, combined vast moral indignation with a pathetic belief in the possibility of achieving a result without paying a price; they ended their petition on another note:

But the Deputation feel it to be their duty to deprecate the practice of war and believe that their wishes may be accomplished by well-directed Public Opinion and by pacific remonstrances urged with the energy of justice and truth.[3]

These resolutions, laid before Peel and Aberdeen, received 'courteous answers'.[4] English antagonism led the French Government

[1] 21 Feb. 1844.
[2] 10, 12, 14, 15 Aug. 1844.
[3] 20 Aug. 1844.
[4] Report for 1844.

to disavow the extreme measures of its admiral, and it was not till 1880 that Tahiti was formally proclaimed a French colony. The London Missionary Society was, nevertheless, driven by French influence from the scene of its earliest missionary labours; its work was continued by the French Protestants of the Paris Missionary Society.

CHAPTER 5

AUSTRALIA

THE DEPUTIES kept a watchful eye on legislation which might tend to reproduce or perpetuate in the colonies the religious inequality of which they complained in England. Their point of view is well set out in the Annual Report for 1847. That Report reminds the Deputies of their duty to their fellow-countrymen scattered throughout the Empire. 'Wherever they go the evils of a State-endowed Church follow them.' Any trouble which the Deputies take in order to secure the benefits of religious equality for the colonists will not be lost. 'Religious freedom may find a clearer theatre in distant parts' and legislation at home in due time may be favourably influenced by colonial experience. This far-seeing prediction has of course been justified. Anglicans who had breathed the freer ecclesiastical air of the colonies realised that Anglicanism in England had at least as much to gain as to lose by the loosening of the connexion with the State.

In 1849 an Australian Colonies Bill caused them great anxiety. Certain definite appropriations of colonial revenues for public worship were to be made (except in South Australia)[1] and the colonial legislatures were not to have power to diminish or refuse these appropriations without the consent of the home Government. The Bill was withdrawn for the session, but the Deputies sent full information for the use of Dissenting ministers in Australia, seeking their guidance and offering advice for future action.[2]

In 1854, when the Constitution of Victoria was discussed, the Deputies tried to prevent an allocation of £50,000 a year for ecclesiastical purposes.[3] A deputation saw Sir George Grey, and

---

[1] The Deputies believed that in South Australia there were only 5 Anglican churches as against 27 Dissenting places of worship (not counting Roman Catholics). Report for 1847.
[2] 20 July and 3 Aug. 1849.   [3] 18 Oct. and 17 Nov. 1854.

pointed out that under earlier legislation only £6,000 a year was to be raised in Victoria for the purpose; that according to a letter from the Rev. Richard Fletcher the proposal to allot £50,000 had occasioned protests, and had only been passed by the votes of the nominated members of the Assembly. Such a matter could have been settled by the free Assembly about to be chosen by the colonists themselves. The new Acts would perpetuate disputes arising from ecclesiastical endowments; and as the Baptists and Independents had refused and would refuse such State help, the scheme became unfair. From Sir George Grey the deputation learnt that Imperial legislation would be needed to authorize the Colonial Bill and that there would be an opportunity for full discussion in Parliament.[1]

Later Lord John Russell consented to see a Deputation on the same matter, but he declined to omit the clause authorizing the £50,000 appropriation.[2]

A Colonial Church Regulation Bill, though it was withdrawn,[3] illustrated the Deputies' attitude to the Anglican Church in the Colonies. The object of the Bill was to give to Episcopalians the same liberty of action as that enjoyed by other denominations. But if the same liberty, why extra privilege? The Deputies suggested that the Bill ought to provide that no bishop or clergyman should ex officio receive a title or authority in a colonial executive or legislature.

[1] 19 Jan. 1855. [2] 19 June 1855. [3] 5 Aug. 1853.

CHAPTER 6

SCOTLAND, WALES, AND IRELAND

Scotland

Scotland occupied comparatively little of the Deputies' attention. They received practically no appeals for advice or help from congregations there. Their principles made them disapprove of the maintenance of an Established Church in Scotland as elsewhere, but the Scottish Establishment differed from that in England, Wales, and Ireland in three important respects. First, it represented until 1843 the overwhelming majority of Scottish Christians, and even after 1843 it was in religious communion with most of the Dissenters. Second, it had never submitted to any great extent to State control. It had maintained the dignity and independence of the spiritual power in a manner almost unique among Established Churches. It had not therefore caused that sacrifice of religion to politics which the Deputies always considered the worst evil of Establishment. Third, the Deputies could not forget (even if the Church of Scotland sometimes could forget) that the Church of Scotland was closely linked in doctrine and tradition with themselves. They did not permit this association to make them play fast and loose with their principles, but it prevented the acerbity that existed in England. The Church of Scotland did not pretend to the same monopoly of churchmanship as the Church of England. It claimed political and social superiority; but it did not deny the religious status of most of the other Churches in Scotland.

Scottish affairs appear in the Deputies' Minutes therefore mainly when some claim of the Established Church had to be resisted or some chance of advancing the cause of religious equality offered itself.

In 1835 the Deputies petitioned both Houses against grants for church endowments in Scotland from the Consolidated Fund, setting out the injustice of such grants to Scottish Dissenters who provided their own churches and alleging that many members of the Established Church considered the measure needless and improper. The abolition of Church Rates in Ireland and the hopes for the abolition of them in England make the present promotion of Establishment in Scotland peculiarly alarming.[1]

In 1838 the Deputies co-operated with a deputation of Scottish Dissenters in agitation in London against more grants. A public meeting at the London Tavern, lectures in London meeting-houses by the Scots and petitions again presented to both Houses were part of the campaign. It was during this time that the Deputies' notice fell on Dr Chalmers's lectures in favour of Church Establishment, and that they arranged for Dr Wardlaw to answer him.[2]

The failure to transcribe the Report for 1843 into the Minutes leaves us in doubt whether the Deputies commented on the Disruption of the Church in that year.

Though the Deputies' attitude to the Church of Scotland is best described in connexion with their general campaign for Disestablishment, one or two special matters may be described here.

In April 1845 Sir David Brewster,[3] representing the Free Church of Scotland, and the Rev. James Taylor, representing the Secession Church, met the Deputies' Committee and secured their co-operation in an endeavour to repeal the Scottish University Test Act.[4] Office holders in Scottish Universities might be required to subscribe to the confession of faith of the Church of Scotland, to promise to practise and conform to its worship, and to submit themselves to its discipline. The Deputies petitioned for the relief of the Scottish Universities and the opening of the Professorships of Literature and Science.[5]

The story is best told in the words of the Report for 1845. It illustrates the Deputies' indefatigable pursuit of Sir James Graham.

The Scotch Deputation had previously issued a circular which startled this country by its concessions on the part of the Scotch to the

---

[1] 9 June 1835.   [2] Report for 1838. See p. 389.
[3] Sir David Brewster was Principal of the University of St Andrews. There was an attempt to remove him from office as a Dissenter.   [4] 28 April 1845.   [5] 5 May 1845.

Church of England, and the injustice to all other Denominations of Dissenters of which till then we had no idea.

After Mr Rutherford's speech on introducing his Bill, so powerful and convincing were his facts and arguments, that it was confidently expected that the Government would yield to the manifest justice of the claims of our Scottish brethren, especially as their appeal was in strict accordance with the principles on which ministers professed to act in reference to the Irish Colleges. At the last moment however Sir J. Graham,—as if to contradict the sincerity of those professions, for which the Government had claimed public support on Irish questions, —sacrificed consistency and the rights of conscience to the fear of giving the slightest encouragement to Free church principles, and of opening the door of the English Universities to all classes of the people.

The result was a melancholy exhibition of the sacrifice of the highest interests of education and science to the arrogant assumptions of a dominant hierarchy; and religious tests, always abandoned when operating against members of the Church of England, were for unworthy purposes rigidly maintained to the disgrace of an enlightened age and the serious injury of science and truth.[1]

In 1872 the Deputies declined to join a deputation from the London Nonconformist Conference to interview the Lord Advocate of Scotland on the Scottish Education Bill.[2]

In 1874 the Deputies petitioned in favour of a Bill for the abolition of Church Rates in Scotland and against a Church Patronage Bill.[3]

In 1905 a joint meeting of the Deputies and the Ministers expressed its sympathy with the United Free Church of Scotland in its 'bitter trials' and assured it of sympathy, help and prayers.[4]

Wales

Wales appears often in the Deputies' records. Most of the references concern interventions to secure elementary justice for some oppressed congregation or individual. These interventions, not being essentially different from interventions in the English counties, have been illustrated in the treatment of burial cases, trustees, brawling and the like.

The campaign for the Disestablishment of the Anglican Church

[1] Report for 1845; cf. Macaulay's speech in the House of Commons, 9 July 1845.
[2] 7 Mar. 1872.   [3] 3 July 1874.   [4] 18 Jan. 1905.

in Wales has been mentioned also. After the ending of Establishment in Ireland the Deputies' agitation tended to centre on Wales. The privileged position of the Church of the minority[1] was in parts of Wales an abuse hardly less flagrant than in Ireland. Moreover it lacked the political defence which could at one time be advanced, however mistakenly, for the Irish Establishment.

The efforts of the Deputies to secure Welsh Disestablishment down to 1906 have been traced. With the Liberal victory in that year the agitation was renewed. More urgent controversies prevented Welsh Disestablishment from securing immediate attention; and some of these nearly concerned the Deputies. In 1909, however, Mr Asquith introduced a Disestablishment and Disendowment Bill. It was withdrawn after the second reading, because the Budget controversy dominated the situation. The Deputies regretted that circumstances had made the progress of the Bill impossible that session and declared that Disestablishment in Wales was urgently demanded.

After the second 1910 Election the Deputies, in congratulating the Government urged it to proceed with Welsh Disestablishment. They gave help in the subsequent campaign which ended in the passing of the Bill in 1915. The war delayed the enforcement of the Act. Long experience had made the Deputies wary even in dealing with their political allies, and when peace came, they immediately resolved to watch closely the action of the Government touching Welsh Disestablishment. In the following year the Liberation Society drew the Deputies' attention to the financial arrangements proposed; and a protest was ordered.

Ireland

Ireland appears more often than Scotland in the Deputies' Minutes. Irish Presbyterianism interested the Deputies both because of its wilful errors and because of its unmerited woes. On the one side, unlike orthodox English Dissent, it maintained a small but reprehensible connexion with the State. On the other side, like orthodox English Dissent, it was the victim of Unitarian influence in high political circles.[2]

[1] E.g. Deputies' resolutions of 17 Feb. 1891 and 25 Feb. 1892.   [2] See p. 92.

The Deputies' concern about Ireland was, however, most often a part of their general concern about Roman Catholicism. Their attitude to Roman Catholicism was the same in Ireland as in England. They supported whole-heartedly Roman Catholic Emancipation because they believed in civil and religious liberty for all. They supported the Disestablishment and Disendowment of Anglicanism in Ireland for the same reason. They even opposed all proposals that the endowments should be shared between the Churches. They petitioned against the *regium donum*, the old State contribution to the Churches in Ireland with which they had the closest kinship. Nevertheless, though active in pressing for justice to be done to the Irish Roman Catholics, the Deputies feared that the Roman Church would never be content with justice. They feared that, as the largest Church in Ireland, it would make dangerous and unjust attempts to secure a privileged position for itself. How well-grounded were their fears later events have proved and illustrated *ad nauseam*.

Already in 1843 an alarm had been sounded. The Deputies had been asked by the Evangelical Voluntary Church Association to assist opposition 'to the proposed establishment of the Roman Catholic religion in Ireland'. The Deputies agreed to co-operate.[1] In 1845 the storm burst round Maynooth College.

Maynooth College was indeed an odd institution. It was founded in 1795, long before Roman Catholic Emancipation, by a Protestant Government, for the training of Roman Catholic ordinands. Until that year, the endowment of any college for that purpose being illegal, many Irishmen had had their training for the priesthood on the continent, especially in France. The war with revolutionary France altered all that. Maynooth came into being to meet the difficulty. English statesmen have never over-valued political consistency, and to have the Irish Roman clergy educated no longer among our enemies 'promised well', it might be supposed, 'for the future loyalty of the priesthood'.[2] The grants first made by the Irish Parliament in time of war were continued after the Union by the United Parliament. But the support of Roman Catholicism by public funds invited criticism, and did not

[1] 25 Oct. 1843. [2] Erskine May, *Constitutional History*, vol. III, p. 271.

invite it in vain. By the middle of the century the College badly needed renovation and improvement. Peel proposed in 1845 to grant £30,000 for the fabric, to increase the annual endowment from £9000 to £26,360, and to allow the trustees to hold lands to the value of £3000 a year. In order to avoid the annual fight for the grant, it was to be charged on the Consolidated Fund. Peel's Government had already shewn in Scotland and in England a capacity for provoking religious strife which amounted to genius; but in Ireland the trouble was ready-made.

Mr Gladstone explained his resignation from office by a reference to the Government's plans for Maynooth. The Deputies at once sent a memorial to Peel. In vigorous language they re-stated their sympathy with the Irish Roman Catholics in being made to contribute to an Anglican hierarchy and Establishment, They 'cordially' detested 'the bigotry and selfishness which have sought to perpetuate the social degradation of the Irish Catholics as such'. But the same principle which made them oppose the Anglican Establishment in Ireland made them oppose 'all appropriation of Public Money raised by compulsory payments to the support of any ecclesiastical institutions whatsoever'. They had therefore always disapproved of the Maynooth grant. The augmentation of the grant and 'the avowed intention of Her Majesty's Ministers to place the College among the Government Establishments superintended by the Board of Works' would place the Roman priesthood in direct connexion with the State. The Roman Catholic grievances cannot be mitigated by aggrieving the consciences of those who already pay for propagating what they deem heretical or erroneous.[1] The memorial was sent to the press and the Deputies resolved to organize a public meeting of Dissenters, to arrange for petitions to both Houses on their own account and from the congregations represented as well as to co-operate with other Dissenters in opposition.[2] They pressed a request to Peel that he would postpone the second reading in order to allow the country time to express its opinion.[3]

The resolutions adopted at a General Meeting of the Deputies

---

[1] 26 Feb. and 5 Mar. 1845.   [2] 19 and 26 Mar., 4 April 1845.
[3] 4 and 8 April 1845.

expressed the same sympathy with the Roman Catholics as had been contained in the memorial and the same condemnation of State subsidy as a remedy. Some new points were made. It had been publicly asserted that until now Dissenters had not opposed the Maynooth grants or the payments made in Ireland and the colonies to Roman priests for services as chaplains in prisons and workhouses. This was merely untrue. The Deputies had 'embraced every suitable occasion of expressing their entire disapprobation'. Moreover they now reiterated their protest against the *regium donum*[1] in Ireland and in England. Should the Commons adopt a Bill 'so repugnant to the feelings of the nation', the Deputies would present a memorial to the Queen asking her to dissolve Parliament to give the nation 'an opportunity of expressing their sentiments on the new and dangerous line of policy'.[2]

A General Committee to oppose the Bill was sitting at Exeter Hall. 'Exeter Hall sets up its bray', said Macaulay in the House of Commons on 14 April 1845. When the Deputies learnt that this Committee had summoned delegates from the country for a meeting on 30 April, they decided to hold the public meeting for Dissenters whilst the country delegates were in town.[3] This 'aggregate meeting' was to be on 1 May. On second thoughts they decided that it would also be 'expedient' to invite the country Dissenting delegates to a public breakfast at the London Tavern at 7 o'clock on the morning afterwards.[4] In order not to clash with the activities of the Exeter Hall conference the aggregate meeting was shifted a day and held after the breakfast on the evening of 2 May at Finsbury Chapel, Moorfields;[5] 750 cards of invitation for the breakfast, free to Deputies and country delegates, were prepared. The greatest pains were taken to ensure full publicity in the press, and it was during this agitation that 'in order to promote the legitimate influence of this Deputation' the press was admitted to General Meetings.[6]

The Deputies had much in mind the need for defeating Peel at the next Election;[7] and the breakfast seems to have been intended mainly to prepare and consolidate Dissenting opinion in the

[1] See p. 387.   [2] 9 April 1845.   [3] 18 April 1845.   [4] 22 April 1845.
[5] 24 April 1845.   [6] 19 Mar. 1845.   [7] See pp. 89 ff., for fuller account.

country for this purpose. The only resolution put at the breakfast declared it the imperative duty of Dissenters so to use the franchise at the next Election as to promote religious equality and freedom from State patronage and interest in ecclesiastical matters.[1] The breakfast cost the Deputies £13 5s. 6d.[2]

In the evening at Finsbury Chapel the 'aggregate meeting' expressed the particular reasons for Dissenting opposition to the Maynooth grant in unanimous resolutions similar in tone to those which the Deputies had already passed.[3] The final resolution noted that the support given from both sides of the House to a 'measure equally hostile to the interests of civil liberty and repugnant to the rights of conscience' demonstrated that the House did not faithfully represent public opinion.

With the object of proving their sincerity and undercutting the criticism that Dissenters themselves received State funds in the *regium donum* the Deputies prepared to petition Parliament to abolish this grant and set up enquiries to ensure that the pensioners should not suffer by its cessation.[4]

In response to a request from an Anti-Maynooth Committee at Salters' Hall the Deputies promised to recommend all their congregations to send representatives to a convention of Evangelical Protestant Dissenters to be held on 20 May.[5]

The Commons passed the Bill. The Deputies therefore petitioned the Lords and agreed to prepare the memorial to the Queen which they had already mentioned.[6] The memorial was drawn up not as from the Deputies in particular but from the London Dissenters who were their constituency. It was circulated to all ministers and congregations and received 20,500 signatures.[7] Copies also went to the Wesleyans and to the central Anti-Maynooth Committee.[8]

The memorial began by expressing the Dissenters' loyalty and their 'admiration of Your Majesty's personal and domestic virtues which afford a bright example to the whole nation and also of Your Majesty's undeviating adherence to constitutional principles in the exercise of the Royal Prerogative'. Then followed a grateful

---

[1] 2 May 1845.   [2] 30 July 1845.   [3] On 9 April 1845. See above.
[4] 9 May 1845; see p. 387, for fuller account.   [5] 9 May 1845.
[6] 28 May 1845.   [7] 16 June 1845.   [8] 30 May 1845.

reference to the protection of Dissenting worship and the removal of many of the civil disabilities of Dissenters 'under the benign government of successive monarchs of the House of Brunswick'. The Dissenters' objection to any State endowment of any form of Christianity made them oppose the Maynooth Bill; but they also believed that a large majority of the people opposed it. It had taken them by surprise; 1,120,000 had signed the petitions to the Commons against the Bill. The Queen was asked to dissolve Parliament so as to give an opportunity for the deliberate judgment of her subjects.[1] The memorial was drawn with skill in such a manner as to appeal to the Queen personally. The Deputies formally approved it,[2] and the Marquis of Breadalbane was asked to present it.[3] He declined.[4] The Committee ordered therefore that it be taken to him, and he be asked to treat it in the same way as similar memorials were treated. If he would not present it, Sir James Graham should be approached.[5] In the event it was reported that Lord Breadalbane had presented it 'through the medium of the Secretary of State' on June 19th.[6] The petition had no result and Maynooth got the money.

In reviewing the whole incident the Deputies commented on the unusual combination of political parties which had secured the success of the Bill.

The measure obtained the support, under various pretexts, of individuals who had been considered the enlightened advocates of religious liberty; but who need to be more fully instructed on that subject by their constituents whenever the opportunity occurs.

Perhaps without very good reason the Deputies claimed that the opposition had 'produced a powerful impression on one at least of the most eloquent advocates for endowing the Roman Catholic church in Ireland'. This was of course Macaulay, whose speech in favour of the Bill is still in its brittle eloquence a delight to read. Macaulay the Deputies quoted as saying to his constituents at Edinburgh:

I do not think that if we had formed a Government we should have entertained the question of paying the Roman Catholic priests of

[1] 30 May 1845. [2] 4 June 1845. [3] 10 June 1845.
[4] 17 June 1845. [5] 18 June 1845. [6] 5 July 1845.

Ireland, as I should have thought it positive insanity to stir the matter.[1]

Much of the agitation no doubt deserved the very hard things which have since been said about it; but, whatever may be said of other people, the Deputies were not moved by sudden passion or spiteful fear. They were acting in accordance with the principles which they had long proclaimed. If they were energetic in their opposition to Maynooth they were not less energetic in support of every movement to give Irish Roman Catholics equal rights with Irish Protestants. Their words were consistent, and their action was as good as their words.

In the same summer the Deputies petitioned against two clauses of the Irish Colleges Bill. This Bill was to make possible the State endowment of new colleges in Ireland. The Governing Bodies were to have power to assign lecture rooms for approved religious teachers and to make regulations for securing the due attendance of students at churches or chapels approved by their parents. All connexion of religion with the State or national institutions is to be deplored. This was as objectionable as the establishment of Roman Catholic Professorships. The supplementing of parental authority by rules for compulsory worship is imprudent and

will inevitably disgust the minds of youth with the solemn observances of religion; a consequence which has uniformly followed whenever the experiment has been tried, and religion has been associated with irksome forms and compulsory regulations.

The power given to endow religious teaching in the colleges was opposed as contrary to the principles of the Statutes of Mortmain and superstitious uses.[2]

The Bill became law, although, as the Deputies tartly commented, the Irish nation did not express any gratitude on the occasion.[3]

In 1852 the Deputies petitioned both Houses in favour of a repeal of the Act of 1845 which had permanently endowed Maynooth College.[4]

In 1856 they declared that all Government subsidies of religion

[1] Report for 1845.   [2] 5 July 1845.
[3] Report for 1845.   [4] 9 Mar. and 16 April 1852.

in Ireland must end. Only so could the Commons extricate themselves from the absurd situation into which they had got by accepting a motion for the withdrawal of the Maynooth grant and by rejecting one for putting an end to the *regium donum*.[1]

General opinion slowly moved nearer to the Deputies' opinion. In the sixties the Disestablishment of the Anglican Church became a question of practical politics. Of course the Deputies welcomed it; but they were fearful lest instead of complete Disendowment there should be some sharing of the endowments with the Roman Catholic and Presbyterian Churches. The Deputies wanted the State to leave all the Churches alone, not to attempt to shower its favours more equitably. How far historical scholarship supported their opinion that endowments were in effect State subsidies it is not our business to enquire. That supposition lay behind much of their thinking.

In 1867 the Deputies petitioned against a Bill about Roman Catholic churches, schools, and glebes in Ireland. Though they desired (and were fighting for) more facilities to enable all denominations to secure sites for Church work, they opposed the loan of public money and the extensive repeal of Mortmain laws in this Bill. The Bill failed.[2]

A general resolution of this year opened the new campaign. It condemned three things: all State Establishment of religion, as opposed to New Testament teaching; the peculiar injustice of establishing the religion of the minority in Ireland; the proposal to buy off opposition by offering a share of the revenues of the Establishment to other Churches.[3] A petition to this effect followed,[4] and a sub-committee which represented the Liberation Society was set up to give effective expression to this view. Mr Gladstone's own speeches in the Commons made it unnecessary to send any deputation to him,[5] but the sub-committee advertised an appeal for support for him.[6] The Deputies promised their support at the General Election to candidates who supported Disestablishment and the Disendowment of all Churches in Ireland.[7]

The Election satisfied them, as did the 'wise, liberal and compre-

[1] 21 April 1856.   [2] 12 June 1867.   [3] 31 July 1867.   [4] 26 Feb. 1868.
[5] 19 Mar. 1868.   [6] 31 Mar. 1868.   [7] 29 July 1868.

hensive' measure introduced by Gladstone in the new Parliament.[1] When the Lords by amendments reduced the Disendowment proposals to a shadow and tried to establish concurrent endowment of other Churches, the Deputies joined in the outcry by resolutions on their own account[2] and by helping in a meeting of protest at Cannon Street Hotel. At this Gladstone's policy was supported by representatives of almost all the Dissenting Bodies, including the Quakers, Wesleyans, United Presbyterians, and Unitarians.[3] For his defeat of the Lords as for his success in the General Election Gladstone owed much to the enthusiastic support of Dissent. The Bill ended the *regium donum* and the Maynooth grant on terms of compensation similar to those accorded to Anglican clergy and trustees.[4] The Deputies opposed proposals to lend public money for the purchase of glebes and parsonages in Ireland.[5]

After the Disestablishment of Anglicanism the danger to religious liberty in Ireland came from the claims of Roman Catholics to a specially privileged position. These claims mainly concerned university education.

Rumours that the Government were about to endow a Roman Catholic College or University caused the Deputies to send a memorial to Gladstone. The proper course was to abolish all religious inequalities in Trinity College, Dublin. Gladstone reassured the Deputies,[6] and later they approved Henry Fawcett's Bill for reforming Trinity College.[7]

This problem remained. More facilities for university education were demanded; and the Deputies sympathized with the demand. The difficulty was that the overwhelming strength of the Roman Catholic Church made it difficult to ensure that new institutions would not be in practice sectarian. When Conservative and Unionist Ministers were in office the Deputies seem to have been particularly nervous. The policy of Conservatives in English elementary education shewed that they had no dislike of denominational education as such. In 1879 the Deputies reasserted their hostility to the establishment by the State of any Roman Catholic

---

[1] 4 Mar. 1869.   [2] 28 June 1869.   [3] 2 July 1869.
[4] The Bill is conveniently summarized in F. W. Cornish, *The English Church in the Nineteenth Century*, vol. II, p. 310.
[5] 21 July 1870.   [6] 18 Jan. 1872.   [7] 22 Feb. 1872.

or other denominational College; having assisted in getting religious equality in Ireland they will oppose any retrograde policy.[1] For this reason they opposed a Bill introduced by The O'Conor Don: under cover of promoting secular education it would endow denominationalism.[2] The division of opinion about the Bill among Liberal M.P.s led the Committee to organize its opposition by personally approaching individual M.P.s rather than by public meetings.[3] Among the questions to be put to all Parliamentary candidates at the General Election was one about endowing sectarian education in Ireland.[4]

Ten years later, in 1889, the Deputies took alarm at the Government's intention to 'satisfy all the legitimate aspirations of the Roman Catholics' of Ireland in regard to higher education. They feared that this was a euphemism for sectarianism. They would resist any measures which were opposed in principle to the legislation which removed ecclesiastical tests from Oxford, Cambridge, and Trinity College, Dublin.[5] A decade later, when the Conservatives were again in office, the Deputies deplored the Government's education policy, mentioning its willingness to create and endow an Irish University which would be more or less under the control of Roman hierarchy.[6] Earlier in the same year they passed a resolution in favour of establishing a national and undenominational university in Ireland.[7]

---

[1] 25 Feb. 1879.   [2] 20 May 1879.   [3] 17 June 1879.   [4] 2 Jan. 1880.
[5] 10 Oct. 1889.   [6] 27 April 1898.   [7] 16 Feb. 1898.

CHAPTER 7

THE RIGHT OF APPROACH
TO THE THRONE

NO PRIVILEGE of the Deputies has been more highly valued or more often challenged than their traditional privilege of presenting Addresses to the Throne. At times the monarch received representatives personally; on other occasions they were submitted through the Home Secretary, with the traditional answer that the sovereign had been pleased to receive them 'in the most gracious manner'. The occasions that called for an Address were very different: great national occasions, domestic events in the Royal Family, situations which concerned religious affairs, in this country or outside, of special concern to Protestant Dissenters.

The nature of the privilege is rooted in the origin of the Deputies. For the General Body of Ministers from which the lay Deputies was originally an offshoot, had been accustomed from the time of the Revolution to appear at Court in large numbers to pay their respects. About 90 ministers were introduced to William of Orange in 1688 by the Earl of Devonshire, Lord Wharton, and Lord Wiltshire, and presented an Address in which they stated that 'although they did now appear in a distinct company, they did not on a distinct account, but on that only which was common to all Protestants'.[1] On the accession of Queen Anne they adopted the more sensible plan of sending a small deputation; Dr Daniel Williams led four Presbyterians, three Baptists, and three Independents, who presented an Address to the Queen in 1702. The Presbyterians, who had originally outnumbered the others by two to one,[2] claimed precedence on these occasions, and continued to present Addresses on behalf of the United Body down to 1835.[3]

[1] Colligan, *Eighteenth Century Conformity*, 1915, p. 5.
[2] Coomer, *English Dissent under the Hanoverians*, 1946, p. 59.   [3] See above, p. 21.

But the whole procedure was a matter of custom, and on many occasions down to the 19th century, as we shall see, the whole Body of Ministers attended at Court.

When the lay Deputies were at first constituted, they seem to have left it to their ministerial brethren to represent the Three Denominations at Court. But they assumed from the first the right to speak as ambassadors of Dissent on behalf of their brethren overseas. In 1746, and again in 1751, they conveyed Addresses from the North American colonists in Connecticut and 'the Massachusetts' to George II, and were clearly regarded on both sides as the correct intermediaries. In 1746 Dr Avery consulted the Duke of Newcastle about procedure, and apologized to the Committee for not having 'desired the Committee or a competent number of them to have gone with him', but the 'Duke of Newcastle had told him that he had better present it alone or at most not bring more than one with him'. In 1751, as we have seen,[1] 'The Dr read an address of Condolance to his Majesty on the death of the late prince of Wales from the Ministers at Connecticutt' and another to the Princess Dowager of Wales which he had received from New England.

From the tone of Dr Avery's apology one might imply that the Committee were already accustomed to attend at Court; but the first occasion on which we have evidence that they did so on their own behalf was in 1789, when the recovery of King George III from madness called forth general rejoicings. Four Deputies presented congratulatory Addresses to the King and Queen in person at Windsor, praying that the King's health might be continued

---

[1] Above, p. 408. This Prince of Wales was the one whose death is also commemorated by the lines:

> 'Here lies Prince Fred
> Gone down among the dead.
> Had it been his father
> We had much rather;
> Had it been his mother
> Better than any other;
> Had it been his sister
> Few would have missed her;
> Had it been the whole generation
> Ten times better for the nation;
> But since 'tis only Fred
> There's no more to be said.'

and his reign prolonged over a 'free, loyal, and united people'. The Protestant Dissenters, they assured the King,

yield to none of their Fellow Subjects in Zeal and Affection for your Majesty and our Glorious Constitution as their Loyalty and Attachment to your Majesty's August Family and Government are founded in Principle and trust have ever been manifested in their Conduct.

The King replied:

Your dutiful and affectionate congratulations on my recovery from my late indisposition and your expressions of attachment to my Family and Government are very agreeable to me. The Protestant Dissenters will always experience my favor and protection.

To the Queen the Deputies presented a separate Address, assuring her that

the many amiable virtues by which your Majesty has engaged the hearts of the British Nation and the affections of our most Gracious Sovereign,

had led them to share her feelings first of anxiety and now of peace. They prayed for her happiness, and that she might

continue a bright example of those Conjugal and Maternal virtues which eminently distinguish your Majesty.

The Queen graciously replied, and the Deputies had the honour to kiss their Majesties' hands.[1]

After the attempt on the King's life in 1795, the Deputies congratulated him on his 'very providential and happy Preservation from the late traitorous and wicked attack'. They lamented that there should exist persons capable of 'so atrocious and diabolical a Design'. 'Esteeming the safety of Your Majesty's Person and the Security of the Constitution to be inseparable', they asserted in truly Whiggish spirit their loyalty and affection, and prayed for a long life for the King.[2] Two members of the Committee presented this Address, and kissed the King's hand.[3]

Much is said in the text-books about the revolutionary inclinations of the Dissenters; and doubtless Dr Price's sermon on 'The True Love of one's Country' represented the views of some of them at all times, and of all of them at some times. The accident

---

[1] 16 and 22 April 1789.   [2] 18 Dec. 1795.   [3] 29 Jan. 1796.

that one of the greatest writers of English chose that sermon as the text for his *Reflections on the French Revolution* has perhaps given undue prominence to one side of Dissent in the late 18th century. Some persons, more ingenious but not more accurate than the text-books, have attempted to draw a firm line of distinction between the sluggish, conventional patriotism of the orthodox Dissenters and the clear-eyed, prophetic, revolutionary doctrine of the Unitarians. Such a distinction cannot survive examination; for at the very time when the Deputies spoke for the whole body of Protestant Dissenters[1] with such perfervid affection for the King and the Constitution they were probably more under Unitarian than any other influence.

On 5 August 1814 the Deputies resolved that it was 'expedient' to congratulate the Prince Regent on the peace. On 13 April Napoleon had ratified the Treaty of Fontainebleau which banished him to Elba. The Deputies congratulated the Prince Regent

on the successful and glorious termination of the late tremendous Contest;—protracted by the gigantic efforts of a mad and unprincipled ambition till Europe had been convulsed to its centre, and millions involved in misery and ruin. While we admire [they continued] the fortitude and bravery of our illustrious Allies, we cannot but exult in the accession of glory which Britain has obtained from the conflict; nor do we less applaud that spirit of magnanimity and moderation which rules the Allied Counsels in the hour of triumph and contributed so largely to the accomplishment of a Pacification on which we trust that we may safely build the hope of permanent Peace and Happiness.

Feeling on these topics only in common with their fellow-subjects, the Deputies went on to express the peculiar attachment felt by the Protestant Dissenters to the family of Brunswick, remembering especially

that it was reserved for the latter period of His Majesty's reign to extend Religious Toleration beyond all example of former times.

With a spirit greatly to their credit, the Deputies concluded by mentioning the Slave Trade:

in the midst of a scene at once so consoling and so splendid, we deeply regret any Shade should exist.

[1] 22 April 1789.

The treaty between England and France of 30 May 1814 had prohibited foreigners from taking slaves to French colonies, but allowed the French to take them until 1 June 1819. In Africa, the Deputies observe,

increased Desolation is about to prevail, and our concern is only alleviated by the assurances of your Royal Highness that the influence of your Government, corroborated as it is by the loud and universal voice of the Nation, shall be exerted to the utmost to avert the impending evil from that unfortunate Quarter of the Globe.

The opinion represented by the Deputies influenced British policy. It did much to secure the general acknowledgement at the Congress of Vienna that the Slave Trade should be abolished as soon as possible. It also helped to procure the more particular and more effectual measures against the trade which were gradually put into force through British influence.

No special Address marked the final fall of Napoleon, but late in 1815 the persecution of Protestants in France roused the Deputies. At a special meeting on 1 December 1815 they used their congratulatory Address as a means of pointing a moral. After expressing 'indignant regret' at the necessity of so soon again 'appealing to the sword' they find cause for exultation and gratitude:

The Arms of His Majesty and his Allies under the Command of the most distinguished Hero of this Military Age have in a just Warfare been again crowned with prompt and decisive Success.

Yet again their joy has 'a large Alloy of poignant concern' as they observe that

The perverse and mischievous spirit of religious intolerance should even now have burst forth in a neighbouring Kingdom with such barbarous and sanguinary fury. From the allies of Protestants in the very crisis of the most brilliant and important success, the persecution of Protestants was surely not to have been expected.

Imaginary guilt is imputed in order that unmerited punishment may be inflicted:

These transactions do not appear to have been the transitory excesses of an ignorant and deluded Populace,

and the Deputies beseech the Prince Regent to exert his powerful intercession with the French Government 'in such manner as to your Wisdom shall seem meet' to suppress the outrages which disgrace it.

Observing the general Temper which has appeared to prevail among those great Powers by which the councils of Europe have been directed, we have indulged the cheering expectation of such an Extension of the principles of religious Liberty as should remove universally the civil Disabilities inflicted on account of religious Profession; and we trust that the Calamities now flowing from the prevalence of the opposite principle will have a strong tendency to accelerate its accomplishment.

It was characteristic of the Deputies that their interest in the French Protestants did not end when they had exhorted someone else to do something for them. Collections for the sufferers were planned throughout the country.

The spirit which dictated the terms of the settlement at Vienna has come in for much facile abuse from text-books and orators. We note that Dissenters were at one with other Englishmen in approving warmly most of what was done. The spirit of 'magnanimity and moderation in the hour of triumph' commended by the Deputies on 5 August 1814 was not displayed at any time after 4 August 1914 in such a manner as to shew to disadvantage the treaties of a century earlier.

By far the greatest number of Addresses refer to domestic events in the Royal Family. On 12 July 1816 the recent marriage of Princess Charlotte and the Prince of Saxe-Coburg called forth three Addresses: one to each of them and one to the Prince Regent. The Address to the Prince Regent well illustrates which is the main and constant point of interest in the Addresses of this class: the Deputies lose no chance of emphasizing the peculiar loyalty to the House of Hanover felt by the Dissenters, and their evergreen memories of 1688 and the Old and Young Pretenders.

Accustomed as we have been [say the Deputies in 1816] to regard with hereditary veneration the principles of that glorious revolution in consequence of which the August Family of your Royal Highness was seated on the throne of these realms, and entertaining sentiments of the most lively and respectful gratitude for the benefits which Protestant Dissenters as a distinct Body have received from the successive Princes of the Brunswick line, we feel peculiar pleasure in contemplating an event which tends to perpetuate a Rule founded on Bases so favourable to the happiness of Great Britain and of Mankind.

On 7 February 1817 the escape of the Prince Regent from the 'outrageous violence' of the attack on his carriage as he returned from opening Parliament drew forth an Address of congratulation which William Smith and two other Deputies presented at the Levée of 21 April. Next came a series of Addresses of condolence: on 19 December 1817 to the Prince Regent and the Prince of Saxe-Coburg when the Princess Charlotte died; on 18 December 1818 to the Prince Regent on the death of his mother, the Queen; on 18 February 1820 on the deaths of George III and the Duke of Kent, an Address of 'mingled emotions'—congratulations to the new King, and condolence on the loss of his father and brother. It is to be feared that George IV had not fully benefited from the admirable sentiments expressed, especially at the time of his mother's death, concerning the 'Unerring Wisdom' of the Almighty in giving

an important and striking Lesson to Mankind by visiting those in the highest Sublunary Stations with domestic Misfortunes in a degree rarely to be paralleled even in the humbler walks of Life.

It is greatly to the Deputies' credit that even in the 'grateful and seasonable Occupation' of congratulating the new King they offered no word of insincere or formal admiration for a character which, in fact, they could not admire; they skated on thin ice with their usual agility. They praised the merits of George III; they praised the merits of the Duke of Kent; they praised the services of the House of Hanover and 'that excellent Constitution which has arisen out of the Union of the three estates of the Realm'. They were full of hopes and good wishes for the new King's reign; but they said no word that sycophancy might suggest and for which honesty might blush.

Opinion was divided on the propriety of presenting an Address to the Queen 'on account of her Accession to the Royal Dignity of Queen Consort'. The Bill to dissolve her marriage with George IV on account of her alleged immorality had been abandoned on 10 November 1820, and there was great public sympathy for her.

On 26 January 1821 the Committee, after a division, referred the question to a General Meeting specially summoned for 9 February; after discussion the proposal was withdrawn.

When on 30 July 1830 the Deputies considered their Address to congratulate William IV on his accession, they discreetly made no reference to the character of his predecessor:

We would not unnecessarily dwell on the solemn and painful Event which calls us to present ourselves to Your Majesty, but gladly rather avert our Attention from it to indulge in dutiful Congratulations.

They dwelt on the vigorous loyalty of the Dissenters, on the expansion of their liberties under George III and George IV, and on their good wishes for the new King and Queen.

But when they asked for permission 'to present the Address to His Majesty on the throne', Sir Robert Peel refused. He denied the Deputies' right, declaring that he could not advise the King to depart from the established rule which had hitherto governed the presentation of Addresses to His Majesty 'on the Throne' and 'in the Closet.' Many bodies were seeking this privilege, and if he were to recommend a departure from the ancient usage in any one instance, he would be exposed to the greatest embarrassment.

No such objection was made to the presentation of an Address by the Ministerial Body. On 26 July 1830, Peel informed their secretary that their Majesties would receive the Addresses on Wednesday 28, before the Levée.[1]

These were the arrangements:

1. That the members of the Body should go to court as they had done in the preceding Reigns in the habits usually worn by them in the discharge of their public clerical duties.

2. That the Address to the King, being upon his accession, and carried up by the Body in their collective capacity, should as on former occasions be received *upon the Throne.*

3. To avoid confusion in so numerous a deputation, the Secretary, after being himself introduced by the Minister presenting the Address (Mr Aspland) should as the official organ of the Body introduce the other members severally by name to their Majesties to kiss hands.[2]

---

[1] Ministers' Minutes, 28 July 1830.
[2] Ministers' Minutes, vol. IV, p. 161.

But this was too much for Sir Robert. He objected to 'so numerous a body kissing hands' and pointed out that other deputations had been satisfied with having a few representatives presented. The secretary of the Ministers claimed the honour as having been allowed 'on every previous occasion', and asked how many Sir Robert would suggest. Sir Robert 'declined to fix any number as proper to be presented' and in the end all the Ministers were presented to the King, but only seven of each denomination to the Queen.

The ministers, 95 in number, then proceeded to St James's in private carriages, and being introduced into the Presence Chamber with the usual formalities, were received by the King, seated upon the Throne and surrounded by the great officers of State . . . the King having listened to the Address with fixed attention, and to some parts of it with emotion, read his Answer with considerable force and feeling.

After his formal reply, the King made an extempore speech. The whole feeling induced by this occasion is that the presentation of Addresses was a matter still in the process of solidifying into a formal right governed by exact ceremonial, and this impression is intensified by the report of the Ministers' next visit, on Wednesday, 30 April 1834. On this occasion, by arrangement with Lord Melbourne only six members of each denomination attended.

Before the Levée the deputation were conducted to the Royal Closet by Lord Melbourne where His Majesty awaited them, surrounded by the great officers of the Household.

The Address was read in a distinct and impressive manner by Dr Cox. When he had concluded, there seemed to be an expectation that the deputation should withdraw, the King being provided with no written answer. His Majesty, however, perceiving that the deputation did not move, with great self-possession addressed to them an extemporaneous reply—He reminded the deputation that he had shown himself a friend of Religious toleration—but added that placed as he was at the head of the established Church of England, it was his duty to watch over its interests. He could at present, he added, say no more than that he should, as was his duty, consider such very respectful and proper representation as the deputation had made to him.

His Majesty having concluded his reply, the deputation expected to have the honour of kissing hands as usual—No indication being given of this ceremony, the Secretary spoke to Lord Melbourne and claimed the honour for the deputation as a privilege always allowed them on such occasions—His Lordship immediately mentioned this matter to the King, and he without hesitation held out his hand. . . .

As the deputation was retiring, the Secretary applied to Viscount Melbourne for a copy of His Majesty's answer, which it was usual to deliver to the Minister presenting the Address—his Lordship objected, alleging the difficulty of giving the copy of an extemporaneous address —but the Secretary claiming it as a matter of privilege, which had never been refused—his Lordship promised that it should be written out and forwarded to the Secretary's address. . . .

From the irregularities which attended the presentation of the Address, it was apparent to the deputation that there had been a good deal of official neglect in the department to which the business pertained. . . .

In acknowledging the receipt of the King's answer, the Secretary deemed it right, in order to guard against such irregularities in the future, to explain fully to Viscount Melbourne the situation in which the Body stood in relation to the King's Court, the privileges always conceded to them in approaching the Royal presence—and the course of proceeding usually adopted in the presentation of its addresses to the King.[1]

Meanwhile, the lay Deputies on their part were not willing to let their own right go by default. When Queen Victoria succeeded William IV, the Deputies' Chairman sought an interview with Lord John Russell about the presentation of an Address; and as a result the Deputies met to agree on an Address, which it was resolved the Chairman and three other Deputies should present in person.[2]

The Address assured the Queen of their

unabated attachment to the principles of civil and religious freedom which placed your August Family on the Throne of these realms. . . . We rely with confidence upon your Majesty's gracious avowal of a determination to secure to all the full enjoyment of religious liberty.

The Address ended with a prophetic wish, which by the end of the Queen's reign had been in great part fulfilled:

---

[1] Ministers' Minutes, vol. IV, p. 353 (20 April 1834).
[2] Deputies' Minutes, 13 July 1837.

May your Majesty's reign be signalized by a removal of whatever vestige remains of the intolerant or mistaken legislation of former ages.[1]

The ground so won was held. In 1840[2] the Deputies, by two representatives, presented personally to the Queen an Address on the occasion of her marriage. In an Address to Prince Albert they reminded him that his own ancestors had shewn a firm attachment to the principles of civil and religious freedom; and in an Address to the Duchess of Kent they expressed their obligations to her

for having inculcated on the mind of our gracious Sovereign those Christian and Constitutional principles which make Her Majesty's reign a blessing to this great and powerful country.

Five other Addresses were presented in this same year. The Deputies congratulated the Queen and Prince Albert on their escape from an attack made on them, and they congratulated the Queen, the Prince, and the Duchess of Kent on the birth of the Princess Royal. These Addresses were not presented in person; but on 17 November 1841 three members were appointed to present personally the Deputies' congratulations on the birth of the Heir Apparent. In their Addresses to the Prince and the Duchess of Kent, as well as in the Address to the Queen, they laid emphasis on their expectation that the future King would be educated 'in those free and liberal principles which adorn Your Majesty's reign'. They anticipated 'with delight' Prince Albert's co-operation in educating him in the principles of the British Constitution. The experiences of King Edward VII give a certain poignancy to this ingenuous delight.

More congratulations to the Queen and the Prince Consort followed in the next year[3] when a second attempt to assassinate the Queen failed. The Queen received her Address through Sir James Graham. It is interesting, if not significant, that on this occasion the Tories were in power.

After twenty years the death of the Prince Consort drew from the Deputies an Address of condolence.[4] Besides their hope for the religious consolation of the Queen they set their confidence that Prince Albert 'will be regarded as one of the highest of the

[1] 5 July 1837.   [2] 4 Mar. 1840.   [3] 1 June 1842.   [4] 12 Feb. 1862.

great men who have left their stamp in the improvement of their age'. This Address was not presented personally.

The marriage of the Prince of Wales with the Danish Princess Alexandra delighted the Deputies, who noted in their Address to them that

this is but the renewal of an alliance between two noble northern nations distinguished for their uniform and unwavering attachment to the principles of civil and religious liberty.

They hope that the Prince and Princess 'holding firmly the broad principles of the Protestant faith' may promote freedom. To the Queen they expressed their hopes for the Prince of Wales, hopes that

virtues nurtured and cherished with so much parental care may descend to future generations.[1]

The birth of a son to the Heir Apparent caused a renewal of the discussion about the Deputies' right to approach the Queen. To the Queen the Deputies expressed their prayer and expectation that

similar care and parental solicitude will be evinced in the education of the young Prince for the discharge of the constitutional duties of his exalted station as were bestowed by Your Majesty and His Royal Highness the late lamented Prince Consort on the education of his father, the Prince of Wales.

To the Prince and Princess of Wales the Deputies repeated the hopes for an education in the 'free and liberal principles of the British Constitution' which they had cherished for the education of the Prince of Wales himself.[2]

Meanwhile the Ministerial Body, too, had prepared an Address; but on writing to Sir George Grey for an audience, they received a reply, dated 3 March 1864, expressing

his regret that the Protestant Dissenting Ministers did not inform him sooner of their desire to present an Address . . . as in that case a deputation . . . would probably have been received by Her Majesty on Saturday last at Windsor, when several Addresses were presented . . . Sir George Grey does not think it probable that any early day can be fixed for the reception of other addresses.[3]

Lieutenant-General Knollys wrote similarly from Marlborough

[1] 25 April 1863.　　　[2] 6 April 1864.　　　[3] Ministers' Minutes, 7 Mar. 1864.

House that the Prince of Wales had 'already received on two different days three public bodies'. But the Ministers persisted, and at last won their point; the Queen received them in audience at Windsor on 23 June; but only three members of the deputation were presented to the Queen, and the Address was not read, nor the Queen's reply.

The Deputies had been even slower off the mark than the Ministers, and did not learn until the last moment that the Ministers had been granted an audience. When they discovered this, they wrote to Sir George Grey asking permission to present their own Address at the same time as the Ministers; but the Home Office declined to admit the Deputies' right to present to the Queen in her Closet without proof that such a right existed. The Deputies convinced the Home Office from their records that they had personal access to the Queen; but the Home Office replied that the presentations had been made *at Levée*, and not *in the Closet*.[1]

For the rest of Queen Victoria's reign the Deputies made no personal presentation, although they continued to frame Addresses which had to be forwarded through the Home Secretary. These covered a surprising range of occasions, from the time when the Duke of Edinburgh escaped assassination in the East while in command of the frigate *Galatea*;[2] when the Prince of Wales recovered from a dangerous illness;[3] when Princess Alice died;[4] when an attempt to injure the Queen failed;[5] and when the Duke of Albany died.[6] Of the Duke of Albany the Deputies spoke with special regard, if with slight gaucherie: his 'thoughtful and cultivated mind' had been devoted to the service of his country, especially to efforts to help the poorer and struggling classes.

Their Jubilee Address in 1887 the Deputies wished to present personally, but on enquiry the Lord Chamberlain intimated that the Queen could see no more deputations, and they had to content themselves with 'the usual way through the Home Secretary'.[7] The Ministers, however, were informed that the Queen would

---

[1] 6 July 1864.   [2] 10 June 1868.   [3] 22 Feb. 1872.
[4] 20 Dec. 1878.   [5] 7 Mar. 1882.   [6] 2 April 1884.
[7] 19 July 1887.

receive 'a deputation of not more than ten persons' at Windsor on 16 May.[1]

In 1893 and 1894, however, the Ministers too showed some anxiety lest their ancient privilege might be impaired. On the marriage of the Duke and Duchess of York they decided 'after some correspondence with the Secretary of State' to 'send the Address by post . . . presuming this will not be made a precedent to disturb our ancient privilege'. Eventually the Duke and Duchess agreed to receive a deputation of ten persons from the Ministerial Body.[2]

In 1894 the Ministers' request to present an Address to the Queen on the birth of a child to the Duke and Duchess of York was answered politely; the Queen was going to Osborne immediately, and 'will not expect the General Body . . . to send a Deputation so far for the purpose of presenting the Address'.[3] Again the Ministers made enquiries about the practice of other bodies, and found that all except the Corporation and Commission of Lieutenancy of the City of London had been prevented from presenting Addresses personally.

But the biggest tussle for both the lay and Ministerial Bodies came with the Diamond Jubilee. On 22 April 1897 the Home Secretary told the Ministers that he could not yet name a date for presenting the Address; and in July that

> Her Majesty having felt unequal to receiving all the privileged bodies on this occasion has asked the Prince of Wales to act in her behalf in certain cases.

The Ministers received this news with 'surprise and disappointment' and objected particularly to being classed with 'certain cases', reminding the Home Secretary that Nonconformists 'constitute a majority of Her Majesty's subjects' and that they would be prepared to wait until the autumn if necessary, but 'must sustain the long established right to approach the Queen in person'.[4]

After these strong representations, the Queen agreed to see a deputation of not more than 20 persons at Windsor on 15 July.

[1] Ministers' Minutes, 13 May 1887.　　[2] *Ibid.* 26 Sept. 1893.
[3] *Ibid.* 19 July 1894.　　[4] *Ibid.* 12 July 1897.

The Deputies were less successful. In preparing their Address, they observed that their Minutes indicated that they had a right of personal approach, and that they resolved to take steps to use it. But again the Home Secretary refused to admit the right, and the Address had to be sent to him.[1]

In spite of these rebuffs, the Deputies had throughout the latter part of Queen Victoria's reign had their part in the increasing national recognition of Dissent. In 1872 they thanked the Lord Chamberlain for procuring tickets of admission to St Paul's Cathedral for the thanksgiving for the recovery of the Prince of Wales.[2] Tickets were sent to them also for the Jubilee Celebrations of 1887 and 1897 at Westminster Abbey, and were distributed by ballot among members of the Committee. The newly established National Free Church Council, however, to some extent modified the traditional function of the Deputies to represent Dissent in relation to the State. This is reflected in the arrangements made when Queen Victoria died. Three days after her death the Deputies appointed a Committee to act with the Committee of the National Free Church Council in allotting seats to Nonconformists if there were any public function on the occasion of the Queen's funeral.[3]

They also asked to be allowed to present their addresses of condolence and congratulation to King Edward in person with other Nonconformist bodies.[4] The Home Office promised to take his Majesty's pleasure; and, on being stirred up by the Secretary, reported that the King would not, on this occasion, receive the Deputies in person; but as a result of this application, the Lord Chamberlain agreed that, if the Ministerial Body would consent, the King would in future recognize a joint approach by the Deputies and that Body.[5] Perhaps it was their concern about this traditional right which made the Deputies, in December 1902, decline as 'not opportune' a suggestion (apparently coming from the Free Church Council) that the King should be approached about the Education Bill. For this the representations made direct to Queen Victoria about the Maynooth grants in 1845 would have

[1] 26 Oct. 1897. [2] 7 Mar. 1872. [3] 25 Jan. 1901.
[4] 17 May 1901. [5] 4 April 1902.

afforded a precedent; but that precedent could not raise hopes of any good results.[1]

The Deputies were disturbed, on the occasion of the Coronation of King Edward VII, to find that Nonconformists had not been invited to the Abbey; and as the Lord Great Chamberlain did not answer their enquiry, the Secretary was instructed to press the matter.[2] In the end, the Deputies' Secretary and the secretary of the Free Church Council saw the Earl Marshal's secretary, and tickets were sent to the Vice-Chairman of the Deputies and the President of the Free Church Council (the Chairman of the Deputies having the personal right to attend as a Member of Parliament).[3] Two tickets were also sent to the Deputies for the Thanksgiving Service in St Paul's for the King's recovery from illness.[4]

Having re-established the right of Nonconformists to a place in national celebrations, and their own right to represent Nonconformity, the Deputies were next gratified to receive from the Lord Chamberlain in 1905 an invitation to nominate (at the King's suggestion) representatives to attend the Royal Garden Party.[5] Three years later, however, when no invitation was received, 'a letter of respectful protest' was sent to the Lord Chamberlain.[6] After some correspondence on 'the position of the Deputies in the past and present' the Lord Chamberlain promised to note the claims of the Deputies;[7] but as there was no Garden Party the following year (1909) the Deputies could not tell whether their claims had been effective.[8]

In that year, however, a compromise was reached over the right of approach. The Deputies were permitted to unite with the Body of Ministers in presenting Addresses; and accordingly in 1910 they presented an Address to King George V on his Accession; in 1919 they presented an Address on the conclusion of peace; and in 1924 they were received by the King and the Duke of York (afterwards King George VI) on the occasion of the Duke's marriage.

In 1936 the Home Secretary approached the National Free

[1] 28 May 1845. [2] 4 April 1902. [3] 13 June 1902.
[4] 3 July 1902. [5] 29 June 1905: they named 5 divines and 10 laymen.
[6] 26 June 1908. [7] 23 Oct. 1908. [8] 20 April 1909.

Church Council with a proposal that the Free Churches should present a United Address of condolence and congratulation to the King, rather than that the special Free Church Bodies which have an historic right of approach should present separate ones. The Home Secretary insisted that if this was done, it would not prejudice in any way the historic right of separate approach of the constituent Bodies, and it was suggested that the deputation should consist of about 25 persons. The proposal was accepted, and the deputation was to represent the Federal Council, the Deputies, the Ministers of the Three Denominations, the Presbyterian Ministers, and the Free Church Council. Whilst it was agreed that the Moderator of the Federal Council should present the Address on this occasion, the Chairman of the Deputies stipulated that it should not be taken for granted that this would always be the case.

In 1945, on the conclusion of hostilities in Europe, the Deputies considered the presentation of an Address; but as it was intimated that on this occasion the King could not receive Addresses personally, the Deputies' Address, made jointly with the Ministers, was sent through the Home Secretary. In 1947 the Deputies were received, with other Nonconformists, on the occasion of Princess Elizabeth's marriage to the Duke of Edinburgh.

It was not only to the British Throne that the Deputies addressed their congratulations and exhortations. When the Crimean War was nearing its end, Victor Emmanuel, King of Sardinia, soon to be proclaimed King of a united Italy, visited 'our beloved Queen' at Buckingham Palace. The policy of his Minister, Cavour, which pointed to a reduction of the political privileges of the Roman Church in Victor Emmanuel's dominions, commended itself to the Deputies, and they thought the moment opportune for encouraging the liberal King and for explaining to him the benefits which his country might expect from an extended programme of religious toleration.

The Deputies' Address to the King first expressed gratitude for his efforts in the face of opposition to give civil and religious liberty to his subjects. It then explained that few religious inequalities survived in England, and that, as these had diminished, national unity had increased. English experience has shewn that freedom in the teaching and profession of religion was not only safer for the civil government, but more favourable to the intellectual, social, and religious development of the nation than a policy of persecution or patronage on account of religion. The Deputies prayed that the King might be spared to give yet more liberty to his people, and to see in consequence concord and loyalty among them.

The Deputies were not unheard. The Ambassador, in acknowledging the Address, replied that the King's predecessor, Charles Albert, when he gave constitutional government, intended also to add religious equality. Victor Emmanuel had followed his example. He was much pleased to see that his policy of impartial toleration was approved by English public opinion.[1]

The incident has value in illustrating the attitude of England to the unification of Italy, and to the liberal policy accompanying the unification.

[1] 25 June 1856.

CHAPTER 8

PUBLIC AFFAIRS

THE EFFECTIVENESS of the Deputies depended on the care with which they confined themselves to their own concerns. They have always been extremely cautious about expressing themselves on public questions; even the general Whig sympathies which most of them had were carefully veiled. A good example of this caution was the issue of slavery, for the Evangelical leaders had made this cause their own, and the Deputies were after all concerned with liberty. Yet it was only once or twice, under extreme pressure, that they made any public pronouncement on it.

In 1807, for instance, they noted the Abolition Bill before Parliament. No steps were proposed to support it, but it was

Resolved that in the event of the passing of the above Bill it will be desirable that the Protestant Dissenters should publicly express their Gratitude to Almighty God for the deliverance of our Country from that National Sin.[1]

A sub-committee was set up for that purpose, but a month later it was decided that 'under all circumstances it does not appear necessary to proceed any further'.[2]

In 1814 the terms of the Treaty of Paris provoked the Deputies to protest, and petitions were presented on their behalf to Parliament by Lord Holland and Wm. Smith, M.P.

From the commencement of the Discussions on the Slave Trade, Your Petitioners have ever held that inhuman Traffic in the utmost abhorrence and have exerted their best endeavours to procure its abolition—That in consequence they exulted with the most heartfelt satisfaction in the sentence pronounced upon it by the legislature of Great Britain . . . and therefore could not but feel extreme regret at that article of the late Treaty with France in which Great Britain is

[1] 14 Mar. 1807.   [2] 28 April 1807.

made consenting to the renewal of that murderous and desolating practice to an indefinite extent. [In the view of the Deputies, England could not expect the protection of God if] the manifest extension of his goodness to us be made the occasion of renewing in any degree a system of oppression and desolation unparalleled in the Annals of the World for cruelty and injustice.[1]

But when the question of slavery again came up some years later, it was on William Smith's advice that the Deputies resolved not to petition,

it being a measure in which they may more properly co-operate with the public at large, as a question of humanity, not affecting them particularly as Dissenters.[2]

Not all the Deputies, however, accepted the Chairman's point of view, and during the next few years, the crucial years of agitation between 1830 and 1833, we find the reservations giving way, and at one moment (25 April 1833) a meeting called by special requisition, and therefore presumably against the view of the Committee, to consider the question of slavery.

In 1830 the Deputies recommended Dissenters throughout the United Kingdom to petition for the speedy abolition of slavery 'throughout every part of his Majesty's Dominions'. The Deputies' own petition adopted the same standpoint, noting the failure of the law of 1823, and demanding complete abolition, with a specific reference to the West Indies:

Slavery can never be upheld but at the tremendous sacrifice of the most sacred principles of our Religion and the most imperative of moral Duties, and it is therefore equally a Reproach to our national Character and an Anomaly in our Constitution.[3]

At this point the Deputies decided to render every assistance to the Anti-Slavery Society, which gratefully acknowledged their support. In December 1830, and again in May 1832, further petitions were prepared. The second of these (drafted by John Wilks) affirmed that the Deputies

cannot be indifferent as Men—as Britons—as Protestant Dissenters—or as Christians to the sufferings of any of their fellow subjects

and complained that

---

[1] 14 July 1814. [2] 24 Feb. 1826. [3] 28 May 1830.

even these moderated attempts to mitigate the Condition of the oppressed and wretched are met by Complaint and Remonstrance, by
Defiance and Scorn.

Evidence of this will be found in the chapter on Jamaica; and
indeed it was on the specific ground of the danger to religious
liberty that the special General Meeting justified the memorial
which it addressed to Lord Grey in 1833:

A large part of the Colonists chuse to declare that a profitable Sugar
Cultivation demands that the Negro should be retained in their
brutalizing Bondage. . . .

To the undeniable proof of these Imputations, extraordinary and
almost incredible as they must appear, your Memorialists beg to
refer not merely to common Fame uncontradicted, or to the most
authentic private Testimony, but to the irrefragable Documents in the
Colonial Office.[1]

The Deputies' references to slavery close, with their usual
practical directness, with a suggestion that part of the £20,000,000
voted as compensation to the planters on the abolition of slavery
should be used to replace chapels destroyed during the troubles.
The Baptists, however, who had chiefly suffered, refused when
approached to touch the money, and the proposal was dropped.

Another matter in which the Deputies felt themselves justified
in interfering as a body was that of religious persecution abroad.
In 1847, in the Canton de Vaud in French Switzerland, all religious
meetings outside the national Church were prohibited under penal
threats; and the Deputies asked Palmerston in a memorial to give
friendly advice and use his influence for religious freedom. He
replied that he had already instructed the chargé d'affaires to use
unofficially all proper influence with the Swiss Government; but in
spite of this the Deputies' Report for 1848 declared that the spirit
of intolerance had not yet subsided, and asked for sympathy and
prayers for the Swiss brethren. In March 1854 we find the Deputies listing seven cases of persecution in Germany, Switzerland, and
Denmark, and in December of the same year French Protestants
who were seeking religious liberty were supplied by the Deputies
with a statement on the position in England.

[1] 2 May 1833.

The Reform Bill was a more difficult matter. On 15 March 1831 the Committee considered the wish of 'many Dissenters' that a General Meeting in support of the Bill should be held; but finally decided unanimously against it. No doubt Dissenters 'in their individual and parochial capacities' would be among the foremost in supporting 'the laudable endeavours' of the Government, but they did not think it compatible with the objects of the Deputation to interfere as a separate body 'in a matter purely political' in which they have only the same interests as their fellow-citizens.

But to Lord John Russell the Deputies owed a special debt; the Annual Report for 1831 describes him as 'a nobleman for whose services in their behalf Protestant Dissenters can never feel too grateful', and his part in securing the Repeal of the Test and Corporation Acts led to proposals to help in his Election campaign in Devonshire. At first the Deputies feared that their interference might rather prove injurious than beneficial to his Lordship's interest. But when two Ministers expressed the view that their co-operation was desirable, they threw caution to the winds and opened a fund which by 15 May 1831 stood at £926 8s. The Deputies were indeed ahead of events, for it remained uncertain what sum, if any, would be needed; but Lord John, in a private letter and a public one in *The Times*, expressed his gratitude for their 'prompt liberality'. In their Annual Report the Committee state that the return of Lord John was effected 'at the small expense of about £350' the whole of which was defrayed out of the fund; and the absence of opposition was attributed to the prompt and spirited manner in which the Dissenters came forward. We learn elsewhere that retaining horses from the New London Inn for the two candidates cost £600, and that this was not thought exorbitant.

It was inevitable that the franchise, once achieved, should be thought of as a weapon for extending religious liberty. In 1834 we find the Deputies assuming an unusually militant tone. The Annual Report concluded with a warning against the Duke of Wellington and his party, against being 'lured by the hollow pretence of their adopting liberal measures' and prophesying that 'for many, many years to come' the Deputies would seek redress of grievances and a more extended freedom. 'There can be no doubt that our numbers are such that if united we shall be able to turn the scale on the present occasion.'

There follows a period in which the modern technique of questioning Parliamentary candidates is evolved. In 1841 the Deputies decided to set up committees in each Metropolitan Borough to secure the right M.P.s; in 1845 they consulted with country Dissenters about tactics at the next General Election, and later in the year decided that, since the disadvantage of the Dissenters were attributable to lack of Parliamentary representation, a Committee to secure representation must be formed. When in July 1847 they got down to the business of drawing up an approved list of candidates, they found some difference of opinion among themselves and a certain liveliness in discussion. They voted £100 to the Dissenters' Parliamentary Committee and submitted four questions:

1. Would the candidate vote for extending civil rights to all?
2. Would he oppose all grants of public money for any religious purpose?
3. Would he support the abolition of church rates and ecclesiastical courts?
4. Would he oppose any system of general education *more especially any* which compelled the catechism or attendance at worship? [The italicized words inserted later.]

The adoption of this questionnaire and the publication in July 1847 of a list of approved candidates did not, however, mean that a settled policy of intervention in Elections was decided. In 1852, for instance, and again in 1895 the Deputies decided to take no part in the Election. All the same, there is a very decisive change from the timidity of the political tone of the Deputies in the 18th century.

One thing especially to be noted in the later 19th century is the doubt which shews from time to time about the soul of the Liberal party. The Deputies were exceedingly bitter about what they regarded as Mr Gladstone's betrayal of their interests in the Education Act of 1870. Yet they could hope for little except through the Liberals, and it is significant that in 1879, when the Deputies conducted a joint campaign with the Liberation Society, it was Liberal candidates only whose views were to be ascertained; and where candidates had not been chosen, an active policy of providing suitable ones was recommended.

By 1900 their disgust with the Liberals had given way to fury with the Conservatives; and they resolved that the policy of bolstering up denominational schools must be met by fighting the next Election. In 1903 they called on every constituency to return Members pledged to amend the Education Acts of 1902-3 as a gross infringement of the rights of conscience. The overwhelming defeat of the Conservatives in 1906 was undoubtedly due in part to the strength of Dissenting feeling; in 1910 the Deputies heartily congratulated the Government on its success.

As late as 1919 the Deputies carried the educational struggle to the L.C.C., resolving to question candidates and to support those favouring religious equality. But in the pattern of politics as it emerged after the First World War there was little place for the Deputies' intervention as a body. It is interesting to note that in 1918 they recommended Lord Grey's pamphlet on a League of Nations, and in 1920 made the League the subject of their annual address, which was given by their old opponent Lord Hugh Cecil.

To conclude the account of the Deputies' interventions in politics, it is only necessary to mention one or two particular instances.

The Deputies have shared and expressed religious scruples about gambling. In 1919, for instance, they condemned Premium Bonds as encouraging the gambling spirit, and in 1923 they sent a memorandum to the Committee on the Betting Tax.

The Deputies have always carefully scrutinized the provisions of the Poor Law, particularly for religious discrimination; they were anxious lest a national service should be turned into the exclusive privilege of the State Church. In 1819 they got William Smith to watch a Bill to prevent the misapplication of the poor rates, under which children of Dissenters who applied for parochial relief might come under such rules and regulations as a select vestry might appoint in regard to instruction. The House of

Lords, however, rejected the Bill. The Poor Law Amendment Bill in 1834 needed a clause to give inmates power to attend worship where they pleased. In 1838 the appointment of chaplains came up because of restrictions placed on a Mr Dixon who was not allowed to give religious instruction at Dunmow except to members of his own denomination. After six years of renewed petition and agitation, the Poor Law Commissioners promised at an interview in 1844 to do something to meet Dissenting grievances; to allow Dissenting burial for Dissenting paupers; to consider the admission of Dissenting teachers; and to remove the opprobrious term 'licensed' as applied to Dissenting ministers. The Commissioners refused, however, to fix chaplains' salaries or to exempt children from the Church of England catechism; and the Deputies in consequence continued their agitation in Parliament, until the reorganization of the old Poor Law.

One legislative reform found the Deputies among its earliest and most persistent supporters. In 1850 they petitioned for the first time in favour of a Bill to legalize marriage with the sister or niece of a deceased wife. They carried on their agitation for more than half a century, in the later stages assisting the Marriage Law Reform Association; there is reference to the subject in 1855, in 1861, 1869, in 1883 and 1884, in 1897, in 1904 and again in 1906. With this characteristic instance of the Deputies' tirelessness we may conclude.

In the 20th century practical grievances have died away, with an alteration in the temper of men perhaps larger than we yet understand. The anomalies in the complicated pattern of English life are still there, but we accept them with more pride than regret. The Protestant Dissenting Deputies have reached a point in their history when they pause to consider the nature of their future functions. At such a point, they may look back with some pride to the changes which have been effected since their foundation, when the Dissenter, surrounded by the implications of a grudging toleration bestowed with the stigma of inferiority, was unable to hold office under the Crown, to send his child to a university or public school, to be married or buried in his own way except on sufferance, and liable to contribute to the upkeep of the National Church without always being secure in the possession of his own meeting-place. We have now concluded our attempt to describe the part of the Deputies in changing all this, by an informal political activity behind the scenes of Parliaments and Courts of Law of a kind which has been too little studied; and contributed something, we hope, to a picture of Dissenting life through more than two centuries.

APPENDICES

APPENDIX I

OFFICERS OF THE DEPUTIES

Chairman:

Samuel Holden	1732-5
Dr Benjamin Avery	1735-64
Jaspar Mauduit	1764-71
Thomas Lucas	1771-7
William Bowden	1777-80
Nathaniel Polhill	1780-2
George Brough	1782-5
Edward Jeffries	1785-1801
Ebenezer Maitland	1801-5
William Smith, M.P.	1805-32
Henry Waymouth	1832-44
J. Remington Mills, M.P.	1844-53
Sir Samuel Morton Peto, M.P.	1853-5 and 1863-7
Apsley Pellatt, M.P.	1855-63
Sir Charles Reed, M.P.	1867-74
Henry Richard, M.P.	1874-89
William Woodhall, M.P.	1889-1901
W. S. Caine, M.P.	1901-3[1]
John Massie, M.P.	1907-25
Sir Murray Hyslop, M.P	1925-35
C. T. Le Quesne, Q.C.	1937-

Vice-Chairman:

John Gurney	1805-16
Joseph Gutteridge	1816-25
Henry Waymouth	1825-32
Thomas Wilson	1832-42
Benjamin Hanbury	1842-4
Thomas Pewtress	1844-56

[1] The Chairmanship was vacant from 1903-7 and in 1936.

Vice-Chairman:

Apsley Pellatt, M.P.	
(jointly with Thomas Pewtress)	1853-6
Sir Robert Lush	1856
James Low	1857-63
Sir Charles Reed, M.P.	1863-7[1]
John Glover	1869-77
Henry Wright	1877-84
S. R. Pattison	1884-94
Col. J. T. Griffin	
(jointly with Samuel Pattison)	1890-4
Sir Evan Spicer	1894-1945
MacAdam Eccles, M.D.	1945-7
S. W. Carruthers, M.D., Ph.D.	1947-

Treasurer:

Dr Benjamin Avery	1738-48
Nathaniel Carpenter	1748-53
Michael Dean	1753-65
Thomas Lucas	1765-71
James Bogle French	1771-93
Thomas Boddington	1793-1805
Joseph Gutteridge	1805-16
James Collins	1816-28
William Hale	1828-36
John Remington Mills	1836-44
Benjamin Hanbury	1844-63
William Gover	1863-9
Samuel R. Pattison	1869-84
William Holborn	1884-1905
Samuel Watson	1905-18
A. Pomeroy	1918-31
Joseph King	1931-43
[vacant 1943-7]	
W. Winterbotham	1947-

Secretary:

William Hodgkin	1732-43
Nathaniel Sheffield	1743-67

[1] The Vice-Chairmanship was vacant in 1868.

Secretary (cont.):

Thomas Cotton	1767–88
Bayes Cotton	1788–95
John Webster	1795–1822
Robert Winter	1822–35
Robert Fletcher	1835–9
Hull Terrell	1839–63
Charles Shepheard	1863–78
Alfred J. Shepheard	
(jointly with Charles Shepheard)	1877
	1878–1928
Harold B. Shepheard	1928–
J. Ormerod Greenwood (jointly	
with Harold B. Shepheard)	1947–

APPENDIX II

SOME NOTABLE DEPUTIES

CAINE, William Sproston:
(Chairman, 1901-3). Born at Seacombe, Cheshire, in 1842, the son of a Liverpool merchant, he entered Parliament in 1880 for Scarborough, after four attempts; became a Civil Lord of the Admiralty; he opposed Gladstone on the Home Rule issue, but returned to his allegiance in 1890. He was an authority on India, and President of the National Temperance Federation.

CONDER, Josiah:
Born 1789, the son of an engraver; he lost an eye by smallpox in childhood. Became a bookseller, first as assistant to his father, then alone. He edited the *Eclectic Review* (1814-37), the *Patriot* newspaper (1835-55) and 30 Volumes of the *Modern Traveller* (1825-9). He made an *Analytical View of All Religions* in 1838. Died 1855.

HANBURY, Benjamin:
(Vice-Chairman, 1842-4; Treasurer, 1844-63). Born 1778. Author, editor of Hooker, Nonconformist historian, and first treasurer of the Congregational Union. Died 1864.

JEFFRIES, Edward:
(Chairman, 1785-1801). A distinguished surgeon, and medical superintendant of St Thomas's Hospital.

LUCAS, Thomas:
(Chairman, 1771-7). Also a doctor, and connected with Guy's Hospital.

LUSH, Sir Robert:
(Vice-Chairman, 1856). Born 1807 and trained in a solicitor's office; became a barrister in 1840, Queen's Counsel in 1857, and Sergeant-at-Law in 1865. He was Justice of Queen's Bench 1865-80, a member of the Judicature Commission and the Commission on the Penal Code. He was one of three Judges who sat in the Tichborne Case, 1873-4. He had just been appointed a Lord Justice of Appeal when he died in 1881.

MILLS, John Remington:

(Treasurer, 1836-44; Chairman 1844-53). Born in 1798 and died, a millionaire, in 1879. He was a silk manufacturer, and after retiring from business in 1840 devoted himself to politics and philanthropy. He sat in Parliament as Member for Leeds, Finsbury, Wycombe.

MORLEY, Samuel:

(Committee-man). Another of the Victorian merchant princes. Born in Hackney, 1809, he became a hosier, and built mills at Loughborough, Leicester, Heanor, Daybrook, and Sutton-in-Ashfield. He became the largest textile employer in the world, with 8,000 employees. He was chairman of the Deputies' Parliamentary Committee; he built chapels and contributed largely to the Memorial Hall; and was indefatigable in religious and philanthropic work. He sat on the London School Board and in Parliament, and was active in the Temperance movement. He refused a peerage. He died in 1886, and Morley College perpetuates his name.

PELLATT, Apsley:

(Vice-Chairman 1853-6; Chairman 1855-63). Born 1791. His father was a glass manufacturer of note and owner of the Falcon Glass Works, Southwark. He entered the family business and showed the same aptitude for it, taking out patents for inventions in the manufacture of glass while in his twenties, and re-discovering in 1851 the secret of Venetian crackle glass. His firm still flourishes. He was a Common Councillor of London and M.P. for Southwark, introduced the Dissenters' Marriages Bill and other measures, including a Bill to define the law about crossed cheques, which passed in 1856. He wrote on glass manufacture, and a 'Brief Memoir of the Jews in relation to their civil and municipal disabilities'. He died in 1863.

PETO, Sir Samuel Morton:

(Chairman 1853-5 and 1863-7). Born in Woking, 1809; he was apprenticed to his uncle, a builder, who left him half the business when he died. Peto became one of the great builders of Victorian London. He built Hungerford Market, the Lyceum and St James's Theatres, the Reform and the Conservative Clubs, as well as the G.W.R. works near Hanwell. He was responsible for the erection of the Nelson column. Then he turned to railway contracting. Besides British railways he built the Victoria Docks and was active in places from Norway to Australia. During the Crimean War he built a railway from Balaclava to the trenches. In 1866 he went bankrupt. He was M.P. for Norwich, Finsbury, and Bristol, and became a baronet in 1855.

REED, Sir Charles:

(Vice-Chairman 1863-7; Chairman 1867-74). He was the son of an eminent Congregational Minister, hymn-writer and author. He was apprenticed to a woollen manufacturer, but went into printing. He was M.P. for Hackney and St Ives, but was even more notable as a London politician. He sat in the Common Council, and the scheme for a City Library and Museum was due to him. He was also Chairman of the London School Board. Sunday School organization was among his special interests.

RICHARD, Henry:

(Chairman, 1874-89). Born in Tregaron, Cardiganshire, 1818, he studied at Highbury, and became pastor of the Marlborough Congregational Chapel in the Old Kent Road. He was secretary of the Peace Society, 1848-85, attended many International Congresses and got an Arbitration Clause inserted in the Treaty of Paris. He was M.P. for Merthyr for twenty years and was called in affection the 'Member for Wales'. He became Chairman of the Congregational Union.

SMITH, William:

(Chairman, 1805-32). The Father of the Deputies, and in a more personal sense of a distinguished family from which were descended Florence Nightingale and Barbara Smith of Girton College. He was a lover of art and literature, patron of Opie and Cotman, and owner of Reynolds's 'Mrs Siddons as the Tragic Muse' and of a famous library. He sat as M.P. for Norwich.

WAITHMAN, Robert:

A distinguished citizen of London whose services are commemorated by that famous landmark, the obelisk in Ludgate Circus.

WILLIAMS, John Carvell:

Secretary of the Liberation Society for thirty years (1847-77) and became Chairman of the Congregational Union. He was equally assiduous as a member of the Deputies' Committee.

WILKS, John:

Founder of the Protestant Society, was the son of the minister of Moorfields, and himself endowed with an extraordinary power of eloquence. He was a lover of art and literature, possessed of a fine library and a collection of works of art. He sat as Radical M.P. for Boston. Not to be confounded with John Wilkes, M.P. for Middlesex.

WOODHALL, William:

(Chairman, 1899-1901). Born in 1832, and educated in the Crescent Congregational Schools, Liverpool. As manager of the Burslem Gas Works, he was responsible for the introduction of gas into the Potteries. His services to the district included the building of the Wedgwood Institute opened in 1869, with a Free Library and Museum. The town raised a fund as a testimonial to him, and he devoted the fund to the Institute. In London he served as Chairman of the School Board; he was an M.P. and Financial Secretary to the War Office. He was a great traveller, and wrote about his travels; he was one of the first to enter Paris after the siege of 1871.

LIST OF WORKS CONSULTED

ANONYMOUS PUBLICATIONS:

A Brief Statement of the Regium Donum and Parliamentary Grant to Poor Dissenting Ministers, by the Trustees, n.d., c. 1835.

A Narrative of the Proceedings of the Protestant Dissenters of the Three Denominations, relating to the Repeal of the Corporation and Test Acts, n.d., c. 1732.

An Impartial Account of the later transactions of the Dissenters, in reference to their Committee and deputations, 1734.

Historical Memoirs of Religious Dissention, n.d.

Proceedings at a Dinner to Commemorate the Abolition of the Sacramental Test, 1828.

Proceedings in Reference to the Preservation of the Bunhill Fields Burial Ground, published by order of the Corporation of London.

Report to the Deputies by the Committee of Enquiry and Proposals, n.d., c. 1734.

Sketch of the History of the Protestant Dissenting Deputies, London, 1813.

BLACK, K. M., *Scots Churches in England*, 1906.

BRIGHT, JOHN, *Speeches on Questions of Public Policy*, ed. J. E. Thorold Rogers. (2 vols, London, 1869.)

CARLYLE, THOMAS, *Critical and Miscellaneous Essays*, vol. III, London, 1899.

CLOUGH, A. H., *Poems*, 3rd edn., London, 1871.

COLLIGAN, J. HAY, *Eighteenth Century Conformity*, London, 1915.

COOMER, DUNCAN, *English Dissent under the Early Hanoverians*, London, 1946.

CORNISH, F. WARRE, *The English Church in the Nineteenth Century*, London, 1910.

GOW, H., *The Unitarians*, London, 1939.

GREAVES, R. W., *The Corporation of Leicester, 1689-1836*, Oxford, 1939.

HAMMOND, J. L. and BARBARA, *Lord Shaftesbury*, London, 1923.

HORNE, C. S., *Story of the London Missionary Society*, London, 1928.

LLOYD, W., *Protestant Dissent and English Unitarianism*, 1899.

MACAULAY, T. B., *History of England*, vol. III, London, 1857.

MAY, ERSKINE, *Constitutional History of England*, 2 vols, 1863, continued by FRANCIS HOLLAND, 3 vols, London, 1906.

MORLEY, JOHN, *Life of W. E. Gladstone*, 1908 ed.

PARKER, C. S., *Life and Letters of Sir James Graham*, 1907.

PEEL, DR ALBERT, *These Hundred Years*, London, 1930.

PLUCKNETT, T. F. N., *A Concise History of the Common Law*, 1936.

SKEATS, H. S. and MIALL, C. S., *A History of the Free Churches of England, 1688-1891*, 1891.

TREVELYAN, G. O., *Life and Letters of Lord Macaulay*, 2 vols., London, 1876.

WALPOLE, SIR SPENCER, in *Cambridge Modern History*, vol. XI, Cambridge, 1909.

WOODWARD, E. S., *The Age of Reform, 1815-1870*, Oxford, 1938.

YOUNG, G. M. (ed.), *Early Victorian England*, 2 vols., Oxford, 1934.

INDEX

All *cases* are under the general sub-heading of C A S E S ; all *Bills and Acts of Parliament* under
A C T S. The abbreviation D.D. is used for Dissenting Deputies.